Reading Graphic Design in Cultural Context

Reading Graphic Design in Cultural Context

**GRACE LEES-MAFFEI AND
NICOLAS P. MAFFEI**

BLOOMSBURY VISUAL ARTS
LONDON • NEW YORK • OXFORD • NEW DELHI • SYDNEY

BLOOMSBURY VISUAL ARTS
Bloomsbury Publishing Plc
50 Bedford Square, London, WC1B 3DP, UK
1385 Broadway, New York, NY 10018, USA

BLOOMSBURY, BLOOMSBURY VISUAL ARTS and the Diana logo
are trademarks of Bloomsbury Publishing Plc

First published in Great Britain 2019

© Grace Lees-Maffei and Nicolas P. Maffei, 2019

Grace Lees-Maffei and Nicolas P. Maffei have asserted their right under the Copyright, Designs and Patents Act, 1988, to be identified as Authors of this work.

For legal purposes the Acknowledgements on p.xii constitute an extension of this copyright page.

Cover design: Louise Dugdale
Cover image © Bettina Erwert / EyeEm / Getty Images

All rights reserved. No part of this publication may be reproduced or transmitted in any form or by any means, electronic or mechanical, including photocopying, recording, or any information storage or retrieval system, without prior permission in writing from the publishers.

Bloomsbury Publishing Plc does not have any control over, or responsibility for, any third-party websites referred to or in this book. All internet addresses given in this book were correct at the time of going to press. The author and publisher regret any inconvenience caused if addresses have changed or sites have ceased to exist, but can accept no responsibility for any such changes.

A catalogue record for this book is available from the British Library.

A catalog record for this book is available from the Library of Congress.

ISBN: HB: 978-0-8578-5800-9
PB: 978-0-8578-5801-6
ePDF: 978-1-3500-1558-6
ePub: 978-0-8578-5802-3

Typeset by Deanta Global Publishing Services, Chennai, India
Printed and bound in Great Britain

To find out more about our authors and books visit www.bloomsbury.com and sign up for our newsletters.

Contents

List of illustrations vi
Acknowledgements xii

Reading graphic design in the expanded field: An introduction 1

PART ONE On message and off message 15

1. Branding as sign system: Semiotics in action 17
2. The responsive brand: Uniformity and flexibility in logo design 36
3. Whose wall? From posters to digital displays and the colonization of public space 52
4. Slogan T-shirts: Billboards of identity politics 68

PART TWO On legibility and ambiguity 81

5. Seeing clearly? Legibility, word and image in postmodern print design 83
6. Signifying orientalism, chinoiserie and japonisme: Fashion photography in *Vogue* as a case study 103
7. A good read? Corporate literature and brand stories: Alessi SpA as a case study 125
8. Information overload: Negotiating visual complexity in a data-rich world 144

PART THREE On paper and on screen 159

9. How to? Visual techniques of persuasion in guidebooks and manuals 161
10. Driving sales: Print and TV advertising of cars to women drivers 175
11. Picturing music: The rise and fall of music packaging 192
12. E-Book, iBook, weBook, youBook: Declensions of digital design 207

Index 221

List of illustrations

Figure 1.1　Diagram of the Saussure / Peirce sign. 19
Figure 1.2　Panzani advertisement, analysed by Roland Barthes, 'Rhetoric of the Image' (Barthes 1977: 32–51), Plate XVII. 21
Figure 1.3　Pepsi mosaic on soft drinks vending machine, Las Vegas, 2018, photograph by Jo Turney, with permission. 26
Figure 1.4　Advertisement for Belair cigarettes from the collection of Judith Williamson, with permission. 28
Figure 1.5　Unilever logo 1970–2004. Design Research Unit. Unilever Archives, Port Sunlight, Merseyside. © Design Research Unit, Scott Brownrigg. 29
Figure 1.6　Unilever logo, designed by Miles Newlyn and Lee Coomber for Wolff Olins, 2004. 30
Figure 1.7　Pharmacia & Upjohn logo, 1995–2000, Newell and Sorrell, photograph and permission Jeremy Winkworth. 32
Figure 2.1　Peter Behrens, trademark for AEG, registered 1908. 38
Figure 2.2　IBM eight stripe logo designed by Paul Rand in 1962 and introduced in 1972, permission IBM. IBM and the IBM logo are trademarks of International Business Machines Corp., registered worldwide. 40
Figure 2.3　Nike swoosh on gravestone outside Camp Perrin, Haiti, n.d, photograph and permission Paul Bick. 43
Figure 2.4　Gap logo generator ca. 2010, design and permission James Yu, maker of digital things in San Francisco. 44
Figure 2.5　MIT Media Lab identity, design and permission E. Roon Kang and TheGreenEyl, 2011. 46
Figure 2.6　Ollo logo iPad app, design and permission Bibliothèque, 2011. 47
Figure 2.7　Tate logo designed by North, 2016 with permission. A re-fresh of the original Wolff Olins word mark. 48
Figure 2.8　Chart of Variations on the 'Responsive W', Whitney Museum of American Art, design and permission Experimental Jetset, 2013. 48
Figure 2.9　Mock-up of 'Responsive W' in situ, Whitney Museum of American Art, design and permission Experimental Jetset, 2013. 49
Figure 3.1　Electrically Illuminated Billboards, New York City, 1898, Outdoor Advertising Association of America Archives Digital Collection, John W. Hartman Center for Sales, Advertising and Marketing History, David M. Rubenstein Rare Book and Manuscript Library, Duke University with permission./SLB4676 – OAAA Slide Library Digital Collection, John W. Hartman Center for Sales+C31/. 53

LIST OF ILLUSTRATIONS

Figure 3.2 Lynchburgh Bill Posting Co., undated, Outdoor Advertising Association of America Archives Digital Collection, John W. Hartman Center for Sales, Advertising and Marketing History, David M. Rubenstein Rare Book and Manuscript Library, Duke University with permission./BBB3296. 54

Figure 3.3 "Wake Up, America!' Civilization calls every man, woman and child!' 1917, James Montgomery Flagg, poster, colour lithograph, sheet 103.8 × 69.8 cm. Library of Congress Prints and Photographs Division Washington, D.C. 56

Figure 3.4 'American Way' billboard on US Highway 99, California. Nation-wide advertising campaign sponsored by the National Association of Manufacturers, March 1937, photograph by Dorothea Lange, Library of Congress, Prints & Photographs Division, FSA/OWI Collection, (reproduction number, e.g. LC-USF34-9058-C). 57

Figure 3.5 'See Britain First on Shell', poster with image of Stonehenge, Edward McKnight Kauffer, 1931, Design Council Slide Collection, VADS, © Simon Rendall with permission. 59

Figure 3.6 'Hello Boys' Wonderbra, reduced version of 48-sheet poster, 1994, Nigel Rose (Art Director), Ellen von Unwerth (photographer), permission from TBWA\London (advertising agency), featuring the model Eva Herzigová. 61

Figure 3.7 Empty Sao Paulo billboard, photograph and permission Tony de Marco, ca. 2007. 62

Figure 3.8 Times Square, New York, NY, February 2015, photograph by Grace Lees-Maffei. 64

Figure 4.1 Prime Minister Margaret Thatcher greets fashion designer Katharine Hamnett, wearing a T-shirt with a nuclear missile protest message, at 10 Downing Street, 1984, permission PA Archive/Press Association Images. 69

Figure 4.2 James Dean poses for a Warner Brothers publicity shot for his film *Rebel Without a Cause*, 1955, Los Angeles, California. Photograph and permission Michael Ochs, Michael Ochs Archives/Getty Images. 70

Figure 4.3 Vendor with Che Guevara T-shirts, Santa Clara, Cuba, 2017, photograph by Kaldari. CC0 1.0. 71

Figure 4.4 Hunt Memorial Potlatch T-shirt, designed by Corrine Hunt, 1992, photograph and permission by Aaron Glass. 75

Figure 5.1 Proof sheet for the Universal typeface ca. 1926, designed by Herbert Bayer 1925, Victoria and Albert Museum, National Art Library, London. 86

Figure 5.2 *This Is a Printing Office*, by Beatrice Warde, 1932. Broadside. 'Set in Centaur and Arrighi types by Westcott & Thomson and reprinted for the Type Directors Club of New York on the occasion of their dinner honoring Mrs. Warde on April 28, 1950'. 87

Figure 5.3 Jan Tschichold, *Die neue Typographie*, 1928, title page and interior spread showing correct and incorrect layouts. 88

Figure 5.4 'Meet the Cast', film poster for *Helvetica*, directed by Gary Hustwit, Plexifilm/Swiss Dots, 2007. Design and permission Experimental Jetset, 2006. 89

Figure 5.5 Neville Brody, *The Face*, no. 39 (July 1983). 93

Figure 5.6 The Factory, poster 30" × 40", 1978, design Peter Saville. 95

Figure 5.7 Pull-out life-size self-portrait for 'Does it make sense?' *Design Quarterly* no. 133 (1986). Design and permission April Greiman. 96

LIST OF ILLUSTRATIONS

Figure 5.8 David Carson, 'ra6belaisian without a clue', single page spread, *Ray Gun* 26. 99
Figure 6.1 Model Hiroko Matsumoto wearing Hanae Mori clothing, *Vogue* (UK), June 1972: n.p. Photograph by Lord Snowdon (Anthony Armstrong Jones), permission Condé Nast Publications, 2017. 110
Figure 6.2 'Chinoiserie by Beaton' showcases antique cheongsams purchased in a 'Beverly Hills antique shop' by Tina Lutz, described as defying 'both date and place' (*Vogue* 1973: 74–7). 15 April 1973 issue, p. 75. Cecil Beaton/*Vogue* © The Condé Nast Publications Ltd. 111
Figure 6.3 '*Vogue* in China', cover 1 October 1979. Model Esmé Marshall in a Mao suit and peaked cap. Alex Chatelain/*Vogue* © The Condé Nast Publications Ltd. 112
Figure 6.4 Chinatown, Gerrard Street, London, 27 September 2015. Photograph by Grace Lees-Maffei. 115
Figure 6.5 Spring/Summer 1993 campaign Yves Saint Laurent Rive Gauche, in *Vogue* March 1993: n.p. photograph by Helmut Newton. Image © The Helmut Newton Estate/Maconochie Photography. 117
Figure 6.6 'Cool Khaki'. *Vogue* (UK), May 1994, pp. 160-9. Fashion Editor Kate Phelan. Hair by James Brown and make-up by Lucia Pieroni. Kim Knott/*Vogue* © The Condé Nast Publications Ltd. 118
Figure 7.1 Photograph of Alessi employees outside the factory, Crusinallo 1935. Frontispiece to Officina Alessi catalogue 1995. Graphic Design: Sottsass Associati. Permission Alessi Press Office, Alessi S.p.A., Crusinallo, Italy. 128
Figure 7.2 Carlo Alessi Anghini, 'Bombe' tea and coffee set, 1945. Reproduced in electro-plated stainless steel in 1983 as part of the Antologica Alessi range. Meret Gabra-Liddell, ed. 1994. *Alessi: The Design Factory*, p. 83. London: Academy Editions. Permission Alessi Press Office, Alessi S.p.A., Crusinallo, Italy. 129
Figure 7.3 Graves Family, showing Michael Graves' 9093 Kettle (1985), aka 'Kettle with a Whistling Bird', sugar bowl and milk jug. Permission Alessi Press Office, Alessi S.p.A., Crusinallo, Italy. 131
Figure 7.4 Alessi family portrait, Frontispiece, Gabra-Liddell, Meret, ed. 1994. *Alessi: The Design Factory*. London: Academy Editions. Alessi Press Office. Featuring the 'Juicy Salif' lemon squeezer, designed by Philippe Starck (1990), Permission Alessi S.p.A., Crusinallo, Italy. 131
Figure 7.5 Family Follows Fiction objects, including 'Christy' conical sugar bowl with thermoplastic resin feet. Designed in metal by Christopher Dresser in 1864, and reinterpreted in plastic by Centro Studi Alessi in 1993; Nutty the Cracker nutcracker; Diabolix bottle opener, Permission Alessi S.p.A., Crusinallo, Italy. 132
Figure 7.6 Traditional local crafts. Meret Gabra-Liddell, ed. 1994. *Alessi: The Design Factory*, p. 10. London: Academy Editions, Permission Alessi S.p.A., Crusinallo, Italy. 134
Figure 7.7 Cover of Officina Alessi catalogue 1995, showing the Bauhaus Dessau campus (1925-6) rebadged with the Alessi name. Permission Alessi S.p.A., Crusinallo, Italy. Graphic design by Sottsass Associati. 136
Figure 7.8 Designers Roland Kreiter (left) and Philippe Starck (right) with Kreiter's mysqueeze lemon reamer for Alessi, 2010, Permission Alessi S.p.A., Crusinallo, Italy. 140

LIST OF ILLUSTRATIONS

Figure 8.1 Charles-Joseph Minard's (1781–1870) flow map (1861) of Napoleon's March on Russia of 1812–13, printed 1869, Paris. Bibliothèque nationale de France, département Cartes et plans. 146

Figure 8.2 Charles Booth's *Maps Descriptive of London Poverty 1898–99*. Colour-coded chromolithographs indicating the class of household street by street: darker colours for poverty and lighter ones for financial stability. Close-up crop of East Central District. 147

Figure 8.3 Isotype 'Picture dictionary' leaf from binder, Gerd Arntz, 1929–33, 300 x 225 mm, permission Otto and Marie Neurath Isotype Collection, University of Reading. 149

Figure 8.4 'Medical Care Expenditures', explanation graphics for *Time* magazine, 1979. Design and permission Nigel Holmes. 150

Figure 8.5 Network Models. Three proposed models of the internet: centralized, decentralized and distributed, designed by Paul Baran, 1964. Permission from the RAND Corporation. 154

Figure 8.6 Selection from an atlas of 64 maps, 'Atlas of the Habitual', 2010–2011, atlasofthehabitual.tlclark.com, design and permission Tim Clark. 155

Figure 8.7 Selected pages from 2010 *Annual Report*, http://feltron.com. Design and permission Nicholas Felton. 156

Figure 9.1 'The Kitchen Buffet', illustration by James Kingsland. Mary and Russel Wright, *Guide to Easier Living*, New York: Simon and Schuster, 1954 (1950). Permission Russel Wright Studios CC-BY. 165

Figure 9.2 'Vulgarity', portrait by John Deakin, jugs photographed by Elsie Collins, in Alan Jarvis, *The Things We See No. 1 Indoors and Out*, West Drayton, Middlesex: Penguin, 1946, 47. Permission Design Council / University of Brighton Design Archives. CC-BY. 166

Figure 9.3 Cover, illustration by Ésme, *The Creda Housecraft Manual*, Stoke-on-Trent: Simplex Electric Co. and London: Odhams, 1958. Permission IPC Media, a Time Inc. Company. CC-BY-NC-ND. Copyright TI Media Ltd. 168

Figure 9.4 Cover, illustration by Ésme, Woman *Week-End Book*, London: Odhams Press, [1949] 1950. Permission IPC Media, a Time Inc. Company. CC-BY-NC-ND. Copyright TI Media Ltd. 168

Figure 9.5 Cover, illustration by Ésme, Woman *Week-End Book Number Two*, London: Odhams Press, 1949. Permission IPC Media, a Time Inc. Company. CC-BY-NC-ND. Copyright TI Media Ltd. 169

Figure 9.6 Teen decorator, image 'Courtesy Dow Chemical Company', in *Teen Guide to Homemaking*, edited by Barclay, Marion Stearns and Frances Champion, New York and London: McGraw-Hill Book Company Inc., 1961, p. 205. Courtesy Dow CC-BY-NC. 170

Figure 10.1 'Somewhere West of Laramie'. Advertisement for Jordan Motor Car Company, Cleveland, Ohio. Original artwork by Fred Smith Cole, founder of the Jordan Motor Car Company. 23 June 1923. 11.5 × 8.5 inches. With permission from the Collections of The Henry Ford. 176

LIST OF ILLUSTRATIONS

Figure 10.2   Renault 'Nicole-Papa' campaign for the Clio car ran for seven years from 1991. Image Courtesy of the Advertising Archive. 182
Figure 10.3   Advertisement for Canon Ixus, Permission from Canon, UK. 183
Figure 10.4   'Your Car Madam'. Advertisement for Volkswagen Beetle. 1961. Permission from adam&eveDBD. 184
Figure 10.5   'Discover the fragrance of Umwelt by Volkswagen'. Appeared in *The Tatler* magazine, April 1993. Photography and permission Chris Simpson. 185
Figure 10.6   'Tattoo' Peugeot 106 Independence advertisement, published as a centrefold in *The Observer*, June 1997. Part of a campaign for the 106, 206 and 306 initiated in 1993 to target women. Photo Peugeot / Euro RSCG Wnek Gosper. Photography and permission by Nadav Kander. 186
Figure 10.7   'Shaved' Peugeot 106 Independence advertisement poster. This also appeared in a two-page format in magazines and newspapers including *The Guardian*, July 1997. Photo Peugeot / Euro RSCG Wnek Gosper. Photography and permission by Nadav Kandar. 187
Figure 10.8   'Obsession from Laboratoires Volkswagen'. Advertisement for The New Passat, Volkswagen. Printed in *The Guardian*, April 1997. This image mixes references to fragrance (Calvin Klein's Obsession) with shampoo (from Laboratoires Garnier) with stereotypes of German technical excellence. Photography and permission by Chris Simpson. 188
Figure 11.1   Andy Warhol, Billy Name, Craig Braun, John Pasche, Rolling Stones Records, Album cover for The Rolling Stones *Sticky Fingers*, 1971. New York, Museum of Modern Art. Lithograph with metal zipper, 12 x 12" (30.5 x 30.5 cm). Committee on Architecture and Design Funds. Inv. n.: 847.2014.© 2017. Digital image, The Museum of Modern Art, New York/Scala, Florence. 194
Figure 11.2   Thomas Edison portrait on wax cylinder case, ca. 1902-1912, Victoria and Albert Museum, National Art Library, London. 195
Figure 11.3   Elvis Presley album cover for *ELVIS*, released 1956 by RCA. Photograph and permission from Michael Ochs Archive/Getty Images. 196
Figure 11.4   The Beatles, *Sgt. Pepper's Lonely Hearts Club Band*, album cover, design by Peter Blake and Jann Haworth, 1967, Parlophone, UK. Courtesy Getty Images. 198
Figure 11.5   Bow Wow Wow, *See Jungle! See Jungle! Go Join Your Gang, Yeah! City All Over! Go Ape Crazy*, album cover, 1981, RCA. Photography and permission by Andy Earl. 200
Figure 11.6   Teenager's bedroom with LPs on the wall, Norwich, photograph and permission by Martin Devenney, 2016. 203
Figure 12.1   Third-generation Amazon Kindle e-reader showing text from the novel *Moby Dick*, 2010. Photograph by NotFromUtrecht - Own work, CC BY-SA 3.0, https://commons.wikimedia.org/w/index.php?curid=11658040. 208
Figure 12.2   Discrete (Chunk Style) hypertext from Ted Nelson's *Computer Lib/ Dream Machines,* 1974 (faxed copy from Ted Nelson Studios 10.28.1998). Permission Ted Nelson. 211

LIST OF ILLUSTRATIONS

Figure 12.3　Gutenberg Bible, Johann Gutenberg, ca. 1455. Lenox Copy, New York Public Library, Rare Books Division, photo by NYC Wanderer (Kevin Eng). CC BY-SA 2.0.　213

Figure 12.4　*Tree of Codes*, by Jonathan Safran Foer, London, 2010. Permission Visual Editions.　214

Figure 12.5　*Composition No. 1*, by Mark Saporta, London, 2010. Permission Visual Editions.　214

Figure 12.6　Espresso Book Machine, permission On Demand Books.　218

Acknowledgements

This book is dedicated to the thousands of students that we have taught, over more than two decades, at the University of Hertfordshire and at Norwich University of the Arts and elsewhere, and to our children Jay and Laurel. We are grateful to our editor, Rebecca Barden, for intelligent and patient support of this book, and to Claire Constable for her unwavering assistance. Sincere thanks to the institutions, designers and photographers who kindly allowed us to reproduce their work in this book. Thanks to our indexer, Róisín Nic Cóil.

Grace thanks Sylvia Lees for giving me her collection of British *Vogue* magazine which formed the basis for Chapter 6; Nic for leading on the significant task of assembling the image permissions; the Swiss Design Network for inviting me to beautiful Giessbach, Switzerland, to deliver a keynote talk for the Unfrozen conference in January 2016 which became the introduction to this book; Peter Saville for giving me a generous telephone interview in February 2018; and members of the TVAD Research Group at the University of Hertfordshire – especially Dr Steven Adams, Dr Barbara Brownie and Prof Rebecca Houze (Northern Illinois University, USA) – for reading and commenting on an early draft of Chapter 6. The TVAD Research Group also warmly welcomed Nic when he visited to deliver Chapter 2 as a TVAD Talk in March 2017. Thanks also to Reaktion Books for permission to update, develop and extend the following essay as Chapter 10: Lees-Maffei, Grace. 2002. 'Men, Motors, Markets and Women', in *Autopia: Cars and Culture,* ed. Peter Wollen and Joe Kerr, 363-370. London: Reaktion.

Reading graphic design in the expanded field: An introduction

Grace Lees-Maffei

In his essay 'Soap Powders and Detergents', published in French in *Les Lettres Nouvelles* in November 1954, post-structuralist French theorist Roland Barthes points out that advertisements for laundry products which promise to clean deep down are based on the notion that cloth is deep 'which no-one had previously thought' (Barthes (1957) 1972: 37). Barthes makes this point in order to draw attention to how and why advertisers and marketers had imagined this notion of depth. Conversely, *Reading Graphic Design* was prompted by a desire to probe misconceptions of superficiality in graphic design. Graphic designers are too often dismissed as mere messengers, concerned only with surface appearance, packaging, beautifying and delivering and content for others. This book shows that far from being superficial, graphic design is deep: it functions as a social lubricant, allowing designers and consumers to communicate with others and to express themselves. This introduction reflects on the development of a professional field of graphic design and two impetuses for the writing of this book, before briefly introducing the chapters within the context of the relationship of theory and practice in graphic design education.

Graphic design: A professional field

The initial impetus for this book was increasing frustration with a sense that, notwithstanding the processes of professionalism, graphic designers are wrongly perceived, in educational contexts and in the public sphere, as mere messengers, engaged in superficial window dressing, beautifying and delivering content for others, who are classed as originators. This prejudice is built on a number of stilts, the primary one of which is the continuing influence of modernism. If graphic designers are (rightly or wrongly) perceived as being involved in prettifying the world, making it more acceptable, beautiful and saleable, then they are engaged in an anti-modernist practice. Graphic designers' concern with surface appearance is at odds with the modernist design principle of form following function (to paraphrase architect Louis Sullivan, 1896). If there must be a visible relation between form and function, it follows that a concern for surfaces is anti-modernist, as the historian of design and architecture Nikolaus Pevsner made clear in his book, *Pioneers of Modern Design* (1975 (1936)). This point carries even though many graphic designers across the current and previous centuries have been engaged in the modernist project of making the world more legible (see Chapter 5 on Legibility, Modernism and Postmodernism).

The professionalization of graphic design developed throughout the twentieth century in the United Kingdom, the United States and elsewhere. It was given a boost in the United States through the setting up of professional gate-keeping organizations such as the American Institute of Graphic Arts (AIGA, founded 1914). Graphic designers were not alone in feeling a need to actively professionalize their field; other designers were engaged in the same task around the same time. However, the work of fostering a professional design identity was difficult, as Jonathan Woodham has noted:

> the widely felt uncertainty of terms commonly used in the interwar years such as 'commercial art' or 'graphic design', 'industrial art' or 'industrial design' reflected the inability of designers to establish a clearcut professional identity or status. (Woodham 1997: 167)

For the United States, Ellen Mazur Thomson has distinguished between the drive to professionalize and the achievement of status:

> By 1920 members of graphic design associations had achieved a sense of professional solidarity and pride, but they continued to grapple with problems of status. Graphic design, like other applied and popular arts, held an ambiguous place in the American cultural hierarchy. (Thomson 1997: 104)

Some clarification in terms of status was achieved when William Addison Dwiggins coined the term 'graphic design' in 1922 (Thompson 1997: 35). This new label separated graphic designers from printers, on the one hand, and commercial artists, on the other. Following the setting up of various governmental and independent design organizations in the United Kingdom (Lees-Maffei 2008: 7), the Designers and Art Directors Association was founded in 1962. The International Council of Graphic Design Associations (ICOGRADA) was set up the following year. The latter merged with ICSID (the International Council of Societies of Industrial Design) in 2003 to form the International Design Alliance (IDA). A third partner, the International Federation of Interior Architects/Designers (IFI) joined IDA in September 2008.

Even as the process of professionalization was gaining ground, so graphic designers had to contend with the competition of amateur practitioners. Amateur involvement has always been part of the history of graphic design, from the jobbing printers (untrained in graphic design) who set type prior to the twentieth-century process of professionalization, to the assemblers of punk fanzines who revelled in the rough and ready appeal of their work. If industrialization led to the development of graphic design as a discrete field of activity, by allowing the separation of design and realization, the further technological developments that produced desktop publishing and a suite of digital aids for graphic design facilitated amateur engagement. Users of PCs and Macs were able to make their own business cards and logos much more easily than before. By the end of the twentieth century and during the first decade of the twenty-first century, some graphic designers felt threatened by the introduction of desktop publishing and the notion, underpinned by the spread of personal computers, that 'everyone is a designer' (Gerritson and Lovink 2010). However, professional design practice has more recently taken on board developments which privilege users, including user-centred design, or people-centred design, co-design and issues of social inclusion and sustainable design.

Yet, art and design schools and colleges operate under an unspoken and almost unspeakable hierarchy, with fine art at the top and then the 'hard' design subjects, industrial design, product design, and the 'soft' design subjects at the bottom. The fact that it is difficult to gather evidence of this hierarchy in action does not mean that it does not exist. It exists in ephemeral phenomena such as attitudes, gestures, offhand comments, newsletter stories and the amount of space allocated at the end of year shows, and the names of some institutions, such as the Royal College of Art. Graphic design courses are sometimes regarded as 'cash cow' programmes, attracting large numbers of fee-paying students while at the same time being relatively cheap to resource. Graphic design courses recruit well, perhaps because of public perceptions of the employment opportunities in the field. But one function of a degree is to encourage and allow space for critical thinking. Consultations with design agencies and other employers of graphic design graduates routinely confirm that critical thinking is a valued graduate attribute. Tutors in higher education institutions can adopt the mandate to pursue employability unquestioningly, or they can work to complement the marketization of higher education through developing their students' skills of critical analysis. Increased numbers of students in design higher education have provided a base for increasing academic publishing in design, so the infrastructure exists for there to be more space in which to do the work of graphic design history.

Graphic design and design history

A second impetus for writing this book was the complaints we heard from colleagues – design educators and design historians – from roughly 2008 onwards, that graphic design history lags behind design history more generally in terms of published studies. Such complaints have been expressed at, for example, the Annual General Meeting of the Design Studies Forum at the College Art Association in the United States. These complaints surprised me because I have used a range of excellent sources with my graphic design students since I started teaching in higher education in 1995. I used the series *Looking Closer: Critical Writings on Graphic Design* beginning in 1994 (Bierut 1994), and David Crowley and Paul Jobling's *Graphic Design: Reproduction and Representation since 1800* (1996), and later Rick Poynor's prolific journalism and books (e.g. 2013 (2003)), among others. At that time, I also taught students on programmes called 'Software Systems for Arts and Media' and 'Contemporary Applied Arts', both groups which were much less well served at that time, in terms of suitable textbooks, than the graphic design students.

Was the disparity between my US colleagues' sense of a lack of graphic design literature, and my sense of relative abundance, a result of different literatures being available in the United Kingdom and the United States? It seems not. Design history developed first in the United Kingdom, whereas discreet design history programmes remain rare in the United States, and leading design historian Victor Margolin reported that he got the first US design history PhD (Lees-Maffei 2016: 350). Yet, Margolin himself recognized the existence of 'a plethora of publications' on graphic design as early as 1994 (Margolin 1994: 236), although he lamented their failure to distinguish between graphic design, typography, art direction and illustration and the resultant narrative problems within graphic design history.

I began to wonder whether complaints about the lack of design historical writing on graphic design, or more specifically, the lack of a history of graphic design, related not to the quantity of writing or – crucially – to its quality, but rather to its content. The College Art Association is home, principally, to educators in art and design and art history with design historians forming a small minority of members and delegates, and graphic design historians an even smaller constituency of that subset. US higher education delivers survey courses that require survey textbooks (Lichtman 2009). Colleagues' complaints were perhaps more specifically about the lack, at that time, of a survey textbook for graphic design history courses. Indeed, even as recently as 2017, Carma Gorman has complained that 'design historians still await a truly authoritative account of the development of visual identity design (aka graphic identity design or corporate identity design) in the United States' (Gorman 2017: 371). The fact that these complaints have focused on graphic design history suggests that it has not developed in the same way as design history more broadly.

Design history emerged as a discrete subject in response to, among other things, the development of art history of the mid- to late-1970s and as a response to Nikolaus Pevsner's aforementioned *Pioneers of Modern Design*, which had been published in 1936 and remained influential as a promoter of modernism in design, with subsequent editions in 1949, 1960 and 1975. Design historians initially followed Pevsner's model by focusing on modern design, promoting modernism and writing heroic accounts of modernist design. However, a backlash ensued in which the centrality of modernism in design historical discourses was challenged with, for example, Clive Dilnot calling attention in 1984 to the limited nature of focusing on 'who said what to whom at the Museum of Modern Art in 1956' (Dilnot 1984: 20). Pevsnerian heroicizing was similarly unfashionable, and turns to consumption and everyday life developed as alternatives.

As D. J. Huppatz and I have noted (2013: 312), design historians have consciously sought to reject their roots in art history, which has been narrowly understood as being 'focused primarily on aesthetic quality and creative geniuses – the cults of iconic objects and personality' and the decorative arts. Design historians have distanced themselves from the work of 'fetishists and idolaters' (Fallan 2010: 21) and what Denise Whitehouse has termed 'Pevsnerian and art historical practices of canonization and connoisseurship, and the privileging of the innovative designer, aesthetic form, and zeitgeist' (Whitehouse 2009: 58). Design history's early focus on production and designers was followed by consumption and mediation turns, which have facilitated a more diverse, inclusive and contextualized understanding of design (Lees-Maffei 2009).

Herbert Spencer's *Pioneers of Modern Typography* of 1969 (revised 1982; third edition, 2004) was clearly named as a companion to Pevsner's own *Pioneers of Modern Design*. We might then ask: did it function in the same way for the field of graphic design history as Pevsner's *Pioneers* did for design history more broadly, that is, firstly as an influence and then as a model to rail against? Yes and no. Spencer's *Pioneers* did not have the same far-reaching influence as Pevsner's in terms of promoting a canon of modernist designers, and nor is it clear that Spencer's book has been subject to the same backlash against the heroicizing promotion of modernism and the development of graphic design-focused versions of the various turns design history in general has undergone. Without a Pevsnerian model against which to develop, graphic design history has been in danger of continuing to produce hagiographic, producer-oriented accounts and has therefore lacked more contextualised studies.

Design historians have worked for four decades to understand design inclusively and in context. Have these same developments been seen in graphic design history? Not as much as we might hope. If graphic designers are wrongly perceived as engaged in superficial window dressing, then to what extent are graphic design discourses complicit in this through their formalist, aesthetic focus? Andrew Blauvelt has written that graphic design's ephemerality has

> contributed to the object-oriented nature of most, if not all, histories of graphic design. This orientation developed as an inheritance of art history, which itself developed out of the connoisseurship, historical attribution and classification of objects. For graphic design this has meant the selection of objects which testify to the value of design, or more appropriately the cultural capital of 'good design'. (Blauvelt 1994: 208)

Supporting the emphasis on appearance in understanding graphic design are the leading textbooks which have foregrounded the history of styles. The standard text for US graphic design history courses since its first publication, Philip Meggs' classic *A History of Graphic Design*, was first published in 1983 during the early years of design history's development (Meggs 1983). It maintained a chronological arrangement and followed an earlier model for survey textbooks of art history such as Helen Gardner's *Art through the Ages* (1926) with its many subsequent editions, Jansons' *History of Art* (1962) and E.H. Gombrich's *The Story of Art* (1950). Huppatz has noted the way in which design history, interior design history and graphic design history survey textbooks borrow narrative motifs from art history (Huppatz 2010, 2012). Yet, the history of styles had been superseded in art history in the 1970s by the social history of art and the new art history (see Harris 2001). As with these other perennial textbooks, so Meggs' book has been updated in successive editions that have attempted to respond to new currents in scholarship, and a second author has revised the fourth and fifth editions (Meggs and Purvis 2011). A challenger to Meggs, Stephen J. Eskilson's *Graphic Design: A New History* (2007) was fiercely critiqued and quickly revised for a second edition of 2012 (Lees-Maffei 2012: 3, 12). Even the most recent revisions of these survey texts show that historians of graphic design remain transfixed, perhaps understandably, on the most arresting or innovative examples of work by notable designers.

But there might be another reason why graphic design history has not broadened its focus as design history in general has. Spencer writes in the closing paragraph to his introduction for *Pioneers of Modern Typography*:

> The debates about typefaces, about serifs, and other typographical minutiae which, during the late 'twenties and subsequently, have often surrounded modern typography, have sometimes obscured its fundamental characteristics and the advantages, in terms of visual fluency and clarity, which flow from the imaginative use of contrast and asymmetry. This book records some of the achievements of those pioneers of modern typography who, in a period of war and revolution and of political and economic instability, with slender resources but fierce determination and unwavering dedication, created a new and richer visual vocabulary. (Spencer 2004: 67)

Spencer is aware of the obscurantist pitfalls of debates about 'typographical minutiae'. His focus is on individuals who have 'created a new and richer visual vocabulary'. His visual preoccupation is demonstrated in the main body of his book where text often cedes entirely to illustrations and functions as a series of, admittedly rather elaborate, captions. Rick Poynor has described Spencer as having 'a connoisseur's taste for aesthetic experiments' (Poynor 2004: 5). I wonder, then, whether the attention to detail which is the hallmark of writing on typography has endowed the field of graphic design history with a formalist tendency, and the status of micro history (focused on the details and small case studies), rather than the meso and macro histories (broadened contextually) being produced for other fields of design?

Spencer's Pevsnerian celebration of his 'pioneers' waned in influence as the interest in modernism of the 1960s ceded to postmodernism, but his book was perhaps the foremost expression of an approach to the history of graphic design which influenced art school students such as Malcolm Garrett and Peter Saville. They responded to modernism as a stylistic influence, ranging from Russian Constructivism to Italian Futurism. Poynor's *No More Rules* (2013 (2003)) picks up this aesthetic preoccupation and critiques postmodernism in graphic design as a series of theoretically informed appropriations and pastiches, and an aesthetic project.

For examples of writing in both the micro and macro camps we can turn to the designer and writer Paul Shaw, whose forensic 'dissections' in his 'Blue Pencil' blog were born out of disappointment about the decline in 'editorial quality of books on graphic design and typographic history'. In this detailed critical work, Shaw identifies and publishes about the errors – 'typographical, orthographical and factual' – in books on graphic design history and typography (Shaw 2016). Similarly, Shaw's monograph on the graphic identity of New York's subway (Shaw 2011) minutely details a slow evolution from the rationalization of the subway's multifarious identities to a commitment in the 1960s first to the typeface Standard (Akzidenz Grotesk) and then in the 1980s and 1990s to the extensive use of Helvetica. Here Shaw is a detective, amassing visual and documentary evidence to deconstruct a typographical myth. In contrast, his edited book *The Eternal Letter*, on the archetypal classical roman lettering and its influence over 2000 years, is macro-historical in scope even if the individual chapters are detailed (Shaw 2015).

Other broadened histories of graphic design include Hannah Higgins' *The Grid Book* (Higgins 2009) and Rebecca Houze's *New Mythologies in Design and Culture: Reading Signs and Symbols in the Visual Landscape* (2016), both of which address the grid. Higgins places a chapter on the grid in the histories of graphic design and typography within the diverse context of chapters addressing architecture, bureaucracy and information networks, among other things, while Houze's study of the grid examines construction toys alongside other chapters which interrogate greenwashing in contemporary corporate identity and bring together MacDonald's Golden Arches and the Jefferson memorial in St Louis, Missouri, to name but two examples. Houze's book is a prime example of graphic design being understood within context, as part of an expanded field, as Houze sought to replicate Barthes' project of understanding the everyday scene as mythologically rich, albeit from the standpoint of a woman living in the United States in the twenty-first century. Further examples of analyses of graphic design in an expanded field include *Megastructure Schiphol: Design in Spectacular Simplicity* (Berkers et al. 2013), in which the signage at Schiphol airport is considered alongside its architecture, infrastructure, reception and mythology; *Print Culture: From Steam Press to Ebook* (2013) in which Frances Robertson has avoided a formalist focus by examining print culture as encompassing everything from newspaper plants to postage stamps and posters; and Jesse Adams Stein's oral history of the New South Wales Government Printing Office, which combines graphic design history with the history of technology, labour history and business history (Stein 2016). This work shows what we already know, that design is a complex social process involving design teams and input from clients and users, but this has not always been sufficiently recognized in graphic design history. One exception is Shaun Cole's *Dialogue: Relationships in Graphic Design* which explores designer and client relationships and collaboration through examples of outputs (Cole 2005).

I have described the preoccupation with mediation on the part of early-twenty-first-century design historians 'as a third stream' in design history, with three currents:

> First, the mediation emphasis continues the consumption turn within design history by exploring the role of channels such as television, magazines, corporate literature, advice literature and so on in mediating between producers and consumers, forming consumption practices and ideas about design; second, the mediation emphasis examines the extent to which mediating channels are themselves designed and therefore open to design historical analysis – indeed, these channels have increasingly constituted the design historian's object of study; third, the mediation emphasis investigates the role of designed goods themselves as mediating devices. (Lees-Maffei 2009: 351)

Clearly, graphic design is particularly important in all three currents of mediation. Graphic designers construct the print media, such as magazines, catalogues, ephemera, and billboard advertisements, via which so much consumer education has been channelled. Along with the print media, mediating channels par excellence created by graphic designers include packaging and, latterly, web design. Indeed, it is the very multiplicity of graphic design that prompted Victor Margolin, writing in 1994, to claim that discrimination between the various fields of work which the extant graphic design history has homogenized would enable us to:

> understand better how graphic design practice has been shaped by borrowings and appropriations from other discourses instead of seeing it as a single strand of activity that embraces a multiplicity of things. By recognizing the many routes into graphic design from other fields and practices, we can learn to see it as more differentiated than we have previously acknowledged it to be. This will enable us to better relate emerging fields of endeavor such as information design, interface design and environmental graphics to what has come before. (Margolin 1994: 242–3)

We would amplify this in a call for graphic design history to speak to other disciplines outside of design history including sociology, history of technology, cultural history and others. Graphic design, a predominant form of communication in a capitalist society, plays an essentially social role. In communicating messages, whether personal or instructional, individual or corporate, graphic designers and their designs, have a social impact from the individual to society. Graphic design allows people to communicate with one another, as the chapter on T-shirts in our book shows so clearly, and it is therefore undeniably significant socially and sociologically.

Our project is consistent with Margolin's approach in other ways. The book's chapters on discrete fields and practices allow insight into the media with which graphic designers engage, from T-shirts to books and billboards. In this way, our project addresses the problem of viewing graphic design as one thing – one practice – rather than appreciating the diverse skills, artefacts and expressions that graphic design actually encompasses. Gorman points to something of the diversity of graphic design in the expanded field in her discussion of terminology: 'Historians use the terms "visual identity design", "corporate identity design", and "graphic identity design" somewhat inconsistently and interchangeably to refer to the practice of visually unifying or coordinating the appearance of all of a business's or organization's products, properties, and communications' (Gorman 2017: 385, n. 1). Gorman prefers the broader term 'visual identity design' 'because readers often understand the term "corporate" to mean design specifically for corporations, and the term "graphic" in "Graphic identity design" to refer only to the coordination of printed materials' (Gorman 2017: 385, n.1).

Graphic design cannot be understood in isolation from the other design fields because design fields do not operate in isolation. The notion of *Gesamtkunstwerk* and the architectonic function of architecture are relevant here; consider the ways in which designers from Charles Rennie Mackintosh to Karim Rashid have achieved a total design environment. Theatre design and film design are both, obviously, ensemble efforts but so is graphic design. *Reading Graphic Design* recognizes that graphic designers work as parts of teams, with art directors, illustrators, photographers, advertising and marketing professionals and so on, in providing the advertising, marketing and packaging for product design, automotive design, service design and all the other design fields. In so doing they carry manufacturer and producers' messages and precondition consumer responses to the wealth of designed goods they represent. Graphic designers thereby engage with all other forms of design in a significant, constitutive way as many of the chapters in this book demonstrate, including examples such as the advertising of cars to women, the packaging of music and the narratives communicated in corporate literature. Just as graphic designers need to understand how illustration and photography work, so illustrators and photographers need to understand the graphic design contexts within which their work will be situated. *Reading Graphic Design* therefore provides examples of how these phenomena work collectively to create messages. While a chapter on fashion photography may seem odd in a book on graphic design, narrowly understood, if graphic design is recognized as a collaborative practice distributed across a number of creative specialisms and operating in an expanded field, then its relevance should be clear.

Reading graphic design in the expanded field

This book approaches graphic design as a vital channel of discourse between individuals and society. Unlike some other treatments of graphic design, *Reading Graphic Design* does not focus on iconic or celebrated examples, but rather our emphasis on design in social contexts means that the book interrogates a great deal of everyday and even anonymous graphic design, which is the stock-in-trade of the jobbing designer. Our approach here avoids aesthetic value judgements and a tendency to focus on the most celebrated work, however this might be determined. We do not set out to focus on the most beautiful, or iconic work in graphic design, although we have examined aesthetics (Lees-Maffei 2014a; Maffei 2003) and iconicity (Lees-Maffei 2014b) in design elsewhere.

Rather, following in the wake of work in design history and neighbouring fields such as Science and Technology Studies (STS) and the history of technology which has countered a latently canonical approach by foregrounding everyday design, design failures (Petroski 1985) and amateur design practices, we show how even the most demotic example of graphic design can be effective in performing social labour. A greetings card, which would be dismissed as kitsch in the art colleges and design studios populated by innovative and creative designers, can be just as effective in expressing the card giver's care for its recipient as a design which would garner art and design school approval. By looking beyond recognized aesthetic norms, and standard chronologies of graphic design, we can recognize graphic design as socially profound. We advocate reading graphic design as situated within an expanded field, by which we mean in interaction with other design fields and in ways informed by ideas from related fields such as cultural sociology, the history of technology, semiotic and post-structural theory, as well as design histories of modernism and postmodernism. We do not advocate departing from formalist analysis entirely, as is shown in the chapters on semiotics among others. Rather, we propose an approach that combines detailed formalist analysis with contextual understanding of graphic design in action (not to be confused with action research). In this way, we underline the ubiquity of graphic design in contemporary life and its social function. The book asks how does graphic design function in society? What messages are delivered through these graphic designs and why?

The structure and contribution of this book

The book is carefully structured to emphasize some of the ways in which graphic design succeeds in communicating socially important messages between people and groups. The chapters provide twelve case studies of graphic design examined in social and cultural context, and drawn from different parts of the graphic design industry. Contextual chapters on semiotics, modernism, postmodernism and legibility, situate the book theoretically. Other chapters deal with issues of context and identity as they are played out in relation to different graphic design media, from advertising hoardings to eBooks and other digital contexts, greetings cards to fashion photography. The book is divided into three parts in order to focus the discussion onto three important defining characteristics of graphic design.

The chapters in Part 1, On Message and Off Message, variously address the ownership of graphic design messages. The first chapter introduces semiotics and structuralism, and the notion of branding as a sign system. It therefore paves the way for chapters 2 to 5, which take up the story of the development from structuralism to post-structuralism through various case studies. Chapter 2 explores the historical shift from static to dynamic logos, from universal international brand identities to more flexible and responsive corporate personalities within the context of the emergence of the critical consumer, the development of the responsive corporation, and the co-creation of brands in online landscapes. Chapter 3 surveys the history of outdoor advertising, from the diffusion of handbills and posters to the proliferation of, and resistance to, city and roadside billboards, to the more recent phenomena of out-of-home electronic displays, including those that survey, record and target consumers. Key design issues broached here include the tension between commercial activity and environmental protection, the role of the landscape in national identity, freedom of expression and the limits of privacy, the visual dynamism of the modern city and highway, and critiques of the morally and visually polluting effect of billboards by reformers. Chapter 4 examines slogan T-shirts as facilitating social needs. They aid social organization, express cultural meanings and act as expressions of political resistance. They are key channels for the communication of identity politics.

Part 2 explores the semantic richness of graphic design, and the medium's affordance in terms of communicating complexity, contradiction and competing meanings at various times and at once. Chapter 5 tackles two key issues for graphic designers: a shift from modernism to postmodernism and varying interpretations of legibility promoted within these cultural tendencies. Globalization is one of the defining characteristics of twenty-first-century design and culture, economics and politics. But it is not entirely new. Chapter 6 introduces readers to some key theories of postcolonialism in a semiotic analysis of orientalism, chinoiserie and japonisme as they are represented in British *Vogue* over the last fifty years. Chapter 7 considers the functions of corporate identity through the narrative potential of corporate publishing, using Italian household goods manufacturer Alessi as a case study. The proliferation of information – its collection, interpretation and graphic depiction, whether for the purposes of bureaucratic communication, editorial design or personal expression – has been a key aspect of the late-modern period and contemporary life. Chapter 8 investigates the origins of information graphics and data visualization and the evolution of infographics into infotainment. Central issues in this chapter are the necessity of balancing function and form, the universal and the unique, and education and entertainment.

The final part comprises chapters that collectively open up the cross-media nature of graphic design as a field. Chapter 9 examines the interplay of text and image in advice books, noting the ways in which visual techniques are used both in mutually supportive ways *and* in ways in which image subverts the text. The tenth chapter reviews how advertisers working for car manufacturers have targeted women purchasers through the use of techniques from fashion and beauty advertising, with reference to theories of gender and social and cultural history. The penultimate chapter examines the development of the twelve-inch LP cover, as the visual face for performers and as an expression of consumer identity. The chapter considers the impact of the digital music commodity on traditional music packaging. The closing chapter also considers what is gained and lost as a result of a series of technological innovations centred upon a shift to digital delivery, in this case with the advent and take-up of eBooks. While reviewing predictions on the future of the book, the chapter explores a range of profound transformations affecting the digitally distributed text, including the separation of the object from content, audience interactivity, algorithmic content, on-demand publishing and the integration of the physical and the digital.

There are, of course, many other examples we could have put in our book and did not, including those relating more explicitly to graphic design's interplay with illustration, such as the affective labour performed by greetings cards, whether aesthetically directional or beyond the stylistic pale, and the social conditioning function of children's book illustration. The chapters that appear here relate closely to our research and therefore form evidence of our approach to research-informed teaching, which creates a virtuous circle of mutually informative conversations about the things that interest us and our students. And there are many more international examples we might have explored. As it stands, the book's chapters address graphic design in the United Kingdom and the United States principally, alongside further examples from outside the United Kingdom and United States, such as Clean City laws in São Paulo (Brazil), and examples of multinational brands and themes of interest globally. We hope that *Reading Graphic Design* will be of interest in wherever graphic design is taught.

Conclusion: Mutuality in history, theory, practice

This introduction began with two converging catalysts for our book, identified through our experiences of teaching graphic design students and our readings and writings in design history: the tendency to dismiss graphic design as superficial and complaints about the lack of critical writing on graphic design. I have explored these issues and the relationship between them in a brief historiographic survey of design history and the literature of graphic design history. In addition, this introduction has explained the book's structure and the twelve chapters and the selected case studies. The chapters address different areas of the field of graphic design practice, showing it to be part of an expanded field. In responding to specific empirical pedagogic and scholarly impetuses, this book will be a tool for students of graphic design and design history, among other fields, to read, or understand and analyse, different parts of the industry, from music to publishing.

Graphic designers need to understand the contexts in which their work is mediated and consumed. We do not simply propose a shift from aesthetics to context in graphic design history, but that these are mutually informative. Here, we provide fledgling graphic designers with examples of graphic design in action, graphic design out in the world, when it leaves the designer's digital desktop to arrive at the desktops of mediators and consumers, and the billboards, TV screens, magazine pages and shopping bags of consumers. This book will inform graphic designers and historians of graphic design alike, along with those working in the range of fields mentioned. In proposing the use of this book in both studio and theory contexts, we are contributing to the range of debates about the use of theory and history in studio teaching and the benefits of embedding contextual understanding in design programmes (Lee 2011; Pollen 2015).

We close with the issue of mutual influence. If graphic design is understood through contextual reference to work in sociology, cultural history, urban studies and so on, then graphic designers and graphic design historians need to demonstrate, in turn, the relevance of their work to audiences in other fields. In turning to sociology to understand a slogan T-shirt we must ask the correlative question: why should a sociologist care about a graphic T-shirt? Ultimately, our approach poses a new challenge to graphic design historians, which is how and what can the field of graphic design history contribute to allied areas of study such as cultural sociology, cultural history, communication sciences, architectural history and the history of technology, among others which form part of the expanded field. We avoid aesthetic judgements to explore how graphic design performs important social functions in Western consumer cultures. By emphasizing communication and context, *Reading Graphic Design* complements an existing history of styles approach and rewrites the ways in which graphic design history is told.

References

Barthes, Roland. [1957] 1972. *Mythologies*. London: Jonathan Cape.
Berkers, Marieke, Koos Bosma, Iris Burgers, Karel Davids, Abdel El Makhloufi, Heidi de Mare, Anna Nikolaeva, and Jan Willem de Wijn. 2013. *Megastructure Schipol: Design in Spectacular Simplicity*. Rotterdam: Nai010.
Bierut, Michael.1994. *Looking Closer: Critical Writings on Graphic Design*. New York: Allworth Press.
Blauvelt, Andrew. 1994. 'An Opening: Graphic Design's Discursive Spaces'. In 'New Perspectives: Critical Histories of Graphic Design'. *Visible Language* 28 (3) (July): 205–16.
Cole, Shaun. 2005. *Dialogue: Relationships in Graphic Design*. London: V&A Publications.
Crowley, David, and Paul Jobling. 1996. *Graphic Design: Reproduction and Representation since 1800*. Manchester: Manchester University Press.
Dilnot, Clive. 1984. 'The State of Design History Part II: Problems and Possibilities'. *Design Issues* 1 (2): 3–20.
Eskilson, Stephen J. 2007. *Graphic Design: A New History*. London: Laurence King. Second edition, *Graphic Design: A History*. 2012. London: Laurence King.
Fallan, Kjetil. 2010. *Design History: Understanding Theory and Method*. Oxford: Berg.
Gardner, Helen. 1926. *Art Through the Ages*. New York: Harcourt, Brace & Company.
Gerritson, Mieke, and Geert Lovink. 2010. *Everyone is a Designer: Manifest for the Design Economy*. Amsterdam: BIS Publishers, B.V.
Gombrich, Ernst. H. 1950. *The Story of Art*. New York: Phaidon Publishers Inc.
Gorman, Carma. 2017. 'The Role of Trademark Law in the History of US Visual Identity Design, c. 1860-1960'. *Journal of Design History* 30 (4): 371–88.
Harris, Jonathan. 2001. *The New Art History: A Critical Introduction*. Abingdon: Routledge.
Higgins, Hannah B. 2009. *The Grid Book*. Cambridge, MA and London: MIT Press.
Houze, Rebecca. 2016. *New Mythologies in Design and Culture: Reading Signs and Symbols in the Visual Landscape*. London: Bloomsbury.
Huppatz, Daniel J. 2010. 'The Cave: Writing Design History'. *Journal of Writing in Creative Practice* 3 (2) (December): 135–48
Huppatz, Daniel J. 2012. 'The First Interior? Reconsidering the Cave'. *Journal of Interior Design* 37 (4) (December): 1–8.
Huppatz, Daniel J., and Grace Lees-Maffei. 2013. 'Why Design History? A Multi-National Perspective on the State and Purpose of the Field'. *Arts and Humanities in Higher Education* 12 (3) (July 2013): 310–30.
Janson, Horst Waldemar 1962. *History of Art: A Survey of the Major Visual Arts from the Dawn of History to the Present*. New York: Abrams.
Lee, Chae Ho. 2011. 'Applying Oral Sources: Design Historian, Practitioner, and Participant'. In Grace Lees-Maffei (ed.), *Writing Design: Words and Objects*, 163–74. London: Berg.
Lees-Maffei, Grace. 2008. 'Introduction: Professionalization as a Focus in Interior Design History'. In *Professionalizing Interior Design, 1870-1970*, special issue. *Journal of Design History* 21 (1): 1–18.
Lees-Maffei, Grace. 2009. 'The Production-Consumption-Mediation Paradigm'. *Journal of Design History* 22 (4): 351–76.
Lees-Maffei, Grace (ed.) 2012. *Writing Design: Words and Objects*. Oxford: Berg.
Lees-Maffei, Grace. 2014a. 'Design History and Theory'. In M. Kelly (ed.), *The Oxford Encyclopedia of Aesthetics*. Second edition, 350–54. New York: Oxford University Press.
Lees-Maffei, Grace (ed.) 2014b. *Iconic Designs: 50 Stories about 50 Things*. London: Bloomsbury.
Lees-Maffei, Grace. 2016. 'Victor Margolin'. In Clive Edwards (ed.), *Bloomsbury Encyclopedia of Design*, 350–1. London: Bloomsbury.
Lichtman, Sarah A. 2009. 'Reconsidering the History of Design Survey'. *Journal of Design History* 22 (4): 341–50.

Maffei, Nicolas P. 2003. 'The Search for an American Design Aesthetic: From Art Deco to Streamlining'. In Charlotte Benton, Tim Benton and Ghislaine Wood (eds.), *Art Deco: 1910-1939*, 361–9. London: V&A.

Maffei, Nicolas P. 2014. 'Mobility Scooter, USA (Allan R. Thieme, 1968)' and 'Streamlined Pencil Sharpener, USA (Raymond Loewy, 1933)'. In Grace Lees-Maffei (ed.), *Iconic Design: 50 Stories about 50 Things*, 50–3 and 122–5. London: Bloomsbury.

Margolin Victor. 1994. 'Narrative Problems of Graphic Design History'. *Visible Language* 28 (3) (July): 233–43.

Meggs, Philip B. 1983. *A History of Graphic Design*. New York: Van Nostrand Reinhold.

Meggs, Philip B., and Alston W. Purvis. 2011. *Meggs' History of Graphic Design*. 5th revised edition. London: Wiley & Son.

Petroski, Henry. 1985. *To Engineer is Human: The Role of Failure in Successful Design*. London: Macmillan.

Pevsner, Nikolaus. 1936. *Pioneers of the Modern Movement from William Morris to Walter Gropius*. London: Faber and Faber.

Pevsner, Nikolaus. 1975. *Pioneers of Modern Design: from William Morris to Walter Gropius*. London: Penguin.

Pollen, Annabella. 2015. 'My Position in the Design World: Locating Subjectivity in the Design Curriculum'. *Design and Culture* 7 (1): 85–105.

Poynor, Rick. 2004. 'Foreword'. In Herbert Spencer (ed.), *Pioneers of Modern Typography*, 4–5. London: MIT Press.

Poynor, Rick. 2013 (2003). *No More Rules: Graphic Design and Postmodernism*. London: Laurence King Publishing.

Robertson, Frances. 2013. *Print Culture: From Steam Press to Ebook*. London and New York: Routledge.

Shaw, Paul. 2011. *Helvetica and the New York City Subway System*. Revised edition. Cambridge, MA and London: MIT Press.

Shaw, Paul. 2015. *The Eternal Letter: Two Millennia of the Classical Roman Capital (Codex Studies in Letterforms)*. Cambridge, MA: MIT Press.

Shaw, Paul. 2016. The Blue Pencil blog. http://www.paulshawletterdesign.com/category/blue-pencil

Spencer, Herbert. 1969. *Pioneers of Modern Typography*. London: Lund Humphries.

Spencer, Herbert. 2004. *Pioneers of Modern Typography*. London: MIT Press.

Stein, Jesse Adams. 2016. *Hot Metal: Material Culture and Tangible Labour*. Manchester: Manchester University Press.

Sullivan, Louis, 'The Tall Office Building Artistically Considered' (1896). In Robert Twombly (ed.), *Louis Sullivan: The Public Papers*, 103–12. Chicago: University of Chicago Press, 1988.

Thomson, Ellen Mazur. 1997. *The Origins of Graphic Design in America, 1870-1920*. New Haven and London: Yale University Press.

Whitehouse, Denise. 2009. 'The State of Design History as a Discipline'. In Hazel Clark and David Brody (ed.), *Design Studies: A Reader*, 54–63. Oxford: Berg.

Woodham, Jonathan M. 1997. 'Design Promotion, Profession, and Management'. In Jonathan M. Woodham, *Twentieth-Century Design*, 165–81. Oxford: Oxford University Press.

PART ONE

On message and off message

1

Branding as sign system: Semiotics in action

Grace Lees-Maffei

Semiotics, the analysis of signs, was an extremely influential method of understanding words and images developed in the twentieth century, from the publication in 1915 of Ferdinand de Saussure's lectures on semiotic approaches to linguistics (Saussure 2013), to the early work of Roland Barthes in the middle of the century, such as his 'An Introduction to the Structural Analysis of Narrative' of 1966 (Barthes 1977: 79–124). Structuralists sought to understand the underlying structures by which societies and cultures are organized. Structuralism and semiotics have been criticized for being too static, for taking insufficient account of the fact that societal structures and the meanings of signs are subject to constant change. Barthes' thinking and writing shifted towards influential and dynamic post-structuralist understanding of meaning in culture in order to better recognize the constantly changing nature of cultural meanings. Post-structuralism as a name implies what comes after structuralism, as both a rejection of, and a continuation of structuralism. Semiotics continues to offer many useful techniques to graphic designers including the model of the sign, distinguishing connotation from denotation, and the mutually constitutive relationship between *langue* (a system of language) and *parole* (an individual utterance). Like the shift from modernism to postmodernism in design, examined in Chapter 5, the move from semiotics and structuralism to post-structuralism and deconstruction in cultural analysis is not only of historical interest, it informs the way design and culture are understood in our own century. This chapter introduces semiotics and structuralism, and the notion of branding as a sign system. It therefore paves the way for the following chapters 2 to 5, which take up the story of the move to post-structuralism through various case studies.

Introducing semiotics

In the modern period, which extends from the introduction of the printing press into Europe in the sixteenth century to the last days of the industrial period in the West, Western culture has prized originality of thought. At the same time, in the industrializing, industrialized and post-industrial phases of our societies, invention and innovation have been lauded, and in many cases rewarded. So, when two or more people make similar innovations, it is remarked upon as surprising, even though the very notion of originality is questionable and much innovation occurs collaboratively. Concorde, for example, was the product of collaboration between British and French engineers, while the paper clip, the light bulb, and even the Coca-Cola bottle (launched in 1915, the same year that Saussure's *Cours de linguistique générale* – Course in General Linguistics – was first published) have contested origin stories (Lees-Maffei 2014). Semiotics, the study of signs (aka 'semiology'), derives from linguistics and was developed by two original thinkers, Charles Sanders Peirce (United States, 1839–1914) and Ferdinand de Saussure (Swiss, 1857–1913). Saussure's term 'semiology', and 'semiotics' which is used to refer to the Peircean tradition, are nowadays often bundled under the term 'semiotics' (Nöth 1990: 14).

Peirce was a polymath who made significant contributions to a number of fields including philosophy and mathematics as well as semiotics. Peirce's theory of the sign, published in 1867, is complex, extensive and remains important in the field of linguistics (Pierce 1992). However, Saussure's structural linguistics has exerted more influence in the study of cultural production and specifically design because his writings in French influenced the French structuralists, chiefly Roland Barthes, and the community of French theorists of literature and culture including such towering figures as Michel Foucault (1926–84). It is therefore understandable that in seeking to chart the development of *Modern Criticism and Theory* in his anthology of that name, a leading English Literature scholar, David Lodge, begins his chronological arrangement of texts with Saussure (although a subsequent edition put Marx before Saussure), while Peirce is represented not by his writings but rather by a couple of mentions in passing in the work of others (Lodge 1988; Lodge and Wood 2013).

Peirce proposed three categories of signs: iconic, indexical and symbolic. The iconic sign is a resemblance or representation, such as a drawing, a map, a photograph or a pictogram. Pictograms are the oldest form of writing, while contemporary examples are seen in road signs and other public places. Pictograms are distinct from the more abstract ideograms, which are indexical signs. The indexical sign has a physical connection to its referent (to which it refers), such as metonymy (the part representing the whole) as in the use of smoke to represent fire, and the pen to represent writing, learning and reason as in 'The pen is mightier than the sword'. Ideograms are learnt signs; examples are found in Egyptian hieroglyphics and Chinese writing. Peirce's symbolic sign stands for, or represents, something else and relies entirely on convention for its meaning. Examples include the Christian cross and the warning triangle traffic sign. Symbols entail suggestive and subjective interpretations: an image may mean different things to different people. Peirce's sign categories overlap; an image may present a naturalistic figure with a secondary conceptual or symbolic meaning.

We can apply these ideas to the notional example of a greetings card designed to mark the birth of a baby. The card might feature a dummy, or pacifier, and two different cards might be available, one pink and one blue, based on a learnt, conventional association with girls and boys, respectively. The image of the dummy is iconic. It functions as a metonymical symbol of the baby who may suck the dummy. The baby is therefore indexically implied. The card's symbolic message is one of welcoming a new baby and wishing her or his parents well.

For Saussure, each instance of language, called *parole*, forms part of the *langue*, or system of language, and must be understood in that context. A sign is made up of a signifier (a word, whether written or spoken, or an image), a signified (the idea put into the mind of the receiver when contemplating the denotation) and a referent (the thing referred to). (Figure 1.1) Breaking the sign down into constituent parts in this way is useful for comprehending the difference between denotation (words or sounds in messages) and connotation (the meanings indicated by the messages). The relationship between a thing and its sign is learnt and arbitrary, not natural or innate. However, through familiarization and habit, signs can come to seem natural or inevitable. In English, trees are indicated by the letters t-r-e-e, forming the word 'tree', and by the sound 'tree'. In France the same tree would be indicated by the name 'arbre' or the sound of that word. The fact that different languages have different words for the same things serves to highlight the arbitrary nature of the connection between word or image, sign and the thing it indicates.

Saussure posited two ways of understanding language, the syntagmatic and the paradigmatic. In the former, combinatory relationships are explored, so that individual phonemes or sounds are seen to work in combination with others, as in 'c-a-t', for the word 'cat', and individual words combine with other for the meaning of phrases, as in 'cat-sat-on-mat' for the phrase 'The cat sat on the mat'. Paradigmatic approaches emphasize difference; we understand words through their difference from others in the same language system. We understand 'cat' because it is not 'sat', 'mat' or 'bat'. Saussure's work has been criticized by some for its use of a synchronic approach, which takes a slice of time, the contemporary moment, and examines the evidence available in the present, rather than a diachronic approach which considers development over time. Synchronic models do not take account of the fact that language, culture and meaning change over time.

But what about signs, which resemble the thing, or concept, to which they refer? Onomatopoeia is the term for a word mimicking the sound of the thing it denotes, such as 'sizzle', 'bang', 'miaow' or 'squeak'. Again, the existence of different onomatopoeic words in different languages points to their arbitrary nature. The dominance of English as a global language means that English onomatopoeic words are increasingly found in other languages. However, these loan words accompany indigenous onomatopoeic words which are often quite aurally distinct, such as the

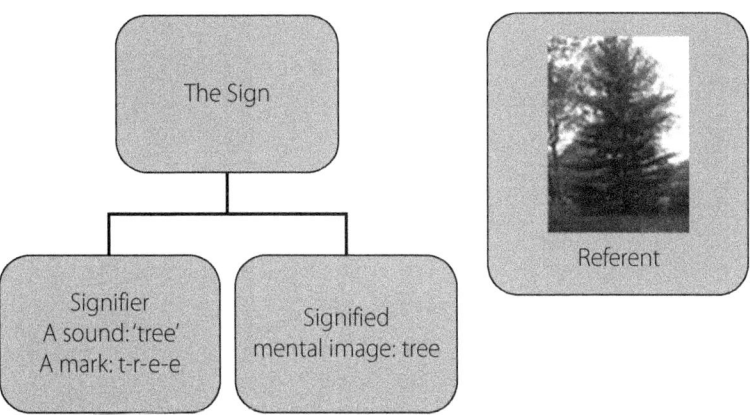

FIGURE 1.1 *Diagram of the Saussure / Peirce sign.*

Turkish 'hev hev' or the Russian 'gav gav' (гав-гав) for 'woof woof'. Saussure compares a 'French dog's *ouaoua* and a German dog's *wauwau*' to illustrate that 'onomatopoeia is only the approximate imitation, already partly conventionalised, of certain sounds' and that, furthermore, 'onomatopoeic and exclamatory words are rather marginal phenomena, and their symbolic origin is to some extent disputable' (Saussure in Lodge 1988: 13).

How does this apply to visual resemblance? Wouldn't a drawing of a tree, for example, have a more natural or inevitable connection with the thing it represents, because it *resembles* a tree? Again semiotic distinctions are useful. A visual signifier, in the form of a drawing of a tree, might prompt the signified of a generic tree, and the category of vegetable matter that we group together as trees. This would be the case however individuated the drawing of the tree might be, even if it was drawn from life or a photograph of a specific tree, unless the recipient knew the tree in question, in which case the signifier would communicate the signified of that specific tree. In certain contexts, a drawing of a tree might connote home, England (for an oak tree, perhaps), Canada for a maple tree, roots, family trees, mother, father, friend, nature, specific gardens or gardeners, and so on.

Peirce's notion of indexical signs is useful here. An indexical sign indicates a thing (or idea) and the connection between the sign and the thing is learnt. For example, a sign showing smoke affords a learnt indexical connection with fire. Smoke is not fire, but as we know proverbially, there is no smoke without fire. Smoke is therefore a sign for fire. An exception would be the group of 'No smoking' signs which show smoke in order to debar its production via cigarettes.

Semiotics and structuralism

Saussure's structuralist linguistics formed the basis of a structuralist approach to understanding society and culture. Structuralists have sought to explain the underlying structures by which diverse societies have been organized, and the myths devised to understand and explain those structures. A key exponent was the anthropologist/ethnologist Claude Levi-Strauss (Belgian, 1908-2009). In works such as the first volume of his *Mythologiques*, called *The Raw and the Cooked*, which appeared in French in 1964 and in an English translation in 1969, Levi-Strauss examined 187 indigenous American myths, noting convergence around repeated binary oppositions such as raw and cooked, nature and culture, with cooking being a process whereby 'nature' becomes 'culture'. Explaining Levi-Strauss' work, Roland Barthes (1915–1980) notes that 'the constituent units of mythical discourse (mythemes) acquire meaning only because they are grouped in bundles and because these bundles themselves combine together' (Barthes 1977: 86). Binary oppositions have been used extensively to understand cultural meaning as well as social organization. It has been suggested that these pairings of opposites can provide insights into hierarchies of value and throw into relief preferred options as in good and bad, male and female, black and white, old and new. However, the fate of binary oppositions provides a metonymic case in part or a microcosmic case in miniature of the intellectual history of its parent field of structuralism.

Barthes was born in the year that Saussure's *Cours* first appeared in print. His intellectual development exemplifies a shift from structuralism to post-structuralism, revealed in Stephen Heath's edited selection of Barthes' writings from 1961 to 1973. 'The Photographic Message' of 1961 demonstrates the utility of attention to connotation. 'Rhetoric of the Image' provides a virtuoso analysis of the semantic possibilities of one print advertisement for Panzani Italian foods (Figure 1.2), noting that 'all images are polysemous; they imply, underlying their signifiers, a "floating chain" of signifieds, the reader able to choose some and ignore others' (Barthes 1977: 39). 'Introduction to the Structural Analysis of Narratives' (1966) describes how to apply semiotic approaches to cultural analysis. 'The Death of the Author' (1968) and 'From Work to Text' (1971) work as a pair, in that the former argues against the primacy of authorial intention in cultural

FIGURE 1.2 *Panzani advertisement, analysed by Roland Barthes, 'Rhetoric of the Image' (Barthes 1977: 32–51), Plate XVII.*

production and the latter proposes that if the author is dead, the cultural artefact is no longer the work of an authorial individual but rather a cultural text, available for interpretation. Foucault responded to Barthes' 'Death of the Author' with his own essay 'What is an author?' which ends with the notion that if the author is really dead, texts will circulate anonymously and be understood only within the context of discourse (Foucault (1969) 1979). Foucault's notion may be seen to have been realized in the internet 'memes' which are circulated and recirculated on social media with little attention paid to their origination. Taken together, these essays represent a paradigm shift in approaches to cultural production in the twentieth century, from a structuralist model of reading culture and society for evidence of underlying organizational frameworks, which has been criticized as static, to a more dynamic post-structuralist approach which allows for semantic flux and changing interpretations.

Barthes provides ample evidence of the value of a post-structuralist cultural analysis in his collections *Mythologies* ((1957) 1972) and *The Eiffel Tower and Other Mythologies* (1979). While the core material selected by editor Stephen Heath for *Image-Music-Text* derives from academic journal articles, the brief essays in *Mythologies* are gathered from Barthes' journalism, written for an informed general reader of literary magazine *Les Lettres Nouvelles*. D.J. Huppatz has characterized the contribution of *Mythologies* as 'a new method of reading cultural artifacts in terms of their supplementary meanings, exposing the rich connotations embedded in everyday life' (Huppatz 2011: 86). Huppatz notes that 'Barthes used the term "myth" in his analysis of consumer culture and its artifacts in order to reveal that even in the sophisticated technological society of post-war France, objects were organized into meaningful relationships via narratives that expressed collective cultural values' (Huppatz 2011: 88). For example, in *Mythologies* readers are told that red wine signals France in multiple ways and that 'cars today are almost the exact equivalent of the great Gothic cathedrals ... the supreme creation of an era, conceived with passion by unknown artists, and consumed in image if not in usage by a whole population which appropriates them as a purely magical object' (Barthes 1972: 88). Barthes influentially moved the analytical frame to include the serious analysis of popular culture.

Semiotics, structuralism and graphic design

How are Barthes' analyses of literature and popular culture relevant to the understanding of design? In providing exemplary analyses of designed products such as the Citroën D.S., and plastic as a material category, *Mythologies* (1957) and its successor volume *The Eiffel Tower and Other Mythologies* (1979) demonstrate how meanings may be decoded from cultural products such as designed goods, with the implication that such meanings are also already encoded. In his essay 'Myth Today' which appears at the end of *Mythologies*, Barthes notes the omnipresence of designed meanings:

> The development of a publicity, of a national press, or radio, of illustrated news, not to speak of the survival of a myriad rites of communication which rule social appearances makes the development of a semiological science more urgent than ever. In a single day, how many really non-signifying fields do we cross? Very few, sometimes none. Here I am, before the sea; it is true it bears no message. But on the beach, what material for semiology! Flags, slogans,

signals, sign-boards, clothes, suntan even, which are so many messages to me. (Barthes 1972: 112, n. 2)

Barthes' work is therefore of value in the production and mediation of design as well as in design consumption. Reading Barthes we see a modernist concern for authorial expression and intention cede to a postmodern interest in interpretation. Post-structuralism puts meaning in the eye of the beholder. A shift from the systematizing of semiotics as a science of signs, and structuralism, to the 'incessant sliding' of post-structuralism has allowed for, and recognized, the role of readers and viewers in making meaning in graphic design, as in other areas of cultural production. In the twenty-first century, post-structuralism can be seen as socially inclusive, in terms of allowing for the importance of meaning created by end users. Subsequent chapters will examine the related shift from modernism to postmodernism in design, and review a rejection of branding exemplified by the subversive tactics of *Adbusters* and Naomi Klein's *No Logo* (1999).

Understanding the three distinct parts of a sign (signifier, signified and referent) can inform a designer's command of the difference between denotation and connotation. Both Saussure and psychoanalyst Jacques Lacan pointed to what Lacan called 'the notion of an incessant sliding of the signified under the signifier' (Lacan 1988: 87). A designer may seek to minimize any 'sliding' or slippage between denotation and connotation in a vitally important message about, for example, fire safety. Or she/he may exploit the gap between denotation and connotation by embracing ambiguity in, for instance, double meanings such as punning or suggestive, risqué double entendre. The connotation of a visual design can provide a subversive or polemical subtext. The possibilities for propaganda and advertising, particularly, are rich: 'The invitation to buy any item becomes part of a wider signifying process that involves the product being encoded with reference to metaphors, puns, myths and dreams' (Jobling 2005: 3). Illustrator Alan Male asserts that 'visual communication relies on semiotics. This is where the audience interprets and translates signs and symbols, often by association and the deciphering of those meanings can be subconscious' (Male 2007: 19). However, rather than leaving the process of interpretation to the audience, some designers and design educators believe that they should design with an awareness of semiotics.

The Hochschule für Gestaltung (HfG) was founded in 1951 in Ulm, Germany, with a strong interest in theoretical approaches to design, shown in the work of Tomás Maldonado and Gui Bonsiepe (Bonsiepe 1963). Graphic design historian Stephen J. Eskilson notes that Otl Aicher and Inge Scholl, who founded HfG Ulm with Max Bill, 'pioneered the semiotic analysis of graphic design at a time when few outside the HfG were operating at such a high intellectual level' and 'attempted to establish a credible academic theory for their design practice' (Eskilson 2012: 298). However, Eskilson observes little visual difference between Otl Aicher's work redesigning the identity of German airline Lufthansa (1969), for example, and Paul Rand's corporate identity work in the United States. Describing Yale professor Rand as 'less scholarly' than Aicher, Eskilson asks 'what role the theory of graphic design can play in the actual practice of the profession' (Eskilson 2012: 299). Unfortunately, Eksilson's question goes unanswered in his book.

When Eskilson expects graphic design which results from a theoretical approach to *look* different from 'less scholarly' approaches, he misses the point. Theoretically informed graphic design need not differ visually, although it may do. Rather, the ways in which the work is approached, undertaken and understood benefits from theoretical – specifically, in this case, semiotic – awareness. Paul Rand (1914–1996) and Otl Aicher (1922–1991) were contemporaries. Graphic designers, whether informed by semiotics or ignorant of it, might well produce similar-looking work as a result of shared contextual factors, such as being roughly the same age, sharing features in graphic design education, reading the same magazines, attending the same conferences, working with the same international group of leading practitioners and watching the same films, among other things.

The HfG theoretical approach to design persists, for example, in Bernhard E. Bürdek's 2005 textbook which provides a history of HfG Ulm, based in part on Bürdek's experiences as a student there, and contains sections on both 'Design and Methodology' and 'Design and Theory' informed by Bürdek's experience as a professor at the Hochschule für Gestaltung Offenbach. Bürdek insists that 'the designer must understand these languages; then, he must be able to teach the objects to speak (Bürdek 2005: 231). Edward Triggs has averred that 'judicious application of selected concepts of rhetoric and semiotics is an effective means of determining new forms unrestricted by allegiance to conventional models; that is, a form which arises naturally from an argument the designer has developed as a persuasive entry point for reading of the text' (Triggs 1995: 86).

The continuing relevance of Barthes' ideas is shown in reappraisals and continuations of his work (Huppatz 2011; Houze 2016). Designers Ellen Lupton and Abbott Miller introduce both Saussure and Barthes into their book *Design Writing Research* ((1996) 1999) which elaborates their understanding of deconstruction as relevant to the practice and understanding of graphic design, discussed in Chapter 5. Also published in 1996, Gunther Kress and Theo van Leeuwen's influential textbook *Reading Images: The Grammar of Visual Design*, ((1996) 2006) acknowledges their debt to Roland Barthes even while they refuse the arbitrary status of the sign, preferring instead to draw attention to the extent to which signs are motivated. Kress and Theo van Leeuwen's work has, in turn, been influential. For just one example of work which uses their method, see Tresidder's semiotic analysis of the website for Michelin-starred restaurant Le Manoir Aux Quat'Saisons which shows how 'a particular ideology and construction of hospitality that are embedded and reinforced' in the restaurant's website in such a way as to 'elevate the notion of food and hospitality to that of the sacred' (Tresidder 2011: 80).

Sean Hall's *This Means This, This Means That* ((2007) 2012) is unusual in that an introduction which reviews the importance of wide variety of contexts for determining semiotic meaning is followed by around seventy questions which are asked of the reader in order to demonstrate semiotic principles, keywords and concepts in action, such as genre, style and stereotypes. This brilliant tactic has the advantage of engaging us, as readers, in the process of semiotic analysis but the modular approach does not allow for comparison across the keywords and concepts. For example, Hall defines ideology, discourse and myth in very similar ways: 'Ideologies are about ideas: what they are and how they are formed'; 'Discourses help to form our ideas about the world through regulated forms of use'; 'Myths help us to understand the world' (Hall (2007) 2012: 162, 164, 166). Hall's theory-in-action approach is useful nevertheless, and his conclusion that 'in semiotics we don't simply decipher a coded meaning and leave it at that. Instead, we are asked continually to reinterpret, reformat, rework, rethink and reinvigorate the meanings that we find around us' (Hall (2007) 2012: 189) provides a convincing account of the practice of post-structuralist approaches to meaning in contemporary culture.

Some commentators argue strongly against theory in graphic design. As Robin Kinross asserts:

The realm of detail remains stubbornly out of reach of the theorizing and polemic that has surrounded recent typography. Ligatures and word-breaks can't be grasped by big, single-tack ideas about the death of the human subject, the end of grand narratives, the terrors of the Enlightenment, the tyrannies of Western metaphysics. Such details are just too small, too mundane, too material, too much just a matter of keyboard layouts and pixels. The kind of theory that matters for word-breaks is not poststructuralist semiotics, which hopes to describe pretty much everything in the universe, but rather what is useful here is the workaday grammar and etymology of a particular language. (Kinross 1997: 93)

The idea that semiotics has a scalar tendency that renders it unsuitable for appreciating details is not sustained by even the most cursory reading of Saussure's work. On the contrary, semiotics *affords* detailed comprehension and is an analytical frame which facilitates the analysis of formal aspects both large and small. In the preface to the 1970 edition of *Mythologies* Barthes explains that having just read Saussure, he saw a way to 'account *in detail* for the mystification which transforms petit-bourgeois culture into a universal nature' (Barthes 1972: 9). Kinross' argument above is not really about scale – that position is unsustainable – rather it is about the theory/practice divide. Kinross argues that there are areas of practice which cannot be accounted for in theory. This may be true of haptic (touch-centred), experiential, tacit (known but unstated) and non-verbal areas of experience, but it is not true of typographic details. In any case, the demand for semiotics is high: writing in 2010, Arthur Asa Berger notes the extensive publications in print and online that deal with semiotics (Berger 2010: 5).

Branding as a sign system

Some areas of graphic design seem to be made for a semiotic analysis, such as road signs and branding (Manning 2010). Branding as a category, genre or sub-field of design can be seen as a langue, a language system in Saussure's terms. Branding forms part of the wider category of corporate identity and it includes not just logos and logotypes but the entire appearance of each brand that a company might own. For example, the branding for Coca-Cola includes the logotype 'Coca-Cola' in a script typeface underlined by the 'dynamic ribbon device' (aka wave), and the 'Coke' logotype as well as the bottle shape. Each of these visual cues contributes to the Coke brand. The Coca-Cola Company's logo clearly resembles the logo of its original and strongest brand, as does its name, to the extent that the Coca-Cola Company and the Coca-Cola logos could be indistinguishable to a casual observer. Yet, while Coke's brand identity is consistent, the Coca-Cola Company owns 350 other brands including Dasani water and Minute Maid orange juice, each with their own brand identities, so that a drinks vending machine or a restaurant can offer an apparent variety of differentiated drinks choices all supplied by the Coca-Cola Company. The same is true of Pepsi-Cola (Figure 1.3). Branding can be seen, therefore, as a balancing act of similarity and difference.

Each individual brand can be seen as a parole, or utterance which is understood through its difference from others. That process of distinction is part of the work of the graphic design and

FIGURE 1.3 *Pepsi mosaic on soft drinks vending machine, Las Vegas, 2018, photograph by Jo Turney, with permission.*

branding specialist. Although brands exist to communicate difference, even where none or little might exist (Coke is not Pepsi), brands form clusters of similarity, from the insignia of quality and assurance seen in luxury branding to the identikit appearances of the many brands which use Helvetica for their logotypes, from the troubled American Apparel to Crate & Barrel. Not all brands are associated with commerce, in the manner of trademarks. Some brands are perhaps better described as tags, or labels of personal or group identity or ownership. Graffiti tags are one example, and the 'branding' of terrorist organizations, from al-Qaeda to the Tamil Tigers, is another (Beifuss and Bellini 2013).

Per Mollerup has made a detailed study of similarity and difference in branding with his *Marks of Excellence: The History and Taxonomy of Trademarks* (1997). Mollerup's book is clearly informed by semiotics: it begins with a quotation from Peirce and reviews some core ideas of communication theory from Claude E. Shannon and Warren Weaver ((1949) 1964), Charles Morris (1946), Roman Jakobson (1960), Pierre Guiraud (1971) as well as Peirce, in an attempt to list all the potential functions and requirements of trademarks. These inform Mollerup's taxonomic categories in which a large number of trademarks are arranged first by formal qualities (e.g. picture marks, letter marks) and then by linguistic characteristics (e.g. non-acronym initial abbreviations) while motifs follow (e.g. arrows, lions). Mollerup avoids the static nature of the taxonomy representing a slice of time (synchronic) with a section on trademark development, showing how a number of trademarks have developed over time (diachronic) and place, with geographical variations.

Just as Saussure made clear the ways in which language functions through difference (in that the word 'cat' is similar to, but distinguishable from 'mat' or 'bat') so Judith Williamson has demonstrated the function of advertisements in communicating difference in the products they depict. While advertising and marketing are distinct from corporate identity and branding, they work to suggest and reinforce messages and stories about brands. Williamson's starting point for her now-classic instance of the application of semiotics to the understanding of design, *Decoding Advertisements* (1978), was her concurrent readings of Marx and consumer magazines. She combines Marxist analysis of ideology with semiotic analyses of advertisements as signs, seeing past surface meanings in favour of deep explorations of the mythologies they encode. Product difference, like linguistic difference, is established via association. So, Williamson shows, an advertisement for Belair cigarettes (Figure 1.4) overcomes the empirical fact that cigarettes taste anything but fresh (with the possible exception of menthol cigarettes) by associating the brand with fresh produce: 'We are shown foods which we *know* are fresh-tasting, and invited to ride on the accuracy of this information to the assumption that the other oral pleasure invoked, smoking Belair, is also fresh-tasting. How can a *cigarette* really be "fresh"? Yet it seems to be, because of the dewy drops on the cucumber' (Williamson 1978: 33). Although the intellectual tide in the neoliberal West has turned away from Marxist cultural analysis in the twenty-first century, Williamson's amalgam of Marxism and semiotics remains a classic for the clarity with which the methods of semiotics and structuralism are applied to cultural analysis. More recently, Bernhard Kettemann has provided a concise statement that we consume meanings not goods. This happens through a transfer of meaning from an advertisement 'We have bought a meaning, not a function' (Kettemann 2014: 47).

A salient case study of the reach of branding is the bottled water industry (Wilk 2006). In much of the West, clean tap water is freely available at a low cost. Yet, an enormous industry has developed to sell bottled water. Consumer appeals are based on the superior taste and/or purity of bottled water, even though some bottled waters, such as Coca-Cola's Dasani and PepsiCo's Aquafina are simply filtered tap water (*Consumer Reports* 2012). Bottled water is also sold for its convenience, to the extent that Kane Race has shown how the ideological construct of hydration – that we must drink all the time or risk becoming dehydrated, even though this is not a real risk for people living in temperate climates – convinces consumers to drink on the go (Race 2012). However, the environmental costs of bottled water consumption are prompting campaigns to counter the marketing of bottled water (van der Linden 2015).

FIGURE 1.4 *Advertisement for Belair cigarettes from the collection of Judith Williamson, with permission.*

In focus: Unilever

Barthes' essay 'Soap Powders and Detergents' was one of a series written between 1954 and 1956 that were collected in the book *Mythologies*. In this essay Barthes sets the Persil and Omo brands in opposition, just as he places soap powders and detergents in separate camps. The binary oppositions continue, at a microscopic scale, in Barthes' semiotic analysis of Omo advertising. Readers learn that in order to accept advertisers' claims that Omo detergent cleans deep down, we must first accept that fabric is deep: deep and shallow, clean and dirty are some more binary oppositions engaged in this advertising strategy.

Around the time that Barthes was writing about Omo's advertising, Wally Olins was recruited from Oxford University, where he read History, via National Service, to SH Benson, 'one of the London agencies that backed Ogilvy & Mather, the US firm founded by the British adman David Ogilvy, and eventually became part of it' (York and Damazer 2014). As a young advertising industry professional, Olins worked on campaigns for Unilever's detergent Omo centred upon the idea that Omo 'was able to add "brightness to whiteness" because "whiteness alone is no longer enough"' (Olins, 2003: 59). This campaign furthered the binary oppositions and specious claims Barthes noted, adding to the opposition of whiteness and blackness, brightness and darkness, the idea that brightness and whiteness may be distinguished as markers on the cleanliness continuum. In 1957, the year that *Mythologies* was first published, Olins was posted to Ogilvy & Mather's operation in Mumbai, India. Five years later he returned to London and set up the Wolff Olins branding consultancy with designer Michael Wolff. Barthes concludes his 'Soap Powders and Detergents' essay that 'there is a plane on which Omo and Persil are one and the same: the plane of the Anglo-Dutch trust Unilever' (Barthes 1972: 38).

Unilever had been formed in 1929 by the merger of the Dutch company Margarine Unie and British soap manufacturer Lever Brothers. Even before the merger, Lever Brothers operated a brand structure. Lever's leading brand, Sunlight soap, gave its name to Port Sunlight, England, a model village for employees erected as part of Lever's enlightened business practice. Other brands included Lifebuoy, which emphasized hygiene, and Lux, which traded on Hollywood glamour. Unilever's brand structure grew to the extent that considerable pruning was felt to be necessary. For the twenty-first century, Unilever launched a 'Path to Growth' strategy, to concentrate on Unilever's portfolio of brands in terms of product type and profitability. Unilever cut its holdings from 1600 brands to 900 brands by 2001, selling assets such as premium cosmetics brand Elizabeth Arden. Unilever now owns 400 brands, one quarter of its previous holdings. Among the most successful of these are Hellman's, Lux and Surf, each of which relate to Unilever's original product categories of oil- and fat-based consumer products, plus other products such as Lipton's tea.

Unilever did not adopt a coherent global corporate identity until 1967, when the Design Research Unit produced a logo intending to communicate stability and seriousness as well as the British and Dutch twin pillars of Unilever Ltd and Unilever NV (Figure 1.5). The logo appeared in grey until 1989 and in blue from 1990, when the name 'Unilever' was added for clarification (Unilever ND). Following the attacks of September 11, 2001 on the World Trade Center, the 'twin towers' aspect of the Unilever logo was unwelcome. As part of 'Path to Growth' the Wolff Olins

FIGURE 1.5 *Unilever logo 1970–2004. Design Research Unit. Unilever Archives, Port Sunlight, Merseyside.* © *Design Research Unit, Scott Brownrigg.*

agency was commissioned to redesign the Unilever logo. The new logo was rolled out in 2004, for the company's seventy-fifth anniversary (Figure 1.6). Wolff Olins had grown to become a global, leading brand consultancy even as Wolff left in 1983 and Olins sold the company in 2001. Just as the notion that the 'Path to Growth' lay in consolidation and the reduction of Unilever's brand roster by 75 per cent, from 1600 to 400 brands, is counter-intuitive, so Unilever's approach to its company identity is similarly unexpected. The Coca-Cola Company's identity strongly resembles that of its leading brand, Coke, and therefore pulls a diverse range of brands together around one identity. Unilever, on the other hand, adopted a new logo which recognized the diversity of a company which in 2014 had a turnover of $48.4 billion, with 400+ brands and 172,000 employees, while also seeking to achieve focus around the notion of vitality. Unilever's holding company logo of 1970 was not widely published, but in a bid for greater transparency, the new logo now appears on all Unilever products and advertising. Unilever's 'vitality mission' was intended to provide a focus for all of Unilever's products and brands. It influenced not only which brands Unilever bought and sold, but also the ingredients in the product ranges: 'Over the course of 2004, Unilever's leading brands grew by 3.7% under the "Vitality Mission" while operating profit grew at an average of 15% a year, for four consecutive years' (Wolff Olins 2015).

The 2004 logo was drawn by Miles Newlyn, working with Lee Coomber. While Coomber has praised Miles Newlyn's typographic expertise in using positive and negative space in the design so that the many icons within the 'U' remain legible (Coomber 2012), in practice the 2004 Unilever

FIGURE 1.6 *Unilever logo, designed by Miles Newlyn and Lee Coomber for Wolff Olins, 2004.*

logo works differently in different contexts and platforms. The U can be read at a distance, or at smaller sizes than the icons which are best seen close up, such as in print media, or at larger sizes. Unusually, the Unilever logo communicates diversity rather than similarity with twenty-five constituent motifs including sunlight, a bee, a DNA helix, a hand, hair, a palm tree, a flower, a whirlpool, a spoon, a cooking pot, a chilli, a fish, water, a bottle, clothing, ice particles, a heart, bubbles, a tea plant, a recycling symbol, a mouth, an ice cream, a dove and a star/sparkle. The icons form a sans serif 'U' shape, for Unilever, atop a wordmark showing 'Unilever' in a handwritten script style. This multiple denotation gives rise to a wide range of connotations.

At the time of the launch, one commentator suggested that the 2004 Unilever logo resembled the Pharmacia and Upjohn logo designed by Newell and Sorrell (Weinberger 2004). This logo (Figure 1.7) showed a hand, a bird and a star figured on a rock and was in use from the merger of Pharmacia and Upjohn in 1995 until their merger with Monsanto in 2000, to form Pharmacia Corporation (later bought by Pfizer). 'According to the 160-page Pharmacia & Upjohn Corporate Identity Guideline book the symbols on the rock reflect the qualities of humanity, innovation and aspiration' (Winkworth 2015). The simple, impressionistic way in which the symbols are applied or incised prefigures the motifs in the Unilever logo and their arrangement is also similar.

For viewers who scrutinize the Unilever logo close up, each of the twenty-five constituent symbols functions as an individual iconic sign. The bird in the Unilever logo is intended to represent the successful 'Dove' brand of soap and beauty products, but it can also connote peace and nature. The bee can connote honey, sweetness, nature, pollination and agriculture, among other things. The palm tree can refer to palm oil, or to paradise, while the bubbles are sufficiently impressionistic in their rendering that they could indicate particles in scientific research as well as bubbles in a bubble bath. Examples of how some of these motifs are rich with meaning are found in Martin Kemp's book on contemporary icons; Kemp includes the heart and DNA (as well as Coke) among twelve focal examples (Kemp 2012), while a study of iconicity in design includes Dubai's Palm Islands and Coke among its fifty examples (Lees-Maffei 2014).

However, an important level of meaning here derives from the relationships between the constituent symbols. Collectively, the symbols may be read as indicative of certain areas of human experience, such as engagement with nature (sunlight, water, bees, fish, birds, trees, flowers) or food (ice cream, cooking pot, chilli, fish, frozen food) or cleanliness (sunshine, water, bottle of detergent, perhaps, laundry, bubbles, recycling) or beauty (hair, lips, plants and flowers). Narrative connections may be made; contiguous icons suggest sequential meanings such as the mouth and the ice cream, the water and the bottle (which may contain laundry detergent), the cooking pot and the chilli, and the sunshine and the bee. One intended example of such a micro-narrative is provided by an ice crystal being shown next to a plant with an arrow, to suggest the freezing of fresh produce.

If the Unilever logo enables the construction of several narratives, not all of these are intended. Like the BP logo of 2002, which shows a green and yellow flower motif that connotes green ecological values at odds with the environmental threat represented by the oil industry (BBC 2000; Houze 2016), Unilever's logo emphasizes natural phenomena alongside its manufactured goods in a way that might invite criticism. Although chemicals are drawn from nature, the natural and chemical can be situated in a binary opposition that this logo fails to collapse and unite. With this logo, Unilever has tried to address the fact that its strength in personal and household hygiene products is difficult to reconcile with ecological principles. Karin Wagner has written a social

FIGURE 1.7 *Pharmacia & Upjohn logo, 1995–2000, Newell and Sorrell, photograph and permission Jeremy Winkworth.*

semiotic analysis of food packaging which notes the importance of symbols in the constricted space of the food package. She notes that the heart symbol can connote health and love, and that the use of symbols denoting organic, or otherwise responsible, production methods, and those representing recycling affordances, are connected to a wider practice of greenwashing which draws on colour, keywords such as 'natural', and materials such as cardboard and the reduction in the use of plastic (Wagner 2015).

The Unilever logo works on many levels, both formally, as a 'U' and as twenty-five constituent symbols, and in terms of the way in which each symbol works semiotically with its own referents, as well as working collectively to promote areas of experience and micro-narratives. A further layer of context for the Unilever logo is provided in the *langue* of branding in general, and the brands of fast-moving consumer goods (fmcg) and household multinationals particularly.

Conclusion

Semiotics is only one method through which graphic design may be understood – there are a range of other suitable methodological approaches including ethnography and audience reception analysis – but it is extremely useful for understanding cultural meaning. This first chapter has introduced some key proponents of semiotic analysis, including Ferdinand de Saussure, Roland Barthes and Judith Williamson. It reviewed some basic semiotic principles such as the constituent parts of the sign, the arbitrary, iconic and indexical nature of signs, the relational function of signs as instances of *parole*, or utterances, which make sense within a *langue*, and structuralist techniques such as identifying binary oppositions and understanding culture in aggregate for evidence of convergence or trends.

Saussure was a product of the nineteenth century, although his work achieved its widest audience during the following century. Barthes' life and career spanned much of the twentieth century and yet his legacy continues to be felt in the current century. His work displays a shift from the relatively static model of meaning which underpins structuralism and semiotics, to the more dynamic understanding of meaning upon which post-structuralism depends. In our current century, the design industry is preoccupied with methods centred upon distributed responsibility in the form of co-design, participatory design and user-centred design. These design methodologies seek to involve users in the design process, They can be seen, therefore, as more or less directly informed by post-structural theory in that they all allow for interpretation and consumption as part of the design process, as the following chapters will show.

References

Barthes, Roland. [1957] 1972. *Mythologies*. London: Jonathan Cape.
Barthes, Roland. 1977. *Image-Music-Text*. Translated by Stephen Heath. London: Fontana.
Barthes, Roland. 1979. *The Eiffel Tower and Other Mythologies*. Translated by Richard Howard. Berkeley and Los Angeles: University of California Press.
BBC News. 2000. 'BP Goes Green'. *BBC News*, Business, Monday 24 July. http://news.bbc.co.uk/1/hi/business/849475.stm. Accessed 29 May 2015.
Berger, Arthur Asa. 2010. *The Objects of Affection: Semiotics and Consumer Culture*. New York: Palgrave Macmillan.
Beifuss, Artur, and Francesco Trivini Bellini. 2013. *Branding Terror: The Logotypes and Iconography of Insurgent Groups and Terrorist Organizations*. New York: Merrell.
Bonsiepe, Gui. 1963. *Gestammelter Jargon: Industrial Design und Charles Sanders Peirce*. Ulm 8/9.
Bürdek, Bernhard E. 2005. *Design: History Theory and Practice of Product Design*. Third edition. Basel: Birkhauser.
Consumer Reports. 2012. 'Knowing Where Your Bottled Water Comes From.' *Consumer Reports Magazine*, July. http://www.consumerreports.org/cro/magazine/2012/07/do-you-know-where-your-bottled-water-comes-from/index.htm. Accessed 30 May 2015.

Coomber, Lee. 2012. Comment on 'Unilever Icons Explained'. LogoDesignLove, 1 December 2011. Comment posted 11 January 2012 at 16:51. http://www.logodesignlove.com/unilever-icons. Accessed 29 May 2015.

Eskilson, Stephen. 2012. *Graphic Design: A History*. Second edition. London: Laurence King.

Foucault, Michel. [1969] 1979. 'What Is an Author?' (1969). In Josué V. Harari (ed.), *Textual Strategies: Perspectives in Post-Structural Criticism*. Ithaca, NY: Cornell University Press, 1977. Reprinted in Lodge 1988. 197–210.

Guiraud, Pierre. 1971. *Semiology*. London: Routledge & Kegan Paul.

Hall, Sean. [2007] 2012. *This Means This, This Means That*. London: Laurence King.

Houze, Rebecca. 2016. *New Mythologies in Design and Culture: Reading Signs and Symbols in the Visual Landscape*. London: Bloomsbury.

Huppatz, D. J. 2011. 'Reconsidering: Roland Barthes, *Mythologies*'. *Design and Culture* 3 (1): 85–100.

Jakobson, R. 1960. 'Linguistics and Poetics'. In T. Sebeok (ed.), *Style in Language*, 350–77. Cambridge, MA: MIT Press.

Jobling, Paul. 2005. *Man Appeal: Advertising, Modernism and Menswear*. Oxford: Berg.

Kemp, Martin. 2012. *Christ to Coke: How Image Becomes Icon*. Oxford: Oxford University Press.

Kettemann, Bernhard. 2014. 'Semiotics of Advertising and the Discourse of Consumption.' In Beate Flath and Eve Klein (eds.), *Advertising and Design: Interdisciplinary Perspectives on a Cultural Field*, 45–60. Bielefeld: Transcript.

Kinross, Robin. 1997. 'Where the Dear God Lives'. In Michael Bierut, William Drenttel, Steven Heller and D. K. Holland (eds.), *Looking Closer 2*. New York: Allworth Press.

Kress, Gunther, and Theo van Leeuwen. [1996] 2006. *Reading Images: The Grammar of Visual Design*. Abingdon: Routledge.

Lacan, Jacques. 1988. 'The Insistence of the Letter in the Unconscious'. In David Lodge (ed.), *Modern Criticism and Theory: A Reader*, 80–106. Harlow: Longman.

Lees-Maffei, Grace (ed.) 2014. *Iconic Designs: 50 Stories about 50 Things*. London: Bloomsbury.

Lodge, David (ed.) 1988. *Modern Criticism and Theory: A Reader*. Harlow: Longman.

Lodge, David, and Nigel Wood (eds.) 2013. *Modern Criticism and Theory: An Introduction*. Third Edition. Abingdon: Routledge.

Lupton, Ellen, and J. Abbott Miller. [1996] 1999. *Design Writing Research: Writing on Graphic Design*. London: Phaidon.

Male, Alan. 2007. *Illustration: A Theoretical and Contextual Perspective*. Lausanne: AVA.

Manning, Paul. 2010. 'The Semotics of Brand.' *Annual Review of Anthropology* 39: 33–49.

Mollerup, Per. 1997. *Marks of Excellence: The History and Taxonomy of Trademarks*. London: Phaidon.

Morris, Charles. 1946. *Signs, Language and Behavior*. New York: George Braziller.

Nöth, Winfried. 1990. *The Handbook of Semiotics*. Bloomington, IN: Indiana University Press.

Olins, Wally. 2003. *On Br@nd*. London: Thames and Hudson.

Peirce, Charles S. 1992. *The Essential Peirce: Selected Philosophical Writings Volume 1 (1867-1893)*. Edited by Nathan Houser and Christian Kloesel. Chichester: John Wiley & Sons.

Race, Kane. 2012. '"Frequent Sipping": Bottled Water, the Will to Health and the Subject of Hydration'. *Body & Society* 18: 72–98.

Saussure, Ferdinand de. 1988. 'Nature of the Linguistic Sign'. In David Lodge (ed.), *Modern Criticism and Theory: A Reader*, 10–14. Harlow: Longman.

Saussure, Ferdinand de. 2013. *Course in General Linguistics*. Edited by Roy Harris. London: Bloomsbury Academic.

Shannon, Claude E., and Warren Weaver. (1949) 1964. *The Mathematical Theory of Communication*. Urbana: University of Illinois Press.

Tresidder, Richard. 2011. 'Reading Hospitality: The Semiotics of Le Manoir aux Quat'Saisons'. *Hospitality & Society* 1 (1): 67–84.

Triggs, Edward. 1995. 'Visual Rhetoric and Semiotics'. In Teal Triggs (ed.), *Communicating Design: Essays in Visual Communication*. London: Batsford.

Unilever. Not Dated. 'Unilever Logo' Information Sheet produced by Unilever Archive and Records Management (UARM).

Van der Linden, Sander. 2015. 'Exploring Beliefs About Bottled Water and Intentions to Reduce Consumption: The Dual-Effect of Social Norm Activation and Persuasive Information', *Environment and Behavior* 47 (5): 526–50.

Wagner, Karin. 2015. 'Reading Packages: Social Semiotics on the Shelf'. *Visual Communication* 14 (2): 193–220.

Weinberger, David. 2004. 'Unilever: 25 Times Friendlier'. May 17. *Speak Up* [blog]: *The Archives, August 2002–April 2009*. Archive ID 1953. http://www.underconsideration.com/speakup/archives/001953.html. Accessed 2 June 2015.

Wilk, Richard. 2006. 'Bottled Water: The Pure Commodity in the Age of Branding'. *Journal of Consumer Culture* 6 (3): 303–25.

Williamson, Judith. 1978. *Decoding Advertisements: Ideology and Meaning in Advertising*. London: Marion Boyars.

Winkworth, Jeremy. 2015. 'The Merger with Pharmacia'. *Upjohn Memories* http://www.upjohn.net/corporate/merger/merger.htm. Accessed 2 June 2015.

Wolff Olins. 2015. 'Unilever'. http://www.wolffolins.com/work/33/unilever. Accessed 29 May 2015.

York, Peter, and Mark Damazer. 2014. 'Wally Olins Obituary'. *The Guardian*. Tuesday 15 April. http://www.theguardian.com/media/2014/apr/15/wally-olins. Accessed 29 May 2015.

2

The responsive brand: Uniformity and flexibility in logo design

Nicolas P. Maffei

From the uniformity of modernism to the embrace of difference, this chapter explores the historical shift from static to dynamic logos, representing a development from universal international brand identities to more flexible and responsive corporate personalities. The transformation charted in this chapter occurred over a period extending from the nineteenth century to the present, including the roots of branding, the ideals of modernism, the emergence of the critical consumer, the development of the responsive corporation, and the co-creation of brands in online landscapes. From Peter Behrens' designs for the German Allgemeine Elektrizitäts-Gesellschaft (AEG) 1907 – considered the first corporate identity – to Paul Rand's flexible and humanizing identity developed for International Business Machines Corporation (IBM) after the Second World War, this chapter charts the rise of the unchanging logo and, in turn, the multivalent brand-mark. In addition, the design responses of corporations to the vocal and ethically informed consumer are surveyed via the anti-branding movement, which has targeted Starbucks and McDonalds among other corporations. Nike is examined through local reinterpretations of the global brand. Gap's failed logo of 2010 shows the power of the online consumer and the need for companies to listen and respond. Finally, brand reactions to the responsive consumer – characterized by chameleon-like logo transformation and an emphasis on user interaction and co-production of meaning, are investigated through the designs for telecommunications company Ollo by Bibliothèque 2012, the identity for the Tate museums by Wolff Olins 1999, and Experimental Jetset's Responsive 'W' for The Whitney Museum (2011).

Fixed ideas: Brands as unifying

A static logo – an unchanging brand-mark – is never physically or conceptually fixed; it moves as it is carried on everything from letterheads to livery, and it is interpreted variously depending on its audiences and contexts (see Chapter 1). The static logo is, therefore, always conceptually and materially unstable. The post-war pioneers of corporate identity F.H.K. Henrion and Alan

Parkin understood the slipperiness of brand meanings, expressing the complex contexts in which corporate communication occurs in their early branding primer *Design Coordination and Public Image* (1967):

> A corporation has many points of contact with various groups of people. It has premises, works, products, packaging, stationery, forms, vehicles, publications and uniforms, as well as the usual kind of promotional activities. These things are seen by customers, agents, suppliers, financiers, shareholders, competitors, the press, and the general public, as well as its own staff. The people in these groups build up their idea of the corporation from what they see and experience of it. An image is therefore an intangible and essentially complicated thing, involving the effect of many and varied factors on many and varied people with many and varied interests. (Henrion and Parkin 1967: 7)

This quotation is significant for two reasons. First, it shows that even a static logo is not immobile. It makes many journeys and has many encounters as it travels across time, space and media. Secondly, in addition to its physical movement is its fluid signification: it is uniquely interpreted by a multitude of people across varied physical and temporal contexts. So, in this respect a fixed brand-mark on a letterhead has as much semantic potential as an animated one on a website.

One of the main purposes of a logo is to identify a brand, but also to maintain longevity and relevance. Some logos are so recognizable that they do not need to name the institution or company that they represent. The NBC peacock of 1985 by Chermayeff and Geismar or the Nike swoosh designed by Carolyn Davidson (1971) typify this phenomenon. Implying the need for stasis and familiarity in logo design, in 1966, the former president of the Japan Graphic Designers Association, Yusaku Kamekura explained, 'A long lifespan is demanded of trademarks and symbols. It would not do for them to look old-fashioned soon after they have been designed' (Kamekura 1966: 4). While the 1908 logomark for AEG, for example, may be regarded as exemplary of the use of enduring design to achieve brand recognition, recent developments in shape-shifting digital logos seem to undermine this fundamental strategy of visual identity. What has changed to challenge these long-held branding precepts?

Some of the first brand-marks were precious metal hallmarks, paper watermarks and ceramic marks. They emerged before industrialization and were meant to indicate quality, status, origin or contents. Nineteenth-century technological innovations in printing, packaging and production and the introduction of selling pre-packaged goods allowed for mass branding to flourish after the 1890s in Europe and the United Kingdom. Whereas shopkeepers had previously measured and bagged loose goods, increasingly national and international companies were able to control their image through the graphic design of their packaging. In the history of branding this development is significant, as it allowed the 'surface of a product to be used as a communicative site in a consistent and systematic way' (Moor 2007: 16–18, 18). This enabled companies for the first time to use graphic elements (for example, image, type, colour, form) to communicate meanings and associate specific values with their brand names. These early brand-marks were never in fact static; they were circulated on signs, packaging and advertising as well as in the minds of consumers.

As Moor has observed, following Benedict Anderson's notion of 'imagined communities', mass distribution and mass access to identically packaged goods facilitated the development of national consciousness through shared experiences of consumption, not only of the product but also of the meanings communicated by the brand (Moor 2007: 20). For British citizens at the end of the nineteenth-century imperial imagery on branded goods might have been a source of national pride during a time of global decline. For early-twentieth-century American immigrants consistent brand imagery may have offered a sense of stability in an unfamiliar country (Moor 2007: 21–2). In this way, national symbols communicating ideologies ranging from British Imperialism to American capitalism could be controlled and orchestrated by producers and transmitted to consumers. Critics of branding, however, suggest that corporate branding resulted not in the creation of an authentic national consciousness but in the co-construction of false communities (Klein 1999: 6–7).

From modernist universality to corporate personality: What AEG taught IBM

The German architect and designer Peter Behrens is regarded as the grandfather of corporate identity for his rigorous application of a consistent house style at AEG, and for his influence on successive designers, including Paul Rand at IBM (Heller 1999: 147). At the turn of the nineteenth century in Europe and America, a rapidly expanding consumer economy and resultant glut of cheap and varied goods were seen by some cultural commentators as symptoms of a moral crisis in which capitalist values appeared to trump all others. One way to address this concern, many modernists felt, was to pursue universal and timeless design. This included the rejection of historical styles and a search for an enduring aesthetic based on pure geometric forms. Behrens' corporate identity for AEG was seen by his contemporaries as an antidote to the detrimental effects of capitalism, especially the selling of goods based on historical styles and the use of novelty and excessive marketing to increase sales (Schwartz 1996: 155).

In 1908 the AEG logotype (Figure 2.1) was praised by influential critic Karl Scheffler as a harbinger of a reformed capitalism:

> We have a new sign [*Zeichen*] that the bourgeois enterprising spirit [*Unternehmungsgeist*], which till now has only been concerned with the accumulation of material gain ... is beginning to feel the need to make ... [its work] moral by considering its duty to beauty; and that it is, in this way, becoming truly aware of its modernity. (Scheffler quoted in Schwartz 1996: 153)

FIGURE 2.1 *Peter Behrens, trademark for AEG, registered 1908.*

This modernist appreciation of AEG's logo as a moral corrective to the dynamic reality of consumer culture, which prized fashion and constant transformation, can be contrasted with examples of visual identity from the early twenty-first century which have sought visual elasticity in order to relate to engaged consumers. Both approaches show a moral concern with the needs of people, while addressing them in seemingly opposite ways.

Eliot F. Noyes, IBM's first consultant director of design, was largely responsible for its post–Second World War corporate identity. Noyes' role was not dissimilar to that of Peter Behrens at AEG. Hired in 1956, Noyes was charged with coordinating the redesign of everything at IBM, from its logos and interiors to its computers and buildings. Both Noyes and Behrens completely remade a large twentieth-century firm's visual and material identity. However, Noyes, an architect and product designer, handed graphic design responsibilities to Paul Rand (Harwood 2011: 3). IBM's makeover was not merely aesthetic; it had significant public relations advantages. According to Walter Gropius, Noyes' mentor at Harvard University and a former employee of Behrens, good design benefitted business, workers and society. This view was shared by Thomas J. Watson Jr. chairman and CEO of IBM (Harwood 2011: 3).

Reflecting on his initial impression of IBM, Noyes described a confused and outdated corporate identity:

> When I first met IBM the large main company showroom in New York was a sepulchral place, with oak-panelled walls and columns, a deeply coffered painted ceiling, a complex pattern of many types of marble on the floor, oriental rugs on the marble and various models of black IBM accounting machines sitting uneasily on the oriental rugs. These accounting machines, I might add, often had cast iron cabriole legs in the manner, I believe, of Queen Anne furniture … . It said IBM about twelve times on the façade … . It also said, 'World Peace through World Trade' and many other slogans. (Noyes 1976: 146 quoted in Bruce 2006)

The cacophony of styles, materials and messages resulted in semantic chaos. Noyes thought that the corporate character of IBM should originate not from its past but rather from its core business of 'controlling, organizing and redistributing information in space'. To reconceptualize IBM as a provider of expertise and a producer of communication, management and measurement technologies (e.g. typewriters, time systems, punch-card tabulators and later computers) meant that the firm's technology was at the heart of America's modern corporations (Harwood 2011: 5, 7).

In 1955 Rand was commissioned by Watson to produce an in-depth study of IBM's printed materials (Harwood 2011: 39). Rand was highly critical of IBM's graphic identity. Noting an 'inconsistent' typographic style and a logo lacking in distinction, Rand concluded that the absence of 'family resemblance' across the company graphics made 'it difficult satisfactorily to establish a "company personality"'. Rand argued that what was required was a centralized and coordinated integration of design standards across the organization (Rand 1955).

The first step in achieving this goal was the redesign of the company trademark, which Rand considered 'commonplace' and lacking in 'precision and definition'. It needed to 'express dignity, authority, efficiency and modernity'. But in order to maintain familiarity and family resemblance it should not diverge greatly from the existing logo (Rand 1955). Because IBM's technologically sophisticated goods were beyond most consumers' comprehension, Rand felt the logo was essential as a symbol of technological dependability and innovation.

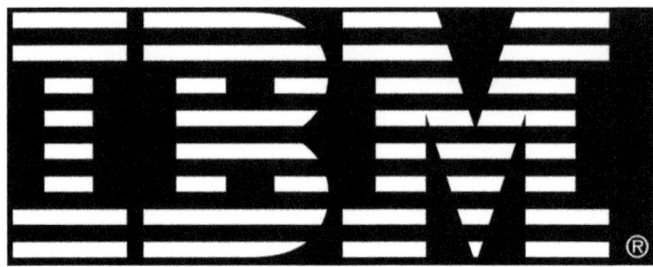

FIGURE 2.2 *IBM eight stripe logo designed by Paul Rand in 1962 and introduced in 1972, permission IBM. IBM and the IBM logo are trademarks of International Business Machines Corp., registered worldwide.*

Rand understood that the logo achieved its power not through fixing its meaning but through being flexible and open to a range of meanings. As early as 1955 he indicated that the IBM logo would benefit from visual variation. Not satisfied with a singular approach to the design of the logotype, he wrote, 'some graphic feature, when possible, might be added to give the mark even more distinction and to increase its flexibility' (Rand 1955). Rand would later create many variations of the IBM logo, ranging from the addition of horizontal stripes to its reinterpretation as a rebus. However, in the *IBM Design Guide* (1960), Rand forbid staff to tinker with the new corporate symbol, 'Multiple versions of a logo, like multiple versions of a signature, confuse its meaning and dilute its power. Don't alter the IBM logo ... even in humor' (Rand 1994: 21; Harwood 2011: 40, 41, 51). Considering Rand's later logo variations, this warning may seem hypocritical, but it reflects Rand's emphasis on centralized control of design in order to maintain a coherent visual identity.

Although not used until 1972, in 1962 Rand introduced eight horizontal stripes to his logo design, resulting in the familiar brand-mark that is now widely recognized as the company signature (Figure 2.2). Rand did not consider the lines to have any representational value, but believed that their rhythm resolved an inherent visual awkwardness in the design without lines. Nevertheless, the logo carries a range of meanings. In fact, IBM executives interpreted the horizontal bands as prison stripes, a prejudice that delayed the logo's introduction and acceptance. The horizontal strokes and gaps can be associated with communication and technology and can be read as the dashes and spaces of telegraphy as well as the on-off logic of computer language. In 1972 Rand designed a thirteen-striped version that perhaps more explicitly suggested speed, repetition and movement (Harwood 2011: 52–4). Rand later created a witty interpretation of the letters 'IBM' as a rebus of an eye, a bee and the striped letter M, in a 1981-poster for an in-house event. The striped 'M' from the City Medium typeface was easily recognizable as that of IBM. However, IBM's management disliked the playful engagement with the firm's logo, failing to appreciate that this single act helped to humanize what some people saw as a faceless corporation (Heller 1999: 156).

Challenging the logo: The postmodern consumer and Nike reinterpreted

Seeing a corporation as faceless and inhuman can make it easier to rebel against. While IBM was not a target of the anti-corporate movement of the late nineties, other global firms such as

McDonalds, Nike and Starbucks were. This brand rebellion was a response to issues ranging from the corporate degradation of the environment to the exploitation of labour in developing countries. It was characterized by consumer empowerment, culture hijacking and consumer resistance to brands, and stimulated by the activist rhetoric and brand spoofs or subvertisements of Kalle Lasn's Canadian-based *Adbusters* magazine (1989). It was documented in Naomi Klein's *No-Logo: Taking Aim at the Brand Bullies* (Klein 1999). As the anti-corporate movement developed, marketers could not explain this brand rebellion. The most successful companies, and the ones which most closely adhered to the advice of marketing theorists – such as Nike, Coke, McDonalds, Microsoft and Starbucks – were vilified by anti-branders (Holt 2002: 70). How could this be explained?

To understand the origins of this brand rebellion, we need to reflect on the history of mass-culture criticism. After the Second World War an influential group of mass-culture critics, collectively known as 'The Frankfurt School', developed the 'cultural authority model', in which the producers of brands were understood as cultural engineers who controlled society (Horkheimer and Adorno (1944) 1996). Consumer society, they claimed, was organized around the cultural authority of marketers who were part of a wider 'culture industry'. Those consumers who accepted this state of affairs allowed firms to organize their tastes. The 'culture industry', typified by post–Second World War mass media (television, music, film, advertising and branding) and consumer goods, had 'defanged political opposition by restructuring it as taste' (Holt 2002: 71). In this new system former acts of resistance such as the labour conflicts which accompanied early industrial capitalism were quelled by mass-culture industries. Branded purchases acted as the basis for the expression of personal identity and the creation and reproduction of a narrow range of market segments and, it was argued, left little room for unique, idiosyncratic individuality (Horkheimer and Adorno 1996: 123).

However, a more positive take on the cultural authority model can be associated with the cultural studies approach in which the postmodern consumer resisted and reworked the meanings offered by marketers and brands (Firat and Venkatesh 1995). These acts of resistance are at the heart of the anti-branding movement, enacted through public protests against global brands (e.g. the Seattle, Washington, World Trade Organization protests of 1999) and the culture jamming of *Adbusters* and others. The brand parodies of *Adbusters* can be seen as a form of psychological resistance to the postmodern experience where pervasive advertising clutter contributes to a feeling of an increased speed of life, fragmentation of the self and the decentering of individual identity. However, the postmodern condition has also produced the active postmodern consumer who redefined the roles of producers and consumers by constructing his/her own symbols (Firat and Venkatesh 1995: 252; Rumbo 2002: 127) and recombining existing ones.

Jeff Murray and Julie Ozanne have outlined ways that consumers can break free of the chains of brand-imposed social values (1995). They follow Jean Baudrillard (1998), who considered consumer culture to be made up of a consumption code (see the section 'Branding as a Sign System' in Chapter 1 above), a system of meanings the market embeds in goods, and Jürgen Habermas (1985), who recognized an imbalance in the control of this code favouring the marketers (e.g. in the form of brand consultants, advertisers, etc.), who produce and disseminate it and consumers who have no option but to engage in it. Ozanne and Murray believe that freedom within such a system is only possible if consumers become aware of the code and separate out the manipulative marketers' messages from the actual use value of the product (Ozanne and Murray 1995: 522–3). Fuat Firat and Alladi Venkatesh have extended this analysis and placed it within the context of postmodernity. They argue that we are in a phase where divergent and multiple consumption styles are increasing and these will emancipate society from the control of marketers. They recognize that consumers, rather than depending on brands to produce their cultural worlds, are now beginning to produce their own values, identities and culture outside of those provided by the often domineering and restrictive brands (1995). In anthropology this idea of bricolage, where myth, artefacts, and so on are modified and mixed to create an individual outlook and attire was developed by Claude Levi-Strauss in *The Savage Mind*. It was later applied by Dick Hebdige in *Subculture: The Meaning of Style* to explain the cut and mix approach to expressing style among groups ranging from punks to skinheads (1979: 103).

The Nike swoosh became one such symbol that was vulnerable to acts of postmodern bricolage. The Nike 'tick', as it is also known, has become a potent and ubiquitous global symbol. This is perhaps in part due to its consistent and enduring use as an unchanging stand-alone symbol. Nike's marketing strategy has been based on a contract with the consumer: purchase this authentic symbol via the goods we manufacture and you will be associated with greatness and achievement, Nike's brand values.

However, purchases of genuine Nike goods are not necessary to build a Nike identity, as Paul Bick and Sorina Chiper have observed in their study of counterfeit Nike goods and refashioned Nike logos in Haiti and Romania. In fact, as the Nike swoosh is transformed – rescaled, stretched, and so on – through its application on unofficial handbags and hoodies, new meanings coalesce. In Romania the Nike tick has become a 'V' for victory or is seen as a horizontal 'J' for the basketball player and Nike sponsor Michael Jordan (Bick and Chiper (2007) in Lees-Maffei and Houze 2010: 502) (Figure 2.3). Used on a gravestone in Haiti the swoosh takes on local connotations in a religious context, appearing as 'a warm and comforting version of the icon – thick bodied, gracefully curved, pale blue and lying at rest on its side [...] like a Caribbean wave' (Bick and Chiper 2007: 506). The design of the swoosh, its simplicity, its independence from text, its ambiguous shape, facilitate a range of meanings even in illiterate or non-English speaking communities. This semantic openness and conceptual flexibility allows local meanings to be inscribed on this international symbol (Bick and Chiper 2007: 502).

So, how can a symbol that is so accommodating to a diverse range of meanings be such a marketing success? While this kind of reappropriation of brand imagery is rarely seen outside of the developing world, it does not mean that people in Haiti and Romania do not understand the marketed meanings of the Nike brand. They have understood that the symbol can accommodate additional layers of meaning in ways appropriate to their specific local and historical contexts. The core meaning of the Nike brand remains beneath these strata of signification (Bick and Chiper 2007: 506). Following Zygmunt Bauman's view that within global capitalism the greatest injury to the impoverished is a lack of mobility, whether physical, social or spiritual, the authors recognize the Nike logo as providing *imagined* mobility associated with American prosperity (Bick and Chiper 2007: 507; Bauman 2004: 97):

> Within the context of this widening breech, the swoosh may be employed as a kind of living icon of that mobility and freedom, a sacred homage to the reality-defying lightness of a soaring Michael Jordan, and spiritual link, however fragile, to the hope and prosperity of the mythical American promised land, where everything moves with speed and grace, and everyone wears Nike shoes. (Bick and Chiper 2007: 507)

FIGURE 2.3 *Nike swoosh on gravestone outside Camp Perrin, Haiti, n.d, photograph and permission Paul Bick.*

In *Nike Culture: The Sign of the Swoosh*, Goldman and Papson (1998 (2000)) discuss the visual omnipresence of the Nike swoosh, its global recognition and its affordance of signifying excellence in sports, self-determination, and 'hip authenticity' even without the word 'Nike'. However, the authors also discuss the problem of 'overswooshification', where the more ubiquitous the logo becomes, the less value it has (Goldman and Papson 2000: 1). Overswooshification – the overexposure of a mass-distributed commodified symbol – can result in a free-floating logo untethered from its original commercial meanings. The ease with which the Nike logo has been reinterpreted and recontextualized in developing countries is perhaps a direct result of its symbolic overextension, resulting in its accommodation to, and adoption of, local meanings.

Gap's gaffe and the birth of the responsive logo

While the Nike logo led to local and global variations, a recent Gap brand-mark resulted in an online outcry, and stasis. The failed launch of Gap's new logo in 2010 exemplified the influence of online feedback on brand design. It also underlined the consumer devotion and importance of personal

Why hire an expensive firm to rebrand?

Right click, "Save Image As" to save your logo.

Crap up another logo!

FIGURE 2.4 *Gap logo generator ca. 2010, design and permission James Yu, maker of digital things in San Francisco.*

meanings endowed in logos. The clothes retailer's unveiling of a new corporate symbol resulted in a storm of negative online feedback, culminating in the reinstatement of its previous logo. The about-face illustrated not only the power of consumers to influence the visual identity of brands, but also demonstrated the remarkable speed at which this can occur. Before the internet became a feature of daily life, a corporate response of this kind would have taken months; now brands must react instantly.

In 2010 Gap, Inc. junked its logo of nearly twenty years. Misreading consumer attachment to its old corporate symbol, the new one, designed by Gap with Laird and Partners, New York, appeared on gap.com on 6 October and was quickly derided across the internet (Figure 2.4). The new Gap logo looked very different from the old one: it stood outside of the 'iconic' blue box, which was diminished in size, set in the background, and moved to the upper right behind the lowercase 'p'.

Initially, Gap put on a brave face and sought a positive spin in its corporate response: 'We know this logo created a lot of buzz and we're thrilled to see passionate debate unfolding!' But as the volume of criticism grew, Gap quickly expressed defeat on its Facebook page, 'We've heard loud and clear that you don't like the new logo.' The retailer concluded, 'We're bringing back the Blue Box tonight.' Shortly afterwards the president of Gap North America, Marka Hansen added, 'We are clear that we did not go about this in the right way. We recognize that we missed the opportunity to engage with the online community' (all quotations from Elliott 2010).

The Gap gaffe has become part of branding lore: a stark warning symbolizing the dangers of online branding and the need to respond to consumers instantaneously. Developments in communications technology, most notably the internet and social media networks such as Facebook and Twitter, have challenged the erstwhile one-way communication of traditional branding, toppling the cultural authority model typified by top-down corporate control. As a result, the form and concept of the static logo has been rethought by branding professionals and graphic designers. Global CEO at Interbrand, London, Jez Frampton noted in 2012, 'Today's consumers can connect with many brands through multiple channels. And many of these channels fall outside marketers' control. No longer are consumers simply influenced by brands. Now, brands themselves are being reviewed, shaped and even co-created by consumers' (Frampton 2012).

In 2014 the branding pioneer Wally Olins expressed a similar concern, but rather than adopting the model of co-creation, where consumers and producers collaborate, he reflected on both the unruly consumer and the consumer-as-producer. 'Does the rise of digital technology mean that corporations will increasingly be on the defensive because customers will not only answer back but will be able to make their own brand and market it – like self-publishing? And, if it does, where does that leave the multinational corporation?' (Olins 2014: 7) Interbrand and Wolff Olins exemplify a professional consensus that the internet has profoundly changed the relationship between brands and their publics.

In the pre-internet age organizations were thought to hold the balance of power in the production of brand meaning. They produced and promoted the product, while the consumer's role was limited to using it (Asmussen et al. 2013: 1474). With the advent of online communities consumers had become powerful brand influencers, co-creating brand meaning. A 2013 report showed that clicking on Facebook's 'like' button is worth $174.17 for a brand page (Wang and Hajli 2014; Scissons et al. 2013), suggesting that considerable brand value is created by online consumer actions. Social commerce (the combination of customer-focused computer technology and the rise of social networks) results in an environment where consumers have become brand ambassadors, thus aiding or damaging a company's image (Asmussen et al. 2013). Social media and mass access to the internet and brand democratization put consumers in command, as online reviewers and critics, whether of new products or loved logos, such as Gap's. They (we) now have the tools to control and change their relationships with brands from purchaser, to designer, ad creator, critic or promoter with access to blogs, social networking sites, wikis, video sharing sites, and product review sites (Asmussen 2013: 1474).

The concept of co-creation has taken on central importance in branding theory and branding practice. In co-creation, consumers and companies collaboratively create brand meanings (Prahalad and Ramaswamy 2004). Co-creation is seen as a paradigm shift and includes the concepts of co-production and consumer involvement (where consumers and companies interact to create value), prosumption (where consumers create their own products), consumer empowerment (through education), culture hijacking (such as *Adbuster* parodies) and consumer resistance (where consumers outflank marketers through defiant or oppositional consumption) (Pongsakornrungsilp and Schroeder 2011: 304). In response to such developments brand strategists have suggested a user-generated branding approach where firm-sponsored, brand-related, user-produced content is carefully edited and integrated into brand communications. This company-centric approach to generating content, however, does not ring true to users as genuine, non-sponsored, user-produced content. It is instead seen as carefully orchestrated, albeit user-derived, content and is thus consistent with the 'industrial age, company-control-centric paradigm' (Asmussen 2013: 1474).

Responsive visual identities, however, offer a way to visually communicate that a company is flexible, nimble and aware. Responsive design has multiple meanings. It can refer to the way in which graphic elements can change in ratio to different mobile devices from iPhones to iPads. However, it can also refer to how the brand identities can respond to user interaction – a click, a swipe, a tap or an IP address. The origins of responsive logo design can be traced to 2001 when Marcus Weisbeck and Frank Hauschild of Surface.de produced the logo for Rhizome, the media art blog begun in 1996. Surface.de's generative Rhizome logo was made up of radiating coloured lines of differing lengths (2001). Proclaimed as the first generative logo, it never looked the same twice because it was generated 'on the fly' whenever viewed, depending on the last four IP addresses of the website visitor (Rhizome 2001).

In recent years there has been a proliferation of logos which move and change shape, represented by the various building shapes of Casa da Musica by Sagmeister and Walsh (2007); the rotating box kite of Doyle and Partners Cooper Union logo (2009); MIT Media Lab's ever-changing searchlights by E. Roon Kang and TheGreenEyl (2011) (Figure 2.5); and Siegel+Gale's purple waving flag for Monster.com (2014). On the one hand, the recent trend in flexible visual identities is the result of the need to respond to different digital media environments. However, a dynamic logo also suggests that the brand is responsive not only to different media but also to its consumer. Can these shape-shifting logos be understood as a visual symbol of a company that listens, a new attitude towards the postmodern consumer, especially in the internet age?

Illustrating the continuation of this trend in technology-driven, responsive design is the 2012 brand identity for the telecommunications company Ollo by Bibliothèque, London. The Ollo logo was promoted as the first to exploit the new multi-touch hardware of smart phones and tablets (Bibliothèque 2012). An iPad app was released that allowed users to pull and stretch the logo, but when let go it returned to the original 'Ollo' word mark (Figure 2.6). Yet, even when stretched to an unrecognizable line Ollo's distinctive rainbow colour palette retained the visual DNA of the brand.

The brand guidelines called the logo 'soft, responsive and alive' and suggested that it mirrored the brand strategy of 'infinite possibilities' (Bibliothèque 2012). When interviewed about the benefits of brand co-creation, Timothy Beard, founder of Bibliothèque, replied that because brand execution was presently in a 'state of flux' and consumers could more easily compare products, brand allegiance had become 'short term':

> So, encouraging consumers to have a direct influence over a brand, or the products a brand produces, enables another level of direct interaction where the consumer feels like they are in control. Thus creating engagement, and emotion – which any strong brand is looking for. (Beard interviewed in Wood 2015)

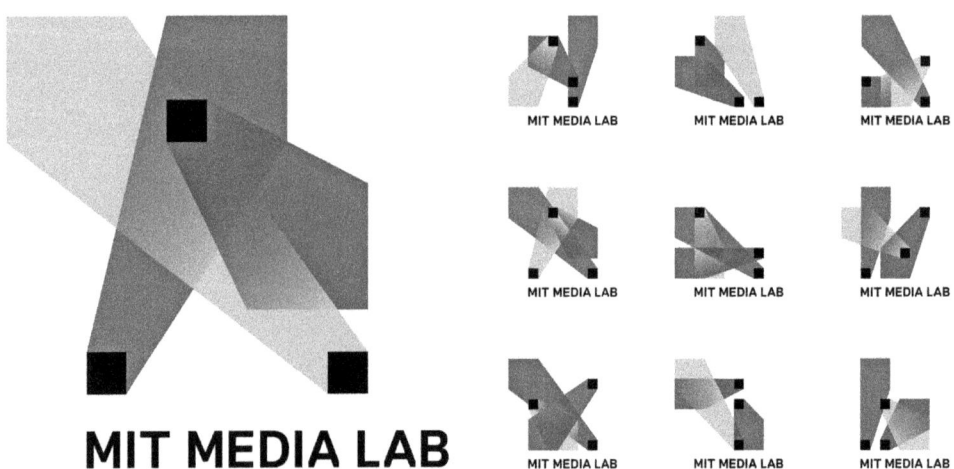

FIGURE 2.5 *MIT Media Lab identity, design and permission E. Roon Kang and TheGreenEyl, 2011.*

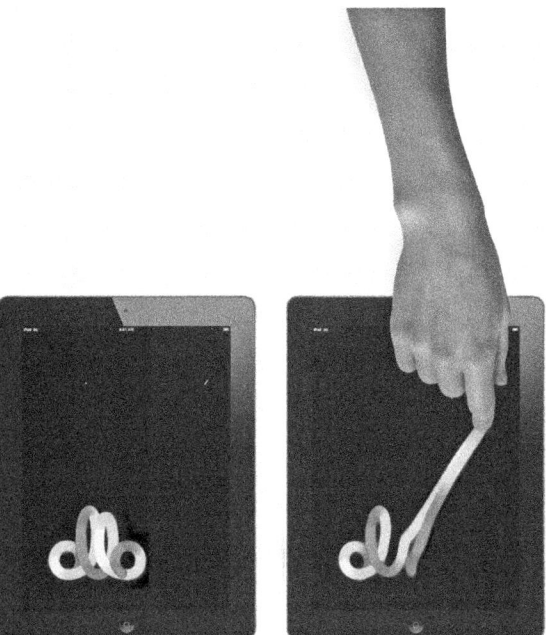

FIGURE 2.6 *Ollo logo iPad app, design and permission Bibliothèque, 2011.*

Reflecting on the impact of the anti-branding movement and the recent Gap U-turn, the emphasis on making consumers feel in control while seeking an emotional bond makes strategic sense. The Ollo app lets users play with the logo, literally transforming the brand identity, and symbolically reshaping the actual brand, at least within the context of the iPad app. This kind of imaginative engagement in the form and meaning of a brand is one type of aesthetic co-creation. This is a long way from the brand rebellion of anti-brand activists. However, it diverges from the top-down, one-way communication mind-set of twentieth-century big brands. Just how much this appearance of control might satisfy a real user desire for corporate flexibility and audience interaction remains to be seen.

Wolff Olins' 'radical' visual identity of 1999 for the Tate museums (Tate Britain, Modern, Liverpool and St. Ives) was an early example of a major art institution engaging in flexible branding. It included a recognizable family of logos that moved in and out of focus while suggesting the museum's dynamic and democratic ethos. The new identity was intended to visually unify its geographically dispersed sites, present them as exciting and varied destinations, and appeal to a wide and diverse audience (Figure 2.7). According to the designer of the identity, Marina Willer, it needed to be 'fluid and very open', 'not imposing', 'always changing' and 'embracing different points of view' (Williams 2011). Suggestive of diversity and flexibility this set of visually adaptable logos indicated a departure from traditional museum practice.

In 2013 the Whitney Museum in New York revealed its new visual identity designed by Experimental Jetset, a Dutch design group with a reputation for theory-derived design. Diverging from the tradition of the static logo, the new design makes central use of a shape-changing black Neue Haas Grotesk 'W', that stretches and extends to fit around visual and textual content (Figure 2.8; Figure 2.9). The 'Responsive W', as the designers called it, replaced a ten-year-old Whitney identity designed by J. Abbott Miller of Pentagram. While this may seem

FIGURE 2.7 *Tate logo designed by North, 2016 with permission. A re-fresh of the original Wolff Olins word mark.*

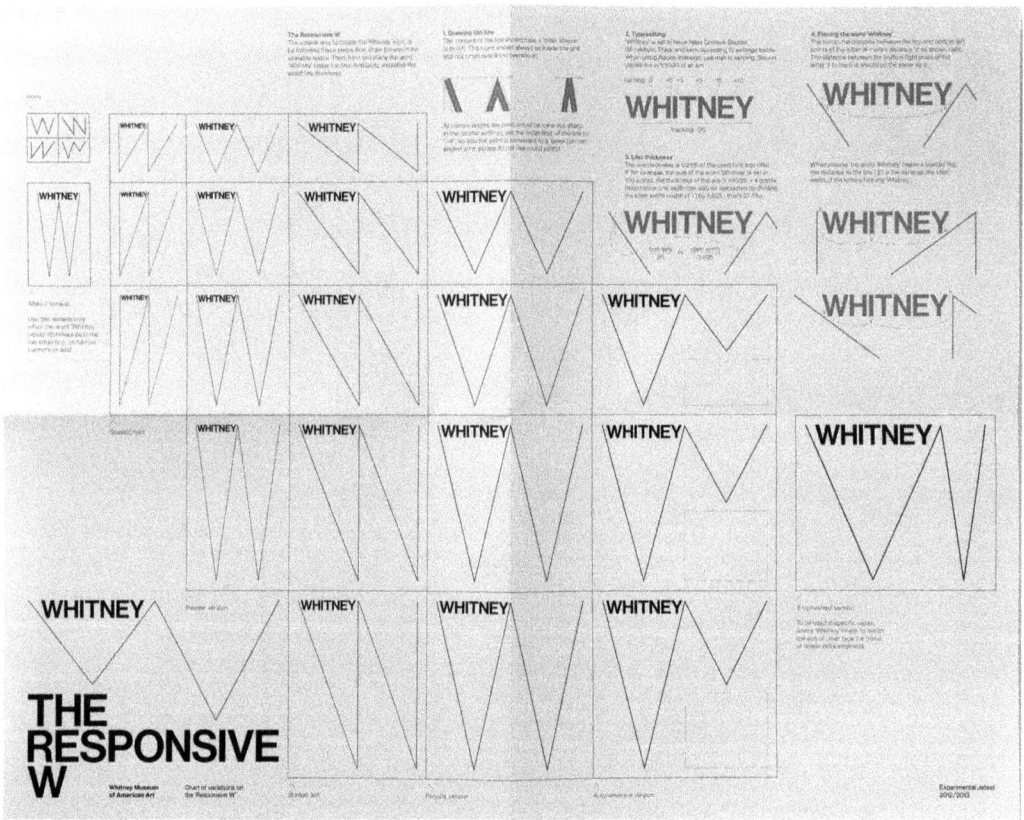

FIGURE 2.8 *Chart of Variations on the 'Responsive W', Whitney Museum of American Art, design and permission Experimental Jetset, 2013.*

a short time after which to introduce a rebrand, in the context of co-creation, the postmodern consumer and the new museology, which emphasizes public engagement, it is appropriate. A long-held goal of museums has been responsiveness to their public, something museums have arguably not been very good at since their inception (McLean 1997: 75). More recently museums have embraced digital capabilities to engage remote and local publics, ranging from

FIGURE 2.9 *Mock-up of 'Responsive W' in situ, Whitney Museum of American Art, design and permission Experimental Jetset, 2013.*

accessible online collections to interactive technology in the museum setting. A responsive and up-to-date visual identity is consistent with the active audience that twenty-first-century museums seek.

Conclusion: Flexible uniformity, co-created balance

Branding balances the needs of commerce with those of consumers. Increasingly, this is achieved through a feedback loop between firms and their markets. During the twentieth century, companies sought varying methods to maintain this balance. In the case of AEG and IBM, pleasing aesthetics communicated an ethical concern for the betterment of society. According to his contemporaries Behrens used his AEG design to counter the visual degradation wrought by uncontrolled capitalism. With humour and wit Paul Rand humanized IBM, a faceless, technological giant. Gap's 2010 failed logo was a stark warning to listen to consumers, proving that a blue box and three letters held powerful, personal meanings for many. Nike's text-free swoosh aided its accrual of new meanings in global contexts, while, more recently flexible digital logos, including those for Ollo and The Whitney Museum, suggest real-time responsiveness to a brand's audience.

Balancing the relationship between user engagement and company goals is a requirement in developing and maintaining brands. However, brands should be considered not only 'company controlled but also as socially constructed entities', complex, sociocultural phenomena, made up of interrelated brand meanings (Asmussen 2013: 1474). These brand meanings might indicate social betterment, as in the case of AEG and IBM, as well as personal achievement, a brand value associated with Nike. However, unpredictable user actions (e.g. online critiques, anti-globalization protests, etc.) may derail a firm's attempt to control its brand messages. Companies may control the manifestations of their brand to a certain extent in the form of products, visual identity, and so on. However, 'each person ultimately develops his or her own personal brand understanding based on various individual as well as socio-cultural factors' (Asmussen 2013: 1474). As Henrion and Parkin noted in 1967, visual identity is 'intangible' and 'complicated' and is influenced by 'many and varied factors on many and varied people with many and varied interests' (Henrion and Parkin 1967: 7). Brand meaning is not only dependent on a complex web of contextual factors, but at its most fundamental it is the productive collaboration between firms and their audiences. If the balance becomes unequal it can also be destructive. Perhaps aware of Barthes' idea of the death of the author – the view that cultural artefacts are open to interpretation by audiences – brand managers have shown an increasing awareness of co-design, making use of digital technology and dynamic identities (whether generative or responsive) to both respond to audiences and visually represent consumer engagement.

References

Anderson, Benedict. 1991 [1983]. *Imagined Communities: Reflections on the Origin and Spread of Nationalism*. Revised edition. London: Verso.
Asmussen, Bjoern, Sally Harridge-March, Nicoletta Occhiocupo, and Jillian Farquhar. 2013. 'The Multi-layered Nature of the Internet-based Democratization of Brand Management'. *Journal of Business Research* 66: 1473–83.
Baudrillard, Jean. 1998. *The Consumer Society: Myths and Structures*. Newbury Park, CA: Sage.
Bauman, Zygmunt. 2004. *Identity: Conversations with Benedetto Vecchi*. Cambridge: Polity.
Bick, Paul B., and Sorina Chiper. 2007. 'Swoosh Identity: Recontextualizations in Haiti and Romania'. *Visual Communication* 6 (1): 5–18.
Bruce, Gordon. 2006. *Eliot Noyes: A Pioneer of Design and Architecture in the Age of American Modernism*. London: Phaidon.
Elliot, Stuart. 2010. 'Gap Inc. Puts 'GAP' Back in Logo'. *New York Times*. 12 October, 2.21pm. http://mediadecoder.blogs.nytimes.com/2010/10/12/gap-inc-puts-gap-back-in-logo/?_r=0. Accessed 13 May 2015.

Firat, A. Fuat, and A. Venkatesh. 1995. 'Liberatory Postmodernism and the Reenchantment of Consumption'. *Journal of Consumer Research* 22 (3): 239–67.
Frampton, Jez. 2012. 'Branding in the Post Digital World'. *Lecture Abstract*. October. http://www.ie.edu/alumni/lifelong-learning/agenda/clubs/functional/882b31367688a310VgnVCM1000004b01050aRCRD?_adptlocale=en_US. Accessed 27 April 2015.
Goldman, Robert, and Stephen Papson. 1998. *Nike Culture: The Sign of the Swoosh*. London: Sage.
Habermas, Jürgen. 1985. *The Theory of Communicative Action*. Boston: Beacon.
Harwood, John. 2011. *The Interface: IBM and the Transformation of Corporate Design, 1945-1976*. Minneapolis and London: University of Minnesota Press.
Hebdige, Dick. 1979 (2003 reprint). *Subculture: The Meaning of Style*. London and New York: Routledge.
Heller, Steven. 1999. *Paul Rand*. London: Phaidon Press.
Henrion, Frederick Henri Kay, and Alan Parkin. 1967. *Design Coordination and Public Image*. London: Studio Vista.
Horkheimer, Max, and Theodor W. Adorno. [1944] 1996. *Dialectic of Enlightenment*. New York: Continuum.
Holt, Douglas B. 2002. 'Why Do Brands Cause Trouble? A Dialectical Theory of Consumer Culture and Branding'. *Journal of Consumer Research* 29 (1): 70–90.
Kamekura, Yusaku. 1966. *Trademarks and Symbols of the World*. London: Studio Vista.
Klein, Naomi. 1999. *No-Logo: Taking Aim at the Brand Bullies*. Vintage.
Lees-Maffei, Grace, and Rebecca Houze (eds.) 2010. *The Design History Reader*. Oxford and New York: Berg.
Levi-Strauss, Claude. 1966. *The Savage Mind*. London: Weidenfield and Nicolson.
McLean, Fiona. 1997. *Marketing the Museum*. London: Routledge.
Murray, Jeff B., and Julie L. Ozanne, 'Uniting Critical Theory and Public Policy to Create the Reflexively Defiant Consumer'. *American Behavioral Scientist* 38 (4): 516–25.
Moor, Liz. 2007. *The Rise of Brands*. Oxford: Berg.
Olins, Wally. 2014. *Brand New: The Shape of Brands To Come*. London: Thames and Hudson.
Pongsakornrungsilp, Siwarit, and Jonathan E. Schroeder. 2011. 'Understanding Value Co-creation in a Co-consuming Brand Community'. *Marketing Theory* 11 (3): 303–24.
Prahalad, C. K., and Venkat Ramaswamy. 2004. 'Co-Creation Experiences: The Next Practice in Value Creation'. *Journal of Interactive Marketing* 18 (3): 5–14.
Rand, Paul 1955. 'IBM Presentation…1955', ACCN 1745/200-M-133, Box 22, Folder 'IBM 1962-66 (1 of 2), *Paul Rand Collection*, Yale University Archives.
Rand, Paul and IBM Corporate Brand Management. 1994. *The Spirit and the Letter*. Armonk, NY: IBM.
Rhizome. 2001. 'The World's First Generative Logo?'. http://rhizome.org/editorial/2001/sep/5/the-worlds-first-generative-logo/. Accessed 1 May 2015.
Rumbo, Joseph D. 2002. 'World of Advertising Clutter: The Case of Adbusters'. *Psychology and Marketing* 19 (2): 127–48.
Scheffler, Karl. 1908. 'Kunst und Industrie'. *Kunst und Künstler* 6 (10): 343. Trans. Frederick J. Schwartz.
Schwartz, Frederick, J. 1996. 'Commoditiy Signs: Peter Behrens, the AEG, and the Trademark'. *Journal of Design History* 9 (3): 153–84.
Scissons, M., M. Kalehoff, and R. Laufer. 2013. *The Value of a Facebook Fan 2013: Revisiting Consumer Brand Currency in Social Media*. New York: Syncapse.com.
Wang, Yichuan, and M. Nick Hajli. 2014. 'Co-creation in Branding through Social Commerce: The Role of Social Support, Relationship Quality and Privacy Concerns'. In *Proceedings of the Twentieth Americas Conference on Information Systems*, 1–16. Savannah: Georgia.
Williams, Eliza. 2011. 'Branding the Art World'. *Creative Review*. October. http://www.creativereview.co.uk/back-issues/creative-review/2011/october/branding-the-art-world. Accessed 20 May 2015.
Wood, Timothy. 2015. 'Brand to the Future: How is the Future of Branding Adapting to Changing Technology'. BA Thesis, Norwich University of the Arts, Norwich.

3

Whose wall? From posters to digital displays and the colonization of public space

Nicolas P. Maffei

Throughout its history the billboard has been a focus of public critique and legislation. This chapter surveys the history of outdoor advertising, from the diffusion of handbills and posters to the proliferation of, and resistance to, city and roadside billboards, to the more recent phenomena of out-of-home electronic displays, including those that survey, record and target consumers. This investigation explores key design issues including commercial activity versus environmental protection; the role of the landscape in national identity; and freedom of expression and the limits of privacy. In the nineteenth century, operatives from the printing trades produced what we now call graphic design. In the early twentieth century commercial and graphic artists refined the use of design to compete with the visual dynamism of the modern city, later adapting to the mobile perceptual experience of the highway. Throughout its history, outdoor advertising has been attacked as morally and visually polluting by reformers, yet defended as informative and democratic by the advertising profession. Today print-based outdoor advertising competes with a proliferation of digital displays, some with interactive and sensing technology which can record and react to consumers. In this changed landscape the question persists: can a balance be maintained between individual freedom and commercial necessity?

The progressive response to outdoor advertising

In the United States of the early and mid-nineteenth centuries, outdoor advertising attracted little controversy. Temporary posters for travelling entertainments, including circuses and medicine shows, and more permanent site-specific shop signs were already well established. Better printing technologies and the increased production and sale of commercial goods in the late nineteenth century helped to multiply and extend these small-scale and local practices. While Phineas Taylor Barnum, the showman and entrepreneur, is often credited with innovating the large-scale, graphic billboard, the

Philadelphia department store pioneer, John Wannamaker is more responsible for establishing the vigorous and widespread practice of outdoor advertising, carving and painting his shop's name on street crossings, large rocks and rooftops as early as 1869 (Fox 1984: 25–7; Baker 2007: 1189).

The rise of the department store is seen to have greatly stimulated advertising of all kinds in late nineteenth century (Schudson 1993 (1984): 152). By 1870 a range of technologies including the paper-folding machine, the web perfecting press and lithography allowed the poster to proliferate in the United States. At this time posters were normally 42 x 28 inches (106 x 71 cm). In the following decades aggressive and widespread billposting (the circulation and display of poster advertising) became an urban commonplace practice, coinciding with an explosion in advertising of all kinds. In the United States by the 1890s outdoor advertising (including billboards and street posters) had hugely altered the urban landscape as one of the earliest and most pronounced examples of the commercialization of public space. With the advent of electric illumination, billboards and signs could communicate twenty-four hours a day, making them omnipresent and unavoidable (Baker 2007: 1188, 1191) (Figure 3.1).

By the 1890s billposting was marred by duplicitous practices, especially on the part of patent medicine producers, attracting vociferous critics and reformers. This was the case in both England and the United States (Richards 1991: 168–204). Attempts to improve the reputation and profits of advertising posters, while regulating the industry for consumers, led to the creation of professional groups within the advertising industries. In their defence, the producers of billboards, posters and electric signs stressed not only their commercial value, but also their contribution to a cohesive American society. Relying on the popular belief that pictures were more universally

FIGURE 3.1 *Electrically Illuminated Billboards, New York City, 1898, Outdoor Advertising Association of America Archives Digital Collection, John W. Hartman Center for Sales, Advertising and Marketing History, David M. Rubenstein Rare Book and Manuscript Library, Duke University with permission./ SLB4676+31/.*

FIGURE 3.2 *Lynchburgh Bill Posting Co., undated, Outdoor Advertising Association of America Archives Digital Collection, John W. Hartman Center for Sales, Advertising and Marketing History, David M. Rubenstein Rare Book and Manuscript Library, Duke University with permission./BBB3296.*

understood than written language, billboards were promoted as ideal for mass, illiterate and non-English speaking markets, and for cutting across linguistic, ethnic and class lines while stimulating consumerism and patriotism (Baker 2007: 1189–90).

By the early 1890s it was possible to create displays of up to 12 feet high with the use of multiple sheets of paper. These developments accompanied increased urbanization, industrialization and mass consumption resulting in a 'billboard eruption' (Wilson 1987: 396) (Figure 3.2). At the time it was not unusual to encounter a billboard of 100 feet along the edge of construction site. In 1899, it was estimated that Chicago contained 50,000 running feet of billboards. One might also witness double-deck boards of 18 feet or triple-deck ones of 26 feet, as well as signs on buildings, some of which were illuminated. In large cities, entire facades of old buildings were leased for large signs. By 1908, billboards in the United States stretched over 1,600 miles (Wilson 1987: 396). Between 1893 and 1903, the billboard business in the United States and Canada had grown from $200,000 to $5,000,000, and this figure increased to $35,000,000 by 1921. Critics complained of the commercial conquest of natural and civic space as urban monuments and natural wonders, including Niagara Falls, were increasingly the sites of advertising (Baker 2007: 1191).

Twentieth-century reformers' response

American billboard reformers were inspired by the Society for Checking the Abuses of Public Advertising (SCAPA) founded in England in 1893. SCAPA campaigned effectively in the press against the degradation of the urban and rural landscape and considered visual pollution equivalent to other outlawed nuisances to the senses. They called for tighter regulation, including restrictions on advertising in specific scenic sites and boycotts of products advertised on billboards. SCAPA influenced the founders of the American Park and Outdoor Art Association (APOAA), founded in 1897, and later the American Civic Association (ACA) looked to SCAPA for inspiration and worked at the national level to curb what were considered billboard excesses (Wilson 1987: 396).

By 1917, US reformers were able to get exclusionary zoning laws enacted, keeping billboards from many residential parts of big cities (Baker 2007: 1195). Cultural commentators echoed the views of the City Beautiful Movement, expressing a desire for an urban landscape of moral, aesthetic and environmental improvement, where the images and messages of one's surrounding would uplift the masses (especially working class and immigrant populations), and all-encompassing city planning would combat vice and excessive commercialism (Gudis 1999: 165). This would be achieved through the creation of urban beautification projects, including landscaped boulevards, parks, and monumental classical architecture and statuary, in order to foster civic responsibility and impart a civilizing influence, something it was feared outdoor advertising would only diminish (Wilson 1987: 399).

Critics of billboards complained they could catch fire, crush pedestrians, reduce house prices, and threaten family morals. They stole air and light and attracted garbage at their feet while hiding criminals and criminal acts in the dark recesses behind the boards. It was feared that their morally corrupting and seemingly inescapable promotion of alcohol, cigarettes and cheap theatre appeared wherever people gathered, from churches to parks to boulevards and schools, threatening urban refuges from commerce and persuasion (Wilson 1987: 401, 402).

Billposters and their allies countered the attacks on their industry, arguing that billposting must exist within a commercial era and in a society that protected property rights. Billboards and billposting, they argued, stimulated the economy beyond the sale of goods. Property owners received rents. Sellers of lumber, hardware, paste, and paper gained a livelihood, as did printers and lithographers. Billboards provided a service to society via entertaining and educative advertisements. Countering the criticism that billboards diminished city beauty, bill posters argued that the towering advertisements were more beautiful than many of the views they veiled, whether a trash-strewn lot or an elevated railway; after all, many billboards were designed by trained artists. Unlike the less accessible cultural institutions, such as the art gallery, the billboard functioned as a civilizing, democratic, cultural and aesthetic stimulant (Wilson 1987: 406–10).

By 1910, billposters had begun to promote their work as ethical and responsible, increasingly public service-oriented and safety-conscious. In the courts they fought off the accusations of City Beautiful advocates that boards were an aesthetic nuisance. Court battles against the poster men centred on the community's power to act on behalf of the morals, safety, health or general welfare of the population. In the first years of the century attempts to ban billboards near public parks failed, due in many cases to the refusal by the courts to rule on grounds of aesthetic nuisance, which was seen as a matter of luxury rather than necessity. However, around the same time courts across the country began to impose regulations on billboard height, size and placement in relation to building and streets, safety and decency. By the 1920s zoning laws provided the main billboard regulation. Eventually, the public became reconciled to billboards in part due to the patriotic posters of the First World War (Wilson 1987: 410–19).

The First World War posters and billboards

During the First World War, the employment of popular poster artists and the distribution of collectable, commemorative outdoor posters, fostered public goodwill for advertisers. By delivering public service messages alongside commercial advertisements outdoor advertisers successfully sold the medium, as well as the messages, to the public. Pro-war campaigns instilled patriotism and convinced the populace of the importance of the billboard in art and

FIGURE 3.3 *"Wake Up, America!' Civilization calls every man, woman and child!' 1917, James Montgomery Flagg, poster, colour lithograph, sheet 103.8 × 69.8 cm. Library of Congress Prints and Photographs Division Washington, D.C.*

FIGURE 3.4 *'American Way' billboard on US Highway 99, California. Nation-wide advertising campaign sponsored by the National Association of Manufacturers, March 1937, photograph by Dorothea Lange, Library of Congress, Prints & Photographs Division, FSA/OWI Collection, (reproduction number, e.g. LC-USF34-9058-C).*

education (Gudis 1999: 29). One of the most prominent poster campaigns was for Liberty Bonds; it included the painter James Montgomery Flagg's poster produced in a run of close to 2,000,000 (Figure 3.3 shows one of Flagg's many patriotic First World War posters).

Liberty Bond posters would later be exhibited in the Metropolitan Museum of Art and the New York Public Library. The campaign resulted in about 40,000,000 more Liberty Bond posters being plastered in cities and towns across the United States, thereby marketing both outdoor advertising and public service messages in support of the war (Gudis 1999: 30). In the United States in the following decades billboard and posters producers continued to promote patriotic messages, for example defending the 'American Way' of consumerism as a civic duty during the economic depression of the 1930s (Figure 3.4) and using posters to lift public spirits and promote home front wartime efforts during the Second World War. Thus by the 1950s outdoor advertising had become a politically powerful force able to fend off, for a time, highway beautification regulations (Gudis 1999: 31).

Highways and buyways

At the beginning of the twentieth century, with the advent of automobile ownership and increased road building, the natural landscape was invaded by the first billboards. These towering structures, alluring images and persuasive messages dramatically altered not only the natural and non-commercial environment but influenced the growth of cities and patterns of consumer behaviour. While there were only 500,000 registered motor vehicles in the United States in 1910, that number had increased to 23 million in 1923 (Gudis 1999: 13). In the 1920s and 1930s as many big US cities extended their growth outwards, advertisers imagined highways as 'buyways', connecting people, goods and advertisements (Gudis 1999: 21). Planners and developers of metropolitan areas pushed city development further from the central business districts, while suburbs, small towns and cities grew. Thus outdoor advertising existed as a transformative force in the American landscape and a powerful agent of communication and commerce and the decentralization of the American city (Gudis 1999: 5).

Roadside billboards not only advertised products and services, they changed the perception of what was public. Because they inhabited public space and communicated across it, they challenged the notion of the ownership of the landscape and roadside while pushing the spatial limits of commercial influence (Gudis 1999: abstract). As billboards spread from the cities to the country, American reform groups warned of their impact on spots of scenic beauty. In 1923 the National Committee for Restriction of Outdoor Advertising (NCROA) was formed to save the nation's places of beauty, aiming to establish forest preserves, national parks and limiting the commercialization of the natural landscape, and to prevent billboards invading natural environments by every lawful means. The group considered the billboard a 'blot on nature and a parasite on public improvements' and spread the slogan, 'Save the Beauty of America: The Landscape is No Place for Advertising.' Through an extensive national network of women's groups and access to powerful businessmen and civic leaders the group vigorously lobbied for the conservation of nature and the regulation of the roadside landscape (Gudis 1999: 179, 180). The group was joined by others including the American Institute of Architects who in 1930 argued for the removal of billboards based primarily on aesthetic ground, claiming that billboards had proliferated to such a degree that they 'dull[ed] the sensibilities' of viewers and were 'destructive of natural beauty', and recommended their restriction to zones regulated by public authorities in consultation with 'artistic organizations' (Cable 1930: 522).

These reformers helped to conceptualize the roadside vista as a protected public right, a democratic scenic space owned by all Americans. They often referenced the eighteenth- and nineteenth-century pastoral ideal of painters and poets: an imagined landscape, usually of patchwork fields and wooded hillsides, a sublime and civilizing force that disguised the reality of private property and industrial development. Thus the romantic and picturesque US landscape was sought and preserved in a way that ignored the realities of rapid urbanization, industrialization and immigration. By providing access to these scenic spots highways violently disrupted them. However, the highway was seldom criticized by billboard opponents and was often praised as expressing a kind of sublime technological experience (Gudis 1999: 187–90).

Promoters of billboards argued, on the other hand, that billboards and natural surroundings worked hand in hand; when a motorist is enjoying natural roadside scenes she or he is more susceptible to the allure of advertisements. In addition, billboard agents contended that roadside advertising was important to the health of the nation: it was vital to the flow of money and goods and thus the country's economic well-being. Yet, at the same time outdoor advertisers spoke of improving the nation, large-scale billboard businesses were buying up lesser firms, forcing out smaller, immigrant and family-run concerns (Gudis 1999: 200–12).

Shell Oil's English landscape

In the United Kingdom critics of outdoor advertising included the influential middle-class lobbying groups the Council of the Preservation of Rural England (CPRE) and SCAPA. During a period of environmental transformation, characterized by increased suburbanization and automobile ownership, these and other like-minded groups actively called for the protection of the countryside leading to the Countryside and Footpaths Preservation Conference, Leicester of 1928.

The conference included the photographic exhibition, 'Save the Countryside', where the beauty of the English landscape was contrasted with the visual pollution wrought by hoardings, roadside signs, and billboards, including those advertising Shell products. The conference and exhibition were widely covered in the press, joining a more extensive outcry from preservationists including architects and members of the Design and Industries Association (DIA) in a middle-class campaign to save the English countryside (Hewitt 1992: 127). In this new climate of opinion Shell's promotion of oil and petrol drew the ire of the vocal countryside lobbies and thus alienated one of its core markets, middle-class drivers.

The solution was to promote nature and present the company as a protector of the English countryside. After 1929 Shell worked with the CPRE to remove its outdoor advertisements deemed aesthetically displeasing. Eighteen thousand advertisements, mostly enamel signs and boards, were removed and plans to put up 11,000 were cancelled. In 1930 the DIA and SCAPA praised Shell for its preservation efforts. Shell made good use of these endorsements in the press alongside numerous print advertisements in selected magazines with the copy 'The Proprietors of Shell DO NOT advertise Their Petrol in Places Like This.' However, Shell was able to advertise in such beauty spots through lorry bills, as they were called, mobile hoardings that appeared on the

FIGURE 3.5 *'See Britain First on Shell', poster with image of Stonehenge, Edward McKnight Kauffer, 1931, Design Council Slide Collection, VADS, © Simon Rendall with permission.*

side of Shell delivery lorries. These moving billboards could travel everywhere, never stopping long enough to attract the preservationists' ire.

Shell's lorry bills of the early 1930s constructed a particular notion of 'nature' as the unchanging, rural idyll of England. English flora, fauna, villages and historic landmarks, including Stonehenge, were shown while references to the products of modernization – oil and petrol – produced by the petroleum company were minimized (Hewitt 1992: 128) (Figure 3.5). This idealized image of unchanging Britain contrasted with the realities of the 'artificial, shifting, superficial order of the city' (Hewitt 1992: 130). Indeed, the emphasis on the romantic representation of the English countryside may have veiled the impact Shell products made on the natural environment, which contributed to the rise of automobile ownership and driving, the extension of the city into the country, and increased road building (O'Connell 1998: 156). In this way Shell was able to indirectly market petrol, associate the Shell brand with the English landscape and present the oil company as a protector of nature and the nation (Hewett 1992: 127). But more importantly, Shell's idealized English countryside acknowledged the emergence of a new middle class and aided their consumption of a manufactured idea of English nature, offering them a commodified, unchanging landscape: 'nature became defined as that which was reachable by car, a view, a place, a monument' (Hewitt 1992: 138).

Post-war United States: Regulation and expansion

In the United States after the Second World War efforts to regulate the roadside diminished in part due to the advertising industry's supportive wartime role, a role similar to the one they played during the First World War. By donating poster space to promote the sale of war bonds, and cloaking commercial advertisements in nationalistic jargons, outdoor advertising was reframed as a patriotic service. National reform of outdoor advertising remained dormant until the passing of the Highway Beautification Act of 1965 (HBA), which permitted billboards in areas zoned as commercial and industrial (Gudis 1999: 215). The act was seen as a blow to billboard reformers. It favoured big companies that had sway in local planning decisions and led to increased rental prices for authorized zones, thus forcing out small-scale outdoor advertisers (Gudis 1999: 216). Many outdoor advertisers found ways around the HBA restrictions, for example by creating tiny patches of legally zoned land – small garages and minute parking lots – which acted as bases for hundreds of authorized signs (Patton 1986: 172).

In the decades following the HBA, the billboard industry continued to present an image of corporate responsibility and patriotic duty, while consolidating its businesses. During the energy crisis of the early 1970s, and facing a government-enforced blackout, the billboard industry called for a 25 per cent reduction in its energy usage (Dougherty 1973: 73). In a move reminiscent of the industry's prior support for war bonds, the Outdoor Advertising Association of America planned to use its billboard to promote energy conservation, thus associating the billboard industry with patriotic duty during a national crisis. In 1978 the *New York Times* concluded that the HBA's restrictions had forced many smaller companies to close while aiding the consolidation of the billboard industry. However, while the act discouraged the new construction of billboards, 214,000 illegal boards remained in 1978 due to the cost of their removal (Luxenberg 1978).

Post-feminism and female pleasure: Wonderbra's 'Hello Boys' billboards

As a UK campaign by a British agency (TBWA, London) the 1994 'Hello Boys' Wonderbra billboards differed from the 'local-plus-tobacco' approach of many American outdoor advertisers (Figure 3.6). The Wonderbra billboard campaign has been recognized as a landmark in outdoor advertising. Not only did it increase sales, earn advertising awards, and provoke controversy, it publicly disrupted conventional representations of femininity (Winship 2000: 29). The billboard's image of feminine sexual confidence and its public challenge to gender norms could only have been achieved in the context of post-feminism which, rather than maintaining an oppositional relation to masculinity, and opposing 'conventional femininity', 'embrace[d] a performative, pleasurable femininity' (Winship 2000: 29). The agency responsible for the 'Hello Boys' campaign, TBWA, London considered the Wonderbra consumer to be:

> a powerful image-conscious woman, in control of her life and angered by advertising which did not reflect that she enjoyed *'looking good'* and was a great believer in *'if you've got it flaunt it'* …. She was a liberated 'post feminist' who liked to demonstrate, and exploit, her sexuality.
> (Baker 1995: 269; quoted in Winship 2000: 33–4)

For the campaign the agency used 830 billboard sites in the weeks leading up to Valentine's Day and garnered huge media attention (Winship 2000: 41).

Wonderbra played on the power gained from displaying outdoors an image of a woman taking narcissistic pleasure in her partially naked body. While such images have been a commonplace since the 1960s and were condemned by feminists as degrading in the decades that followed, the significance of such images had shifted by the mid-nineties in the context of women's economic and social accomplishments, the proliferation of more diverse representations of women, and the 'subjection of the men's bodies to the (female) gaze' (Winship 2000: 40). While the Wonderbra

FIGURE 3.6 *'Hello Boys' Wonderbra, reduced version of 48-sheet poster, 1994, Nigel Rose (Art Director), Ellen von Unwerth (photographer), permission from TBWA\London (advertising agency), featuring the model Eva Herzigová.*

advertisement did not escape feminist critique, it provided some evidence of a cultural shift in its 'Hello Boys' copy, which was directed at the male viewer, yet aimed at women, while the speaker is a 'sexually confident' Eva Herzigová.

São Paulo: 'Clean City'

While outdoor advertising proliferated in cities across the globe, in September 2006 the mayor of São Paulo, Gilberto Kassab, passed Lei Cidada Limpa or 'Clean City Law', banning outdoor advertising, including billboards (Burgoyne 2007: 48). The law grew out of a broader need to combat the city's air, water, noise, and visual pollution. While arguments against billboards on aesthetic grounds had failed in the United States, in Brazil they succeeded. Some advertisers condemned the move, but for many this popular law, eventually introduced in January 2007, was seen as a historic blow against advertising clutter in the world's fourth largest city. The images of empty billboard frames documenting the new urban landscape, many by photographer Tony de Marco, seemed to suggest the death of outdoor advertising (Figure 3.7).

The single dissenting vote against the bill was by Dalton Silvano, an advertising businessman, who called billboards both 'art' and 'entertainment', echoing past defenders of advertising. He worried that the city would become a 'sadder, duller place' (Rohter 2015). The Brazilian Association

FIGURE 3.7 *Empty Sao Paulo billboard, photograph and permission Tony de Marco, ca. 2007.*

of Advertisers called the law 'unreal, ineffective and fascist' and argued that tens of thousands of jobs and hundreds of millions of dollars would be lost (Burgoyne 2007: 50). In the weeks before the ban, Clear Channel Communications, which had just bought a Brazilian subsidiary and the rights to a substantial segment of the billboard market, initiated a failed outdoor advertising campaign, pleading, 'There's a new movie on all the billboards – what billboards? Outdoor media is culture' (Harris 2007).

Others believed that the removal of promotional images and slogans would create a more peaceful urban environment. The impact on local design was felt in several ways beyond the loss of corporate advertising. The removal of some billboards revealed long-buried buildings, yet the ban threatened the loss of vernacular graphic design, especially the local lettering of small businesses (Burgoyne 2007: 50). How could businesses devoid of logos and signs communicate to consumers? Many big companies, such as Citibank and Dolce and Gabbana, painted their buildings' storefronts in bright colours and patterns associated with their brands (Garfield 2007). The law was hailed internationally as a unique triumph in the battle against visual pollution. The anti-billboard group, Scenic America, awarded its International Scenic Visionary Award to Kassab in November of 2011. At the same time polls showed that the public, advertisers and business owners supported the ban (Scenic America 2011). The advertisement prohibition occurred just as large-scale electronic billboards became a viable option, revealing foresight in resisting the next generation of outdoor advertising.

Out-of-home electronic displays and billboards

The future of billboards is electronic. In the United States in 2006 there were only 100 digital billboards (Holtz 2006). By 2008 there were around 500, in contrast to the 450,000 non-digital billboards. But since then the electronic billboard market has grown, with thirty-nine states allowing LED billboards and cost dropping from $1 million in 2002 to $200,000 in 2012 (Figure 3.8). Around six to twenty ads can be run on a single billboard, labour costs are low and returns are high. A forecast for 2015 estimated that the number of digital billboards would grow to 16,000 in the United States. However, digital billboards have prompted resistance from politicians and local communities, evidenced by the 2011 bans in Vermont, Alaska, Hawaii and Maine, which also prohibit traditional billboards as do about 1,500 towns across the United States. In 2010 the big billboard companies, including CBS Outdoor, LaMar Advertising Company, Clear Channel and JCDecaux, which own over 400,000 traditional billboards, spent more than $20 million lobbying politicians to allow electronic billboards, considering this medium the future of the industry. In 2011 over three quarters of digital billboards were erected in major metropolitan areas, and usually placed at traffic bottlenecks where, in some cases such as certain spots in San Francisco, they reach over 875,000 people a day (Boer 2011: 28).

In 2007, *Campaign*, the United Kingdom's leading advertising trade magazine, described the huge growth predicted for 'digital outdoor' advertising, especially in airports and London underground and train stations. CBS was set to install digital escalator panels at twenty London underground stations and provide 1,500 cross-track screens. JCDecaux was investing £20 million on over 1,000 screens across the BAA airport network, including Heathrow's terminal 5. Clear

FIGURE 3.8 *Times Square, New York, NY, February 2015, photograph by Grace Lees-Maffei.*

Channel was installing ten large format digital billboards at busy London intersections. It described the developments as a turning point for the medium, when 'out-of-home digital comes of age' (Tylee 2007).

Arguably the twenty-first-century outdoor digital landscape – its pervasiveness, commercial agenda, and ability to survey its audiences – is encroaching on civic freedom and constraining public life. Commentators on contemporary digital urban environments have observed a transition from a twentieth-century citizenry thrilled by the 'bright lights' of the big city, to a technologically networked and surveyed metropolis where inhabitants are 'watchers and watched, mirrored and refracted' (Arnold and Levin 2010). Those who see a benefit in this newly evolving system echo the arguments of the twentieth-century billboard critics. They express an awareness of advertising's invasive nature, but look to personalized advertising models as a solution, including the unobtrusive and often useful 'sponsored links' of Google AdWords. The designers of smart digital signage systems imagine a future of adverts and other communications that are targeted, useful and appreciated. Applied to the outdoor context, the attention spans of consumers would not be overtaxed and the quality of outdoor space could be preserved (Müller and Krüger 2007).

Digital signage, whether billboards or fast-food menu displays, is a 'networked, audiovisual information system that allows remote controlling contents … . It consists of several decentralized digital displays interconnected with a central … content management system and user rights management system.' Such systems are seen as more advantageous than print signage. In particular, digital signage can use sensors, cameras and other technologies to observe and adapt messages to contexts including time, location, demographics and consumer preferences, and so on as well as offering opportunities to interact with the display systems (Bauer, Dohmen and Strauss 2011). The ability to create context-specific content increases the chances of communicating relevant messages to audiences. They are increasingly deployed at points of sale, waiting and transit, by retailers, transit providers, government services, advertisers, and many others. Digital signage networks may count people, recognize faces, as well as gather information about consumers, based on their behavioural, physical and personal characteristics, including age, gender and ethnicity (Dixon 2010: 2). Another key difference between traditional and digital display is interaction where the electronic systems detect and characterize information about the public, adapt information according to audience interests and activities, and detect consumer reactions. Opportunities for consumer engagement are likely to increase through radio-frequency identification, Bluetooth and mobile phones (Bauer, Dohmen and Strauss 2011).

Whereas twentieth-century critics of billboards were concerned about the broadcasting of morally questionable messages and products (e.g. alcohol and tobacco advertising) and the disfigurement of the landscape, those who rail against smart digital signage – with its ability to survey, identify and record – have mostly expressed privacy, rather than content, concerns (Dixon 2010: 2). As of 2010 there was little disclosure about the information collected and analysed. Critics have argued that the result is a 'one-way-mirror society' where consent to be monitored is not sought and the information gathered is not publicly accessible. It is argued that if left unchecked 'sophisticated marketing surveillance' will lead to abuse of the information gathered. The non-profit consumer education group, the World Privacy Forum, recommends a need for better disclosure to consumers; external industry regulation; prohibition of digital signage in bathrooms and health facilities; and restrictions on collection and use of information about and images of children (Dixon 2010: 2).

Conclusion

The examples outlined here illustrate how a critical public has been engaged in a nearly century-and-a-half contest with outdoor advertisers, ranging from billposters to owners of billboards and electronic displays, to curb the reach and content of public commercial messages and images. While reformers have blamed outdoor advertising for corrupting children, degrading nature, spreading ugliness, and commercializing public space, historians and critics of advertising (e.g. Marchand 1985; Lears 1983; Haug 1986) have shown how commercial images and messages are part of a greater social, economic and political system. They have also recognized that such ideal images are not always congruent with lived reality, and instead constrain and widen one's sense of potential (Gudis 1999: 8). While some see empowerment in the post-feminist advertising campaigns such as the Wonderbra 'Hello Boys' billboards, others object to the seemingly inescapable images that create a visual landscape permeated by sexualized imagery. Attempts to curb the apparent visual pollution of outdoor advertising have resulted in efforts such as São Paulo's 'Clean City Law'. However, as sophisticated electronic signage surveys, records and targets audiences, the next frontier of reform will focus on individual privacy, whether in the physical urban landscape or the virtual world through augmented/virtual reality technology.

References

Arnold, Bruce, and Margalit Levin. 2010. 'Ambient Anomie in the Virtualised Landscape? Autonomy, Surveillance and Flows in the 2020 Streetscape'. *M/C Journal* 13 (2): n.p. Online at http://journal.media-culture.org.au/index.php/mcjournal/article/viewarticle/221. Accessed 1 June 2015.

Baker, Chris (ed.) 1995. *Advertising Works 8, Papers from the IPA Advertising Effectiveness Awards, Institute of Practitioners in Advertising, 1994*. Henley-on-Thames: NTC Publications.

Baker, Laura, E. 2007. 'Public Sites Versus Public Sights: The Progressive Response to Outdoor Advertising and the Commercialization of Public Space'. *American Quarterly* 59 (4): 1187–213.

Bauer, Christine, Paul Dohmen, and Christine Strauss. 2011. 'Interactive Digital Signage – an Innovative Service and its Future Strategies'. *International Conference on Emerging Intelligent Data and Web Technologies*, 137–42.

Boer, Marco. 2011. 'Electronic Billboards in the US'. *Wide-Format Imaging* 19 (10) (October): 28–9.

Burgoyne, Patrick. 2007. 'The Naked City: São Paulo: the City That Said No to Advertising'. *Creative Review* (June): 48–50.

Cable, 29 March 1930, 'American Notes of the Week: The Campaign Against Billboards'. *The Spectator*: 522.

Dixon, Pam. 2010. *The One-Way-Mirror Society: Privacy Implications of the New Digital Signage Network*. World Privacy Forum. http://www.worldprivacyforum.org/pdf/onewaymirrorsociety.pdf. Accessed 3 June 2013.

Dougherty, Philip H.. 1973. 'Advertising: More Syndication: Outdoor Ad Men Study Car Traffic'. *New York Times*, 27 December: 64.

Fox, Stephen. 1984. *The Mirror Makers: A History of American Advertising and Its Creators*. New York, NY: William R. Morrow and Company Inc.

Garfield, Bob. 2007. 'Clearing the Air'. *On the Media*. 20 April, podcast transcript. http://www.onthemedia.org/story/129390-clearing-the-air/transcript/. Accessed 17 February 2015.

Gudis, Catherine. 1999. *The Road to Consumption: Outdoor Advertising and the American Cultural Landscape, 1917–1965*. PhD dissertation, Yale University.

Harris, David Evan. 2007. 'Sao Paulo: A City Without Ads'. *Adbusters* 73 (September–October). https://www.adbusters.org/magazine/73/Sao_Paulo_A_City_Without_Ads.html. Accessed 17 February 2015.

Haug, W. F. 1986. *Critique of Commodity Aesthetics: Appearance, Sexuality and Advertising in Capitalist Society*. Minneapolis, MN: University of Minnesota Press.

Hewitt, John. 1992. 'The "Nature" and "Art" of Shell Advertising in the Early 1930s'. *The Journal of Design History* 5 (2): 121–39.

Holtz, Jeff. 2006. 'What's Next? A Zipper Board?' *New York Times*. 2 April: CT2.

Lears, T. J. Jackson. 1983. 'From Salvation to Self Realization'. In Richard Wightman Fox and T. J. Jackson Lears (eds.), *The Culture of Consumption*, 1–38. New York: Pantheon.

Luxenberg, Stan. 1978. 'For Billboards, The Signs Are Bullish: Alternative to TV Some Dropouts "Grab" The Viewer'. *New York Times*. 25 June: F3.

Marchand, Roland. 1985. *Advertising the American Dream: Making Way for Modernity, 1920–1940*. Berkeley, CA: University of California Press.

Müller, Jörg, and Antonio Krüger. 2007. 'Competing for Your Attention: Negative Externalities in Digital Signage Advertising'. In *Proceedings of the 5th International Conference on Pervasive Computing*, 13 May, Toronto, Canada.

O'Connell, Sean. 1998. *The Car In British Society: Class, Gender and Motoring, 1896–1939*. Manchester: Manchester University Press.

Patton, Phil. 1986. *Open Road: A Celebration of the American Highway*. New York: Simon & Schuster.

Richards, Thomas. 1991. *The Commodity Culture of England: Advertising and Spectacle*, 1851–914. London: Verso.

Rohter, Larry. 2015. 'Streets Are Paved With Neon's Glare, and City Calls a Halt'. *New York Times*. 12 December. http://www.nytimes.com/2006/12/12/world/americas/12paulo.html?_r=0. Accessed 17 February 2015.

Scenic America. 2011. 'Sao Paulo Mayor Kassab to Receive Scenic Visionary Award'. *Press Release*, 3 November. http://www.scenic.org/storage/documents/Scenic_America_press_release_Kassab_Award.pdf. Accessed 17 February 2015.

Schudson, Michael. 1993 [1984]. *Advertising, The Uneasy Persuasion: Its Dubious Impact on American Society*. London: Routledge.

Tylee, John. 2007. 'The Growth of Digital Outdoor'. *Campaign*, 26 January: 10.

Wilson, William H. 1987. 'The Billboard: Bane of the City Beautiful'. *Journal of Urban History* 13 (4): 394–425.

Winship, Janice. 2000. 'Women Outdoors: Advertising, Controversy and Disputing Feminism in the 1990s'. *International Journal of Cultural Studies* 3 (1): 27–55.

4

Slogan T-shirts: Billboards of identity politics

Nicolas P. Maffei

Slogan T-shirts facilitate social needs. They aid social organization, express cultural meanings and act as expressions of political resistance. They are key channels for the communication of political identities. The T-shirt has been used by campaigners from Katherine Hamnett's 1984 '98% Don't Want Pershing' T-shirt worn to meet British prime minister Margaret Thatcher at a Downing Street reception (Figure 4.1), to the T-shirt campaign mounted by advocates of gay marriage in the United States and epitomized by American Apparel's 'Legalize Gay' T-shirt of 2008. As well as being deadly serious, T-shirts are humorous ('I'm with stupid') and used as souvenirs of rites of passage such as hen and stag night celebrations, landmark birthdays, college and university education and holidays. As exemplars of modernity, they are affordable, mass producible and accommodate an infinite range of messages. While their generic form suggests the uniformity of mass society, they allow individual expressions from anti-nuclear to pro-hunting. Arguably, the T-shirt has been key to the development of politically engaged 'citizen advertisers' who participate in political discourse through 'embodied citizen display' (Penney 2011: 47, 48). These expressive traits have made the T-shirt a key form of communication, functioning to remind us of past events, experiences and identities, and as a carrier of statements of individual and political expression.

A brief history of the T-shirt

Examining the T-shirt reveals how the worlds of consumer culture and politics are deeply intertwined. The rise of the T-shirt industry after the Second World War resulted from a range of cultural, commercial and political activities, including grassroots protest, political advertising, popular social commentary and fashion retailing. The slogan T-shirt could not have thrived without its acceptance as a form of appropriate public clothing. The wearing of a layer of white undergarments is a centuries-old practice. From 1899, plain white T-shirts were produced by the US Navy as undergarments for sailors. By the Second World War the now familiar, classic cotton T-shirt was standard issue in the US military. It was at this time that T-shirts began to sport the

FIGURE 4.1 *Prime Minister Margaret Thatcher greets fashion designer Katharine Hamnett, wearing a T-shirt with a nuclear missile protest message, at 10 Downing Street, 1984, permission PA Archive/Press Association Images.*

logos and names of particular military units. However, this was a government-sponsored rather than personal expression. It therefore differed greatly from the individualistic slogan T-shirts that would appear some decades later. The lightweight, cotton, often tightly fitting, garment and its association with the military communicated 'strength, and virility', aiding its popularity as a form of expression (Penney 2011: 62). Thus, by the 1950s it was common practice, especially among working-class men in the United States, to sport cotton T-shirts.

The T-shirt's meaning took on particularly rebellious connotations as it became associated with post-war subcultures, including motorcycle and custom car enthusiasts, and as it was worn by Hollywood stars including Marlon Brando in *The Wild One* (1953) and James Dean in *Rebel without a Cause* (1955), two films which are often regarded as establishing the T-shirt as a symbol of youthful rebellion (Figure 4.2).

According to T-Shirt scholar Joel Penney, during this period it was not considered appropriate for adults to wear slogan T-shirts, but children were allowed to wear those with cartoonish designs. The first-known promotional T-shirts were given away at the 1939 premiere of *The Wizard of Oz*. However, this commercial and promotional practice was not common until decades later. The earliest example of a T-shirt worn by children for promotional use in political photo campaign opportunities was the 'Dew-it-with Dewey' T-shirt of 1948 used in the Thomas Dewey presidential campaign. This would become an established practice in the following decades (Penney 2011: 63–4).

With the emergence of the youth counterculture of the 1960s T-shirts sporting rebellious imagery and slogans began to appear. At the start of the decade in Southern California the custom car painter Ed Roth began selling airbrushed T-shirts in the back of hot rod magazines with 'weirdo' monsters and rebellious phrases, including 'Born to Lose' and 'Mother is Wrong.' To publicly communicate a critical point of view towards society through a display of graphic images on one's chest was almost unheard of in the early 1960s, but would become a commonplace by the end of the decade. Roth can be seen as having paved the way for the youth-oriented, graphic T-shirt industry and for bridging the gap between the established practice of shirts using childish imagery and those broadcasting social commentary (Penney 2001: 65–6).

In the late-1960s T-shirts sporting rebellious slogans and imagery were part of a wider set of popular left-wing artefacts including buttons and posters, all of which often shared the same graphic designs, ranging from the peace sign to the Black Panther logo as well as the famous Alberto Korda photograph of Che Guevara, the Marxist revolutionary. Images of individuals wearing

FIGURE 4.2 *James Dean poses for a Warner Brothers publicity shot for his film* Rebel Without a Cause, *1955, Los Angeles, California. Photograph and permission Michael Ochs, Michael Ochs Archives/Getty Images.*

these shirts were photographed by the popular media and further disseminated, amplifying and extending these expressions of protest. The production and distribution of these shirts in the late-1960s was a DIY affair, with production occurring often locally and in small batches. In the 1970s with the development of improved fabric printing technology, including fabric transfer, T-shirt production became more industrialized, allowing for a range of colours and more accurate photographic imagery. As a result of the greater production volume, higher image quality and wider dissemination this period laid the ground for the mass acceptance of the T-shirt as a form of social commentary (Penney 2001: 67–8).

Che Guevara: Revolution or commerce!

T-shirts and other memorabilia have allowed for the collective memorialization of everyone from the peace activist Mahatma Gandhi to the Cuban revolutionary Ernesto 'Che' Guevara. Because he was assassinated while still a young man, Che Guevara's youthful idealism and good looks have been preserved in popular memory and in the products that bear his image. However, the extent to which the commercialization of the Che image (Figure 4.3) has perverted or reinforced his original ideals is debatable, as Anmol Chaddha notes:

> Thirty-five years after dying an anonymous death in a remote region of Bolivia – the culmination of a lifelong struggle for justice and against exploitation by First World countries – Che Guevara has reappeared on $20 T-shirts and on posters in college frat houses in the Land of the Free

FIGURE 4.3 *Vendor with Che Guevara T-shirts, Santa Clara, Cuba, 2017, photograph by Kaldari. CC0 1.0.*

Market. The Latin American revolutionary has paradoxically become an icon in the heart of capitalism, stripping his image of his ideology and allowing any kid from the suburbs to transform himself into a revolutionary – a true hero of the people. (Chaddha 2003: 34)

Chaddha sharply critiques the commodification of political resistance, observing how retailers have used revolutionary figures, ranging from Gandhi to Guevara to sell everything from T-shirts to iPads (Chaddha 2003: 34). Schweimer, on the other hand, is perhaps more circumspect, writing of Guevara as both a historical figure (a Marxist fighter and leader) and a commodifiable symbol (a beret-wearing icon of revolution). A dual image that appeals to the downtrodden as well as the upwardly mobile. 'Che is far more about what he represents than what he achieved, and he seems to represent many things to many people: the poster in the student bedroom, the T-shirt, the fashion icon, the seller of vodka and cars' (Schweimer 2008: 120). Che continues to speak to a public hungry for change, whether in political regimes or seasonal fashions.

The commercial use of revolutionary imagery transforms ideologies of resistance into this season's latest 'must-have'. Summarizing this problematic process of commodification Chaddha observes that once a freedom movement achieves its aims complex revolutionary philosophies are reduced to a single idea, image of phrase: Gandhi equals non-violence; Che equals rebellion. Thus both can be exploited to sell everything from stylish computers to rock music. Third-world rebels are turned into capitalist 'icons, symbols, and mere clichés' (Chaddha 2003: 34). 'When icons of resistance are commodified, they become depoliticized. In essence, dissent is cool as long as it is fashionable, predictable and contained by consumerism. At the same time, actual political and ideological dissent is not really cool at all' (Chaddha 2003: 34). Thus, the process of commodification absorbs and transforms political messages that threaten the dominant ideology.

In parts of Latin America, T-shirts of Che provide a symbol for the fight against enduring poverty and corruption. Near the village where he was killed his death is marked by thousands of visitors. On a visit to such a celebration Schweimer observed the seeming contradiction between the commodification of Che's image and the lasting belief in his revolutionary ideals. 'His face stared out from T-shirts and flags. There were Che mugs and key-rings. While probably he would have flinched at the blatant commercialism of his image, he might have been somewhat surprised that the ideas he fought for … are alive and thriving' (Schweimer 2008: 120). Schweimer suggests that commodification of political imagery can also be a positive political force. It can allow revolutionary ideas to live on. For those in Latin America now fighting against corruption and poverty a Che T-shirt aids their political resistance by reinforcing messages of revolution.

Barrio art T-shirts: montage of Chicano resistance

Another kind of message of cultural identity is reinforced through barrio art T-shirts worn by young Hispanics, depicting themes of Chicano religion, history and culture. A single shirt can include a plethora of contrasting images, ranging from the Virgin of Guadalupe to jail imagery, from low riders to historical figures. Like the Che T-shirt, Mexican-American barrio art T-shirts express political resistance as well as Chicano cultural identity. However, rather than presenting a single iconic image they employ a montage of numerous cultural references to express a history of resistance against the dominant Euro-American culture. The assemblage of multiple contrasting images gives the shirts their particular potency and specific meaning. Hopeful images are contrasted with those of desperation, evidencing the polarized experience of Latino people who suffer pressures of exclusion and assimilation (Goldman 1997: 124–7).

Interviews with the wearers of barrio shirts confirm their paradoxical message: the 'smile now, cry later' philosophy of Mexican-American life, of happiness amidst economic hardship and racism, of cultural affirmations within oppressive conditions (Goldman 1997: 128). Some of the shirts show images of incarceration, suggesting the social and economic 'prison' outside of jail (Goldman 1997: 130). Others suggest fantasies of escape: a low rider car as a symbol of mobility. The stylish, laid back ease of the low-slung, custom car can be contrasted to the dominant Euro-American automobile culture of streamlined speed. Images of strong Aztec warriors can be viewed as symbols of Latino self-determination and a response to socio-economic powerlessness (Goldman 1997: 130–1). Thus the visual iconography of the Mexican-American experience provides a montage of resistance while contributing to ethnic identity.

Barrio art shirts are a potent reminder that the meaning of the graphic T-shirt is dependent upon the identity of the wearer. Arguably, it would be impossible for a Euro-American wearing an barrio art shirt to express Latino cultural resistance and Chicana/o pride and identity. For some, wearing such images would be considered an act of theft and vandalism: an appropriation and transformation of another culture's symbols. It would show deep disrespect. These shirts, however, have gone through their own form of appropriation: wearers have 'borrowed' them from a specifically American form of clothing – the T-shirt – while transforming the shirt's meaning through the application of a barrio sensibility in which ethnic pride and cultural resistance predominate (Goldman 1997: 134–5).

Slutty or sassy sexuality: From Grrrl power to Hurricane Katrina

With their images of scantily dressed women, low riders and prison tattoos, barrio art T-shirts can be read as explicitly masculine expressions of cultural resistance. Riot Grrrl T-shirts, on the other hand, communicate a more feminine form of rebellion. Feona Attwood writes of Madonna, Courtney Love and the rise of the Riot Grrrl persona with its simultaneous performance of 'slutty', DIY, sexualized femininity and its embrace of feminism. Evidencing its popularity Attwood points to the mainstreaming of the Riot Grrrl look in street fashion where T-shirts adorned with phrases such as 'Bitch, Whore, Vixen, Chick, Porn Star' have become an ordinary sight (Attwood 2007: 241). Referring to Rosalind Gill's comments on the hugely popular 'fit chick unbelievable knockers' T-shirt of 2002, such garments have helped to hyper-sexualize women's bodies, contributing to a dominant perception of young women as 'the autonomous, active, desiring subject' (Gill 2003: 105). The performance of youthful sexuality remains a challenge to young women because of the existence of a double standard by which women are encouraged to act freely, as young, assertive and optimistic individuals, while not being too feminine or too masculine. According to some scholars, social norms encourage individually sexualized expressions, for example provocative T-shirts, but these must remain ambiguous in their meaning, avoiding sluttiness while communicating sassiness (Attwood 2007: 242; Griffin 2005: 9).

Alison Jacques has explored the way in which many Riot Grrrls used their bodies as platforms for political expression. Jacques has argued that a lineage can be traced from the Riot Grrrl practice of the early 1990s of writing sexually and politically provocative words such as, 'rape', 'shame' and 'slut' on their bodies to the mass-culture phenomenon of popular 'girl-themed slogans' that appeared on T-shirts in the mid-to-late 1990s. 'So-called "alternative" shops were soon flooded with "baby tees" – tight-fitting T-shirts for girls – emblazoned with sassy, sexy words like "Tasty," "Tart," and "Maneater"' (Jacques 2001: 49). 'Girl power' was further mainstreamed with the mass appeal of the Spice Girls around 1997 and sales of its hugely popular merchandise, including T-shirts.

Such phrases as 'girl power', 'girls rock', or 'girls rule' made appealing slogans for T-shirts and offered an empowering public statement on a personal level. But such arguably superficial acts of communication can be seen as avoiding a commitment to the realities of feminism. The Riot Grrrl ethic was anti-consumerist from the outset. Thus, treating the body like a T-shirt, defacing the female body with pen and politically provocative words countered the dominant image of the female form as perfect and sexualized, thereby addressing issues of women's oppression through body, word and image. According to Jacques, the sale of a baby tee in a commercial context, regardless of the slogan it embodied, undercut any critique of capitalism through its mass production (Jacques 2001: 50).

While the Riot Grrrl T-shirt aesthetic may suggest anything from feminist sassiness to hyper-sexualized promiscuity, it is part of a wider trend in the mainstreaming of provocative sexual expression in T-shirt design. The American clothing retailer Abercrombie & Fitch have embraced such provocation as a marketing and sales strategy in their T-shirt designs. However, they have rejected any hint of Riot Grrrl empowerment, instead courting controversy with slogans such as 'Who needs brains when you have these' and 'I had a nightmare I was brunette.' Such slogans have attracted widespread, albeit negative, media attention. In 2005 a group of teenage girls from Pennsylvania using online media called for a 'girlcott' against the clothing retailer. Their protest snowballed and they soon made their case on major national US media outlets. The media pressure resulted in Abercrombie & Fitch pulling two shirt designs with a promise to replace them with those featuring more empowering slogans. While this may appear a success, for many consumers such controversy increases the company's edgy reputation and thus fuels sales (Kennedy 2005).

Sexism of another kind appeared on T-shirts memorializing Hurricane Katrina. Shortly after the storm struck New Orleans in 2005 T-shirts characterizing the hurricane as a female terror appeared in shop windows of the city's tourist district. Such shirts can be seen as providing a humorous release in the aftermath of a tragedy (Macomber et al. 2011: 525). However, the T-shirt slogans sexualized the hurricane and included, 'Katrina Gave Me a Blow Job I'll Never Forget.' The appearance of lewd language and imagery is perhaps no surprise given the city's former reputation as a hedonistic, party destination.

Material culture and nonmaterial culture are always gendered. Representations of men and women that seem to be the norm have already been 'worked through the hands of the dominant cultural producers' who are normally middle- and upper class, white, heterosexual men. Women are usually depicted as objects of male heterosexual desire, thus limiting how they may express their sexuality (Macomber et al. 2011: 528). Katrina T-shirts cast the hurricane as a 'bitch' for being uncontrollable and as a 'whore' who gave 'blow jobs', because 'she' was actively sexual. Thus these lewd and provocative T-shirts with their powerful rhetoric cast men as inadvertent sufferers of pain and accidental recipients of pleasure and cast women as sexually uncontrollable whores intentionally providing both pain and pleasure (Macomber et al. 2011: 531). Hurricane names are alternately feminine and masculine. We might well ask: would Hurricane Karl have elicited the same set of T-shirt slogans and images?

T-shirts as group belonging: Kwakwaka'wakw tribe and Manchester United Football Club

While the Katrina T-shirts emphasize sexist stereotypes, other shirts aid familial belonging. T-shirts reproduce and reinforce social networks, whether through T-shirt gift-giving ceremonies among indigenous American tribes or through the purchase of sports T-shirts and football tops which link the wearer to a 'family' of fans. Anthropologist Aaron Glass has investigated the use of T-shirts by the Kwakwaka'wakw (Figure 4.4) of British Columbia in 'facilitating social reproduction through the public articulation of memories and identities'. Looking in particular at T-shirts as souvenirs, objects that aid memory of events and express family belonging, Glass shows that T-shirts exist within a network of exchange, including a local economy of 'gift exchanges, fund-raisers and thrift stores' (Glass 2008: 1).

FIGURE 4.4 *Hunt Memorial Potlatch T-shirt, designed by Corrine Hunt, 1992, photograph and permission by Aaron Glass.*

The Kwakwaka'wakw had been producing T-shirts since the 1970s at the same time that paper-based silkscreen prints were produced as part of the growing commerce in indigenous art from the Northwest Coast (Glass 2008: 1). T-shirts – their production and circulation – became a central form of visual expression in societies which emphasized display as an indication of social rank and hereditary privilege, where family crests were displayed on canoes, clothing, hats, house fronts, tattoos and totem poles. T-shirts enter this existing iconography of objects as a syncretic and hybridized form, fusing indigenous design and function with modern materials and technologies (Glass 2008: 2). Glass sees a precedent for the T-shirts in the Kwakwaka'wakw button blanket, where after the mid-nineteenth century mother-of-pearl trade buttons were attached to Hudson Bay Company blankets as a border for appliqued family crest designs. Such blankets are still used today for official ceremonies from school graduations to feasts. Portable button blankets on prefabricated cloth allowed for a wider and freer dissemination of the family crests and hereditary figures, which had previously been found on carved objects such as stationary totem poles or less robust objects of woven cedar bark. In this way, ceremonial display was more widely available to greater segments of Kwakwaka'wakw society (Glass 2008: 2).

Like button blankets, the T-shirts which are now ubiquitous in Kwakwaka'wakw villages, allow for crest display, without needing to be attached to a ceremony. They exist within a broader First Nation 'system of fashion' (Barthes 1983), which includes masks, headdresses, button blankets and high fashion. Printed T-shirts have become a sort of uniform, providing an informal visual indication of aboriginal origin and communicate group belonging: 'What is publicly displayed is not so much the shirt (as an article of clothing) or even the crest image (as an aesthetic design), but the objective basis for claims about personhood and kinship' (Glass 2008: 3).

Numerous events in Kwakwaka'wakw society are marked by the production and distribution of T-shirts: from potlatches – gift-giving feasts – to intertribal football matches. As part of a potlatch, where guests can range from 200 to 1,000 people, families often give shirts to chosen individuals as a token of family belonging. At a 1997 family gathering one of the grand matriarchs, Granny Axu, provided the same T-shirt design in six different colours to relatives, the colours corresponding to six different generations. On the back was a text: 'Descendant of Granny Axu'. In their totality the shirts presented a physical and spatial information graphic, representing generational family belonging and broadcasting kinship connections at a group event (Glass 2008: 10).

The Kwakwaka'wakw example of the social function of the T-shirt provides a refreshing perspective in a design subject dominated by books emphasizing aesthetics qualities. But, of course, this function of providing social glue is not exclusive to Kwakwaka'wakw T-shirts. A person wearing a T-shirt of any kind, whether showing a heavy metal band or sports team, identifies them with a particular group, an extended 'family' which is related by shared interests. A similar clan expression can be found among football fans wearing the same club uniform. Sporting a Wayne Rooney Manchester United shirt signifies one's belonging to a larger group. It identifies the wearer with the values of that group. It requires the cultural knowledge to purchase the correct garment – not last year's kit and not a player who has been sold. It may also indicate social-economic ranking based on purchasing power. Furthermore, a father and son wearing the same top, for example, may indicate hereditary privilege – the favoured son is allowed to engage in a masculine cross-generational ritual of football allegiance.

Ethical T-shirt consumption and the developing world

From football tops to baby tees, T-shirts have an environmental and human cost. With the rise of ethical consumerism there has been an increased outcry aimed more at the manufacturers of T-shirts than the messages the shirts carry. In 1992, as a result of consumer pressure, Nike produced a landmark factory code of conduct for its offshore production facilities. The company required their suppliers to comply with local labour legislation, including outlawing child labour (Bajaj 2013). In some places across the developing world the scale and scope of the garment industry is vast. Two million Bangladeshi people work in the industry, making it the country's biggest. Eighty-five per cent are women and most work ten-hour days. While health and safety conditions have improved, wages are still very low. In 2006, a worker who made T-shirts earned $25.00 a month (*New Internationalist* 2006: 17). More recently the death and injuries of thousands of garment labourers in Bangladesh have brought the issue of ethical clothing consumption once again to the fore, leaving consumers asking, 'What can be done'? (Bajaj 2013)

The production of T-shirts and other clothing can also have a dire impact on the environment. In 2006 it was reported that in the United Kingdom 70 per cent of unwanted clothes ended up in landfill. These items had been washed on average sixty-five times, tumble dried and in some cases ironed, using more energy than their manufacture and distribution (Wells 2007: 90). In 2007 it was estimated that the production of cotton accounted for one-tenth of the global use of pesticides and more than one-fifth of the insecticides used in agriculture. Twenty thousand people in the developing world die each year from the effects of agricultural pesticides, while three million suffer reproductive or acute effects (Wells 2007: 74–5). The city of Tiruppur, India is known for the production of T-shirts (alongside a range of other garments, from blouses to vests). In a 1998 report this export trade was valued at Rs 30 billion per year. But, roughly 2,000 production facilities used chemicals banned in the West (mostly for dyeing and bleaching), thus damaging the environment, ground and river water, agricultural land and natural ecosystems (Thompson and Azariah 1998).

Western consumer excesses have negative economic consequences in developing countries. In the United States, the National Football League (NFL) produces 100,000 T-shirts for each of the teams competing in the annual Super Bowl. Both shirt designs proclaim Super Bowl victory for that team. Of course, only one team wins and as a result 100,000 unsellable T-shirts are donated to developing countries. On the surface this seems to benefit everyone. The NFL gets a tax break and free shirts are given to those in need. However, the vast importation of 'stuff we don't want', including food, toys, clothes, etc., to developing countries impedes economic development. One estimate reckons that the import of used clothing accounted for around half of the decrease in employment in the apparel industry in Africa from 1981–2000 (Kenny 2011: 30–1).

What can consumers do to address these problems? How can the exploitation of labour end? How can the environment be protected? How can local economies be supported? Choosing 'sweatshop free' T-shirts is not easy because there has been little take up by retailers. Most brands and retailers provide little information about the production of their goods. This is often due to complex supply chains where the many shifting layers of contractors, subcontractors and labour pools hide exploitative work practices (Bajaj 2013). Labour activists believe the answer is not to boycott producers of clothing. Boycotts can force the poorest workers to engage in even more arduous and exploitative work. Activists instead encourage consumers to press suppliers for improvements in pay, contracts and working conditions (*New Internationalist* 2006). Such pressure led to Nike instituting its 1992 working practices code, a development that has improved conditions in some factories, but not all. A recent consumer petition helped to improve conditions at H&M's Bangladeshi factories (Bajaj 2013). A UNESCO report argues that developing countries need to enforce their environmental policies, while developed countries should contribute financially to the restoration of the environment (Thompson and Azariah 1998). Clothing by companies like American Apparel are 'sweatshop free' and produced in the United States (American Apparel, 2015). Regarding the importation of used T-shirts, the answer offered by one study is to reconsider this practice in order to allow local garment industries to flourish (Kenny 2011: 30–1). A more radical solution is for consumers to buy fewer cheap T-shirts.

T-shirt futures: Business models and new technology

A T-shirt company that is producing fewer failed designs and thus avoiding the pitfalls of the NFL is Threadless. Founded in 2000, the online T-shirt company has been heralded as a groundbreaking business innovator. Threadless produces products that customers want when they want them; it satisfies micro market segments, and accommodates the ever-changing whims of increasingly diverse customers. This is astounding considering that new products fail at rates of 50 per cent or higher, usually due to a poor understanding of customer needs (Ogawa and Piller 2006: 66).

Threadless achieves its success through customer integration in the design process and advanced customer purchasing commitment. It crowdsources its designs from far and wide; by 2007 it received 125 designs a day from amateur and professional graphic designers. Threadless thereby accesses a pool of talent that is much greater than the company could provide internally. The site's hundreds of thousands of users then vote on the designs, selecting half a dozen each week. Around 1,500 people rate each design. These are then sold in pre-ordered batches of 1,500 and the winning designer is paid $2,000 (Walker 2007: E16). Such customer commitment works especially well for specialized T-shirts where volatile markets and fast-moving trends predominate (Ogawa and Piller 2006: 66).

Threadless' approach is not new. Taking pre-orders prior to production is typical in specialized industrial markets, for example condominiums and flats where customized designs are developed to the owner's specifications and where construction only takes place once there are enough orders (Ogawa and Piller 2006: 67). As a result of access to the internet this approach is now more widespread and is being applied to fast-moving sectors like T-shirt manufacture. It reflects a trend among consumers for a more personalized customer experience and expectations that products should be developed more precisely for the consumers' specific needs.

So, if Threadless provides a future-facing business model for T-shirt development and production, what is the future of T-shirt design? With the advent of flexible displays and microcomputers, communication technology has recently become integrated into T-shirts. Exemplifying this trend is London-based CuteCircuit's high-tech prototype T-shirt that combines a camera, big LED screen, speakers, microphone and accelerometer. Working with the whisky producer Ballantine's, the company has produced a garment that connects a T-shirt to a smart phone to become a 'wearable, shareable, programmable' piece of clothing (Barak 2012: 44). Whereas a traditional T-shirt allows for individual expression and social allegiance through use of a single image, CuteCircuit's T-shirt accommodates up-to-the-minute changes in your identity and allegiances expressed through electronic image and sound. It also allows for interaction between wearers of similar T-shirts. Furthermore, it can be context-sensitive, changing from, say, Che Guevara at a protest rally to a tuxedo T-shirt for a meal out.

Conclusion

The examples outlined above have illustrated how graphic T-shirts are socially significant forms of communication. Not only do their images and written messages communicate group belonging, as exemplified by the Kwakwaka'wakw garments, but they also inform others of one's individual identity – be it sexual or political or otherwise – whether through sassy Grrrl power slogans or the wearing of ethical clothing.

Threadless T-shirts express a kind of hip and creative identity through the wearing of crowd-curated designer graphic T-shirts. But less apparent is the lean and efficient business model at its foundation which makes Threadless ethical simply through its streamlined production and distribution practices, which stands in stark contrast to more wasteful business models such as those practised by the manufacturers of NFL Super Bowl shirts. Just wearing a Threadless shirt could be a way to communicate an allegiance with more ethically minded forms of capitalism. Social communication is made even more fluid in the example of the CuteCircuit T-shirt. Not only does it allow for immediate and shifting expressions of identity and belonging, it also has the ability to contribute to a more ethical system of T-shirt production. It could reduce the number of shirt designs produced and perhaps have less of a negative impact on both the environment and working people. Would it put an end to the T-shirt industry? Would it lead to the end of T-shirt manufacturing as we know it? Would it alleviate the problems of exploitative labour practices in the offshore garment industries? Although not yet in mass production, such a garment could provide new opportunities for graphic designers required to produce the infinite images and slogans for the T-shirt of tomorrow.

References

American Apparel. 2015. 'About Us'. Website page. https://www.americanapparel.net/aboutus/. Accessed 6 June 2015.
Chaddha, Anmol. 2003. 'Cool Commodities; How Many Che T-shirts Does It Take to Launch a Revolution?' *Colorlines* 6 (1): 34.
Attwood, Feona. 2007. 'Sluts and Riot Grrrls: Female Identity and Sexual Agency'. *Journal of Gender Studies* 16 (3): 233–47.
Bajaj, Vikas. 2013. 'Before You Buy That T-Shirt'. *New York Times*. 19 May. SR.10.
Barthes, Roland. 1983. In Matthew Ward and Richard Howard (eds.), *The Fashion System*. New York: Hill and Wang.
Barak, Sylvie. 2012. 'T-Shirt OS –Wearable, Shareable, Programmable Clothing'. *Electronic Engineering Times*. 3 September: 44–5.

Gill, Rosalind. 2003. 'From Sexual Objectification to Sexual Subjectification: The Resexualisation of Women's Bodies in the Media'. *Feminist Media Studies* 3 (1): 100–6.

Glass, Aaron. 2008. 'Crests on Cotton: "Souvenir" T-Shirts and the Materiality of Remembrance Among the Kwakwaka'wakw of British Columbia'. *Museum Anthropology* 31 (1): 1–18.

Goldman, Dorie S. 1997. '"Down for La Raza": Barrio Art T-Shirts, Chicano Pride, and Cultural Resistance'. *Journal of Folklore Research* 34 (2): 123–39.

Griffin, Christine. 2005. 'Impossible Spaces? Femininity as an Empty Category', paper presented at ESRC Research Seminar Series: New Femininities, University of East London, December.

Jacques, Alison. 2001. 'You Can Run But You Can't Hide: The Incorporation of Riot Grrrl into Mainstream Culture'. *Canadian Woman Studies* 21 (4): 46–50.

Kenny, Charles. 2011. 'Haiti Doesn't Need Your Old T-shirts'. *Foreign Policy*. November: 30–1.

Kennedy, Helen. 2015. 'Taking on the Big Guy: Kids Call for 'Girlcott' of Abercrombie & Fitch'. *New York Daily News*. 12 November 2005. http://www.nydailynews.com/archives/news/big-guy-kids-call-girl-cott-abercrombie-fitch-article-1.562607. Accessed 8 January 2015.

Macomber, Kris, Christine Mallinson, and Elizabeth Seale. 2011. '"Katrina That Bitch!" Hegemonic Representations of Women's Sexuality on Hurricane Katrina Souvenir T-Shirts'. *Journal of Popular Culture* 44 (3): 525–44.

New Internationalist. 2006. 'Keep Buying!' *New Internationalist*. 17 April.

Ogawa, Susumu, and Frank T. Piller. 2006. 'Reducing the Risk of New Product Development'. *MIT Sloan Management Review*. Winter: 65–71.

Penney, Joel. 2011. 'Body Screen/Body Politic: The Uses of Political T-Shirts in the Digital Age'. PhD. Thesis, Philadelphia, PA: University of Pennsylvania.

Schweimler, Daniel. 2008. '"Che"'. *Totalitarian Movements and Political Religions* 9 (1): 119–22.

Thompson, Jacob C., and Jayapaul Azariah. 1998. 'Environmental and Ethical Cost of T-Shirts, Tiruppur, Tamil Nadu, India'. In Neno Fukuji and Daryl R. J. Mauer (eds.), *Bioethics in Asia: Proceedings of the UNESCO Asian Bioethics Conference*, 191–5. Christchurch, NZ: Eubios Ethics Institute.

Walker, Rob. 2007. 'Mass Appeal: What One T-shirt Company Has Learned About Community Power – and Avoiding a Design Mobocracy'. *New York Times*. 8 July: E16.

Wells, Troth. 2007. *T-Shirt: One Small Item, One Giant Impact*. Oxford: New Internationalist.

PART TWO

On legibility and ambiguity

5

Seeing clearly? Legibility, word and image in postmodern print design

Grace Lees-Maffei

This chapter tackles two key issues for graphic designers and illustrators: a shift from modernism to postmodernism and varying interpretations of legibility promoted within these cultural tendencies. The modernist quest for legibility is surveyed, from Herbert Bayer's lowercase sans serif modular typeface, Universal (1925), to Beatrice Warde's seminal 1930 lecture published as 'The Crystal Goblet' (2009) in which the invisibility of the text is held up as an ideal for graphic design. These tactics compare with the more playful approach to communication and legibility that characterizes postmodern graphic design and illustration. April Greiman's work will be explored as an example of bricolage and as a precursor of the adoption of computer-aided design in graphics and illustration. David Carson's designs will be analysed as epitomizing a preference for visual communication over textual legibility, for example his layouts for *Ray Gun*. Notwithstanding the social project of modernism, its aims were sometimes expressed through a rarefied and complex aesthetic. Postmodernism sought to offer, instead, attractive, playful and populist cultural artefacts and experiences accessible to the widest possible market. The chapter closes with a reflection on another shift, in the contemporary scene, where postmodern playfulness has ceded to the greater importance, for clients and designers alike, of design ethics, social inclusion and sustainability.

Modernisms

What does 'modernism' mean? It is important for people working in and with design today to understand the complexity of this term, which can mean many things, to the extent that it is more accurate to use the plural 'modernisms'.

First, modernism refers to a period in history, the modern period, as it is used in mainstream history and across the humanities, to denote the period from the sixteenth century to the present. This long period is divided into 'early modern', meaning the sixteenth century to the watershed of the French Revolution of 1789, and 'late modern', meaning the period from 1789 to the present. Historians perceive the very long period of modernism to be distinguished from medieval worldviews by humanism, the enlightenment and post-enlightenment rationalism, science, the Industrial Revolution and Western capitalism. The term 'modern' is used more popularly to mean 'new' or 'current' or 'up-to-date' and is set against 'past' or 'old' in a binaristic, or dual, relationship which ignores its developmental complexity.

In cultural history, modernism is used in a narrower sense to refer to a cultural tendency seen across the arts – including music, literature, theatre and painting – in the period from the end of the nineteenth century to the middle of the twentieth century. In this modernism, self-expression and personal style came to the fore aesthetically and what design historian Kjetil Fallan has described as 'an anti-traditional tradition' prevailed (Fallan 2010: 111). French poet Charles Baudelaire (1821–1867) famously examined modernity as a state, and the quality of being modern as a response to technological and cultural changes in society following the Industrial Revolution.

In design specifically, modernism is associated with the Modern Movement, a twentieth-century phenomenon with roots in the legacy of the Arts and Crafts Movement of the second half of the nineteenth century. The Modern Movement inherited from the Arts and Crafts Movement a concern for the honest, truthful, use of materials exemplified by the elimination of decoration and the necessity for structure or construction to be revealed, and a respect for formal appropriateness and fitness for purpose. Modernist designers sought to achieve a total work of art (*Gesamtkunstwerk* in German) in which all arts worked together. For example, within an interior, all elements should be unified in one style. A key tenet of modernist design philosophy was summarized by architect Louis Sullivan in the phrase 'Form follows function' (1988 (1896)).

Modernism inherited from the Arts and Crafts Movement, in addition, recognition of the relatedness of all the arts, valued equally, as opposed to a hierarchy of the fine arts over the applied arts and crafts. Influential figures such as the designer, novelist and political thinker William Morris sought to improve the lives of ordinary people through design, a project continued by the modernists, who imbued design with social morality, believing that it could counter alienation and transform the economic and social conditions of the masses. This formed part of a broader belief in the inevitability of aesthetic, social biological and technological progress.

However, key distinctions between the Arts and Crafts Movement and the Modern Movement include the latter's embrace of technology. Mass production, standardization and prefabrication enabled the wider dissemination of affordable goods and the achievement, therefore, of democratic design. Modernism was resolutely international, and did not share the Arts and Crafts Movement emphasis on the vernacular. Modernists favoured abstraction, the elimination of figurative or symbolic imagery and a move towards 'pure' form. In so doing, they reduced the function of design to communicate a range of symbolic/expressive meanings, other than those meanings most associated with the values of modernism, such as a celebration of early-twentieth-century technology (Greenhalgh 1990).

The Modern Movement – if it existed as a movement – spanned a broad area of activity from the functional, technological approach to design which communicated a machine aesthetic (celebrating the machine and mechanized manufacture), to the avant-garde performance art of Oskar Schlemmer and the Triadic Ballet. Generations of designers and design historians have equated modernism in design with the Bauhaus design school, which operated in Germany at Weimar and then Dessau, between 1919 and 1933. Bauhaus teaching inculcated the unity of art, craft, design and industry and spanned functionalist and avant-garde modernisms (Whitford 1984; Naylor 1985). It is not accurate, therefore, to think of modernism as a period in the history of design, because it was circulated in a range of ways to different constituencies throughout most of the twentieth century. Nor is it helpful to consider modernism as a style, when it displays such aesthetic and stylistic diversity. Modernism in design is best considered as a cultural tendency (Lunn 1982).

The modernist ideal of 'form follows function' is exemplified in graphic design through the quest for legibility. Three key instances will be considered here as indicative of this quest.

Modernism and legibility: Herbert Bayer at the Bauhaus

One of the most influential art and design schools of the twentieth century was the Bauhaus in Germany. Founded in 1919 by Walter Gropius, who had been involved with the Deutscher Werkbund, the Bauhaus moved in 1925 to Dessau. It was closed by the Nazis in 1933, at which point many Bauhauslers emigrated to the United Kingdom and the United States. The Bauhaus sought to become a 'consulting art centre for industry and the trades' (Bayer, Gropius and Gropius 1975: 12) and to 'rescue all of the arts from the isolation in which each them found itself', (Whitford 1984: 11). Staff and their students who worked in what we would now term 'graphic design' (see the Introduction to this book) reacted against the prevalent German gothic script because they regarded it as heavy and hard to read. László Moholy-Nagy advocated sans serif fonts while Herbert Bayer proposed the use of only one case: 'Why should we write and print in two alphabets? Both a large sign and a small sign are not necessary to identify a single sound. We do not speak in a capital A and a small a' (Bayer, Gropius and Gropius 1975: 147).

Austrian Herbert Bayer (1900–1985) was a Bauhaus member from 1921 to 1928. From 1925 he led the printing and advertising workshop. He left to set up a design studio and worked for the Berlin office of *Vogue* magazine. Following the exhibition of his work in the famous 1937 exhibition of what the Nazi's termed 'Degenerate Art' he emigrated to New York in 1938. Bayer's 'Universal' typeface of 1925 (Figure 5.1) is sans serif and lower case only and uses geometric shapes, the rectangle and the circle, to achieve clarity. Although it was not cast as an analogue face at the time, it was later published as a digital typeface, 'Bayer Universal', with input from Richard Kegler and Denis Kegel for P22 in 1997.

Clarity: Beatrice Warde's Crystal Goblet

In 1930, typographic expert Beatrice Warde (1900–1969) gave an influential lecture 'Printing Should Be Invisible', to the British Typographers' Guild at the St Bride Institute in London. Within a week, the lecture had been published in the trade newsletter *The British & Colonial Printer & Stationer*. It was published as a pamphlet by the Marchbanks Press in 1932 and 1937. In 1955, it appeared in a book *The Crystal Goblet: Sixteen Essays on Typography* (Warde 1955). This influential text used the metaphor of a crystal wine goblet which allows the colour of the wine it contains to be admired as a way of explaining the importance of clarity and transparency in type. Therefore Warde 'uses wine to symbolize the author's words and intentions and the goblet represents typography and the book itself' (Gruendler 2005: 111). Warde argues that 'the most important thing about printing is that it conveys thought, ideas, images, from one mind to other minds' and 'type well used is

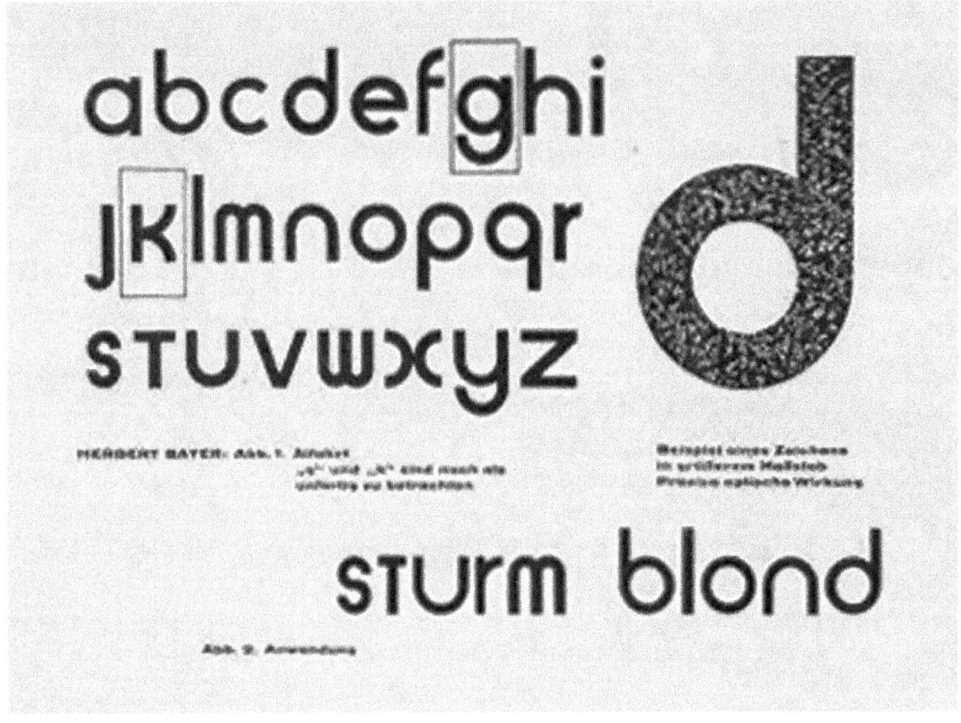

FIGURE 5.1 *Proof sheet for the Universal typeface ca. 1926, designed by Herbert Bayer 1925, Victoria and Albert Museum, National Art Library, London.*

invisible as type, just as the perfect talking voice is the unnoticed vehicle for the transmission of words, ideas' (Warde 2009 (1930): 40, 41).

Shelley Gruendler has noted how the name of Warde's text changed over its various publications from 'Printing Should be Invisible' to 'The Crystal Goblet' and that this exemplifies the power of her metaphor. Indeed, the phrase 'the Crystal Goblet' has become synonymous with the entire concept of clarity in typography (Gruendler 2005: 111). Warde elaborates: 'The book typographer ... may use some rich superb type like text gothic that is something to be looked at, not through. Or he may work in what I call transparent or invisible typography'. She is absolute on the distinction between good and 'bad type', claiming that the 'mental eye focuses through type and not upon it. The type which, through any arbitrary warping of design or excess of "colour", gets in the way of the mental picture to be conveyed, is a bad type' (Warde 2009 (1930, 1955): 42). (Figure 5.2) Warde extends the distinction between good and bad, clarity and excess, to the ego and self-expression of the typographer:

Printing demands a humility of mind, for the lack of which many of the fine arts are even now floundering in self-conscious and maudlin experiments. ... The 'stunt typographer' learns the fickleness of rich men who hate to read. Not for them are long breaths held over serif and kern, they will not appreciate your splitting of hair-spaces. Nobody (save the other craftsmen) will appreciate half your skill. But you may spend endless years of happy experiment in devising

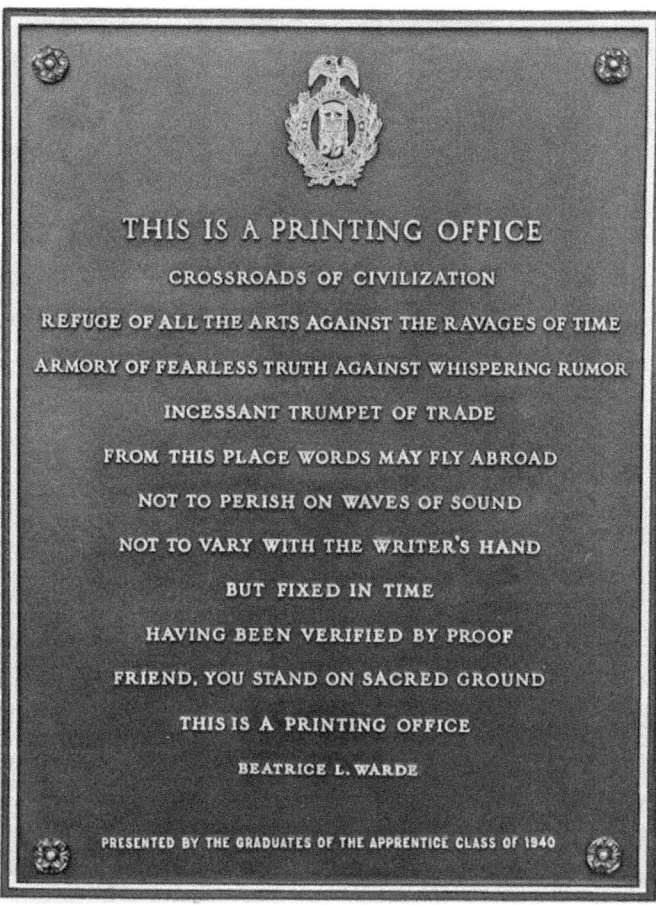

FIGURE 5.2 This Is a Printing Office, *by Beatrice Warde, 1932. 'Set in Centaur and Arrighi types by Westcott & Thomson and reprinted for the Type Directors Club of New York on the occasion of their dinner honoring Mrs. Warde on April 28, 1950'.*

that crystalline goblet which is worthy to hold the vintage of the human mind. (Warde 2009 (1930, 1955): 43)

For Warde, clarity was a modernist project: 'Now the man who first chose glass instead of clay or metal to hold his wine was a 'modernist' in the sense in which I am going to use that term. That is, the first thing he asked of his particular object was not 'How should it look?' but 'What must it do?' and to that extent all good typography is modernist' (Warde 2009 (1930, 1955): 40).

Uniformity: The international influence of Swiss typography

Five years before Warde's lecture, 'Printing Should be Invisible' of 1930, and in the same year that Herbert Bayer designed his 'Universal' typeface, a trade magazine for printers in Germany,

Typographische Mitteilungen, produced a themed issue titled 'elementare typographie'. It included statements by figures variously associated with the Bauhaus including László Moholy-Nagy and El Lissitzky and independent type designer Jan Tschichold (1902–1974). 'Elemental typography' was reduced to essentials consistent with the functionalism of modernist design such as the Dutch De Stijl and Russian Constructivism. Tschichold was extremely influential in the development of this 'new typography' in Germany, where he worked until 1933, and in Switzerland where he spent the rest of his career. Switzerland remained neutral during the Second World War and provided refuge for modernist visual practitioners and for the development of Swiss typography. Tschichold's influence spread internationally as a result of his successful books *Die neue Typographie* (Tschichold 1928) (Figure 5.3) and *Typographie Gestaltung* (1935). However, Tschichold saw a connection between strict functionalism and the totalitarianism he witnessed in Nazi Germany, when he was arrested and had to flee the country. Like Bayer, Tschichold was a victim of the Nazi demonization of modernist visual culture as anti-German. Tschichold subsequently departed from the new typography in favour of a neotraditionalist approach seen, for example, in his work for Penguin Books, where he worked in London from 1947-49. He produced an influential style manual, the *Penguin Composition Rules* (1947) (Shaw 2014). Notwithstanding Tschichold's stylistic departure, a new generation of graphic designers, including Max Bill and painter and designer Richard Paul Lohse, continued the Swiss typographic project.

Swiss Typography, which developed in the 1940s from the new typography of the interwar period, is characterized by the use of a grid to compose layouts of text and image, sans serif typefaces, and photographs and photomontages. Although the grid had long been an organizing tool in text layouts, Swiss typographers gave it a new prominence (Higgins 2009: 177–200). Swiss Typography became internationally important in the 1950s. In 1951, Bill was appointed the founding director of the Hochschule fur Gestaltung (HfG) in Ulm. Swiss designers, among them Josef Müller-Brockmann and Karl Gerstner, became well-regarded practitioners internationally.

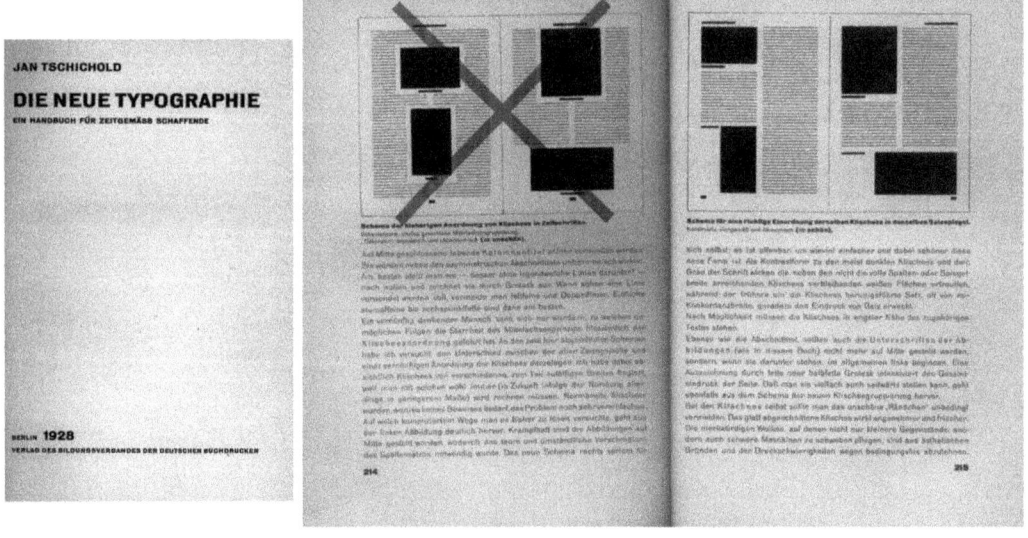

FIGURE 5.3 *Jan Tschichold,* Die neue Typographie, *1928, title page and interior spread showing correct and incorrect layouts.*

FIGURE 5.4 *'Meet the Cast', film poster for* Helvetica, *directed by Gary Hustwit, Plexifilm/Swiss Dots, 2007. Design and permission Experimental Jetset, 2006.*

Helvetica, a typeface designed by Max Miedinger and Eduard Hoffmann in 1957, became the standard choice of corporations seeking associations of contemporaneity and modernity through the development of identities based on the International Typographic Style (Figure 5.4). It has been described as 'that most remarkable of creations: an iconic work whose very success derives from its self-effacing essence' (Purcell 2014: 83). Helvetica's slow burning and eventual dominance of corporate identity was accompanied in the mid-1960s by a turn away from modernist purism towards the pluralism that was recognized in the following decade as postmodernism.

From modernisms to postmodernism

The high modernism of the Bauhaus and of Swiss typography has dominated the discourse and imagery of modernism disproportionately. However, very few people, relatively speaking, adopted high modernism in the first half of the twentieth century. Rather, the mass market accepted a range of popular modernisms. The 'Hollywood style' mediated through movies was a luxurious post-Art

Deco version of modernism associated with celebrity lifestyles and the starlets who attracted such enormous cinema audiences. This luxury style extended to the design of ocean liners, too, for example. In the United Kingdom, society interior decorator Syrie Maugham redefined elegance along moderne lines (the feminizing 'e' distinguishing this modernism from high modern design). 'Moderne' means modernism as a style rather than modernism as a philosophy of design. Writing of the United States, Thomas Hine has used the term 'Populuxe' to describe the democratization of luxury represented by mid-twentieth-century consumerism in the United States (Hine 1986). These popular modernisms seem to have more in common with modernism's heir, postmodernism, than they do with the design ethos of high modernism. The very diversity of popular modernisms prefigures postmodern multiplicity, and their market-led and anti-elitist motivations are similarly in accord with postmodern tendencies, as we shall see.

Kjetil Fallan has described 'isms', with modernism chief among the design 'isms', as both cultural and ideological, in that they are normative: 'They tend to propose or dictate how art/architecture/design should be' (Fallan 2010: 116). But 'isms', he notes, supersede one another fairly frequently, whereas epistemes are deep, fundamental sociological structures which condition modes of thought and understanding (Fallan 2010: 114). Is the shift from modernism to postmodernism simply one of changing 'isms', therefore? Or does it represent the epistemic shift that Foucault posited, in which worldviews change and everything appears to be different?

Evidence of the latter is found in the fact that many modernist designers believed that design could achieve a transformation of consciousness, it could change people's behaviour and psychology. Furthermore, the 'pioneer' phase of modernism was characterized by theological intensity; many pioneer modernists practised Theosophy or explored other mystical belief systems (Maffei 2018: 5–7). Anti-historicism – the rejection of historical styles as a memory of the past – leads to the notion that a designer can have her or his own style. But, some pioneer modernists did raid past design traditions; for example, Le Corbusier's work borrowed from Classical Greek and Roman architecture (Greenhalgh 1990).

High modernism has been criticized and politicized as a totalizing, international style which universalizes design outputs and emphasizes, for example, mass manufacture over local, vernacular, craft traditions. Modernists sought a timeless beauty that could be recognized internationally. Geometric abstraction was a way of achieving this – 'it escaped immediate social contexts and contained the immutable truths of mathematics' (Greenhalgh 1990: 13). This was inconsistent with the polyvalent diversity of postmodernism. Modernism has also been criticized for the extent to which it has privileged men and masculinity (Sparke 1995). Although postmodernism shares with modernism – and Western cultures of the modern period more broadly – a patriarchal base, postmodernism in design occupies a more diverse, commercialized, and therefore arguably feminized, context. Comparing modernism and postmodernism, Ihab Hassan characterizes the former as 'Genital/Phallic' and the latter as 'Polymorphous/Androgynous' (Hassan 1985: 124). We will return to Hassan later in this chapter.

What is postmodernism?

Does postmodernism represent what came after modernism, that is another period, a tool of periodization, or is there more to it than that? For something coming afterwards ('post') to take the name of its predecessor ('modernism') could imply either a total rejection of that earlier entity (postmodernism as a rejection of modernism) or a continuation of that thing. In the case of postmodernism's relationship to modernism, all of these implications are supportable with reference to various cultural instances of these two gigantic isms that have characterized the last 115 years, or more.

Postmodernism can be seen as a continuation of modernism: it evolved from modernism and is, to some extent, defined by its relationship to modernism. Modernist cultural artefacts foreground the processes of manufacture by which they were made, and foreground their own materiality, as do many self-reflexive postmodern cultural artefacts. Like modernism, postmodernism is most usefully regarded as a cultural tendency rather than a period, because postmodern characteristics can be identified retrospectively not only in modernist cultural artefacts, but also even as long ago as the eighteenth century. Then, experimentation with the new format of the novel by authors such as Laurence Sterne displayed characteristics that would now be termed postmodern, such as playfulness, refusal of truth, and self-reflexivity among others (Sterne 1759)

However, whereas modernist cultural production relies on a cult of individuality, postmodern culture is based on multiplicity. If modernism developed in response to mechanization, then postmodernism developed in response to post-industrialism. Walter Benjamin's 1936 essay 'The Work of Art in the Age of Mechanical Reproduction' is useful here (1969 (1936)). What happened to painting when photography was introduced? A focus on the 'aura' of the original intensified, and this is a modernist position. Mass production gave us 'simulacra', or copies without an original, from poster prints to vinyl records (Baudrillard 1983). Acceptance of simulacra – to be unconcerned about the mass production of culture and to cease seeking for the original – is a (proto-)postmodern stance.

Like modernism, postmodernism is seen in all of the arts, from literature to design. For understanding the latter, developments in architecture and architectural theory are key. Steven Izenour, Robert Venturi and Denise Scott Brown's 1968 essay 'A significance for A&P parking lots, or learning from Las Vegas' (1972 (1968)) developed from Venturi's architecture teaching. The essay drew attention to the importance of image over form in US strip mall architecture. Modernist buildings, they argued, were principally about expressive form and volume, whereas the buildings that lined the strips of US non-cities, were principally about surface and decoration. Izenour et al. regarded modernism's focus on form rather than decoration as an exception and the return to decoration in what would come to be known as postmodern design represented a reengagement with what had preceded modernism.

Cultural theorist Frederic Jameson has described postmodernism as 'the cultural logic of late capitalism' (Jameson 1984). For Jameson, and other Marxist and left-leaning critics, postmodern culture is characterized by surface rather than depth, and by the commodity rather than the avant-garde artwork. Postmodern culture is inauthentic, not sincerely felt like modernism. Postmodern culture works like an omnivorous marketing machine, continually commodifying everything, including the avant-garde, in an endless quest for novelty, to stimulate a sated Western market. However, an alternative account of the politics of postmodernism might point to its rejection of overarching metanarratives as part of a wider refusal to recognize value, hierarchy or boundaries. Postmodern culture may be regarded as superficial by modernists but it is inherently inclusive and multi-perspectival; everyone's point of view is levelled albeit within a context of considerable inequalities in terms of resources and access to the market. This approach can be associated with the identification of the needs of a wider range of people in contemporary Western society, so that, for example, cities are being redesigned, to some extent, with children, wheelchair users and the elderly in mind. Furthermore, political weight might be ascribed to the extent to which postmodern culture allows for a consumer who constructs meaning through bricolage and other combinatory practices (Lévi-Strauss 1966 (1962)). Not only cultural producers make meaning, we now understand, following the ideas of Roland Barthes introduced in Chapter 1.

The late cultural theorist Ihab Hassan produced a landmark articulation of 'The Culture of Postmodernism' in his 1985 essay of that name (Hassan 1985). Hassan provides two lists, set side-by-side, of the defining characteristics of modernism and postmodernism. The juxtaposition of these paired characteristics creates a series of binary oppositions, that is pairs of opposites, such as 'off' and 'on'. Binary oppositions emerged from the structuralist linguistics of Ferdinand de Saussure (see Chapter 1; Chandler 2007) and have been used in anthropology as part of the structuralist project of revealing the underlying social structures which condition and characterize societies (Lévi-Strauss 1969 (1964)). They also informed early postcolonial theory, such as Edward Said's *Orientalism* (1978). However, binary oppositions, and binaristic thinking more broadly, have come to be regarded as reductive and polarized, and have been superseded by more complex models of cultural relations such as transculturation (Ortiz 1995 (1940); See also Chapter 6), and hybridity as a dialogue between colonizer and colonized, rather than a binaristic and inflexible relation of centre and margin (Bhabha 1994; Kraidy 2002, 2005; see Chapter 6). Another example is the model of public and private spheres as used, and then rejected, in women's studies and gender studies (McGaw 1989).

Notwithstanding the criticism of binary oppositions as reductively polarized and failing to recognize hybridity, Hassan's approach to understanding postmodernism's complex relationship with modernism remains useful. For Hassan modernism's emphasis on closed form is met with postmodernism's open antiform. Modernism's purpose and design are set against postmodernism's play and chance. If modernism has roots and depth, postmodernism resembles a rhizome and focuses on surfaces. French philosopher Gilles Deleuze and activist Félix Guattari have examined the rhizome as a non-hierarchical, decentralized, modifiable entity (Deleuze and Guattari 1987) – see Chapter 8 of this book, on data visualization. Modernism is associated with creation, totalizing, presence and 'centering' and postmodernism with deconstruction, absence and dispersal. For Hassan, modernism's metaphysics descend into postmodernism's irony, its determinacy into indeterminacy and its transcendence into immanence (Hassan 1985: 123–4). Hassan recalls the semiotics we looked at in Chapter 1 when he attributes to modernism the signified and to postmodernism the signifier, to modernism the 'lisible' or readerly cultural artefact and to postmodernism the 'scriptable' or writerly one; to modernism, semantics, and to postmodernism, rhetoric. Modernism's type is met with postmodernism's mutant, its selection with postmodernism's combination and its genre/boundary with postmodernism's text/intertext. The extent to which these overarching principles are embodied in design practice can be seen, for example, in the catalogue for the major survey exhibition *Postmodernism: Style and Subversion* (Adamson and Pavitt 2011). Here, we consider graphic design specifically.

Postmodern graphic design

By the 1970s and 1980s, the designers who would come to be associated with postmodernism operated without any regard for the staticity of Swiss School typography which had exerted such an influence on their teachers. This was part of a wider cultural refusal of boundaries and categories characteristic of postmodernism. Postmodern practitioners purposefully referenced the histories of design and culture freely referring to popular culture, low culture and high art, sometime with playful intent (Poynor 2003) and sometimes as a critique of contemporary society. Here, we will briefly examine the work of four graphic designers whose practice exemplifies some of the ways in which postmodern graphic design practice might be understood.

Neville Brody

Neville Brody (b. 1957) has achieved commercial success with experimental and innovative work. Brody has explained his philosophy of graphic design as follows: 'Ever since college I've pursued

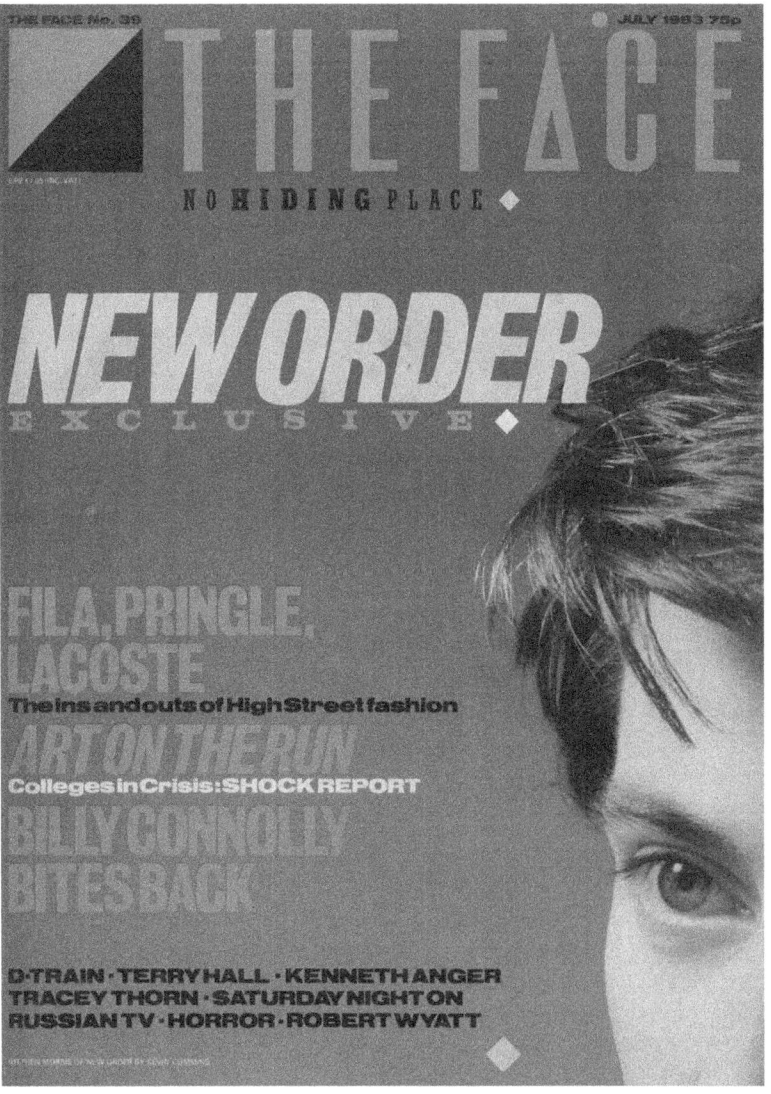

FIGURE 5.5 *Neville Brody,* The Face, *no. 39 (July 1983).*

a no-compromise policy of deep experimentation, whether there is a client involved or not. It comes from my belief that graphic design is a vital tool for expression and for exploring language in the public arena, as opposed to art which is very elitist' (Farrelly 2015). Brody was educated at Hornsea College of Art and then London College of Printing (1976–9). He began designing for the punk community, including work for Rocking Russian, and the independent record labels Stiff Records and Fetish. Brody recognizes the importance of the punk music scene in developing his approach to design and for other designers including Malcolm Garrett and Peter Saville (Dezeen 2009). Of his cover for Cabaret Voltaire's record *Micro-Phonies* (1984), Brody has noted, 'The Cabs' philosophy was about the loss of the human voice in modern society and needed imagery that was ambiguous and disturbing, so elements were hidden behind video textures or barely discernible through repeat patterns' (British Council 1999). Brody's aesthetic can therefore be related to postmodern theories of alienation in a media-saturated world (e.g. Baudrillard 1983).

As well as music graphics, Brody's reputation is built on his magazine work and typography. Brody challenged conventions of editorial design through his work for *The Face* magazine (1981–6) (Figure 5.5) which Peter Saville has hailed as the first style magazine (Saville 2018), *City Limits* (1983–7) and, from 1987, *Arena* magazine. Brody has designed numerous typefaces, including 'Typeface Six' (1986), 'Industria' for Linotype and Blur for Fontshop (1991). He set up Fontworks in 1990 to disseminate digital type. Brody exemplified postmodern ahistoricism in the way he borrowed from the history of art and design to create striking graphics with contemporary relevance. He was influenced by Russian Constructivism and the work of El Lissitzky and Alexander Rodchenko, as well as by the writings of postmodern theorists Jean Baudrillard (1983) and Paul Virilio. He combined street-style influences with the manipulation of images and typefaces into novel, illegible forms (Brody 1988, 1994).

Peter Saville

Like Brody, Peter Saville (b. 1955) also began designing music graphics. He studied graphic design at Manchester Polytechnic (1975–8) with fellow student Malcolm Garrett. Design commentator Rick Poynor noted that Saville used his record covers as ways 'of learning about the history of graphic design':

> Malcolm [Garrett] had a copy of Herber Spencer's *Pioneers of Modern Typography.* The one chapter that he hadn't reinterpreted in his own work was the cool, disciplined 'New Typography' of Tschichold and its subtlety appealed to me. I found a parallel in it for the New Wave that was evolving out of Punk. In this, as it seemed at the time, obscure byway of graphic design history, I saw a look for the new cold mood of 1977–78. … Of course, the whole point with appropriation is knowing what to do and when. (Poyner 1995: np)

Garrett had studied communication design at the University of Reading, but when he transferred to Manchester Polytechnic he brought his reading list with him. Saville and his contemporaries felt that 'punk was not exactly the Russian revolution' but they saw a parallel between that and punk's reinvention of pop (Saville 2018). When Saville and Garrett were at art college together in Manchester, modernism had ceased to be the dominant visual language and it was not on the curriculum. It became, instead, one of many styles available to postmodern practitioners. Saville's practice of appropriation has always included modernism, demonstrating that postmodern practice incorporates modernism as much as it rejects it:

> I was twenty-two and in my last weeks at college, and becoming aware of the great tradition of twentieth century graphics, as well as certain schools such as the Russian constructivists, the Bauhaus and De Stijl. I was really into Jan Tschichold and Die Neue Typographie of the 1930s [*sic*, 1920s], which was exclusively typography and graphics and reflected the mood of the time. Thus my first studies were reflected in the sleeves of my first records. (Nice 1984: np)

The following year Saville became a founding partner and the designer for Factory Records. Like Brody, Saville began his career with no management constraints and so was able to make aesthetics his sole concern:

> At Factory Records I had a remarkably free space in which to express myself. We didn't have clients and quite often no brief, so the New Order covers were a platform for me to express whatever particular idea or concept I was preoccupied with that year. (Saville quoted by Mikhail 2002: np)

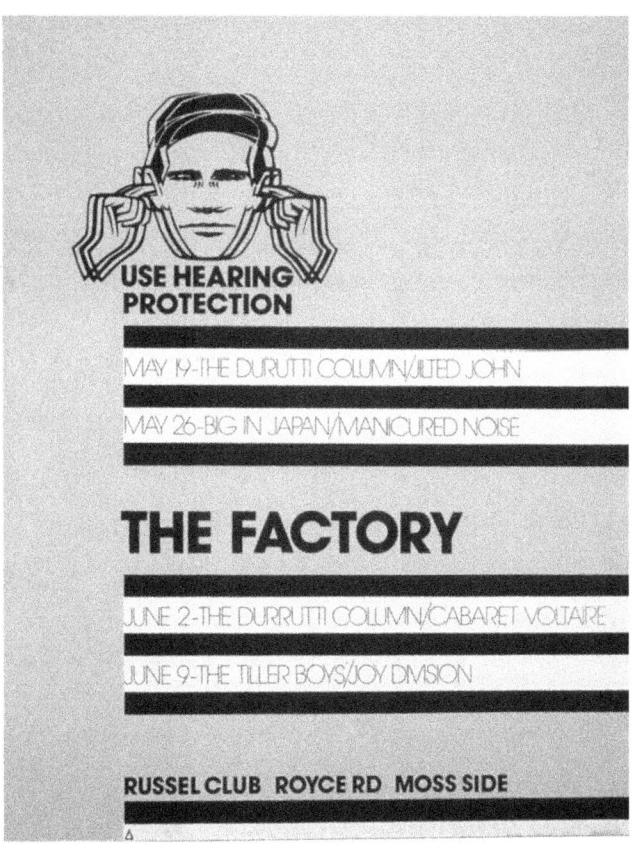

FIGURE 5.6 *The Factory, poster 30" × 40", 1978, design Peter Saville.*

For Saville, the medium of record covers is distinct from other forms of communication design because it offers greater freedom; record covers provide a platform to express ideas about contemporary society (Saville 2018: np). Punk had been something of a coup d'état in design terms, and had allowed young designers an entrée into the design industry, with autonomy (Saville 2018).

Saville has built his approach to graphic design from on the practice of appropriation. In 1984, he described his first work for Factory – the poster 'FAC 1' – as 'constructivist in style' (Figure 5.6) but that was one of several influences in his work and, for example, 'the sleeve for OMD's *Electricity* was more neo-classical' (Nice 1984: np). Saville's early acts of appropriation occurred when he first became aware of postmodernism – 'while working on the second Factory poster':

> On a trip to London I picked up a book of Philip Johnson's proposals for the AT&T building in New York. ... It made me think that maybe I wasn't wrong in wanting to use Tschichold's later work – that and a John Foxx album cover for Ultravox [*Systems of Romance*] with serif type on a black background. Within 12 months, neo-classicism and the influence of architectural post-modernism were everywhere. People in New York were buying columns to put in their apartments. My contribution was the graphic equivalent. (Poynor 1995: n.p.)

In conversation with me, Saville explained that his use of references from the past was a consistent and coherent strategy for expressing annoyance about the shambles of 1970s Britain, the poverty

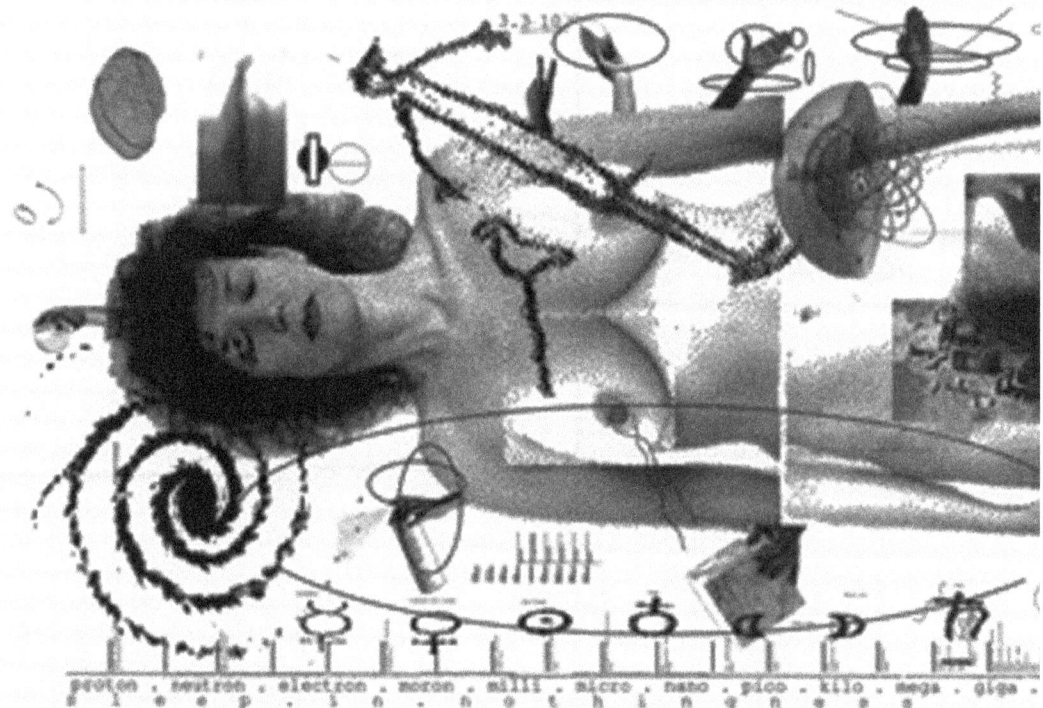

FIGURE 5.7 *Pull-out life-size self-portrait for 'Does it make sense?'* Design Quarterly *no. 133 (1986). Design and permission April Greiman.*

and shabbiness of everyday life (Saville 2018). Saville and his contemporaries quoted from the past purposefully, to express dissatisfaction with the present and to make the everyday scene look better. He was unaware of April Greiman and Wolfgang Weingart who were already exploring 'retrieval and transposition'.

The medium Brody, Saville and Garrett chose was influential upon an impressionable young market and Saville's work was recognized early: in 1981 he won three D&AD awards and has continued to enjoy critical success with, for example, a retrospective at the Design Museum in 2003. Also in 1981, he began working at Dindisc, until, in 1983, he founded Peter Saville Associates. His clients included Roxy Music, Ultravox and New Order, the Whitechapel Art Gallery and the Pompidou Centre. Saville closed his studio in 1990 and joined Pentagram as a partner. He was with Pentagram for two years. Saville did not enjoy the business targets at Pentagram and the emphasis on the role of communication design in creating a veneer of authenticity, credibility and sincerity. Returning to London as a freelancer in 1994 enabled Saville to work for diverse clients ranging from London Records to Mandarina Duck and, particularly, fashion brands including Yohji Yamamoto (see Chapter 6), Jil Sander and Dior. He later worked with Givenchy and has more recently designed a logo for Calvin Klein. In 2004, Saville was appointed creative director for the City of Manchester and although he claims to have had no aspirations to work on place branding (Byrnes 2012) (see chapters 1,2, 6 and 7), he occupied that role for a decade and is currently one of several artistic advisors to Manchester International Festival. In work such as this, Saville has found authenticity. Across his oeuvre, past and

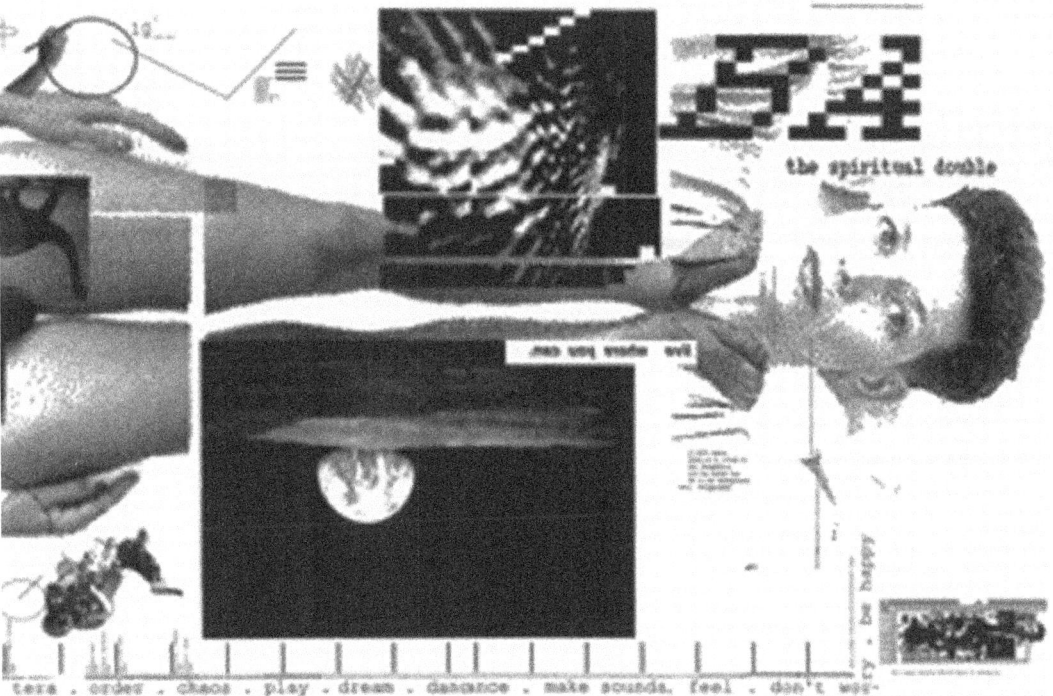

present, commerce and creativity have been negotiated in such a way as to lead journalist Adam Wray to agree with fashion designer Raf Simons that Saville's work is 'timeless' (Wray 2018).

April Greiman

Given the dominance of Apple Mac products in design practice today, it is difficult to imagine that in 1984, when the Macintosh was introduced, 'most designers were skeptical of—if not completely opposed to—the idea of integrating the computer into design practice, perhaps fearing an uncertain future wherein the tactility of the hand was usurped by the mechanics of bits and bytes' (AIGA 1998). It was not only the hand that was usurped. Designers and design educators alike regarded the introduction of computer-aided graphic design as potentially threatening their livelihoods by deskilling the profession and enabling a fully functioning print shop on every desktop. However, as the American Institute of Graphic Artists recognized, 'A visionary few, including April Greiman, recognized the vast potential of this new medium' (AIGA 1998). Greiman (b. 1948) was an early adopter of the Macintosh, and used it to introduce complexity into graphic design practice that would have been eliminated by her modernist forebears. Her intriguing, engaging and meaningful digital collages exemplify postmodern bricolage. In 1990, Greiman published her first book *Hybrid Imagery: The Fusion of Technology and Graphic Design* showcasing six years of her work using the Macintosh (Greiman 1990). Design writer and curator Liz Farrelly has described Greiman as championing duality and diversity:

> Greiman's practice of 'hybridizing' various technologies and aesthetics has significantly reconfigured the concept of 'design for communication' by blurring the boundaries between the disparate disciplines of architecture, interior design, and print and motion graphics … . Her ability to blend words and images with texture and space, mix technology and science with symbol and myth, as well as combine different creative disciplines, has had a fundamental impact on a professional and art form that, until the 1980s, was informed by one overriding, logic-oriented ideology: Modernism. (Farrelly 1998: 8, 9)

Greiman's digital collages make use of what modernist designers would dismiss as visual noise for expressive and communicative purposes. As well as featuring layers of imagery and information, Greiman has made aesthetic use of the degraded effect of pixelated imagery necessitated by the low memory of early Macintosh computers. Furthermore, her refusal of modernism's quest for clarity can be seen in gendered terms as a rejection of masculine aesthetics and logic. Some of Greiman's most notable works have engaged issues of gender explicitly. Design critic Alice Twemlow has noted that Greiman's pull-out life-size self-portrait for 'Does it make sense?' in *Design Quarterly* no. 133 (1986) (Figure 5.7)) was 'a provocative gesture, which emphatically countered the objective, rational and masculine tendencies of modernist design' (Twemlow 2008). This image is both a feminist statement about desexualised nudity and physical individuality, and an exemplar of the technologically determined aesthetic Greiman developed to challenge modernism's emphasis on legibility and universality.

David Carson

David Carson (b. 1954) was inexperienced as an art director when he began designing magazines. Employed as a lecturer in sociology and reaching the status of eighth best in the world at surfing (which is relevant to the material he designed, and the community he served), he developed what was at that time a distinctive and unusual aesthetic that privileged evocative visual layouts over clarity or ease of reading the text. His early work for *Transworld Skateboarding* was considered too radical by advertisers and the title folded. Similarly, *Beach Culture*, designed by and for the surfing community, achieved aesthetic success and critical acclaim but it, too, was dogged by commercial failure and closed due to lack of advertising revenue. Carson's work for *Ray Gun* (1992–5), however, was a

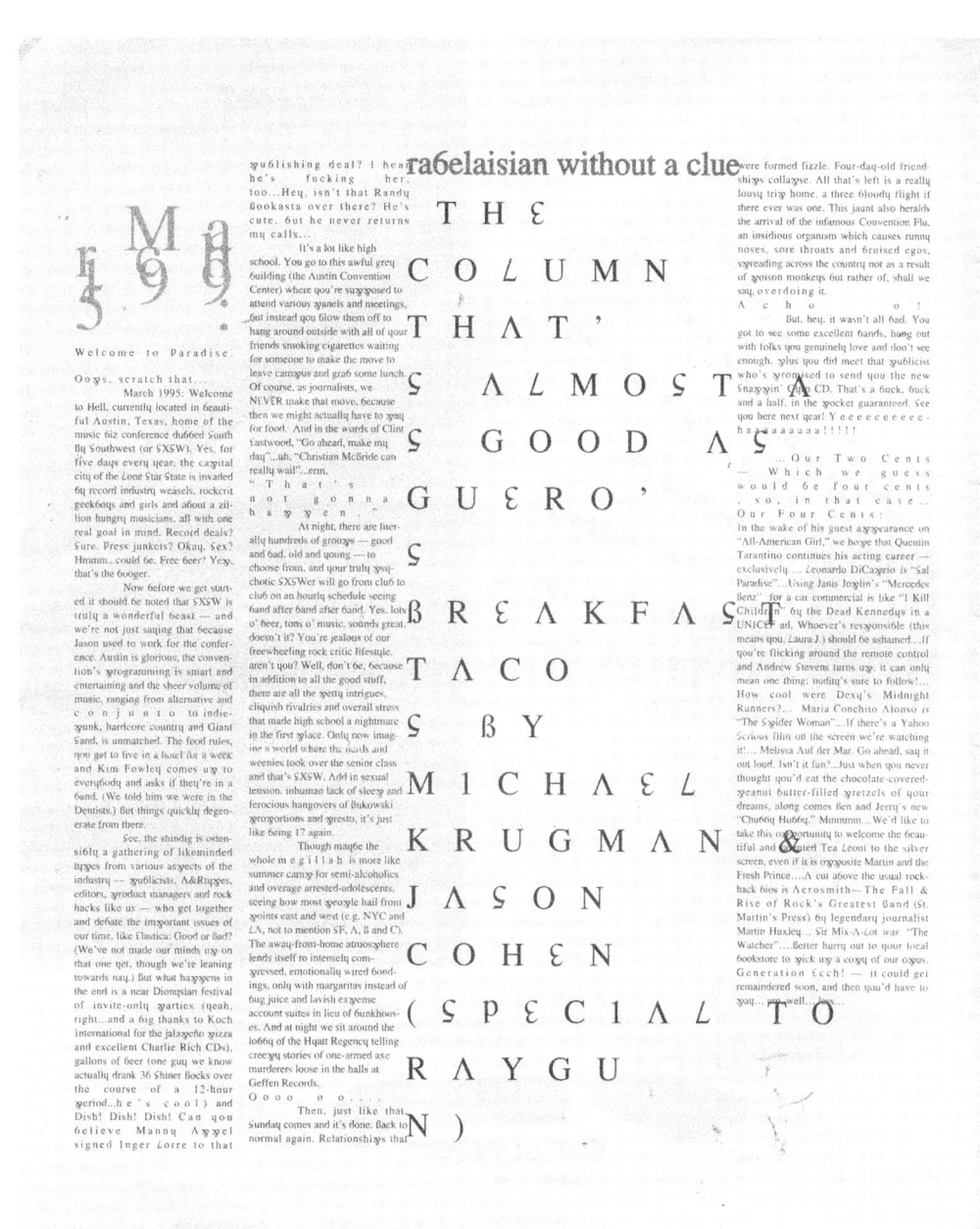

FIGURE 5.8 *David Carson, 'ra6belaisian without a clue', single page spread*, Ray Gun 26.

commercial success and a critical hit (Figure 5.8). This approach can be understood with reference to other landmarks of magazine art direction including Neville Brody's work on *The Face* (1981). Like Peter Saville working for Factory Records, Carson enjoyed complete freedom in design at *Ray Gun*. He developed a distinctive much-copied style there, which refused Sullivan's modernist rule of 'form follows function'. *Ray Gun* had no consistent typefaces or layouts; the masthead was designed anew for each issue, representing a gain in terms of freshness and novelty and a loss in terms of efficiency and brand recognition for the title. Carson collaged these early magazine layouts on paper on his studio floor. Unlike Greiman, Carson turned to digital techniques relatively late (Moszkowicz 2014: 99).

His aim was to communicate the 'feel' of an article rather than to represent it directly or obviously. Infamously, he set one article about Bryan Ferry in the Dingbats typeface composed entirely of symbols rather than letters, thereby rendering it wholly illegible for readers (Hustwit 2007: np). Carson's work epitomizes a preference for what design historian Jeremy Aynsley has called 'Visually driven arrangements of text' (Aynsley 2001: 233). Carson rejects conventional techniques of legibility by using text upside down, layering type and image so that they become indistinguishable, and collaging borrowed, disparate elements. He uses layout to explore meaning. His work divides opinion: it has been applauded as an antidote to modernist neutrality and decried for its illegibility.

Carson's influence is shown in the derivative work that others have produced and in the popularity of his bestselling book *The End of Print* (Blackwell and Carson 2012; see also Blackwell and Carson 1997; Carson and Meggs 1999). Carson's work displays a fascinating shift from producing cut and paste layouts for surfing fanzines to producing large-scale advertising campaigns for global corporate clients such as Pepsi, Coke and Apple. Carson's career therefore exemplifies Jameson's ideas about the impossibility of a postmodern avant-garde in that his early innovative and challenging editorial work has been commoditized in advertising practice, both of his own design, and that of others which bears his influence.

Conclusion: After postmodernism

This chapter has shown how modernism and postmodernism are best viewed as cultural tendencies spanning the arts, rather than historical periods. Postmodernism represents both a rejection of, and a continuation of, modernism. Notwithstanding the social project of modernism, its aims were sometimes expressed through a rarefied and complex aesthetic. Postmodernism sought to offer, instead, attractive, playful and populist cultural artefacts and experiences for the widest possible market. Postmodern culture is commoditized, eclectic, it resists categorization, embraces pluralism, borrowing and collage, playfulness and ahistoricism.

We have examined the work of four graphic designers as exemplary of a number of postmodern graphic design strategies which challenge modernist notions of clarity in various ways. Neville Brody displayed ahistoricist tendencies as he referenced the past in his print designs using Russian Constructivist influences, for example. Peter Saville also displayed mastery of the postmodern practices of appropriation and borrowing. April Greiman was an early adopter of computers in graphic design practice and experimented with the complexity that the Apple Mac facilitated. David Carson went further than most graphic designers in rejecting and reconceiving legibility in apparently illegible arrangements of layers of text and image.

What comes after postmodernism? In the twenty-first century we have seen another shift in which postmodernism playfulness and commercialism has ceded to the greater importance, for clients and designers alike, of design ethics, social inclusion and sustainability. The new ethics in design has been prompted by climate change, diminishing fossil fuels and materials shortages, pressing issues such as food poverty, the inequitable distribution of resources including wealth and education, globalization and global political instability. These problems concern designers who want to be part of the solution. Rather than stipulating modernist clarity or postmodern ambiguity, the new ethics demand that graphic designers achieve political clarity and a way of communicating effectively with audiences about these most pressing issues.

References

Adamson, Glenn, and Jane Pavitt (eds.) 2011. *Postmodernism: Style and Subversion*. London: V&A Publishing.
AIGA (The American Institute of Graphic Arts). 1998. 'April Greiman, Biography by AIGA'. http://www.aiga.org/medalist-aprilgreiman/. Accessed 18 November 2015.
Aynsley, Jeremy. 2001. *A Century of Graphic Design*. London: Mitchell Beazley.
Baudrillard, Jean. 1983. *Simulations*. Paris: Semiotext(e).
Bayer, Herbert, Walter Gropius, and Ise Gropius (eds.) 1975. *Bauhaus, 1919–1928*. London: Secker and Warburg.
Benjamin, Walter. 1969 [1936]. 'The Work of Art in the Age of Mechanical Reproduction'. In Hannah Arendt (ed.), *Illuminations*, 217–52. New York: Schocken Books.
Bhabha, Homi K. 1994. *The Location of Culture*. London: Routledge.
Blackwell, Lewis, and David Carson. 1997. *David Carson 2nd Sight: Grafik Design after the End of Print*. London: Laurence King.
Blackwell, Lewis, and David Carson. 2012. *The End of Print*. Second edition. London: Laurence King.
Brody, Neville, with Jon Wozencroft. 1988. *The Graphic Language of Neville Brody*, London: Thames and Hudson.
Brody, Neville, with Jon Wozencroft. 1994. *The Graphic Language of Neville Brody 2*. London: Thames and Hudson.
Byrnes, Mark. 2012. '"If Your Place Needs a Slogan, It Has a Problem": A Conversation with the Creative Director of Manchester'. *Citylab*. 25 April. Online at https://www.citylab.com/design/2012/04/city-and-its-creative-director-peter-saville-manchester/1822/. Accessed 30 March 2018.
Carson, David, and Philip B. Meggs. 1999. *Fotografiks: An Equilibrium Between Photography and Design Through Graphic Expression That Evolves from Content*. Berkeley, CA: Gingko Press.
Chandler, Daniel. 2007. *Semiotics: The Basics*. Second edition. London: Routledge.
Deleuze, Gilles, and Félix Guattari. 1987. *A Thousand Plateaus: Capitalism and Schizophrenia*. Translated by Brian Massumi. Minneapolis: University of Minneapolis Press.
Dezeen. 2009. Super Contemporary Interviews: Neville Brody. http://www.dezeen.com/2009/06/10/super-contemporary-interviews-neville-brody/. Accessed 19 November 2015.
Fallan, Kjetil. 2010. *Design History: Understanding Theory and Method*. Oxford: Berg.
Farrelly, Liz. 1998. *April Greiman: Floating Ideas into Time and Space*. New York: Watson-Guptill Publications.
Farrelly, Liz. 2015. 'Sound Design UK Music and Graphic Design: Reconstructing an Exhibition'. Blog Post. *Liz Farrelly Visits*. 30 November. http://www.liz-farrelly-visits.org/2015/11/30/sound-design-uk-music-and-graphic-design-reconstructing-an-exhibition/#more-1163. Accessed 30 November 2015.
Greenhalgh, Paul (ed.) 1990. *Modernism in Design*. London: Reaktion Books.
Greiman, April. 1990. *Hybrid Imagery: The Fusion of Technology and Graphic Design*. New York: Watson-Guptill Publications.
Gruendler, Shelley. 2005. 'The Life and Work of Beatrice Warde'. Unpublished PhD thesis, Department of Typography and Graphic Communication, University of Reading.
Hassan, Ihab. 1985. 'The Culture of Postmodernism'. *Theory, Culture and Society* 2 (3) (November): 119–31.

Higgins, Hannah B. *The Grid*. Cambridge, MA: The MIT Press.
Hine, Thomas. 1986. *Populuxe*. New York: Alfred A. Knopf.
Hustwit, Gary, [dir.] 2007. *Helvetica*. [Film.] Plexifilm/Swiss Dots.
Izenour, Steven, Robert Venturi, and Denise Scott Brown. 1972 [1968]. 'A Significance for A&P Parking Lots, or Learning from Las Vegas'. In Steven Izenour, Robert Venture and Denise Scott Brown (eds.), *Learning from Las Vegas*, pp. 3–73. Cambridge, MA: The MIT Press.
Jameson, Frederic. 1984. 'Postmodernism, or the Cultural Logic of Late Capitalism'. *New Left Review* 146 (July–August 1984): 59–92.
Jobling, Paul, and David Crowley. 1996. *Graphic Design: Reproduction & Representation Since 1800*. Manchester: Manchester University Press.
Kraidy, Marwan. 2002. 'Hybridity in Cultural Globalization'. *Communication Theory* 12 (3): 316–39.
Kraidy, Marwan. 2005. *Hybridity: or the Cultural Logic of Globalization*. Philadelphia: Temple.
Lévi-Strauss, Claude. 1966 [1962]. *The Savage Mind*. London: Weidenfeld & Nicolson.
Lévi-Strauss, Claude. 1969 [1964]. *The Raw and the Cooked Mythologiques*, Volume 1. New York: Harper and Row.
Lunn, Eugene. 1982. *Marxism and Modernism: An Historical Study of Lukács, Brecht, Benjamin, and Adorno*. Berkeley and Los Angeles: University of California Press.
Maffei, Nicolas P. 2018. *Norman Bel Geddes: American Design Visionary*. London: Bloomsbury.
McGaw, Judith A. 'No Passive Victims, No Separate Spheres: A Feminist Perspective on Technology's History'. In Stephen H. Cutcliffe and Robert C. Post (eds.), *In Context: History and the History of Technology*. Cranbury, NJ: Lehigh University Press, 1989.
Mikhail, Kate. 2002. 'What's the Big Idea? Peter Saville'. *The Observer*, Sunday September 22. Online at http://www.theguardian.com/theobserver/2002/sep/22/features.magazine167. Accessed 3 December 2015.
Moszkowicz, Julia. 2014. '*Ray Gun*, USA (David Carson, 1992-1995)'. In Grace Lees-Maffei (ed.), *Iconic Designs: 50 Stories about 50 Things*, 96–9. London: Bloomsbury.
Naylor, Gillian. 1985. *The Bauhaus Reassessed*. London: Herbert Press.
Nice, James. 1984. 'Perfect Stylistic Attitude: An Interview with Peter Saville'. Published online http://home.planet.nl/~frankbri/psainter.html. Accessed 19 November 2015.
Ortiz, Fernando. 1995 [1940]. *Cuban Counterpoint: Tobacco and Sugar*. Translated by Harriet De Onís. Durham and London: Duke University Press.
Poynor, Rick. 1995. 'Reputations: Peter Saville'. *Eye* no. 17 vol. 5. Published online at http://www.eyemagazine.com/feature/article/reputations-peter-saville. Accessed 19 November 2015.
Poynor, Rick. 2003. *No More Rules: Graphic Design and Postmodernism*. London: Laurence King.
Purcell, Kerry. 2014. 'Helvetica'. In Grace Lees-Maffei (ed.), *Iconic Designs: 50 Stories about 50 Things*, 80–3. London: Bloomsbury.
Said, Edward. 1978. *Orientalism*. New York: Vintage Books.
Saville, Peter. 2018. Telephone interview with Grace Lees-Maffei. 27 February.
Shaw, Paul. 2014. 'Penguin Books, UK (Allen Lane, 1935 and Jan Tschichold, 1947-49)'. In Grace Lees-Maffei (ed.), *Iconic Designs: 50 Stories about 50 Things*, 76–9. London: Bloomsbury.
Sparke, Penny. 1995. *As Long as Its Pink: The Sexual Politics of Taste*. London: Pandora.
Sterne, Laurence. 1759. *The Life and Opinions of Tristram Shandy*. York: Ann Ward.
Sullivan, Louis. 1988 [1896]. 'The Tall Office Building Artistically Considered'. In Robert Twombly (ed.), *Louis Sullivan: The Public Papers*, 103–12. Chicago: University of Chicago Press.
Tschichold, Jan. 1928. *Die neue Typographie: ein Handbuch für zeitgemäss Schaffende*. Berlin: Verlag des Bildungsverbandes der deutschen Buchdrucker.
Twemlow, Alice. 2008. *The Masters Series: April Greiman*. Exhibition Catalogue. *School of Visual Arts, New York City*, 20 October to 13 December 2008.
Warde, Beatrice. 2009 (1930). 'The Crystal Goblet, Or Why Printing Should Be Invisible'. In Helen Armstrong (ed.), *Graphic Design Theory*, 39–43. New York: Princeton Architectural Press.
Whitford, Frank. 1984. *The Bauhaus*. London: Thames & Hudson.
Wray, Adam. 2018. 'Saville Wrote the Source Code: Home the English Graphic Designer Set the Course for Contemporary Visual Culture'. SSENSE. Online at https://www.ssense.com/en-us/editorial/culture/peter-saville-wrote-the-source-code. Accessed 30 March 2018.

6

Signifying orientalism, chinoiserie and japonisme: Fashion photography in *Vogue* as a case study

Grace Lees-Maffei

Globalization is one of the defining characteristics of twenty-first-century design, culture, economics and politics. But it is not new. The silk routes form a notable example of early commercial, cultural and design globalization through the movement of goods and ideas over large distances before the modern period (Lees-Maffei and Houze 2010: 467–8; Frankopan 2015). Orientalism, too, represents a relatively early example of cultural globalization as an enduring fantasy in literature and design over several centuries. This chapter introduces readers to the relationship between design and national identity, and orientalism in design, as complicating this relationship. It goes on to consider the relationship between the global East and West, and somewhere in between, through some key theories of postcolonialism. We will then turn to the specific case study of magazines, and the ways in which they fuel consumer desire before examining orientalism, chinoiserie and japonisme as they have appeared in British *Vogue* over the last fifty years. Theories of postmodern pastiche (pastiche is imitation without mockery, as discussed later in this chapter) are explored here. The chapter concludes by noting ways in which the model of alterity (otherness) which has characterized understanding of the cultural relations between East and West no longer describes the current situation in which a globalized culture brings people together in shared pursuits from Beijing to Boston and Tokyo to Turin.

Design and national identity

Design has always been an international practice. International Gothic, Byzantine and Romanesque have each spread internationally to become the dominant style of their periods. In the modern period, design has functioned as an important tool in the construction and communication of national identity. As nation states developed, recognizably national styles arose. Postage stamps, currency, a nation's flags and the uniforms of officials often provide foreign observers with their first and lasting impressions of national character as well as functioning as familiar symbols for the nation's inhabitants (Hobsbawm and Ranger 1993). National identity is a sense of belonging, or identification, based on the lived experience of habitation in a nation, or nation state, combined with recognition of the symbolic nation. But international cooperation has always been a prerequisite of export and import trades and is necessary for multinational companies to advance. Standardized time, maritime laws, weights and measures and, eventually, power-sources have all been helpful in this process by allowing manufacturers to cater for more than one national market efficiently.

Design historians have asked a range of questions about national identity in design (Gimeno-Martínez 2016). How can the form, material and technique of a piece of design embody national or international concerns? Can there be national traditions in the system of manufacture? How does a consciously international designer or company approach the organization of their practice? Can the same object contain both a national and an international aspect, or are these mutually exclusive? (Aynsley 1993). Nations wishing to export their goods and services have promoted national identities in the international arena, as in the cases of Danish design (Teilmann-Lock 2016) and the 'Made in Italy' myth (Lees-Maffei 2014). While national identities and stereotypes have extended across the modern period, nation branding has developed as an advanced stage of the relatively recent advertising and marketing professions, and has become more important over the past century, during a period of extensive globalization of trade and culture. The celebrated leading corporate identity consultant, Wally Olins (1930–2014) made a career out of 'nation branding' (Olins 2003). Nation branding involves the identification of a clear message which stands in for the nation metonymically (as the part represents the whole). In this way, nation branding functions like a formalized, official, kind of stereotyping.

Stereotypes are one of the ways in which we understand the world. They are not the concerted efforts of branding and marketing specialists. Rather they emerge and operate in diffuse ways across media and interpersonal communication. Simplification and generalization assist us in recognition, an important safety mechanism whereby we avoid the fear and uncertainty of the unknown (McGarty, Yzerbyt and Spears 2002). Stereotypes are useful, therefore, but they can also be reductive and even damaging. For example, gender stereotypes can dramatically reduce the freedoms ascribed to women and to men. Stereotypes of national identity are dangerous when they intersect with racial, religious and historical prejudices. For instance, stereotypes of England (which often means London) have emphasized royalty, rock and roll and football, including football hooliganism, and bear little resemblance to the multicultural diversity of today's communities. Similar inaccuracies characterize stereotypes of other nations.

Orientalism in design: Theories of East, West and somewhere between

The informal development of national identities and national stereotypes often results in inaccuracies and misrepresentations, as the case of 'orientalism', and the related French terms 'chinoiserie' and 'japonisme' show. These refer to representations of the East made by cultural producers of various kinds (writers, designers) in the West. Orientalism has been identified by literary theorist Edward Said as the tendency by which the West conceptualizes a generalized 'East' as exotic, erotic, feminine and desirable:

> Orientalism can be discussed and analyzed as the corporate institution for dealing with the Orient – dealing with it by making statements about it, authorizing views of it, describing it, by teaching it, settling it, ruling over it: in short, orientalism as a Western style for dominating, restructuring, and having authority over the Orient. (Said 1978: 3)

Orientalism, chinoiserie and japonisme exemplify a fantasy of the East for Western consumption regardless of the facts and particularities of life in East Asia. As such, they have formed part of the drive for novelty which has stimulated consumer society since its origins in the seventeenth and eighteenth centuries in Britain (Brewer and Porter 1992). Orientalism in design, specifically, has been defined as 'the construction of an imaginary Orient to satisfy a western vision of human elegance and refinement within a natural and architectural world of extreme delicacy' (MacKenzie 1995: 109). This fantasy has appeared across a range of product groups including prints (Guth 2015), advertising (Ramamurthy 2003; Moeran 1996), ceramics, furniture, fashion (Bolton 2015) and interior design (Potvin 2015). This chapter examines editorial and graphic design within the context of the visual/textual format of the fashion magazine. Orientalism, chinoiserie and japonisme provide particularly rich examples of the ways in which national identity is expressed in design. In critical writing about design, art and culture more broadly, chinoiserie is used to refer to Eastern influences on Western practice, and representations of the generalized East, whereas japonisme is more often used to refer specifically to the Japanese influence on Western art and design, which was particularly marked during the late nineteenth century (Lambourne 2005). Orientalism has a correlative in occidentalism, and the enthusiasm for Western culture in East Asia, from the sustained rockabilly subculture in China to the popularity of British brands such as Burberry and Paul Smith across the region.

One definition of chinoiserie in the decorative arts is as 'a style in European arts and crafts that reflects the fanciful notions of China which from the Middle Ages have been fostered by travellers' tales and a rather imperfect knowledge of imported textiles, porcelain and objets d'art' (Osborne 1985). The success of medieval trade routes led in 1600 to the setting up of the East India Company by Queen Elizabeth I: 'This move above all others served to establish England's influence in the development of chinoiserie. The East India trade fundamentally altered the drink, dress and artistic taste of the well-to-do classes in England and on the continent' (Jacobson 1993: 17). The European fashion for the Chinese style, stimulated by merchants and importers, influenced Chinese craftsmen who wanted to access the Western market to adapt their designs accordingly: 'Chinoiserie is western, it is a purely European vision of China; a fantasy based upon a China of the imagination' (Jacobson 1993: 27). Jacobson explains that chinoiserie goods sold in the West were the result of 'geographical confusion': Goods from China, Japan, Siam and India were assigned random attributions in a spirit of topographical indifference engendered by the belief that it was all so outlandish out there that little purpose would be served by precision (Jacobson 1993: 31). Impey makes clear that chinoiserie is an amalgam of influences:

> Because it is not always possible to sort out the exact origins of chinoiserie things – they may be descended from a mixture of Chinese, Japanese, Indian or Persian styles, they may even be

> more than second or third hand in descent, as in textiles and porcelain – the name has to be all-embracing. (Impey 1977: 10)

Chinoiserie is geographically generalized; enthusiasts for the style have not cared where it came from. Chinoiserie, therefore, tells us as much about its Western consumers as it does about East Asia. Stacey Sloboda begins her study of chinoiserie in eighteenth-century Britain by noting its capacity 'not only to reflect – but also to shape – taste, identity, and political opinion' (Sloboda 2014: 3). She concludes her book with a slightly different model of chinoiserie as 'at once a product of and a commentary on the global circulation of images and materials in the eighteenth century' (Sloboda 2014: 205).

Chinoiserie has meant different things to its consumers at different times and indeed has meant whatever consumers have wished it to mean, even where these meanings are contradictory and vary over time. Commentators hold differing views about the extent to which chinoiserie is consistent or ever-changing. On the one hand, according to Oliver Impey:

> Much of the iconography of chinoiserie is relatively consistent, so that certain features can be used as diagnostic. In rococo-chinoiserie, for instance, upswept roof-lines, Chinese fret, pagodas, pagods, figures with pig-tails or conical hats, and parasols, singly or in combination, are not only diagnostic, but almost obligatory. (Impey 1977: 11)

Chinoiserie can appear almost timeless. But ironically, Jacobson suggests that it is the ease with which chinoiserie can be modified according to fashionable taste that 'has made it an abiding, if often unrecognised, leitmotif in the design of everyday objects' (Jacobson 1993: 17). In the late nineteenth century, for example 'oriental arts and crafts were used to underpin a variety of standpoints, both modernist and quasi-medieval':

> Some adopted oriental forms precisely because they served as visual representations of their radicalism; others, often accepting secondary influences, did so for what seem like purely aesthetic reasons ... . Among the commentators, some were fervent imperialists, precisely because they identified in imperialism a feudal and artistic atavism that was anti-industrial, anti-urban and certainly anti-socialist. (Mackenzie 1995: 108)

The West's enduring fascination with its fabricated version of the East resides in its ability to combine the apparently contradictory qualities of constancy and mutability at once.

Said's *Orientalism* (1978) focuses on the near- or middle East and on literary representations. Said showed that Western literary representations of the East, or Orient, were both exoticized and generalized, in the sense that they were unconcerned with the specific realities of other cultures. Middle-Eastern and East Asian references have amalgamated in literary and other cultural representations of the generalized 'orient'. Far from evidencing profound interest in particular cultures, orientalist cultural artefacts merely offer a vision of the 'other' for Western consumption. This otherness must be understood within the context of colonialism, a global practice but one in which Europe has been most active, subjugating and absorbing nations and cultures, especially within Africa, Asia, Australasia and the Americas. At its height, the British Empire extended to one quarter of the world's land mass including Egypt, India, Burma, Hong Kong, Malaysia and

Singapore among '43 colonies in 5 continents' (Ferguson 2007: 51). Said's work has provided a bedrock for postcolonial theorists who have examined the political, social and cultural implications of colonialism in retrospect, from the vantage point of the contraction of colonialism from the mid-twentieth century onwards.

If colonialism is something the West has done to the East (and the North to the global South) then orientalism can be understood to engage binary oppositions, that is, pairings of opposites by which significance is habitually understood (see Chapter 1 and Chapter 5). The principal binary opposition at work in Said's understanding of orientalism is that of East and West. This opposition engages further oppositions, including male and female, in which the West is posited as a male viewer and as active, whereas the East is feminized as the passive subject of the gaze.

Postcolonial theorists have learnt much from feminist theories of gender and culture as they have from the civil rights and the Black Power movements of the 1960s and 1970s which mobilized the academic community to deal with issues of race and ethnicity. Peter Wollen has analysed the connection between fashion, orientalism, slavery and gender through the case study of Paul Poiret's designs (1993 (1987)). Nancy Troy has examined Poiret's fashion as fatally caught between the mechanisms of the luxury market and transgressive aesthetic freedoms (Troy 2002). In positing the Western reader as male, the feminized East becomes the subject of what film scholar Laura Mulvey has termed the 'male gaze' (Mulvey 1975). Thus, orientalism operates within a patriarchal Western cultural paradigm in which, as John Berger succinctly put it, 'men act and women appear' (Berger 1972: 47). Mulvey's analysis of the male gaze in film is applicable to fashion photography, in that the model is usually a woman, because womenswear is a larger market generating greater commercial activity and is often, if not explicitly sexualized, then certainly presented attractively in order to be seen and appreciated.

Mulvey's model of the male gaze has been enormously influential (being one of the most reprinted academic articles) but it has also been criticized for its normative and binaristic understanding of gender and film viewing. Similarly, just as Said's analysis of orientalism has achieved tremendous influence within and beyond postcolonial circles of thought and across cultural studies, so it has been extensively challenged and critiqued as binaristic. Writing about orientalism in design in the nineteenth century, John M. MacKenzie concludes that orientalism's 'relationship with imperial power becomes less a matter of Said's "flexible positional superiority" and more a reflection of Victorian doubt and apprehension, suffused with a yearning for a transcultural inspiration' (MacKenzie 1995: 133).

A model in which an increasingly globally dominant West (meaning Western Europe and, latterly, North America) simply exploits the colonized East does not recognize the complexity of these interactions, and has been superseded in postcolonial thought. The histories of textiles and ceramics show, for example, greater complexity than a binaristic model allows. Fernando Ortiz coined the term 'transculturation' to describe how an object or image accrues new meanings in response to changing contexts and locations (Ortiz 1995 (1940)). Homi K. Bhabha sought to overcome a binaristic and inflexible relation of centre and margin with a postcolonial notion of 'hybridity' as a refusal of metanarratives and as a *dialogue* between colonizer and colonized (Bhabha 1994; Young 1995). More recently, Marwan Kraidy has argued for hybridity as a form of 'resistance to domination' while recognizing that cultural hybridity does not preclude unequal power relations (Kraidy 2002: 317; Kraidy 2005; Lees-Maffei 2016a). A more complex and more positive view of cultural exchange is offered by this later postcolonial discourse, with Adam Geczy arguing that fashion offers the clearest departure from the Saidian model (Geczy 2013: 4). Today, the global distribution of economic, political, military and soft (cultural) power has shifted so that the economies of Brazil, Russia, India and China (BRIC) are increasingly important. Postcolonial relations continue to underpin global flows of exchange, in for example the shared language of Portugal and Brazil and their history of colonization, and the continued exchange of population and culture between India and the United Kingdom.

Said's analysis was one of literature. Literature has fuelled our dreams, and as a paraliterary genre, magazines help to form our dreams. Said's literary postcolonial theory can inform understanding of fashion magazines as much as it can the high cultural literary forms of novels, poetry and plays. The postcolonial concepts of transculturation and hybridity apply equally well to design, and specifically graphic design and fashion photography, as this chapter will go on to show.

Magazines and desire

Much of the writing on orientalism, chinoiserie and japonisme concerns ceramics, furniture and interior design, but the mutability of these tendencies is particularly clear in fashion design. Fashion magazines are part of the group of mediating discourses designed to stimulate consumer desires and are therefore of considerable design historical interest (Lees-Maffei 2009: 368–9; Aynsley and Berry 2005; Aynsley and Forde 2007). Graphic designers work with photographers, writers and editors in the production of magazine stories. Fashion magazines relied on illustrators to communicate fashion visually until the beginning of the twentieth century. The spread of photography paralleled the development of advertising. *Vogue* publisher Thomas Condé Nast was in the vanguard of a gradual shift to the dominance of fashion photography which led to the situation which prevails today, when illustration is only occasionally seen in fashion magazines. Now magazines, fashion and advertising rely on photography in a mutually dependent circle (Jobling 1999; Shinkle 2012).

Magazine content can be understood as being combined from two basic categories, words and images, which in turn break down into two further categories: editorial and advertising. Editorial pages are designed by the magazine's staff and, like advertising pages, they exist to inform, entertain and to sell goods and services to readers as assumed potential customers. The boundaries between informing and selling, evaluating and persuading, are porous. Some advertisements in consumer magazines are designed to look like the editorial portions of the magazines in which they appear, to borrow authority from the editorial pages and connect more closely with the magazine's readership. Legally, in the United Kingdom, these pages are required to be labelled as 'advertorial' to help readers to understand the material they are looking at, its derivation and aims, and in the United States, similar material is compulsorily labelled 'advertisement'. Graphic designers are involved in the production of both editorial and advertising content. Designer and writer Steven Heller has described advertising as the 'mother' of graphic design: both practices are 'concerned with selling, communicating and entertaining' (Heller 1997: 119). Anandi Ramamurthy explores the relationship between photography and commodity culture (2015) while Robert L. Craig has explored the complexity of ethnicity and advertising (1991).

In order to sell to readers, magazines not only stimulate desires but also *form* them. Anthropologist Grant McCracken has noted that our dreams are separated from our situation by either space or time; to dream is to wish for a reality that differs from the one we currently occupy (McCracken 1988). We hanker for the past, or for the future, or desire to be somewhere else, rather than here. Magazine content uses both techniques – separation by time and space – in engendering consumer desire. Temporal distancing is engaged by each image of a model wearing a garment. Such images present the reader with an idealized version of her or his future self, the self who has purchased the garment being sold, whether directly in an advertisement or indirectly in an editorial story. Spatial distancing occurs, for example, in the use of far-flung locations for fashion shoots. The reader must imagine her or his future self not only having bought and put on the clothes and accessories being sold, but also having undertaken a journey to an unfamiliar destination. In this respect, fashion magazines function in a similar way to literary works of fiction. They take us on a journey and deposit us in an imagined, unknown place. Said's (1978) work has been particularly influential in understanding the political and ideological connotations of this literary and cultural practice of imagining and desiring when it relates to Western representations of the East.

Orientalism, chinoiserie and japonisme in fashion: *Vogue* 1970–2000

Graphic designers need to understand how signs and symbols work. What follows is a case-study examination of symbols of orientalism in fashion media. My analysis covers each issue of British *Vogue* from 1970 to 2000 identifying as many representations of East Asia as possible, however generalized or specific. Representations of China and Japan were most prevalent, with indiscriminate examples of orientalism, chinoiserie and japonisme. I examined the entire magazine in each case, including food columns (Boxer 1981: 174–6; Boxer 1982: 234–6; Harlech 1981: 113; Lawson 1997: np) and travel pages (Fleming 1973: 178–84; *Vogue* 1980a; Willis 1996a; Ashworth 1996: np) as well as the fashion spreads. Orientalism is a mainstay of Western fashion throughout the twentieth century, along with other perennials such as nautical style, for example.

Notwithstanding the perennial popularity of orientalism in Western fashion, I identified peak periods of interest in orientalism as 1972–6 and 1996–7. The gap between these is the same as that conventionally accorded to a generation so these two periods would have involved two consecutive generations of readers and, ultimately, consumers.

In the first period, we see the UK rollout of clothing labels by Hanae Mori and Kenzo Takada. Kenzo launched 'Jungle Jap' in Paris in 1970 and then his own-name label. Mori launched her label after the Second World War, and enjoyed a successful international design career based on reshaping traditional symbols of Japan, and particularly the butterfly. She became known as 'Madam Butterfly'. Mori's work was launched in New York in 1962, and introduced to the United Kingdom via Harrods' International Room in 1972. *Vogue*'s June 1972 edition showed two of Mori's outfits photographed on model Hiroko Matsumoto by the Earl of Snowdon (Figure 6.1). Here, the designer and the model are Japanese, and the photographer and the publication are British. The orientalism emerges in the magazine design which uses specific language ('Go East! Collect flowers of Japanese couture') and imagery which presents Japanese design for UK consumers. Another notable example from this period is 'Chinoiserie by Beaton' (Figure 6.2)

FIGURE 6.1 *Model Hiroko Matsumoto wearing Hanae Mori clothing,* Vogue *(UK), June 1972: n.p. photograph by Lord Snowdon (Anthony Armstrong Jones), permission Condé Nast Publications, 2017.*

which showcases antique cheongsams purchased in a 'Beverly Hills antique shop' by Tina Lutz, described as defying 'both date and place' (*Vogue* 1973: 74–7). They are seen as timeless and as derived from a generalized East. The copy 'A beautiful Chinese thought even if it is not in the chairman's book', refers to *Quotations from Chairman Mao Zedong*, colloquially known as his 'little red book'. In the 15 September issue of 1976, *Vogue* described a Ballantyne cashmere jumper photographed by Alex Chatelain as 'Ming blue'. It is followed by 'a pair of flowering crepe de chine pyjama pants' and a story photographed by David Bailey showing his wife, Japanese/Hawaiian model Marie Helvin, wearing Bill Gibb's evening dresses, which combine a range of Asian-inspired techniques and shapes (*Vogue* 1976b: 85–91).

On 1 October 1979, *Vogue* UK published a special issue '*Vogue* in China'. The cover showed model Esmé Marshall photographed in a Mao suit and peaked cap by Alex Chatelain (Figure 6.3). The fashion story in this issue, from which the cover image is drawn, showed high fashion garments from labels such as Chloë, Laura Biagotti, Yves Saint Laurent Rive Gauche, Fendi, Thierry Mugler, Norma Kamali, and Jap at Joseph, combined with utilitarian items bought from No. 1 Department Store, Peking. Settings include Tiananmen Square, 'Peking's Democracy Wall', a locomotive factory,

FIGURE 6.2 *'Chinoiserie by Beaton' showcases antique cheongsams purchased in a 'Beverly Hills antique shop' by Tina Lutz, described as defying 'both date and place'* (Vogue 1973: 74–7). *15 April 1973 issue, p. 75. Cecil Beaton/Vogue © The Condé Nast Publications Ltd.*

paddy fields and a Taoist temple. The following year, Chatelain photographed clothes from Milan's ready-to-wear collections including crepe de chine wrap dress and Gianni Versace's asymmetrical camisole with 'branching coral and silver embroidery' (*Vogue* 1980b: 116–9).

Orientalism was evident in street style of the 1980s, in aspects of new romantic aesthetics and in the enthusiasm for conceptual designers such as Rei Kawakubo for Comme des Garçons, Yohji Yamamoto and Issey Miyake. Using Roland Barthes' distinction between image clothing and written clothing (Barthes 1983; 2006), Lise Skov has noted a disjuncture between the appearance of these clothes and the ways in which they were written about in the fashion media. The image clothing comprised 'technically novel conceptions of garments that ignored conventional dressmaking techniques' and 'did not carry any overt aesthetic allusions'. The written clothing was 'a story of exotic Japan. It firmly placed the strange garments in the context of Western Orientalism'. For the image clothing 'sophisticated minimalist deconstruction [was] written up as Japanese tradition and colorful Orientalism' (Skov 2003: 217). She notes how the designers themselves were complicit in this process, with Yojhi Yamamoto, for example, eloquently associating his designs with Zen Buddhism before explaining that he felt coerced into doing so by the press (Skov 2003: 224). Conversely, Peter McNeil sees the minimalism of the late 1980s as 'proto-global' and pits it against the 'refuge' of 'a more local but also romanticised and nostalgic vision' in his study of Australian label Easton Pearson (1989–2016) (McNeil 2011: 139–40).

FIGURE 6.3 'Vogue *in China*', cover 1 October 1979. Model Esmé Marshall in a Mao suit and peaked cap. *Alex Chatelain/*Vogue © *The Condé Nast Publications Ltd.*

However, it was not until the mid-1990s that the orientalizing tendencies witnessed in the mid-1970s were revived completely. *Vogue* fêted British designers for their orientalist and chinoiserie aesthetics, notably John Galliano and Alexander McQueen. In February 1997, *Vogue* ran a story on British designers, fashion-edited by Tiina Laakkonen (Laakkonen 1997: 100–11). She featured Kate Moss photographed by Juergen Teller in a sheer black Alexander McQueen dress embroidered with a dragon. This story was listed on the contents page under the heading 'Chasing the Dragon: A yen for chinoiserie, by Alexander McQueen, in a British designer album'. Here chinoisere is recognized as part of a British visual lexicon. John Galliano's creative direction for the advertising campaign for Dior's Pret-à-Porter autumn-winter 1997–98 collection showed a model in a tailored skirt suit made of bamboo-shoot printed lacquered silk photographed by Nick Knight against a giant bamboo parasol.

Vogue's treatment of orientalism reached a peak in 1997, with related content in almost every issue. In March, Melissa Mostyn reported on the Milan shows in her article 'Eastern Eye: A touch of the Orient puts luxury back in fashion' (1997: 201). Interior designer Kelly Hoppen published her book *East Meets West* in 1997, and was featured in *Vogue* several times that year as a result (Hoppen 1997; D'Souza 1997). In May 1997, a *Vogue* Living feature 'House of the rising sun: Orientalism is the new chic, says Kate O'Donnell' namechecked Hoppen alongside Anouska Hempel (O'Donnell 1997: 55). In November 1997, *Vogue* profiled Dosa, Christina Kim's East Asian-inspired label which launched in 1983 (MacLeod 1997: 199). By June 1998, 'Mood of the moment… Japan' signalled a shift within the orientalist emphasis of *Vogue*'s fashion coverage with a spread showing fashion, accessories, film, food, technology and homewares (*Vogue* 1998c: 96).

Orientalism in fashion magazines: A typology

Where, exactly, in the fashion system does orientalizing occur? There are several loci for the practice of orientalizing. First, the influences that a fashion designer draws upon can include orientalism; second, the shape, material or decoration on a garment can communicate orientalism; third, fashion editing, art direction and magazine design can inject orientalism into fashion media, as can the photography and the choice of location and models. Finally, the viewer can perceive orientalism in fashion design and its mediation.

Visual analysis of *Vogue*'s orientalism across the period may be understood through a typology (Table 6.1). First, the use of a recognizably East Asian location for a fashion shoot is an obvious way of communicating the East. Locations used by *Vogue* UK in the period 1970–2000 have ranged from recognizable places such as the Forbidden City Imperial Palace in Beijing, and the Great Wall of China, to other geographically specific locations which might not be recognized by a Western readership and would therefore connote a generalized orient. Some locations used to connote orientalism are outside East Asia. Pagodas are recognizably Eastern wherever they appear, as the designers of the Chinatowns in London and New York have demonstrated (Figure 6.4). Location shoots can be populated by unknown locals, as representatives of the 'other' cultures engaged in Orientalizing practices. Clearly, travel features based in East Asia have a different relation to their location, in which the location is the focus rather than merely a backdrop to a fashion story. Natural motifs such as a branching cherry blossom have featured in location shoots and in pattern designs

Table 6.1 Typology of Signifiers of Orientalism in Fashion Editorial and Advertising Images

#	Signifiers of Orientalism	Example
1	Location	East Asian location – Great Wall of China – Forbidden Palace, Beijing – Tokyo Cityscape, Chinatown – London, NYC, etc. East Asian signifiers – Zen Garden – Cherry Blossom
2	Models	Apparent Ethnicity Hair styles Make-up
3	Garment Types	Kimono Cheong Sam Mao Suit Nehru Jacket Shalwar Kameez Conceptual Fashion
4	Materials	Silk Lacquer Bamboo Terracotta Jade Pearls
5	Accessories	Zōri Chopsticks Obi Fans Conical Hats Peaked Caps Paper Lanterns Buddha
6	Motifs and Patterns	Pagoda Fretwork Cherry Blossom Flags Calligraphy East Asian Letterforms
7	Colours	Red, White, Black, Pastels

alike. Sarah Cheang has noted that the editor of American *Vogue* from 1963-71, Diana Vreeland, is 'credited with introducing unexpectedly exotic location shoots ... as part of her pursuit of perfect fashion fantasies': 'With the advent of commercial jet planes, distant locations were more accessible, while a new interest in "ethnic" clothing was making unusual non-Western locations more relevant, from Indian palaces to Peruvian temples' (Cheang 2013: 36). Cheang distinguishes

FIGURE 6.4 *Chinatown, Gerrard Street, London, 27 September 2015. Photograph by Grace Lees-Maffei.*

these 'postcolonial *and* neo-colonial' shoots in which the impression given is one of 'going native' with shoots predating the 1960s which occupied a colonial paradigm.

Secondly, fashion editors have sought to communicate orientalism through the employment of East Asian models. Regardless of her clothes, an East Asian model connotes orientalism as it is her or his face, body, gesture and posture which provide the focal visual indicators of the East for the readership, presumed to be Western. For British *Vogue*, more specifically, the readership is assumed to be British. Melanie Clulow has written for *Vogue* about 'the subtle, yet powerful, allure of Oriental women' and 'asks what makes them so enviably cool' (Clulow 1996: 95–6). Sadre-Orafai has examined the ways in which agencies and clients insist that verbal statements about models' ethnicity must be authentic whereas their visual appearance may be ambiguous, ethnically (Sadre-Orafai 2008). This acceptance of ethnic ambiguity mirrors and contributes to the geo-cultural imprecision of orientalism.

A third category of orientalist signifiers in the fashion magazines I examined was formed by the clothes shown. Orientalism may be communicated through the form, or shape, of the clothing and in its material, construction or pattern. Some garments connoting the East are 'so-called traditional costumes of many Asian countries' (Jones and Leshkowich 2003: 5) such as the Chinese cheongsam (Clark 2000) and Mao jacket (Pickering 1994: 120–5), Japanese kimono (Blanchard 1994: 117) and obi, 'the Korean hanbok, and Vietnamese ao dai' (Jones and Leshkowich 2003: 5) whether shown as originals or as reproductions or pastiches. All 'have become familiar in style, if not in name, around the globe and … inspire European and North American designers' (Jones and Leshkowich 2003: 5). Other clothes signifying orientalism feature recognizable construction methods such as the Chinese quilted jacket (*Vogue* 1976a) and embroidery, braiding and beading (*Vogue* 1994a: 19). Still others are adaptations of East Asian garment types and styles.

Also associated with Japan is the group of conceptual designers epitomized by Rei Kawakubo for Comme des Garçons (Skov 1996, Sudjic 1990) and by Issey Miyake. Miyake's APOC (A Piece of Cloth) series confounds initial attempts to associate the garments with the body, as these folded geometric items only take shape once worn. The complexity of these garments on the body belies their simplicity of construction as shown in a *Vogue* spread associating 'intricate cutting and variations' with a 'Japanese influence' (*Vogue* 1999: np).

Fourthly, some feature fabrics associated with the East, such as Shantung silk (Swinson 1996: 155), and silk brocades (*Vogue* 1997: 215), for both clothing and interior design. Silk is associated with the Far East because China pioneered the cultivation of silk worms and protected the process in order to achieve early trade dominance of the international luxury fabrics market (Jarry 1991: 37). Such fabrics are used for Western garments, such as pencil skirts, suits, and button-up shirts to create hybrid forms in which fabric and cut have divergent provenances. A December 1977 story photographed by Lothar Schmid showcased Yves Saint Laurent fashion which used fabrics by Abraham, the Zurich-based manufacturer of silk fabrics, brocades and jacquard weaves (*Vogue* 1977:114–23).

Accessories formed a fifth category of orientalist signifiers, from visual references to foot-binding (Ko 2008) and Japanese zōri shoes (Chaiklin 2014), to artefacts made using traditional East Asian techniques such as lacquer and styles including willow-patterned blue-and-white porcelain. Make-up and beauty pages, too, contributed orientalist signifiers to fashion stories in the period of analysis (Phillips 1997: 146; *Vogue* 1998b: 132–7). The iconic make-up of the geisha, in white, black and red, appeared repeatedly in *Vogue* across the period of analysis.

Across the entire mise-en-scene of the fashion shoot, and the fashion magazine, readers encounter patterns and motifs with East Asian associations. These range from motifs such as dragons, waves, the blue-and-white willow pattern on china or elsewhere, cherry blossoms, Chinese pagodas, pagods, parasols and fretwork, to East Asian typographic characters, calligraphy, flags, coins and other symbols of nations and states. Also characteristic of japonisme is the use of pared-down colourways such as black and white recalling calligraphy and paper screens as room dividers, and scarlet and white, the colours of the Japanese flag, and also the colours of the Geisha's make-up. Black, red and terracotta shades may be used to connote Chinese lacquer. Creamy pastel shades recall silks, and cherry blossom designs. These various visual signifiers appear together and separately to indicate East Asia.

What are the minimum signifiers through which orientalism might be communicated? The red lip of a geisha, the terracotta red of lacquer and the red circle of Japan's flag suggest that the colour red is an orientalist motif. Patrick Cox's red boots with Chinese embroidery (*Vogue* December 1997: 169) are certainly orientalist, but arguably so is the patent red leather of a winkle picker stiletto mule pointed, like a bound foot, such as a red patent mule in Giorgio Armani's Autumn-Winter 2000 collection, advertised in *Vogue* UK. Materials such as jade, silk and bamboo (*Vogue* 1998a) have Eastern connotations regardless of the forms into which they are wrought. The Eastern design philosophy of Feng Shui, which concerns the harmonious alignment of people in their environments (Niesewand 1996), and wabi sabi ('a Japanese design aesthetic and worldview that places value on the transient, unfinished and imperfect nature of life', Jacques 2016: xiii) have been used in a spurious association of Zen religion with minimalism in design.

Indeed, it is in relation to politics and religion that the orientalizing tendencies of Western fashion mediation are most concerning. Clearly, the practice of plundering the generalized East for motifs and forms with which to enliven Western fashion design is as open to critique as the orientalist novels that Said interrogated. But the desire for novelty in consumer society is understandable, if not entirely comfortable. Much less easy to accept, perhaps, is the way in which fashion reportage, as represented by *Vogue* in the years under analysis, used both gender politics and state politics as aesthetic tropes. Eastern spirituality has been similarly misunderstood and misrepresented in Western consumer culture too (see Skov 1996: 147) (Figure 6.5). To use a political ideology or a religious philosophy as fodder for fashion is to conform to the cultural practices which are the focus of the dominant critiques of postmodern culture.

FIGURE 6.5 *Spring/Summer 1993 campaign Yves Saint Laurent Rive Gauche, in* Vogue *March 1993: n.p. photograph by Helmut Newton. Image © The Helmut Newton Estate/Maconochie Photography.*

Postmodern pastiche

In his essay 'Postmodernism or the Cultural Logic of Late Capitalism', Frederic Jameson identifies one of the traits of postmodernism as being pastiche, the practice of mimicry without serious purpose (Jameson 1984). This is distinct from parody, which is mimicry as critique. Postmodern culture borrows from a range of styles for pleasure and novelty, rather than to make political, philosophical or religious points. Fashion designers, particularly, take their inspiration from across cultures (Chambers 1994: 176–84; Willis 1996b). In 1994, *Vogue* quoted Christian Lacroix as saying: 'Mixing cultures, influences and ethnic things is important' (*Vogue* 1994b: 9). The same issue featured a fashion story titled 'Madam Butterfly' with the following introduction: 'Artifice and glamour, the ago-old tools of the courtesan, fill evenings with a heady decadence. Designers open up an erotic past of black lacquer satins, cherry red kimonos and opulent cheongsams, crowned by headdresses of exotic silk flowers' (*Vogue* 1994c: 184). It was followed by a beauty story, 'Colour Vision', featuring models of apparently East Asian ethnicity wearing make-up by Mary Greenwell (*Vogue* 1994d: 192–5).

Consistent with this eclecticism, consumer magazines, and fashion magazines among them, rarely place the fashion they showcase within historical or political contexts and have been criticized for their aestheticized and apolitical stance on subjects such as 'Poverty Chic' (Williams 2002). For instance, Kate Phelan's fashion story 'Cool Khaki' shows photographs by Kim Knott of a Western fashion model dressed in khaki-coloured and other neutrally coloured clothes, some

FIGURE 6.6 *'Cool Khaki'.* Vogue *(UK), May 1994, pp. 160-9. Fashion Editor Kate Phelan. Hair by James Brown and make-up by Lucia Pieroni. Kim Knott/*Vogue *© The Condé Nast Publications Ltd.*

of which are militaristic in shape (Figure 6.6). The story, with hair by James Brown and make-up by Lucia Pieroni, is set in northern Thailand. The contrast between the figure and her context is striking. In this story, military styles are feminized and de-activated as the introduction tells us: 'Army-inspired clothing has gone way beyond the combat gear that once stalked the streets. With the colours of the jungle still at large, these fatigues and drill jackets are newly elegant and easy-going' (Phelan 1994: 160–9).

What is true of postmodern pastiche and of consumer – particularly fashion – magazines is also true of orientalism, chinoiserie and japanisme. Dawn Jacobson notes of chinoiserie that 'the desire for authenticity strikes at the heart of a style that thrives on misunderstanding, allusion and re-interpretation' (Jacobson 1993: 212). In fashion magazines, East Asian philosophies such as Zen and Feng Shui are marketed merely as styles, without reference to religious beliefs. See, for example, Laura Campbell's *Vogue* article 'Orange aid: Hermès is famous for it. It's the Dalai Lama's signature colour. Now designers are hailing orange as the new shade for summer' (Campbell 1996: 73).

Asian fashion became, during the 1990s, 'a noticeable global trend, changing the way that people inside and outside Asia think about and practice dress' (Jones and Leshkowich 2003:1). Jones and Leshkowich caution that while this 'global interest in Asian dress might seem to open up new democratic forms of cultural exchange', 'the processes through which Asian dress has been globalized and celebrated within and outside Asia are also profoundly Orientalizing and feminizing' (Jones and Leshkowich 2003: 5). Orientalism is open to charges of being a reductive and politically incorrect nexus which fosters and consolidates ignorance rather than intercultural understanding:

> From haute couture collections … to renditions of rice bowls and chopsticks aimed at the American middle class by retailers such as Pottery Barn and Pier One, Asian-ness has been reduced from a potentially threatening and unmanageable Other to a mere fashion statement. (Jones and Leshkowich 2003: 19)

Although postmodernism is a set of cultural characteristics associated with twentieth-century cultural texts and artefacts, and orientalism can be explained using postmodern theory, postmodern characteristics are seen in earlier works and orientalism has been a feature of Western culture for centuries. The borrowing of styles purely as styles, rather than as philosophically meaningful symbols was identified and criticized by some leading nineteenth-century design theorists, including Augustus Welby Northmore Pugin, John Ruskin and William Morris, before modernism and postmodernism had emerged. We can reflect, therefore, on whether orientalism, chinoiserie and japanisme have exerted a positive or negative influence on fashion. Williams (2002) has contributed a useful expression of concern about the cultural, political and economic implications of the locations used for fashion shoots. Said's critique of orientalism is powerful, but having a variety of inputs into the fashion system is also desirable creatively, aesthetically and even politically. These influences need to be handled with care, however, if they are to avoid charges of stereotyping, reductionism and even racism.

The intensification of globalization in the current and last centuries has been the subject of sustained critiques. On the one hand, while manufacturing costs in East Asia have given it an apparent monopoly on mass manufacture, the sheer ubiquity of merchandise imported from East Asia to the West has reduced the number of goods from that region which are perceived as exotic. Jones and Leshkowich point out that 'Cross-fertilization between Western and non-western fashion systems has been so extensive as to make a distinction between the two no longer tenable' (Jones and Leshkowich 2003:7). On the other hand, the dominance of global corporations in commercial life has prompted consumers to seek out local, regional and national products as being more authentic than the placeless output of global brands by consumers in East Asia and in the West (Lees-Maffei 2016b). In writing of 'the revival of Japanese Tradition in Modern Japan' Masami Suga perceives a shift from 'Exotic West to Exotic Japan', and has noted that 'the Japanese approach the revival of Japanese tradition from a consumer's orientation. They buy goods and services that represent nostalgia and provide modern convenience at the same time' (Suga 1995: 95). The implications for design here are suggestive: can we design and buy harmony, representation, respect, identity or sound ethics? We can try.

Conclusion: From exotic to everyday

Sloboda concludes her study of chinoiserie in eighteenth-century Britain by asserting that 'while enthusiasm for the style over the past three hundred years has ebbed and flowed with the tides of fashion, the cultural and commercial conditions from which it emerged persist to this day' (Sloboda 2014: 205). She is referring to contemporary conditions such as China's manufacturing power. Indeed, the practice of orientalism has depended on a particular power balance between East and West which has persisted throughout much of the modern period, inclusively understood. However, that power balance has now shifted economically and culturally. Peter McNeil has recognized that 'some Asian cultures, such as those expressed in Singapore, Hong Kong and parts of China have undergone a "reorientalism", in which they buy back the imagery created in the vision of the European colonisers' (McNeil 2011: 139) while Shenaz Suterwalla points out that the appropriation of 'ethnic textiles and design as "authentic" symbols of tradition' within 'the social space of global consumption has served to highlight "whiteness" in capitalist marketing of exotica at both local and global level[s]' (Suterwalla 2011: 151). In her study of fashion and ethnicity in the *Vogue* fashion shoot since 2000, Sarah Cheang concludes more hopefully that 'haute couture fashion culture's strong investment in artistic fantasy and the edgy occasionally provides a space for the successful inclusion of more complex approaches' (Cheang 2013: 43). As evidence, Cheang analyses a Tim Walker shoot published in British *Vogue* in August 2007, in which Huli tribesmen are featured as extensively as the fashion model Gemma Ward, and in which photographer Tim Walker's compositions feature mirrors in a way that signals a complex communication of identity.

Beyond the relatively rarefied pages of *Vogue*, young people in the West today share many cultural references with their East Asian counterparts. They practice karate and judo alongside football and soccer; they play Pokémon video and trading card games at local, regional, national and world tournaments; they eat sushi, noodles and other East Asian foods alongside Western fast food; they watch Disney, Studio Ghibli and anime; they read manga and comics as well as novels. This consumption of East Asian popular culture in the West is distinct from orientalist cultural practices in several ways. Importantly, these artefacts and practices are consumed as part of everyday Western lifestyles, rather than as exotic additions. East Asian cultural products and practices have gained popularity in the West without orientalizing tendencies. This shared culture is genuinely international just as 'World, ethnic and national dress are interrelated in today's global community' (Eicher and Sumberg 1995: 304). Western consumption of cultural artefacts produced in the East, rather than artefacts produced to self-consciously represent the East, facilitates a cultural dialogue based on specificity and authentic authorship, rather than generality and stereotype. It therefore constitutes a more equal dialogue akin to Kraidy's hybridity (Kraidy 2002: 2005), and a way of overcoming the binaristic and reductive orientalizing tendencies of the past. Globalization has legions of detractors, but increased international trade, travel and common cultural consumption also carry the benefit of enhanced understanding which promises recognition of common concerns and shared humanity.

References

Ashworth, Jon. 1996. Asia in *Vogue*. *Vogue* Promotion (advertorial). *Vogue* (UK). October: n.p.
Aynsley, Jeremy. 1993. *Nationalism and Internationalism: Design in the 20th Century*. London: Victoria and Albert Museum.
Aynsley, Jeremy, and Francesca Berry, 2005. 'Publishing the Modern Home: Magazines and the Domestic Interior 1870-1965'. *Journal of Design History* 18 (1): 1–5.
Aynsley, Jeremy, and Kate Forde, 2007. *Design and the Modern Magazine*. Manchester: Manchester University Press.
Barthes, Roland. 1983. *The Fashion System*. Translated by Matthew Ward and Richard Howard. New York: Hill and Wang.
Barthes, Roland. 2006. *The Language of Fashion*. Translated by Andy Stafford. Oxford: Berg.
Berger, John, 1972. *Ways of Seeing*. London: BBC/Harmondsworth: Penguin.
Bhabha, Homi K. 1994. *The Location of Culture*. London and New York: Routledge.
Blanchard, Tamsin. 1994. 'Japan Ease: A New Winter Staple: The Kimono'. *Vogue* (UK). November: 117.
Bolton, Andrew (ed.) 2015. *China Through the Looking Glass*. New York and New Haven: Metropolitan Museum of Art/Yale University Press.
Boxer, Arabella. 1981. '*Vogue* Food: Arabella Boxer Becomes a Japanese Fan'. *Vogue* (UK). May: 174–6.
Boxer, Arabella. 1982. '*Vogue* Food: Rice – a Grain of Truth'. *Vogue* (UK). November: 234–6.
Brewer, John, and Roy Porter (eds.) 1992. *Consumption and the World of Goods*. London: Routledge.
Campbell, Laura. 1996. 'Orange aid: Hermès Is Famous for It. It's the Dalai Lama's Signature Colour. Now Designers Are Hailing Orange as the New Shade for Summer'. *Vogue* (UK). February: 73.
Chaiklin, Martha. 2014. 'Zōri and Flip-Flop Sandal, Japan/World'. In Grace Lees-Maffei (ed.), *Iconic Designs: 50 Stories about 50 Things*, 199–201. London: Bloomsbury.
Chambers, Lucinda. 1994. 'Out of This World: From Morocco to Mongolia, the Far East Is Exerting Its Magical Influence on Designers' Imaginations'. *Vogue* (UK). April: 176–85.
Cheang, Sarah. 2013. 'To the Ends of the Earth: Fashion and Ethnicity in the *Vogue* Fashion Shoot'. In Djurdja Bartlett, Shaun Cole and Agnes Rocamora (eds.), *Fashion Media: Past and Present*. London: Bloomsbury. Kindle Edition.
Clark, Hazel. 2000. *The Cheongsam*. Oxford: Berg.
Clulow, Melanie. 1996. 'East Side Story: Westerner Have Always Been Intrigued by the East, Not Least Because of the Subtle, Yet Powerful, Allure of Oriental Women'. *Vogue* (UK). September: 95–6.
Craig, Robert L. 1991. 'Designing Ethnicity: The Ideology of Images'. *Design Issues* 7 (2) (Spring): 34–42.
D'Souza, Christa. 1997. 'Lady of the House: Kelly Hoppen Tells Christa D'Souza How She Got Ahead in Celebrity Decorating'. *Vogue* (UK). November: 89–92.
Eicher, Joanne B., and Barbara Sumberg. 1995, 'World Fashion, Ethnic, and National Dress'. In Joanne B. Eicher (ed.), *Dress and Ethnicity: Change Across Space and Time*, 295–306, Oxford: Berg.

Ferguson, Niall, 2007. *Empire: How Britain Made the Modern World*. London: Penguin.
Frankopan, Peter. 2015. *The Silk Roads: A New History of the World*. London: Bloomsbury.
Fleming, Kate. 1973. '*Vogue* Travel: Hong Kong'. *Vogue* (UK). September 1: 178–84.
Geczy, Adam. 2013. *Fashion and Orientalism: Dress, Textiles and Culture from the 17th to the 21st Century*. London: Bloomsbury.
Gimeno-Martínez, Javier. 2016. *Design and National Identity*. London: Bloomsbury.
Guth, Christine. 2015. *Hokusai's Great Wave: Biography of a Global Icon*. Honolulu: University of Hawai'i Press.
Harlech, Pamela. 1981. 'Food: Pamela Harlech's Healthy Cooking, the Chinese Way'. *Vogue* (UK). January: 113.
Heller, Steven. 1997. 'Advertising, Mother of Graphic Design' *Eye* 17 (1995) republished in Michael Bierut, William Drenttel, Steven Heller and D. K. Holland (eds.). *Looking Closer 2: Critical Writings on Graphic Design*, 112–9. New York: Allworth Press.
Hobsbawm, E., and T. O. Ranger (eds.) 1993. *The Invention of Tradition*. Cambridge: Cambridge University Press.
Hoppen, Kelly. 1997. *East Meets West: Global Design for Contemporary Interiors*. London: Conran Octopus.
Impey, Oliver. 1977. *Chinoiserie: The Impact of Oriental Styles on Western Art and Decoration*. Oxford: Oxford University Press.
Jacobson, Dawn. 1993. *Chinoiserie*. London: Phaidon.
Jacques, Andrea. 2016. *Wabi Sabi Wisdom: Inspiration for an Authentic Life*. Vancouver, Canada: Kyosei Press.
Jameson, Frederic. 1984. 'Postmodernism or the Cultural Logic of Late Capitalism'. *New Left Review* 146 (July–August): 59–92.
Jobling, Paul. 1999. *Fashion Spreads: Word and Image in Fashion Photography Since 1980*. Oxford: Berg.
Jones, Carla, and Ann Marie Leshkowich. 2003. 'Introduction: The Globalization of Asian Dress: Re-Orienting Fashion or Re-Orientalizing Asia?' In Sandra Neissen, Ann Marie Leshkowich and Carla Jones (eds.), *The Globalization of Asian Dress: Re-Orienting Fashion*, 1–48. Oxford: Berg.
Jarry, Madeleine. 1991. *Chinoiserie: Chinese Influence on European Decorative Art, 17th and 18th Centuries*. London: Sothebys.
Ko, Dorothy 2008. *Cinderella's Sisters: A Revisionist History of Footbinding*. Berkeley, Los Angeles: University of California Press.
Kraidy, Marwen. 2002. 'Hybridity in Cultural Globalization'. *Communication Theory* 12 (3): 316–39.
Kraidy, Marwen. 2005. *Hybridity: or the Cultural Logic of Globalization*. Philadelphia: Temple.
Laakkonen, Tiina. 1997. 'Pretty Edgy: In Their Own Inimitable Style, British Designers Put a Slant on This Season's Most Feminine Looks'. *Vogue* (UK). (February): 100–11.
Lambourne, Lionel. 2005. *Japonisme: Cultural Crossings Between East and West*. London: Phaidon.
Lawson, Nigella. 1997. 'Food: Nigella Lawson Adapts Japanese Cooking for Easy Home Use'. *Vogue* (UK). May: n.p.
Lees-Maffei, G. 2009. 'The Production-Consumption-Mediation Paradigm'. *Journal of Design History* 22 (4): 351–76.
Lees-Maffei, Grace. 2014. '"Made" in England? The Mediation of Alessi S.p.A'. In Grace Lees-Maffei and Kjetil Fallan (eds.), *Made in Italy: Rethinking a Century of Italian Design*, 287–303. London: Bloomsbury Academic.
Lees-Maffei, Grace. 2016a. 'A Special Relationship: The Transatlantic Domestic Dialogue'. In Grace Lees-Maffei and Kjetil Fallan (eds.), *Designing Worlds: National Design Histories in an Age of Globalization*. New York and Oxford: Berghahn.
Lees-Maffei, Grace. 2016b. '"Why Then the World's Mine Oyster": Consumption and Globalization'. In Penny Sparke and Fiona Fisher (eds.), *The Routledge Companion to Design Studies*, 445–56. Abingdon: Routledge.

Lees-Maffei, Grace, and Rebecca Houze (eds.) 2010. *The Design History Reader*. Oxford, Berg.
MacKenzie, John, 1995. *Orientalism: History, Theory and the Arts*. Manchester: Manchester University Press.
MacLeod, Karen Swan. 1997. 'Mega Dosage. LA label Dosa Is Vibing London'. *Vogue* (UK). November: 199.
McCracken, Grant. 1988. *Culture and Consumption: New Approaches to the Symbolic Character of Consumer Goods and Activities*. Indianapolis: Indianapolis University Press.
McGarty, Craig, Vincent Y. Yzerbyt, and Russell Spears. 2002. 'Social, Cultural and Cognitive Factors in Stereotype Formation'. In Craig McGarty, Vincent Y. Yzerbyt and Russell Spears (eds.), *Stereotypes as Explanations: The Formation of Meaningful Beliefs about Social Groups*, 1–15. Cambridge: Cambridge University Press.
McNeil, Peter. 2011. 'Old Empire and New Global Luxury: Fashioning Global Design'. In Glenn Adamson, Giorgio Riello and Sarah Teasley (eds.), *Global Design History*, 138–49. Abingdon: Routledge.
Moeran, Brian. 1996. 'The Orient Strikes Back: Advertising and Imaging Japan'. *Theory, Culture and Society* 13 (3): 77–112.
Mostyn, Melissa. 1997. 'Eastern Eye: A Touch of the Orient Puts Luxury Back in Fashion.' *Vogue* (UK). March: 201.
Mulvey, Laura. 1975. 'Visual Pleasure and Narrative Cinema'. *Screen* 16 (3): 6–18.
Niesewand, Nonie. 1996. 'Good Vibrations'. *Vogue* (UK). (November): 192–5.
O'Donnell, Kate. 1997. 'House of the Rising Sun: Orientalism Is the New Chic, says Kate O'Donnell'. *Vogue* (UK). May: 55.
Olins, Wally. 2003. 'Branding the Nation.' In *Wally Olins. On Brand*, 150–69. London and New York: Thames & Hudson.
Ortiz, Fernando, 1995 [1940]. *Cuban Counterpoint: Tobacco and Sugar*. Translated by Harriet De Onís. Duke University Press (*Contrapunteo cubano del tabaco y el azúcar*).
Osborne, Harold (ed.) 1985. *The Oxford Companion to the Decorative Arts*. Oxford: Oxford University Press.
Phelan, Kate. 1994. 'Cool Khaki'. *Vogue* (UK). May: 160–9.
Phillips, Kathy. 1997. 'Play It Again, Cheongsam: China and the Far East Is the New Inspiration for Bath, Body and Beauty Lines, says Kathy Phillips'. *Vogue* (UK). November: 146.
Pickering, Jayne. 1994. 'Fine China: The Mao Suit's Plan Shape, No-fuss Fabric and Humble Detail Is the Ultimate in Form Following Function. Now It Appears in Luxurious Guises: Sweeping Silk and Bright White, Delicately Decorated'. *Vogue* (UK). May. 120–5.
Potvin, John (ed.) 2015. *Oriental Interiors: Design, Identity, Space*. London: Bloomsbury Academic.
Ramamurthy, Anandi. 2003. *Imperial Persuaders: Images of Africa and Asia in British Advertising*. Manchester: Manchester University Press.
Ramamurthy, Anandi. 2015. 'Spectacles and Illusions: Photography and Commodity Culture'. In Liz Wells (ed.), *Photography: A Critical Introduction*, 231–88. Abingdon: Taylor and Francis.
Sadre-Orafai, Stephanie Neda. 2008. 'Developing Images: Race, Language and Perception in Fashion-model Casting'. In Shinkle, Eugenie (ed.), *Fashion as Photograph: Viewing and Reviewing Images of Fashion*, 141–53. London and New York: I.B. Tauris.
Said, Edward. 1978. *Orientalism*. New York: Vintage Books.
Shinkle, Eugenie. 2012. 'Introduction'. In Eugenie Shinkle (ed.), *Fashion as Photograph: Viewing and Reviewing Images of Fashion*, 1–14. London and New York: I.B. Tauris.
Sloboda, Stacey. 2014. *Chinoiserie: Commerce and Critical Ornament in Eighteenth-Century Britain*. Manchester: Manchester University Press.
Skov, Lise. 1996. 'Fashion Trends, *Japonisme* and Postmodernism, or "What Is so Japanese about Comme des Garçons?"'. *Theory, Culture & Society* 13 (3): 129–51.
Skov, Lise. 2003. 'Fashion-Nation: A Japanese Globalization Experience and a Hong Kong Dilemma'. In Sandra Neissen, Ann Marie Leshkowich and Carla Jones (eds.), *The Globalization of Asian Dress: Re-Orienting Fashion*, 215–42. Oxford: Berg.

Sudjic, Deyan. 1990. *Rei Kawakubo and Comme des Garçons*. London: Fourth Estate and Wordsearch.
Suga, Masami. 1995. 'Exotic West to Exotic Japan: Revival of Japanese Tradition in Modern Japan'. In Joanne B. Eicher (ed.), *Dress and Ethnicity: Change Across Space and Time*, 95–115. Oxford: Berg.
Suterwalla, Shenaz. 2011. 'Response'. In Glenn Adamson, Giorgio Riello and Sarah Teasley (eds.), *Global Design History*, 150–2. Abingdon: Routledge.
Swinson, Antonia. 1996. 'The Silk Route: Once Worn Only After Dark, Shantung Is Emerging into the Daylight'. *Vogue* (UK). March: 155.
Teilmann-Lock, Stina. 2016. 'The Myth of Danish Design and the Implicit Claims of Labels'. In Grace Lees-Maffei and Kjetil Fallan (eds.), *Designing Worlds: National Design Histories in an Age of Globalization*, 156–71. New York and Oxford: Berghahn.
Troy, Nancy. 2002. 'Paul Poiret's Minaret Style: Originality, Reproduction, and Art in Fashion'. *Fashion Theory* 6 (2): 117–44.
Vogue. 1973. 'Chinoiserie by Beaton'. *Vogue* (UK). 15th April: 74–77.
Vogue. 1976a. 'Hooded Quilted Coat, Purple Tulips on Saffron Cotton by Akbar', Photographed by Richard Dunkley. *'More Dash than Cash'*. 1 October: 140.
Vogue. 1976b. 'Your Evening Dress Could Be... Bill Gibb's Confection... Silk Pleats, and Sari Glitter'. *Vogue* (UK). 15th September: 85–92.
Vogue. 1977. 'Yves Saint Laurent Superlatives'. *Vogue* (UK). December: 114–23.
Vogue. 1980a. '*Vogue* Travel: Far Eastern Adventures'. *Vogue* (UK). 1 October: 253–85.
Vogue. 1980b. 'Creaming the Ready to Wear – Milan'. *Vogue* (UK). 1 March: 116–9.
Vogue. 1993. *Vogue* (UK). March: n.p.
Vogue. 1994a. 'Oriental Textures'. *Vogue* (UK). Spring/Summer 1994 *Catwalk Report*: 19.
Vogue. 1994b. 'The Decadent East'. *Vogue* (UK). October: 9.
Vogue. 1994c. 'Madam Butterfly'. *Vogue* (UK). October: 184.
Vogue. 1994d. 'Colour Vision'. *Vogue* (UK). October: 192–5.
Vogue. 1997a. 'Great Good Buys'. *Vogue* (UK). April: 215.
Vogue. 1997b. Advertisement for Patrick Cox. *Vogue* (UK). December: 169.
Vogue. 1998a. 'The New Bamboo'. *Vogue* (UK). October: 25.
Vogue. 1998b. 'Global Beauty: From Sugaring in Damascus to Slimming Rooms in Hong Kong, *Vogue* Seeks out the Essential Beauty Treatments Around the World'. *Vogue* (UK). January: 132–7.
Vogue. 1998c. 'Mood of the Moment... Japan'. *Vogue* (UK). June: 96.
Vogue. 1999. 'Japanese Influence: Intricate Cutting and Variations'. *Vogue* (UK). January/February: n.p.
Williams, Zoe. 2002. 'Poverty Chic'. *The Guardian Weekend* 29 June: 30–31.
Willis, Rebecca. 1996a. 'The Timeless Orient: Rebecca Willis on How to Keep the Far Easy Exotic in the Nineties'. *Vogue* (UK). September: 125–8.
Willis, Rebecca. 1996b. 'View from Abroad: Rebecca Willis Asks British Designers Where in the World They Get Their Inspiration'. *Vogue* (UK). July: 112–5.
Wollen, Peter. 1993 [1987]. 'Out of the Past: Fashion/Orientalism/The Body'. *New Formations* 1 (Spring, 1987), reprinted in *Raiding the Icebox*, pp. 1–34. London: Verso 1993.
Young, Robert. 1995. *Colonial Desire: Hybridity in Theory, Culture and Race*. London: Routledge.

PLATE 1 *Panzani advertisement, analysed by Roland Barthes, 'Rhetoric of the Image' (Barthes 1977: 32–51), Plate XVII.*

PLATE 2 *Pepsi mosaic on soft drinks vending machine, Las Vegas, 2018, photograph by Jo Turney, with permission.*

PLATE 3 *Advertisement for Belair cigarettes from the collection of Judith Williamson, with permission.*

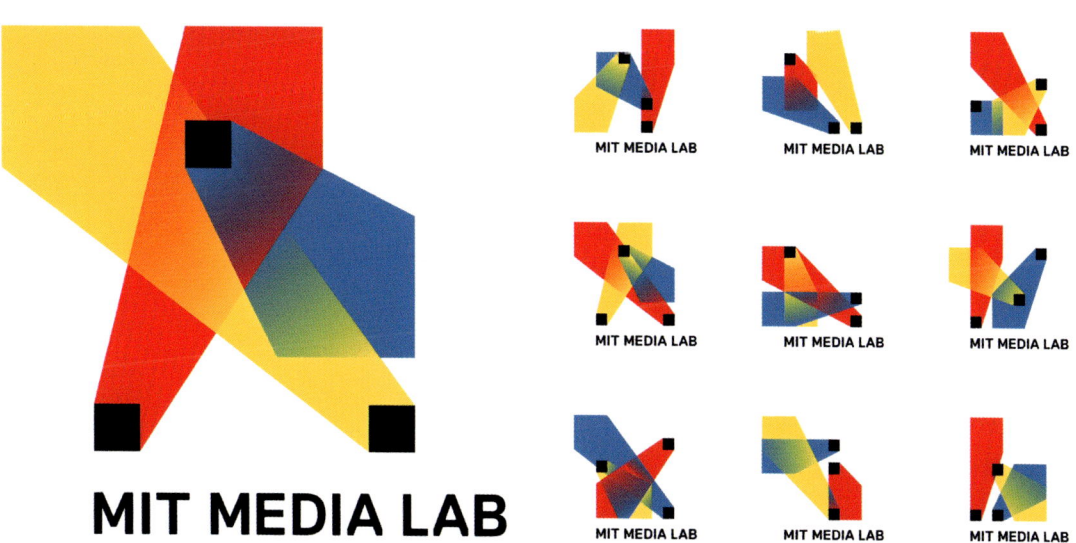

PLATE 4 *MIT Media Lab identity, design and permission E. Roon Kang and TheGreenEyl, 2011.*

PLATE 5 *Ollo logo iPad app, design and permission Bibliothèque, 2011.*

PLATE 6 *"Wake Up, America!' Civilization calls every man, woman and child!' 1917, James Montgomery Flagg, poster, colour lithograph, sheet 103.8 × 69.8 cm. Library of Congress Prints and Photographs Division Washington, D.C.*

PLATE 7 *'See Britain First on Shell', poster with image of Stonehenge, Edward McKnight Kauffer, 1931, Design Council Slide Collection, VADS, © Simon Rendall with permission.*

PLATE 8 *Times Square, New York, NY, February 2015, photograph by Grace Lees-Maffei.*

PLATE 9 Neville Brody, The Face, *no. 39 (July 1983).*

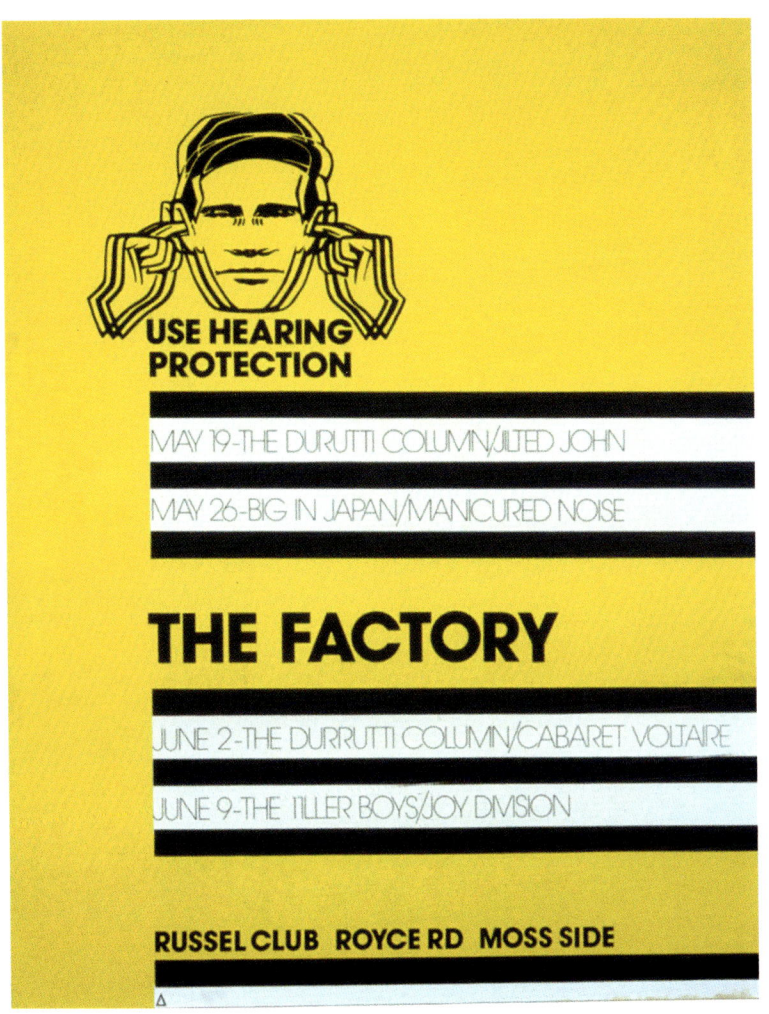

PLATE 10 *The Factory, poster 30" × 40", 1978, design Peter Saville.*

PLATE 11 *Model Hiroko Matsumoto wearing Hanae Mori clothing,* Vogue *(UK), June 1972: n.p. photograph by Lord Snowdon (Anthony Armstrong Jones), permission Condé Nast Publications, 2017.*

PLATE 12 *Chinatown, Gerrard Street, London, 27 September 2015. Photograph by Grace Lees-Maffei.*

PLATE 13 *Spring/Summer 1993 campaign Yves Saint Laurent Rive Gauche, in* Vogue *March 1993: n.p. photograph by Helmut Newton. Image © The Helmut Newton Estate/Maconochie Photography.*

PLATE 14 *'Cool Khaki'.* Vogue *(UK), May 1994, pp. 160-9. Fashion Editor Kate Phelan. Hair by James Brown and make-up by Lucia Pieroni. Kim Knott/*Vogue *© The Condé Nast Publications Ltd.*

PLATE 15 *Family Follows Fiction objects, including 'Christy' conical sugar bowl with thermoplastic resin feet. Designed in metal by Christopher Dresser in 1864, and reinterpreted in plastic by Centro Studi Alessi in 1993; Nutty the Cracker nutcracker; Diabolix bottle opener, Permission Alessi S.p.A., Crusinallo, Italy.*

PLATE 16 *Charles Booth's Maps Descriptive of London Poverty 1898–99. Colour-coded chromolithographs indicating the class of household street by street: darker colours for poverty and lighter ones for financial stability. Close-up crop of East Central District.*

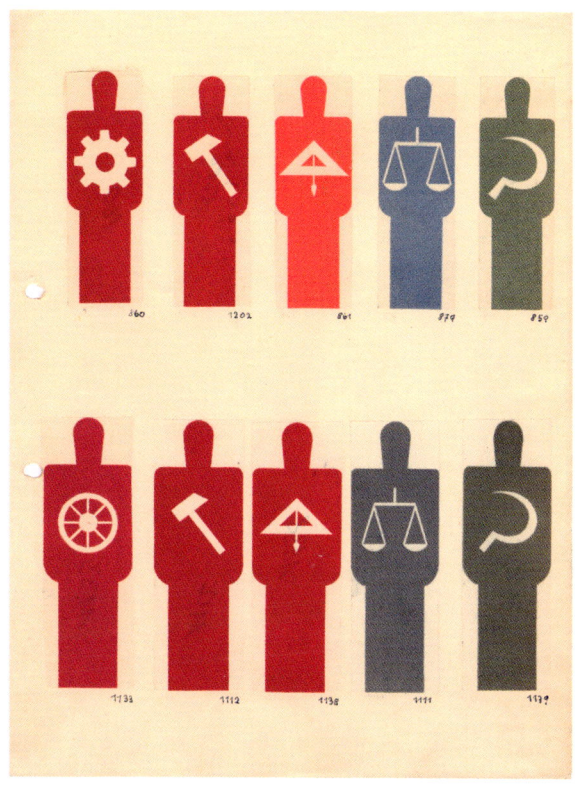

PLATE 17 *Isotype 'Picture dictionary' leaf from binder, Gerd Arntz, 1929–33, 300 x 225 mm, permission Otto and Marie Neurath Isotype Collection, University of Reading.*

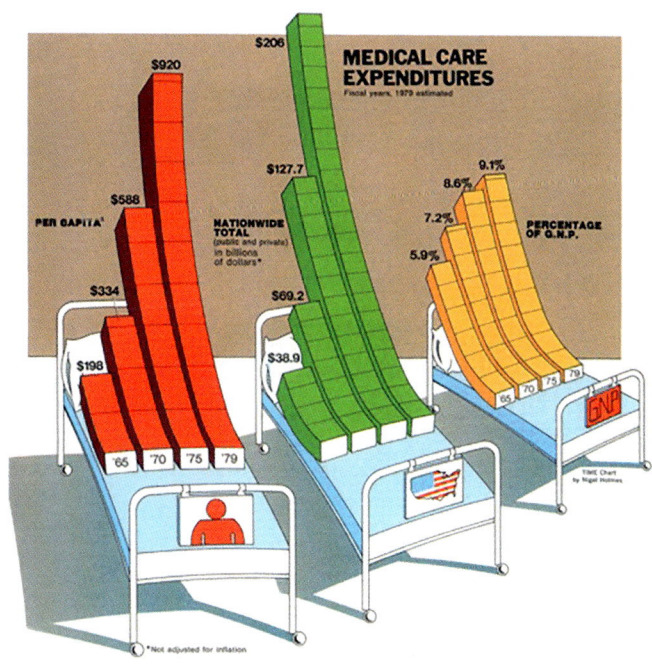

PLATE 18 *'Medical Care Expenditures', explanation graphics for* Time *magazine, 1979. Design and permission Nigel Holmes.*

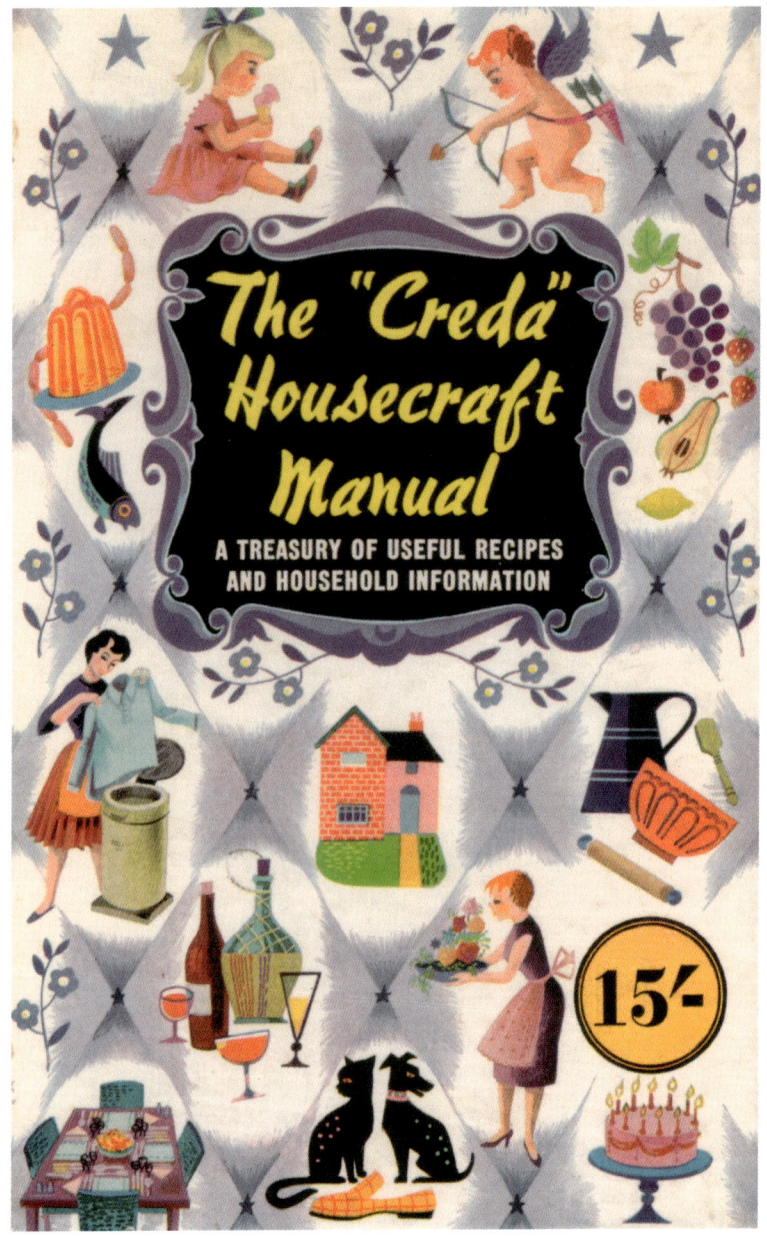

PLATE 19 *Cover, Illustration by Ésme,* The Creda Housecraft Manual, *Stoke-on-Trent: Simplex Electric Co. and London: Odhams, 1958. Permission IPC Media, a Time Inc. Company. CC-BY-NC-ND. Copyright TI Media Ltd.*

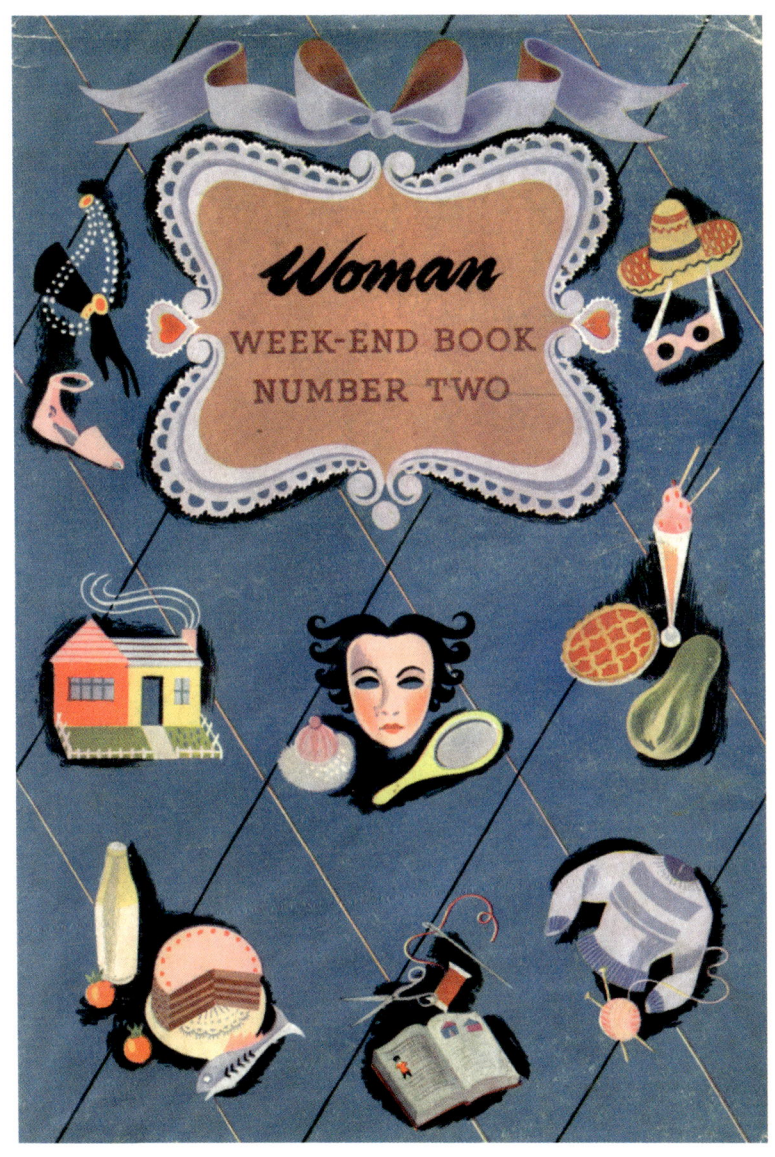

PLATE 20 *Cover, Illustration by Ésme*, Woman Week-End Book Number Two, *London: Odhams Press, 1949. Permission IPC Media, a Time Inc. Company. CC-BY-NC-ND. Copyright TI Media Ltd.*

PLATE 21 *Renault's 'Nicole-Papa' campaign for the Clio car ran for seven years from 1991. Image Courtesy of the Advertising Archive.*

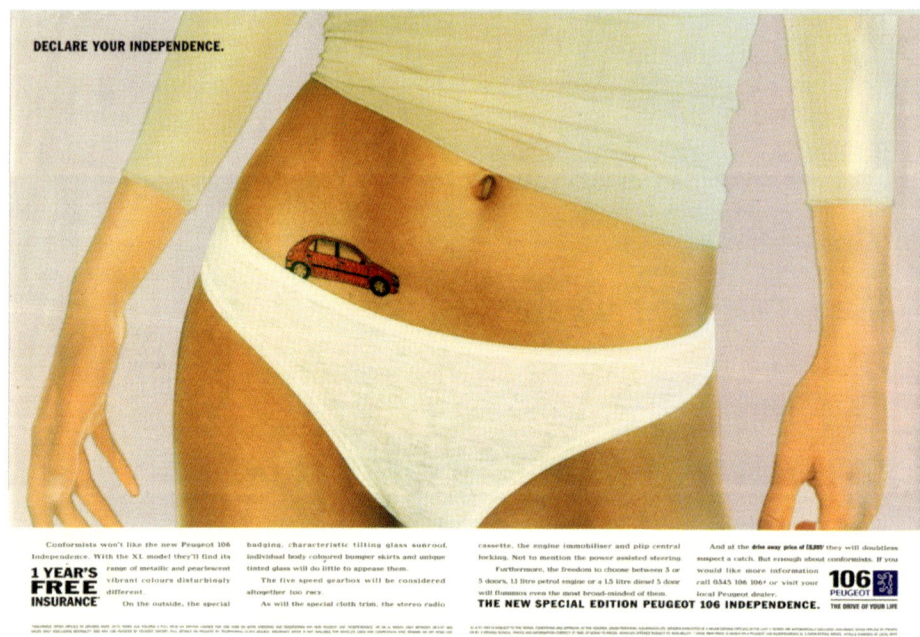

PLATE 22 *'Tattoo' Peugeot 106 Independence advertisement, published as a centrefold in* The Observer, *June 1997. Part of a campaign for the 106, 206 and 306 initiated in 1993 to target women. Photo Peugeot / Euro RSCG Wnek Gosper. Photography and permission by Nadav Kander.*

PLATE 23 *The Beatles,* Sgt. Pepper's Lonely Hearts Club Band, *album cover, design by Peter Blake and Jann Haworth, 1967, Parlophone, UK. Courtesy Getty Images.*

PLATE 24 *Bow Wow Wow,* See Jungle! See Jungle! Go Join Your Gang, Yeah! City All Over! Go Ape Crazy, *album cover, 1981, RCA. Photography and permission by Andy Earl.*

PLATE 25 Composition No. 1, *by Mark Saporta, London, 2010. Permission Visual Editions.*

7

A good read? Corporate literature and brand stories: Alessi SpA as a case study

Grace Lees-Maffei

Visual identity, corporate identity, brand identity, brand stories and logo design work together to tell consumers about the products and services they consume. Through these practices graphic designers seek to unify the visual appearance of businesses or other organizations. In its focus on corporate identity, corporate literature and brand stories this chapter develops some of the issues raised in Chapter 1, on semiotics and branding, and Chapter 2, on uniformity and flexibility in logo design, which explored the variations that can be introduced while maintaining a coherent and recognizable brand identity. This chapter explores corporate identity through the case study of Alessi SpA, an Italian household goods company known worldwide for its design-led approach and output. In particular, this chapter looks at two instances in which corporate literature have functioned to change the narrative of Alessi goods: a shift downmarket in the 1990s and the incorporation of a new product into Alessi's catalogue in 2010. Although Alessi sells product design, the case study here is one of brand stories which will interest graphic designers working for corporate clients of various kinds.

Corporate identity: Origins and development

Forerunners of the contemporary professional practices of corporate identity and today's visual identities are found deep in the histories of design, branding and marketing. The potter Josiah Wedgwood is credited with a number of marketing innovations through which he sold his ceramics. These included celebrity endorsement and product placement: he secured royal patronage for his tableware and made sure his customers knew about this. He sold tickets for entry to his showroom viewings of new product launches. And he promoted loss leaders to raise the desirability of his wares, such as his ceramic recreation of the glass Portland Vase, versions of which he made available at various price points to suit all pockets (Adamson 2014: 154).

Marketing and advertising developed as industries expressly to stimulate consumption. Early advertising techniques ranged from the 'puff' – in which a writer was paid to write a newspaper story mentioning a particular product, as if incidentally – to 'shout louder' type ads where typography was used to give the impression of emphatic persuasion. By 1850, print culture was in full swing: newspapers, magazines and mail order catalogues were all functioning to communicate local, regional and national patterns of consumption to international and global audiences through wide distribution and circulation. Syndication spread messages across nations and internationally. Psychological understanding informed more sophisticated approaches at the turn of the twentieth century, as advertisers learnt to appeal to consumers' dreams and desires rather than to their basic needs (Benjamin and Baker 2004; Lees-Maffei 2016: 448).

Branding exploits the spaces offered by the retailing of ready-packaged goods, from retail environments to packaging surfaces. Branded packaged goods can carry quality assurances to build consumer confidence, and a consistent identity to foster familiarity and trust. When this process is successful, packaged branded goods are perceived as authentic, safe and hygienic and of good quality. Soap manufacturer A&F Pears was at the vanguard of branding goods, along with Lever Brothers' soap brands 'Sunlight' (1884) and 'Lifebuoy' (Lees-Maffei 2016: 448) and these can be compared with the pre-eminent soap brand in Japan, Kāo (Weisenfeld 2004).

We saw in Chapter 2 that Peter Behrens' 1907/8 work for AEG is regarded as the first developed corporate identity. Behrens achieved a distinctive and harmonious visual identity across the AEG organization as a whole. Another game-changing practitioner in the field was Paul Rand; his logo for IBM is a seminal example of post–Second World War corporate modernism. Reflecting on the career of Paul Rand, Jessica Helfand noted his tendency to work alone, as compared with other influential names in US corporate identity including the studios of Pentagram, Landor Associates, and Chermayeff and Geismar (Helfand 2016 [1997]), studios which developed a full service including logo design alongside market research, product positioning and consumer branding. This difference between the sole practitioner (Rand) and the design studios might be explained with reference to the history of the development of corporate identity. Core texts in the field appeared after Rand was established. They included F.H.K. Henrion and Alan Parkin's *Design Coordination and Corporate Image* (1967), James Pilditch's *Communication by Design: A Study in Corporate Identity* (1970) and Wally Olins' *The Corporate Personality* of 1978. These books seek to identify, define and professionalize corporate identity as well as to promote understanding of the need for it in business (Moor 2007: 30–3). Like Rand, Olins was an early and pre-eminent figure in identity design (Balmer 2014), as we have seen in Chapter 1 on branding. Liz Moor nicely characterizes Olin's notion of corporate communications as charged with 'not simply the projection of identity, the *image* of coherence, to an external audience, but the actual *creation* of a group ('corporate') identity' (Moor 2007: 32). This activity extended beyond graphic design and required an interdisciplinary blend of expertise.

The economic power of brands to stimulate consumers and boost sales was recognized in the United Kingdom and the United States in the 1980s, a boom decade for advertisers as well as design agencies. Olins' *Corporate Identity: Making Business Strategy Visible Through Design* (1989) responded to the 'designer decade' in which design was actively promoted as a tool for business in the United Kingdom through the work of the Design Council. During the 1990s, the need for branding to function as a guarantor of quality diminished as consumer advocacy and regulation effectively ensured product standards. Moor notes that at this time, 'the cultivation of more or less abstract values around brands [...relates to...] growing efforts to use consumer affect, and socialized forms of exchange more generally, as sources of value' (Moor 2007: 37).

On B®and (Olins 2003) promotes Olins' understanding of identity as something businesses need as well as consumers, and extends his specialism in nation branding (see Chapter 8, 'Branding the Nation', Olins 2003). Olins refers not only to the ways in which products and brands may carry and promote national associations, but also to work undertaken for national governments in branding specific nation states. In these cases, governments and citizens are branded for the consumption of potential clients such as tourists and foreign businesses (see also 'National Brands and Global Brands' in Moor 2007: 115–41). Olins rode out a shift in corporate identity from a visual emphasis on logo design to identity as brand values and ethos (Balmer 2014).

Corporate and/or visual identity, and advertising, are related but distinct fields which became more extensive, specialized and sophisticated throughout the twentieth century. As I noted in the introductory chapter, Carma Gorman rejects the terms 'corporate identity design' because it is more than merely corporate, and 'graphic identity design' because the practice extends far beyond the preparation of printed materials. She prefers the term 'visual identity design' (Gorman 2017: 385, no. 1) and indeed it seems that corporate identity has been replaced by visual identity as a descriptor used by designers.

Studies of the work of advertising creatives (Nixon 2003) and designers working within advertising and marketing ('Brands, Culture and Economy' in Moor 2007: 39–64) show how intertwined these functions are, while remaining distinguishable. Notwithstanding concerns about how corporate or visual identity would become irrelevant in the digital age (Alderlsey-Williams 2000), it now extends, as does advertising, across multiple platforms and channels from social media networks to installations and environments (Lees-Maffei 2016: 448). The sheer reach of these activities has prompted anti-consumerist activists to employ a variety of means to spread their messages, from direct action to social media, as well as the channels usually associated with corporate identities such as posters, advertisements, branded merchandise such as T-shirts and even corporate reports. The Occupy movement, for example, published posters for its World Revolution Day, in 2015. In addition, designers and artists have exploited the creative potential of the corporate annual report in various ways. Information designer Nicholas Felton produces his own Annual Reports, discussed in the next chapter, while the artist Anish Kapoor worked with design studio Brighten the Corners on lighting company Zumtrobel's 2012 Annual Report (see Sinclair 2012).

Case study: Alessi SpA

We now turn to look at corporate identity in more detail through the case study of Alessi SpA, which has used its corporate marketing programme to promote a brand identity centred upon family, italianità, design history and theory. I will examine two key episodes in the company's design history in which Alessi SpA has used corporate publishing as a vital tool for managing change in its product catalogue through the implementation of brand stories. First was a marked shift in the early- to mid-1990s from the iconic stainless steel high design for which Alessi was fêted in the 1980s, to the introduction of cheaper plastic items. Second was the introduction of a new product marketed as a successor to one of Alessi's most well-known iconic designs, when in fact its origins were very different.

Alessi SpA was set up by Giovanni Alessi Anghini in 1921 in Crusinallo, in the Valley Strona in the Northern Italian lakes region outside Milan, to produce utilitarian household goods in metal, in a region known for metal production (Figure 7.1). The Alessi factory faces the troubled Bialetti factory which produces the famous Moka Express coffee makers. Alessi was founded as part of Italy's relatively belated industrialization surge in the first decades of the twentieth century, and the company's early output was characterized by a gradual shift from manufacturing utility parts and basic pressed goods such as trays, to more technically complex and intellectually challenging projects, starting in 1932. Carlo Alessi's 'Bombe' tea service of 1945 responded to the social context of war (the tea service is rounded like, we might say, bombs) as well as the globular, inflated aesthetic of 1940s design more broadly (Figure 7.2). From 1954, when Italy was almost a decade into its post-war reconstruction and had developed an international reputation for excellence in design, Alessi began to employ designers on a consultancy basis. Representing a new generation in the family firm, Alberto Alessi Anghini joined the workforce as co-general manager in 1970 following a degree in architecture. His Alessi D'Apres art multiples project (1972–7) explored the viability of mass-produced art in stainless steel, and this was the first of a series of projects through which Alberto led the company in the direction of high design. Alessi has continued to produce mainstay products such as its barware, which is used all over Italy and internationally, but it is best known for a range of iconic household goods made largely from stainless steel in collaboration with an international roster of designers. It is this shift which

FIGURE 7.1 *Photograph of Alessi employees outside the factory, Crusinallo 1935. Frontispiece to Officina Alessi catalogue 1995. Graphic Design: Sottsass Associati. Permission Alessi Press Office, Alessi S.p.A., Crusinallo, Italy.*

FIGURE 7.2 *Carlo Alessi Anghini, 'Bombe' tea and coffee set, 1945. Reproduced in electro-plated stainless steel in 1983 as part of the Antologica Alessi range. Meret Gabra-Liddell, ed. 1994.* Alessi: The Design Factory, *p. 83. London: Academy Editions. Permission Alessi Press Office, Alessi S.p.A., Crusinallo, Italy.*

makes Alessi a suitable case study for an analysis of corporate literature as a channel for the narratives that underpin corporate identity.

Mediating Alessi: Marketing the brand

The narratives surrounding Alessi products stem partly from marketing campaigns produced by in-house marketing staff within manufacturing companies, or by hired marketing and PR companies. Alessi uses both strategies for official narratives composed during the design process and through post-project reflections from Alessi HQ, and disseminated internationally via press releases from the marketing company Di Palma Associati, as well as through their catalogues, annual reports and vanity publishing (Lees-Maffei 2014a).

Alessi's bilingual press releases aim to directly shape the brand by giving journalists and bloggers the information and attractive publicity shots needed to inform their articles and blog posts about new products or events. The similarity between press releases and the editorial publicity for those products is not surprising, because one aim of the press release is to direct media coverage. They also sweeten the deal with gifts: 'Alessi sent a specially packaged coffee spoon when they launched their Sottsass cutlery. What design magazine publisher can resist using such seductive and generously bestowed material?' (Griffiths 1992: 56–9, 58).

Furthermore, writing about Alessi has been nurtured by the company itself, through the numerous catalogues and books produced under the aegis of Alberto, a businessman of uncommon historical and theoretical design awareness. Books about Alessi are often produced by people related to the company: Patrizia Scarzella, author of *Steel and Style* (1988), was an employee of the company; *Alessi: The Design Factory* (Gabra-Liddell 1994) is a collection of writings by people working for Alessi; *Paesaggio Casalingo* is by Alessandro Mendini (1979), Alessi design consultant. In addition, Alessi promotes itself through exhibitions many of which are listed in Alessi catalogues, such as the 1979–80 Paesaggio Casalingo exhibition at the 16th Milan Triennale, and 'L'atelier Alessi: Alberto Alessi et Alessandro Mendini: dix ans de design, 1980–1990' at the Paris Pompidou Centre, 1989–90 and, more recently, the Triennale Design Museum Fourth edition, 'Le Fabbriche dei Sogni: Uomini, idée, imprese e paradossi delle fabbriche de design italiano', in Milan in 2011/12.

This vanity publishing and cultural activity shapes retailers', mediators', and consumers' perceptions of Alessi by adding value to the products, and cultivating the company's design history, as we shall see. The audience for the Alessi's corporate literature is unclear, as Laura Polinoro, of the Centro Studi Alessi told me in 1996: 'Who reads them? I don't know. Some designers, many students ... some design theorists ... . I don't know because they are not distributed through bookshops' (Polinoro 1996). Since Polinoro told me this, the situation has changed somewhat: having been published annually between 1998 and 2002 and thereafter by Electa/Alessi, *The Dream Factory* (Alessi 2002) was then published by the mainstream US publisher Rizzoli in New York. Whether self-published or published abroad, Alessi books provide narratives which inform media coverage of the company. This chapter will now explore two examples of this process.

A brand story: From stainless steel to plastic via psychoanalysis

In the 1980s, the designer decade, Italy saw its design brands flourishing, from the long-established manufacturing companies such as Olivetti (f. 1908) and Alessi, to younger but nevertheless successfully established designer brands such as the fashion labels Armani, Versace and Fiorucci. At this time, Alessi experimented with projects influenced by Alessandro Mendini's input as a consultant to the firm, such as 'Tea and Coffee Piazza' (1983). This project involved an international group of invited architects designing tea sets akin to tabletop architecture. The limited edition, the workmanship and materials including silver, suited Tea and Coffee Piazza principally for the museum market. Less rarefied Alessi bestsellers from this decade include Michael Graves' 'Kettle with a Whistling Bird' (1985) (Figure 7.3) and Philippe Starck's 'Juicy Salif' lemon squeezer (to which we will return below) (Figure 7.4). Alessi has been presented as the epitome of 1980s postmodern high design in museum collections and on book covers, which favoured Michael Graves' 'Kettle with a Bird-Shaped Whistle' particularly as visual shorthand for postmodern design. Seventy thousand of the bestselling Graves' whistling bird kettles were produced each year at the height of its popularity (Alessi 1996; Richetti 1996). Victims of their own success in expressing the aspirations and heightened design awareness of the 1980s, these products were rejected by the design cognoscenti at the turn of the decade.

In the 1990s, though, Alessi enjoyed another surge of media coverage for products which replaced the company's characteristic use of stainless steel and silver with colourful plastics.

FIGURE 7.3 *Graves Family, showing Michael Graves' 9093 Kettle (1985), aka 'Kettle with a Whistling Bird', sugar bowl and milk jug. Permission Alessi Press Office, Alessi S.p.A., Crusinallo, Italy.*

FIGURE 7.4 *Alessi family portrait, Frontispiece, Gabra-Liddell, Meret, ed. 1994.* Alessi: The Design Factory. *London: Academy Editions. Alessi Press Office. Featuring the 'Juicy Salif' lemon squeezer, designed by Philippe Starck (1990), Permission Alessi S.p.A., Crusinallo, Italy.*

The Family Follows Fiction range put Alessi alongside brands such as Germany's Authentics and Denmark's Bodum in an interiors trend for design-aware plastics (Figure 7.5). While these cheaper items meant that more people could buy Alessi goods because their entry level products removed high prices as a barrier, they also risked Alessi's reputation for high design and quality. Alessi attempted to solve this problem through its marketing and corporate identity.

FIGURE 7.5 *Family Follows Fiction objects, including 'Christy' conical sugar bowl with thermoplastic resin feet. Designed in metal by Christopher Dresser in 1864, and reinterpreted in plastic by Centro Studi Alessi in 1993; Nutty the Cracker nutcracker; Diabolix bottle opener, Permission Alessi S.p.A., Crusinallo, Italy.*

Alessi, italianità and Family Follows Fiction

Although Alessi is a global brand – it works with an international roster of designers, and retains sales representatives the world over for its global markets – the company has presented itself through vanity publishing as quintessentially Italian. It has done this by communicating several themes through its corporate literature: the importance of family, craft production and the Italian vernacular in design, contextualizing its output as part of canonical design history, and using theoretical references to explain the design process and products. These qualities also underpin Alessi's Family Follows Fiction range, and so the marketing at Alessi which has promoted the brand as Italian has also worked to lend depth, heritage and meaning to the company's move into plastics.

Family saga

In the 1980s, 65 per cent of Italians were dependent upon a family economy (Haycraft 1985: 117). Milan has the highest concentration of private family companies in Italy (Chiesi 1985: 270). Kircherer points to foreign occupation as an explanation for this: 'The Italian understanding of man and society had been shaped over thousands of years by the frequent experience of occupation by foreigners. The family environment has become a stronghold of individuality and self-determination against an imposed system' (Kircherer 1990: 77).

The importance of the family in Italian culture, business and industry is reflected at Alessi across the design, production and marketing of the company's goods. Alberto has described the way in which the family status of the company has impacted upon the design process (Alessi 1994b: 39). Organizational change has been largely generational, as when Alberto joined the company as co-general manager with his brother Michele in 1970. Michele Alessi has emphasized the importance of family relationships to the company's present structure: 'It wouldn't be possible … to match together if we weren't brothers. So that's one of the advantages of, a characteristic, in this case an advantage, of the Italian family companies. We have a lot of family companies' (Alessi 1995).

Family determines both the workings of the business and the development of consciously styled product 'families' and product names. Michael Graves says, 'With Alessi, tradition extends to the idea of the family. As a designer you and your people are brought in and treated as a member of a family.' As well as treating its designers as part of an extended 'family', Alessi products are developed in 'families' such as the Graves Family range, designed by Michael Graves, and Family Follows Fiction (Lees-Maffei 2002: 52–4). (Figure 7.3) Family Follows Fiction foregrounds family in its name, by including the word 'family' and by stating an approach adopted by the Alessi family which favours fiction, meaning narrative, emotions and the opposite of rational modernism. Alberto refers to the fact that 'design' commonly signifies utilitarian and aesthetic problem-solving, and does not imply his companies' cultural concerns (Alessi 1993: 5).

The importance of family is made clear in Alessi's corporate literature. *The Dream Factory: Alessi Since 1921* begins 'Since time immemorial the Alessi family has been firmly established on Lake Orta … . The first Alessi I've traced was called Giovanni; in 1633 he married a certain Caterina Gozano in Luzzogno' (Alessi 2002: 5). Here, long ancestral roots are invoked in order to sell the family firm's household goods. The frontispiece to *Alessi: The Design Factory* (Gabra-Liddell 1994) shows the Alessi family firm (or at least the male members): two older men in suits and ties, and four younger ones with open-necked shirts indicating that the new generation wishes to be seen as relaxed and approachable (Figure 7.4). Alberto is at the front, his brother Michele is rear centre, brother Stefano is seated left and the patriarch is seated in the centre. One sits on an upturned cooking pot and they all brandish Philippe Starck's 'Juicy Salif' lemon squeezer produced by Alessi since 1990. The improbable positioning of the many squeezers, for example tucked into a belt, subverts the dignity of the family portrait with humour and masks the serious business of a corporate board. Wives are absent in accordance with the patrilineal tradition. Alessi markets its familial status as a positive asset, but this can be counterproductive, as with the negative publicity that surrounded the Gucci family collapse (Miller 1994).

Italian crafts

In Italy, Alessi household goods are everyday objects. Alberto explains his relatively high domestic sales with reference to the national character: 'People in Italy are more motivated to buy art through design: they want to use art, to have it close to hand, to experience the emotions of the museum while they are at home' (Alberto Alessi quoted in Walker 1990: 16). Outside Italy, import expenses contribute to the fact that Alessi objects occupy the higher end of the price range for household goods and are perceived as designer housewares in the non-Italian market. Whereas Alessi goods are tantamount to ordinary in Italy, overseas they carry the lustre of italianità: 'We should not be surprised that trade begins with exotica, with goods and objects that acquire value precisely because they are removed from their own context and presented as novelties from afar' (La Cecla 1992: 214, see Chapter 6). For Alessi to market its goods as bearers of italianità, the company needs a self-conscious understanding of how it is viewed elsewhere, and this is expressed not least in its bi- and trilingual catalogues.

Although Alessi offers a broad product range through its medium-sized mass production, the company's catalogues and books emphasize its origins in the context of the Northern Italian craft tradition. Figure 7.6, an image of Northern Italian women spinning and knitting, exemplifies the imagery used by Alessi to locate the brand within a vernacular craft tradition specific to its locale. (Figure 7.6) It has little to do with the reality of production at the Alessi factory, instead representing a myth of italianità, and of local production. The three women might be read as the mythological

FIGURE 7.6 *Traditional local crafts. Meret Gabra-Liddell, ed. 1994.* Alessi: The Design Factory, *p. 10. London: Academy Editions, Permission Alessi S.p.A., Crusinallo, Italy.*

fates, spinning and knitting out the lives of mortals. But the interplay of mass production and craft techniques is prevalent in Italy, which industrialized relatively late when compared with the rest of Western Europe. Alberto has described the company's development as 'a kind of handicraft made with the help of machines' (Alessi 1994a: 9, 11). Examples of attempts to reflect the regional heritage within the Alessi catalogue include the 'Alessofono' saxophone (1983), which pays a tribute both to the metalworking specialism in the Valley Strona and to Alberto and Michele's grandfather Giovanni's involvement in saxophone production, and attempts to revive saxophone production in the area (Sweet 1998: 56).

Design history

Thirdly, Alessi publications present the brand as sitting firmly within the canon of Western design history. Design heritage and company history are emphasized in even the most basic Alessi publications. For example, Alberto's company history *The Dream Factory: Alessi since 1921* places Alessi's current product range within a broader Italian design history and heritage (Alessi 2002: 5). Alessi ranges are organized chronologically, charting design progress, including illustrations of discontinued archive items and extensive bibliographies to contextualize current production. Alessi reproduces work by Italian designers alongside that of foreign designers whose work is aesthetically compatible with the company catalogue, effectively placing Alessi and Italian design within a historical trajectory founded on pre-war design excellence located outside Italy. See, for example, the cover of the Officina Alessi catalogue (Alessi's high end brand) for 1995 (Figure 7.7). It features a photograph of the Bauhaus design school in Germany, with the letters on the outside, 'BAUHAUS' replaced with the name 'ALESSI'. This is humorous, but it also aligns Alessi with the most influential design school. Turning the cover, the frontispiece shows the Alessi factory and workers, photographed in Crusinallo in 1935, again making a clear connection between the Bauhaus and Alessi (Figure 7.1).

Alessi has its own museum, it reproduces design classics such as Marianne Brandt ashtrays, and shows important designs from outside the company's output in its books and catalogues. Several other Italian companies do this too, such as Olivetti, which has a museum and a long-standing programme of cultural activities in the Department of Corporate Image. Kircherer suggests that Olivetti's 'cultural commitment' helped to alleviate 'a situation where nobody was able to locate the human and social consequences of the new technology' and provided consumers with a means of differentiation and recognition (Kircherer 1990: 89). The furniture producer Cassina (f. 1927) reproduced a Le Corbusier and Charlotte Perriand chaise longue in 1965. This was followed with designs by Marcel Breuer, Charles Rennie Mackintosh and Gerrit Rietveld through its 'Cassina i Maestri' collection. Alessi author Enzo Fratelli describes such reproduction as 'an undeniably cultivated act, adding a physical, tangible, three-dimensional and verifiable aspect which complements the cultural contribution of the design historian, who places an object within the framework of his critical analysis' (Fratelli 1994: 92). Featherstone discusses 'the use of art as a vehicle for public relations by large corporations' as a result of the 'aestheticization of everyday life', meaning a widening concern for style and aesthetics (Featherstone 1991: 25).

FIGURE 7.7 *Cover of Officina Alessi catalogue 1995, showing the Bauhaus Dessau campus (1925-6) rebadged with the Alessi name. Permission Alessi S.p.A., Crusinallo, Italy. Graphic design by Sottsass Associati.*

But Alessi goes further in recycling and reinventing canonical design. For instance, the Christy bowl (1993) reinterprets a design by British industrial designer Christopher Dresser (1834–1904) in brightly coloured plastic and therefore extends beyond mere reproduction (Lees-Maffei 2014a). (Figure 7.5). Alessi's Family Follows Fiction range, which has been presented as an innovation designed to facilitate collaboration with younger designers, and has also enabled Alessi to reach a wider market through cheaper goods and a more populist aesthetic, is also informed by the history of Italian design. Italian design of the 1960s featured the seminal production of objects of high-design value made of plastic based on innovations in plastics technology at the Politecnico di Milano.

We can return to the Family Follows Fiction name in the light of this emphasis on design history: it forms a postmodern rewriting of Chicago architect Louis Sullivan's famous Modernist dictum

'Form Follows Function' to underline the playfulness and storytelling elements within postmodern product design, and Alessi's output during the 1990s particularly. Designer Daniel Weil described how the Alessi catalogue 'has taken on the characteristics of an archaeological dig through a century of design. All the different strata are showing, stretching back from postmodernism through the Modern Movement, to the Bauhaus and Arts and Crafts, right back in fact to Christopher Dresser who is widely acknowledged as the world's first industrial designer' (Weil 1994: 142).

Using Baudrillard's suggestion that appreciation of historical objects represents regression into childhood, Michael Collins suggests that Alessi's reproductions of design classics are part of a quest to locate familial origins, and posits Brandt as a mother figure and Dresser as a father (Collins 1990: 15–16). Contrived as this may be, it is nevertheless particularly apt in relation to Alessi because the company presents the family as a motif for understanding its work wherever possible, as we saw above.

In theory

Fourthly, Alessi displays a theorized approach to the design process and the ways in which design is mediated, informed by the architectural training undertaken by Alberto and many of the designers he employs. This means that references to a variety of theoretical ideas are used in Alessi's corporate literature. Nally Bellati summarizes the work of Italian designers as typifying: 'An intellectual approach that unites a humanistic view of culture with science … rather than just a division of industry, design takes on wider intellectual applications, becoming a kind of institution with its own history and dignity' (Bellati 1990: 15).

Family Follows Fiction is an umbrella term for several projects hosted at the Centro Studi Alessi in which psychoanalysis has been used to inspire and explain design. The ideas of child psychologist Donald Winnicott were a major plank in the theoretical recuperation of Family Follows Fiction. This biomorphic range was presented in Alessi's corporate literature as a response to affective codes as delineated by Franco Fornari, and as a group of surrogate transitional objects, a term used by Winnicott to describe the object which a developing child uses to understand, for the first time, that she or he is separate from the mother and specifically, her breast. As Alberto explained:

> Prompted by a number of consultants, and by our own curiosity, we felt the urgent need for an operation which would attempt to balance the authoritativeness, expressive impact and culturalisation of the projects developed for us by the 'great masters' in the 1980s … . The challenge was to reproduce in terms of design the animistic process of an object, common to the world of representation among children and primitive cultures. The process in any case occurs in the reality of all objects, and is spontaneously triggered by personal, or collective, emotive necessities and by the impact of the object itself. We wanted to discover other materials – plastic for example – in order to better explore the world of colour and the sensorial dimension of objects. (Alberto Alessi and Laura Polinoro in Gabra-Liddell 1994: 131; see also Polinoro 1993: 14)

In this story plastic has been chosen for its colour and sensory qualities that set it apart from the company's previous output, not because it is a low-cost material. However, retailers were clear about the benefits of selling Alessi goods at much lower costs, for example FFF bottle stops cost £4.95 thereby removing the price barrier which accompanied much of Alessi's previous output, as noted above (Elphick 1995 and 'Classic Alessi' 1993: 39 cited in Lees 1997: 83).

The theoretical engagement of Italian designers has been associated with the utopianism of a post–Second World War generation led by Ettore Sottsass and Alessandro Mendini. Alessi has been considerably influenced by Alessandro Mendini, one of the company's 'maestri' and father figure to Alberto. Gert Selle has described Mendini as 'theoretician of the Italian avant-garde' redesigning everyday items to inject meaning into them, when they are already replete with meaning and such designed meanings are therefore superfluous (Selle 1989: 55–6). Design at Alessi is guilty of Selle's charge: through the design process, marketing and publications, Alessi invests its objects with ready-made meanings (Lees 1997; Julier 2000: 72 ff.). Sottsass deplores the way in which Italian designers have forgotten the special political dimension of Italian design resulting from post-war reconstruction in favour of consumer seduction and obsolescence (Sottsass 1996). Matteo Thun, for example, spoke for his generation when he proclaimed:

> I'm a servant to the new capitalist system ... simultaneously at the service of Tiffany and Company, Swatch, or Alessi. I want to believe that professional duty asks you not to create subjective poetic messages of personal utopia: the first thing one must do is to permit a client to sell as much as possible, to increase his profits and turnover. (Bellati 1990: 144)

Alessi designers and architects Stefano Giovannoni and Guido Venturini share Thun's disregard for utopianism, the use of design for social improvement: 'We've had enough of erudite designers like Mendini or Branzi, you need to have a degree in architecture to understand their designs' (Alessi 2002: 91). Yet, Thun, Giovannoni and Venturini have all designed for Alessi, and were involved in the Family Follows Fiction project. Alessi's theoretically charged publishing rhetoric enabled the company to remain fashionable in two stylistically and philosophically opposed decades, the 1980s and the 1990s, and to be championed by media sources as the epitome of both.

We have seen how Alessi's corporate literature functioned to manage the introduction of cheaper items in colourful plastics in the mid-1990s into a catalogue which had been dominated by stainless steel until that point. Several themes were promoted in Alessi's marketing materials which explained the product shift in terms of national identity and italianità based on family, craft, design history and heritage, and a theoretical approach to design. Now we will consider a second example in which Alessi's corporate literature was instrumental in introducing a new product into the stable by supplying an origin myth that tied the new product to Alessi's heritage.

Marketing an origin myth: Mysqueeze and Juicy Salif

Our second of two examples of the narratives that form Alessi's corporate identity continues the emphasis on design history and how Alessi has used its own history within a broader design historical context. Just as the reproductions of design classics made by Alessi and Cassina, for example, pay tribute to canonical examples of design history, so Alessi has launched self-reflexive tributes to its own output.

Alessi's 'Juicy Salif' lemon squeezer was designed by Frenchman Philippe Starck and launched in aluminium in 1990. Even though it was relatively expensive, retailing at around ten times the price of a basic lemon squeezer, it sold 50,000 units per year, and between 1990 and 2003, more than half a million Juicy Salifs were sold (Lloyd and Snelders 2003: 238). The Alessi family portrait above highlights Juicy Salif's symbolic rather than utilitarian qualities, its ubiquity, and its importance to the financial success of its manufacturer (Lees-Maffei 2002) (Figure 7.4).

These sales are surprising not only due to the price, however, but also because the Juicy Salif lemon squeezer is not very effective at squeezing lemons. The three legs mean it is prone to tipping when pressure is applied to the top during squeezing. As one user complained of Juicy Salif: 'It's not comfortable, it doesn't feel safe' (Russo and de Moraes 2003: 146–7). Design commentator Guy Julier has noted that 'the cultural baggage of designerly euphoria, its achievements, excesses and wastages converge in the Juicy Salif' (Julier 2000: 79–80). Juicy Salif is not Starck's only design with compromised functionality. His Hot Bertaa kettle (1990) was also criticized because it was heavy when filled and too big to get under sink taps (Gardner 1993) and Alessi withdrew it in 1997. Far from withdrawing Juicy Salif, however, Alessi celebrated its sales success with a gold-plated tenth-anniversary edition in 2000. Gold plate is an unsuitable surface for a lemon squeezer as acidic citrus juice ruins the surface so the use of this material for the tenth-anniversary edition underlines the product's symbolic function.

Gold-plated or not, 'as a best-selling design icon, *Juicy Salif* cannot be evaluated by its effectiveness in squeezing lemons' (González 2009: 305). According to Starck, Juicy Salif is a 'social lubricant' and a conversation starter (Starck 1998 cited in Lloyd and Snelders 2003: 243). Starck has injected it with a range of ready-made meanings which the consumer can comprehend and further embroider (Lees 1997). In asking why 'this disproportioned, menacing-looking, inefficient lemon squeezer is one of Alessi's bestselling products, a design icon, a cultish totem', González suggests that it offers the 'possibility of containing different and often contradictory meanings' and allows for creative consumption or even misuse (González 2009: 306). Juicy Salif might be seen to resemble a spider crossed with a squid, but the fact that it resembles neither very accurately, and that it also recalls space rockets, means that we are at liberty to make of it what we will. By buying or receiving, displaying or otherwise using these objects, we populate our homes and extend our family. And, as we have seen, family is important at Alessi (Lees-Maffei 2014b).

In 2007, Starck contributed seed funding to lastminute.com co-founder Brent Hoberman to launch mydeco.com, an online interiors retailer (mydeco.com 2012a). In 2009 mydeco.com ran a competition, 'Pure Creativity', which was judged by Starck and British designer, retailer and restaurateur Sir Terence Conran. The winner was Roland Kreiter, a Romanian-born designer, educated in Germany. His mysqueeze lemon squeezer, named in honour of the mydeco website, used 3D rapid prototyping to reinterpret the traditional wood or ceramic citrus reamer in stainless steel. Starck arranged an internship in his Paris design studio for Kreiter and 'picked up the phone to Alberto Alessi and told him he'd found his next iconic juicer' (mydeco.com 2012b). Alessi agreed, 'This seemed to me like a worthy tribute to "Juicy Salif" (1990), the most controversial Citrus-squeezer of the twentieth century' (mydeco.com 2012b). Mydeco.com promoted its role in the process: 'Here at mydeco, we're delighted to have played matchmaker between one of our favourite manufacturers and such a talented young designer!' (mydeco.com 2012b). (Figure 7.8)

In 2010 Alessi launched mysqueeze as part of its Object Bijou collection. The launch publicity touts the product as 'the new icon, heir to the "Juicy Salif" designed by Philippe Starck, the citrus

FIGURE 7.8 *Designers Roland Kreiter (left) and Philippe Starck (right) with Kreiter's mysqueeze lemon reamer for Alessi, 2010, Permission Alessi S.p.A., Crusinallo, Italy.*

squeezer produced by Alessi which went on to become one of the most renowned icons of contemporary life in all four corners of the globe' (Alessi.com 2012). But while Juicy Salif arose as a result of a direct commission to Starck from Alessi (albeit for a tray design rather than a lemon squeezer), for Kreiter's mysqueeze the route to production was less direct.

The young student designer Kreiter could not have anticipated that his design would be produced by Alessi. The idea that mysqueeze pays tribute to Juicy Salif was elaborated after Starck had brought the product to Alessi's attention. It is therefore a result of its marketing, and the notions promoted in the literature surrounding the design. The marketing copy makes the succession seem natural. In retrospect, mysqueeze seems to be an obvious candidate for inclusion in Alessi's catalogue. In this, mysqueeze follows a pattern: just as mysqueeze of 2010 pays tribute to Juicy Salif of 1990, so Tea and Coffee Towers of 2003 reprises Tea and Coffee Piazza of 1983; in each case the tribute appears after exactly two decades (Lees-Maffei 2014a). The marketing of mysqueeze as a tribute to Juicy Salif fits with Alessi's corporate narrative of heritage, history, legacy and family, discussed above. The marketing process renders the work of Romanian Kreiter, living in Germany, prepared for a competition hosted by an English online retailer, judged by a French designer, as Italian because it is made by an Italian manufacturer (Lees-Maffei 2014a). The Alessi website now mentions the fact that Kreiter won the 2009 Pure Creativity competition for mydeco.com, judged by Starck and Conran. However, on 27 January 2015, German retailer Monoqi bought mydeco.com in order to expand into the UK market (Howarth 2015). This move covers the traces of the genesis of mysqueeze, and allows Alessi's origin myth to take greater hold.

Conclusion: A happy ending?

This chapter opened with a brief account of the development of corporate identity, and its relationship to the allied fields of marketing and visual identity. It examined corporate identity through the case study of Alessi SpA using two examples: Family Follows Fiction and mysqueeze. Alessi has communicated a series of brand stories through its catalogues, vanity publishing, product blurbs on the Alessi website, and wider marketing. We identified themes or stories through which Alessi's Italian national identity has been mediated – family, Italian craft, design history and theory – and examined the ways in which each of these has been engaged in the task of justifying the plastic Family Follows Fiction range as semantically rich and therefore anything other than cheap. Alessi's engagement with and promotion of design history comes to the fore in our second example, Roland Kreiter's mysqueeze, for which a post-hoc narrative of tribute to Philippe Starck's Juicy Salif has been communicated in sales blurbs on the Alessi and mydeco.com websites. This chapter has explored some of the brand stories communicated in corporate literature at Alessi. Working with advertisers, marketers, manufacturers and other clients, graphic designers play an important part in telling those stories, and communicating corporate identity.

References

Adamson, Glenn. 2014. 'Portland Vase, UK (Josiah Wedgwood, 1789)'. In Grace Lees-Maffei (ed.), *Iconic Designs: 50 Stories about 50 Things*, 152–5. London: Bloomsbury.

Aldersey-Williams, Hugh. 2000. 'Ten Reasons Why Corporate Identity Is Irrelevant'. *Royal Society of Arts Journal* 144 (5495): 4–5.

Alessi, Alberto. 1993. 'The Design Factories: Europe's Industrial Future?', Unpublished Script of Lecture Given for the Design Museum and Pentagram at the Royal Geographical Society, London, June.

Alessi, Alberto. 1994a. 'The Design Factories: Europe's Industrial Future?' In Meret Gabra-Liddell (ed.), *Alessi: The Design Factory*, 9–15. London: Academy Editions.

Alessi, Alberto. 1994b. 'Tea and Coffee Piazza'. In Meret Gabra-Liddell (ed.), *Alessi: The Design Factory*, 38–43. London: Academy Editions.

Alessi, Alberto. 1996. Interview with the Author. Alessi Factory. 20 March.

Alessi, Alberto. 2002. *The Dream Factory: Alessi since 1921*. Milan: Electa and Alessi/F.A.O. SpA.

Alessi, Michele. 1995. Interview with the Author. Royal College of Art. 5 October.

Alessi.com. 2012. http://www.alessi.com/en/2/4916/kitchen-accessories/rk01-mysqueeze-citrus-squeezer. Accessed 11 December 2012.

Balmer, John M. T. 2014. 'Wally Olins (1930–2014), Corporate Identity Ascendancy and Corporate Brand Hegemony. Celebrating the Life of Wally Olins: Leading Corporate Identity Exponent and Prominent Brand Proponent'. *Journal of Brand Management* 21 (6): 459–68.

Bellati, Nally (ed.) 1990. *New Italian Design*. New York: Rizzoli.

Benjamin, Ludy T., and David B. Baker. 2004. *From Séance to Science: A History of the Profession of Psychology in America*. Belmont, CA: Wadsworth/Thomson Learning.

Chiesi, Antonio M. 1985. 'Property, Capital and Network Structure in Italy'. In Rolf Zeigler, N. Stokman and John Scott (eds.), *Networks of Corporate Power: A Comparative Analysis of Ten Countries*, 199–214. Cambridge: Polity.

'Classic Alessi'. 1993. 'Classic Alessi Cuts Tags to Add Mass Appeal'. *HFD – The Weekly Home Furnishing Newspaper* 67 (10): 39. 8 March.

Collins, Michael. 1990. *Alessi*. London: Carlton Books.

Elphick, Caroline. 1995. Interview with the Author. Caz Systems design store, Brighton, UK. October.

Featherstone, Mike. 1991. *Consumer Culture and Postmodernism*. London: Sage.

Fratelli, Enzo. 1994. '"Cronotime" Pio Manzu (1966) 1988'. In Meret Gabra-Liddell (ed.), *Alessi: The Design Factory*, 92. London: Academy Editions.

Gabra-Liddell, Meret (ed.) 1994. *Alessi: The Design Factory*. London: Academy Editions.

Gardner, Carl. 1993. 'Starck Reality'. *Design Magazine* 534 (June): 146–7.
González, Laura. 2009. 'Juicy Salif as a Cultish Totem'. In Barbara Townley and Nick Beech (eds.), *Managing Creativity: Exploring the Paradox*, 287–309. Cambridge: Cambridge University Press.
Gorman, Carma. 2017. 'The Role of Trademark Law in the History of US Visual Identity Design, c. 1860-1960'. *Journal of Design History* 30 (4): 371–8.
Griffiths, Anna. 1992. 'Agenti Segreti in Buona Causa'. *Design World* 24: 58.
Haycraft, John. 1985. *Italian Labyrinth: Italy in the 1980s*. London: Secker & Warburg.
Helfand, Jessica. 2016 [1997]. 'Logocentrism'. *The New Republic*. 29 December. Republished *Design Observer*. 21 July 2016. Available online at http://designobserver.com/feature/logocentrism/38552. Accessed 17 Octover 2017.
Henrion, Frederick Henri Kay, and Alan Parkin. 1967. *Design Coordination & Corporate Image*. London: Studio Vista.
Howarth, Dan. 2015. 'Monoqi Buys Mydeco to Extend UK Reach'. *Dezeen*. 10 February. Online at https://www.dezeen.com/2015/02/10/monoqi-buys-mydeco-extend-uk-reach/. Accessed 23 November 2017.
Julier, Guy. 2000. *The Culture of Design*. London: Sage.
Kircherer, Sibylle. 1990. *Olivetti: A Study of the Corporate Management of Design*. London: Trefoil.
La Cecla, Franco. 1992. 'The Soul and Fetishism of Objects'. *Rebus sic*, 142–250. Crusinallo: FOA.
Lees, Grace. 1997. 'Balancing the Object; the Reinvention of Alessi'. *Things* 6: 74–91.
Lees-Maffei, Grace. 2002. 'Italianita and Internationalism: The Design, Production and Marketing of Alessi s.p.a.'. *Modern Italy* 7 (1): 37–57.
Lees-Maffei, Grace. 2014a. '"Made" in England? The Mediation of Alessi S.p.A'. In Grace Lees-Maffei and Kjetil Fallan (eds.), *Made in Italy: Rethinking a Century of Italian Design*, 287–303. London: Bloomsbury Academic.
Lees-Maffei, Grace. 2014b. 'Juicy Salif, Philippe Starck.' In Grace Lees-Maffei (eds.), *Iconic Designs: 50 Stories about 50 Things*, 184–7. London: Bloomsbury.
Lees-Maffei, Grace. 2016. '"Why Then the World's Mine Oyster": Consumption and Globalization'. In Penny Sparke and Fiona Fisher (eds.), *The Routledge Companion to Design Studies*, 445–56. Abingdon: Routledge.
Lloyd, Peter A., and Dirk Snelders. 2003. 'What Was Philippe Starck Thinking of?' *Design Studies* 24 (3): 237–53.
Mendini, Alessandro. 1979. *Paesaggio Casalingo*. Milan: Editoriale Domus.
Miller, Russell. 1994. 'Gucci: End of a Gilded Dynasty'. *The Sunday Times Magazine*. 9 January.
Moor, Liz. 2007. *The Rise of Brands*. Oxford: Berg.
Mydeco.com. 2012a. 'About Us'. Online at http://mydeco.com/the-magazine/style/mydeco-about-us. Accessed 25 May 2012.
Mydeco.com. 2012b. 'mysqueeze Citrus Juicer'. Online at http://mydeco.com/p/mysqueeze-citrus-juicer-by-roland-kreiter-for-alessimydeco/GB00000012E68CC644B92DC0FE1C75E074CFA8DD/. Accessed 25 May 2012.
Nixon, Sean. 2003. *Advertising Cultures: Gender, Commerce, Creativity*. London: SAGE.
Olins, Wally. 1978. *The Corporate Personality: An Inquiry into the Nature of Corporate Identity*. London: The Design Council.
Olins, Wally. 1989. *Corporate Identity: Making Business Strategy Visible Through Design*. London: Thames & Hudson.
Olins. Wally. 2003. *On B®and*. London: Thames & Hudson.
Pilditch, James. 1970. *Communication by Design: A Study in Corporate Identity*. New York: McGraw-Hill.
Polinoro, Laura. 1993. 'Introduction to the Metaproject F.F.F. for the Workshop: Centro Studi Alessi 1991/1993'. In Giampaolo Guirini and Laura Locatelli (eds.), *Family Follows Fiction Workshop 1991/1993*, 14. Crusinallo: Fratelli Alessi Omegna.
Polinoro, Laura. 1996. Interview with the Author. Centro Studi Alessi, Milan, Italy. 22 March.
Richetti, Carlo. 1996. Interview with the Author. Alessi factory, Crusinallo, Italy. 19 March.

Russo, Beatriz, and Anamaria de Moraes. 2003. 'The Lack of Usability in Design Icons: An Affective Case Study About Juicy Salif'. *Proceedings of the 2003 International Conference on Designing Pleasurable Products and Interfaces*, 146–7. Pittsburgh, New York: ACM Press.

Scarzella, Patrizia. 1988. *Steel and Style: The Story of Alessi Household Ware*. London: The Design Council.

Selle, Gert. 1989. 'There Is No Kitsch, There Is Only Design!' In Victor Margolin (ed.), *Design Discourse: History, Theory, Criticism*, 55–66. Chicago: The University of Chicago Press.

Sinclair, Mark. 2012. 'An Annual Report Full of Light and Colour'. *Creative Review*. 24 August. Online at https://www.creativereview.co.uk/an-annual-report-full-of-light-and-colour/. Accessed 23 November 2017.

Sottsass, Ettore. 1996. Interview with the Author. Sottsass Associati, Milan, Italy. 21 March.

Starck, Philippe. 1998. 'Starck Speaks: Politics, Pleasure Play'. *Harvard Design Magazine* 5 (Summer) cited in Peter A. Lloyd and Dirk Snelders. 2003. 'What Was Philippe Starck Thinking of?' *Design Studies* 24 (3): 237–53.

Sweet, Fay. 1998. *Alessi: Art and Poetry*. Lewes: The Ivy Press.

Walker, Aiden. 1990. 'Serious Make Belief'. *Designer's Journal* 60 (September): 16–17.

Weil, Daniel. 1994. 'This Is Not a Pipe'. In Meret Gabra-Liddell (ed.), *Alessi: The Design Factory*, 140–3. London: Academy Editions.

Weisenfeld, Gennifer. 2004. '"From Baby's First Bath": Kāo Soap and Modern Japanese Commercial Design'. *The Art Bulletin* 86 (3): 573–98.

8

Information overload: Negotiating visual complexity in a data-rich world

Nicolas P. Maffei

The proliferation of information – its collection, interpretation and graphic depiction, whether for the purposes of bureaucratic communication, editorial design or personal expression – has been a key aspect of the late-modern period and contemporary life. This chapter investigates the origins of information graphics and data visualization from Charles Joseph Minard's 1861 depiction of Napoleonic war casualties to Otto Neurath's Isotype system, through which he sought a universal visual language, to Nicholas Felton's *Annual Reports*, which use graphs and charts to depict personal experiences. This chapter explores the evolution of infographics into infotainment, as the illustrated infographic – or more pejoratively, the 'chartoon' – was used to attract and engage in America's first national, mass circulation newspaper *USA Today* in the 1980s. The dangers of depicting data will be explored, on the one hand, through the Victorian visual rhetoric found in Charles Booth's maps of London poverty, and on the other, through the trend towards data visualization ('datavis'), which uses computers to visualize large amounts of data to reveal intricate relationships where complex beauty often trumps clear communication. Maintaining a balance between function and form, the universal and the unique, and education and entertainment, will be central issues in this chapter's investigation of the visual communication of data. Throughout the chapter the rhetoric of graphic depictions of data – its supposed neutrality and scientific tone – will be investigated.

In the spring of 2010 a detailed and visually complex PowerPoint slide depicting the American military strategy in Afghanistan appeared on the cover of the *New York Times* (Bumiller 2010). The slide attempted to represent the complex interrelated forces affecting the conflict across the region. The visually overwhelming slide seemed to confuse more than elucidate and would become infamous as an example of the failure of the graphic portrayal of information while seeming to depict the shifting quagmire of America's military involvement (Galloway 2011: 85). Evidencing a frustration with the complexity of the image, the commander of US military operations in Afghanistan, US General McChrystal wryly commented, 'When we understand that slide, we'll have won the war' (Bumiller 2010: 1). This example typifies the complexity of many contemporary information environments. It serves as a visual reminder of the deliberately obfuscating communication methods sometimes used by those in power, and of the fact that information and its depiction is not neutral, but profoundly ideological.

The rhetoric of information graphics

Despite their apparent transparency and supposed scientific objectivity, information graphics are tools of persuasive rhetoric and highly subjective creations (Kimball 2006: 354). They are ideological constructs containing distortions. Some have suggested that we need a new genre of infographics to reveal these biases (Barton and Barton 1993). Others have argued that designers should re-humanize graphics (Dragga and Dan Voss 2003). However, Kimball persists, 'Most still use, teach, and approach graphics as transparent' (Kimball 2006: 354). It is not that designers 'have yet to see the light' but, rather, that viewers and designers of such graphics have a cultural preference for images of transparency, simplicity and clarity rather than a longing for a complex view of reality (Kimball 2006: 354).

Peter Wildbur observes that the widely held assumption that information graphics are neutral is a fallacy. Following Robin Kinross and Gui Bonsiepe, he argues that 'information graphics is not completely free of visual rhetoric and it is doubtful if information and its communication can be considered completely neutral' (Wildbur 1989: 8; Kinross 1985; Bonsiepe 1965). Wildbur argues that the smallest change to a design can alter its ideological meaning. 'Even within such apparently neutral examples of information graphics as the timetable and directory the decision to emphasize and order certain elements is a means of persuading a reader or user to a course of action' (Wildbur 1989: 10). Wildbur draws an analogy between the rhetorical techniques of politicians, religious proselytizers and street traders and the visual language and tone of information graphics. 'The visual rhetorical devices may seem somewhat muted by comparison but can encompass close control of the sizes and weights of type matter, repetition and the choice and size of paper.' Wildbur goes on to list the factors as: the choice of colours and, in the case of electronic displays, the pace of movement and the use of flashing images' (Wildbur 1989: 10). All of these design elements are used to persuade viewers and direct their actions to ideological ends.

Historical precedents

Tufte traces the origin of the use of 'abstract, non-representational pictures to show numbers' to the period 1750–1800 (Tufte 1983: 9). He credits William Playfair (1759–1823) with developing and refining existing practices of graphic design, replacing 'conventional tables of numbers with systematic visual representations' (Tufte 1983: 9). He outlines numerous methods of visualizing data, from data maps (e.g. use of the map of the United States to represent cancer rates in individual counties over a ten-year period) to space–time-story graphics (e.g. the classic graphic by Charles Joseph Minard (1781–1870) showing the fate of Napoleon's army in Russia) (Figure 8.1). Typical of his often dogmatic and aesthetic-driven method, Tufte critiques the former for using

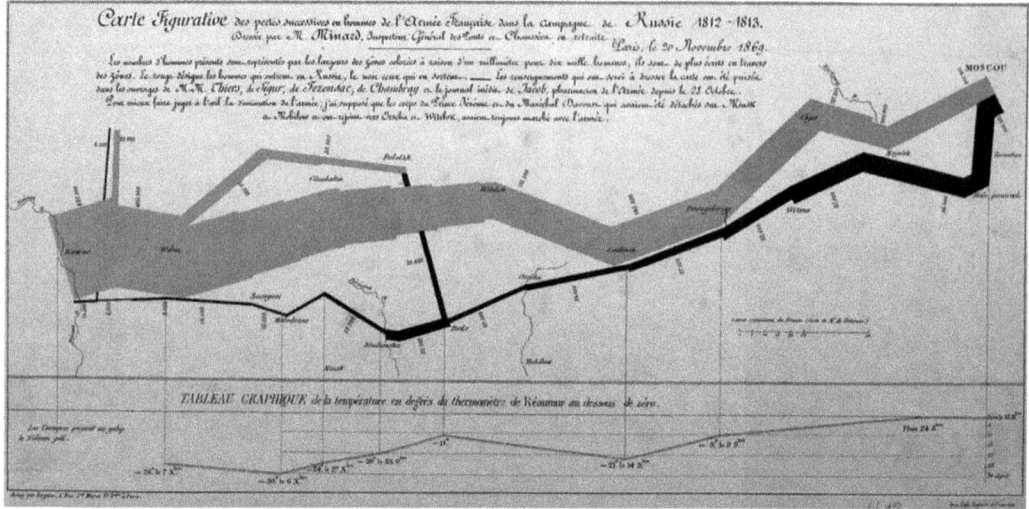

FIGURE 8.1 *Charles Joseph Minard's (1781–1870) flow map (1861) of Napoleon's March on Russia of 1812–13, printed 1869, Paris. Bibliothèque nationale de France, département Cartes et plans.*

inadequate data and praises the latter for its clarity and visual impact (Tufte 1983: 20, 40). Minard's map has been celebrated for its visual elegance, communicative lucidity and its ability to convey multiple levels of information. According to Tufte, Minard's map of 1861, 'may well be the best statistical graphic ever drawn' (Tufte 1983: 40). Using six variables (including army size, locale, direction and temperature) it depicted the decimation of Napoleon's army as it marched to, and then retreated from, Russia (1812-13). Minard's graphics are typical of a genre of information representation known as 'flow maps', which depict movement (e.g. of goods, people, etc.) from one place to another.

While Tufte praised Minard's flow map for its clarity and elegance, the image can also be read metaphorically. The flow map's tapered form representing the army can be seen as a flowing and diminishing tributary. The use of black – meant to indicate a change of direction could be seen to suggest the dark reality of a death march in sub-zero temperatures. Despite its celebrated depiction of factual information, it is arguably the metaphorical power – the visual rhetoric – of the image that secures its graphic impact.

Charles Booth's poverty maps of London (1889–1902) are early and fundamental examples of information graphics, but also significant rhetorical inventions which greatly influenced social policy (Kimball 2006: 355). Booth's maps of economic deprivation accompanied his pioneering, widely read and detailed report on the problem of Victorian poverty (Figure 8.2). Before the publication of Booth's map, many middle- and upper-class Victorians were less able to perceive the poor. Impoverished people were an obscure, but pervasive, problem in the public's imagination: their popular visual and textual depictions relied on existing cultural biases, using metaphors of darkness, submersion, and grime to represent the poor as permanently obscured (Kimball 2006: 356). Booth sought to bring light to this problem. Using census data, his research team's observations and testimonies from the police to the clergy, his voluminous report provided a detailed and groundbreaking sociological survey of life in London from 1889–1903. This, the

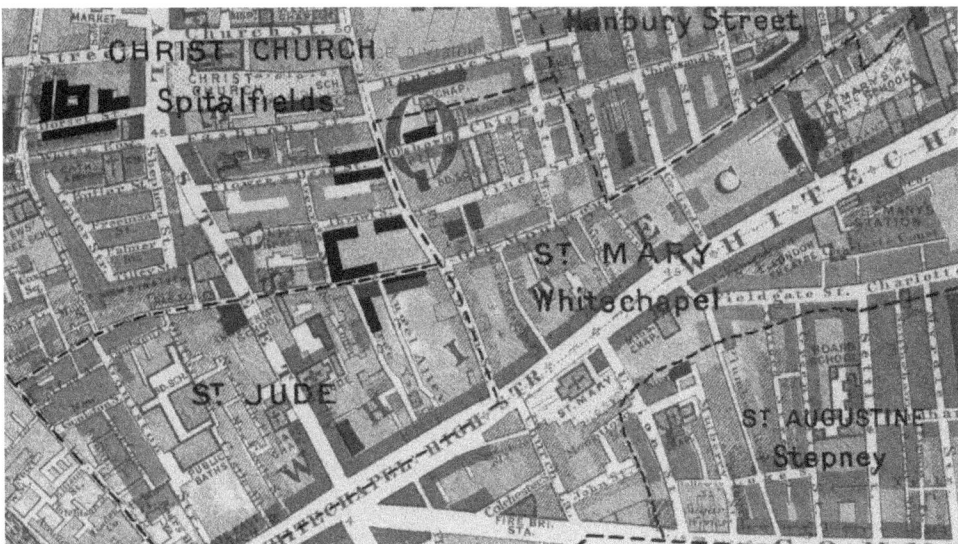

FIGURE 8.2 *Charles Booth's Maps Descriptive of London Poverty 1898–99. Colour-coded chromolithographs indicating the class of household street by street: darker colours for poverty and lighter ones for financial stability. Close-up crop of East Central District.*

world's first large-scale sociological survey, greatly influenced the establishment of universal old-age non-contributory pensions (Kimball 2006: 357).

Booth's contribution to information graphics comprised colour-coded maps printed as chromolithographs that indicated the class of householders street by street. Booth used darker colours to depict poverty (such as black and dark blue) and lighter ones (e.g. pink and yellow) to represent more financially stable classes. The map thus provided a clear, bird's-eye view of concentrations of poverty. Those who viewed the map would have perceived the darker pockets of poverty as a reducible and manageable blot on London society (Kimball 2006: 358, 360). Booth's map thereby visually simplified a complex social problem.

However, his many maps made inconsistent and idiosyncratic use of colour, thereby providing evidence for those who argue that information graphics lack transparency and honesty. It was common practice in Booth's day to use gradations of a single colour for statistical representation, rather than Booth's unusual use of a rainbow-like spectrum. Arguably, the persuasive power of Booths maps 'derive[s] more from visual culture than scientific validity'. They are convincing because they 'invoke and extend an existing visual rhetoric in Victorian culture' (Kimball 2006: 365). Due to of the inconsistencies in the mixing of colours and cultural biases in their use, as well as Booth's role as an amateur painter, the maps could be considered more of an aesthetic undertaking – paintings of London – rather than transparent visualizations of statistical reality.

In the face of such cultural biases and technical inconsistencies why did viewers want to believe Booth's maps? Arguably it was because the 'the color scales of Booth's maps participate in a broader cultural visual rhetoric that consistently presented poverty as obscured in darkness and pictured comfort, salvation, and wholesomeness in terms of brightness' (Kimball 2006: 370–371). Booth's maps rely on a public knowledge of a popular visual language where economic deprivation was represented as a dark underworld as seen in popular paintings, engravings and illustrations from Gustave Doré to William Holman Hunt; whereas salvation was depicted as luminous (see Chapter 5 on binary opposites). Booth used the same colour scale and, therefore, the same visual semantics as these artists. However, through an inversion in their use he showed that the dark populations of poverty were in the minority and surrounded by a luminous sea of bright and colourful light. Thus his maps presented a hopeful picture of a manageable, but major, societal problem: poverty in London.

Isotype: Modernist ideology visualized

The increasing impact of modernism in the first decades of the twentieth century entailed an embrace of internationalism and a quest for a universal visual language. Isotype was a system of visualizing data that brought these two developments together. Based on an acronym of the **I**nternational **S**ystem **O**f **TY**pographic **P**icture **E**ducation, Isotype relied upon simplified pictographic symbols to communicate social and economic data. Beginning in the 1920s, Isotype was developed by Otto Neurath, a Viennese philosopher, social scientist and economist, working with Gerd Arntz, a designer, and Marie Neurath, who as the primary 'transformer' analysed data and formed it into draft examples of graphics (Burke 2009: 215; Neurath and Kinross 2009: 6). Otto Neurath was keen to make the pictograms as universally comprehensible and timeless as possible, while being memorable and attractive (Burke 2009: 214, 215; Neurath, 2010: 125) in order to compete with other visual stimuli. Otto Neurath believed that statistics were potentially empowering. He considered words with some suspicion, even claiming that 'words divide, pictures unite' and aimed his designs at schoolchildren, uneducated adults, and international audiences (Burke 2009: 212). Neurath considered Isotype internationally comprehensible; for him, it had 'grammar' and a 'vocabulary' (Neurath 2010: 102). However, he did not consider it an independent language or intend it as a replacement for language. Isotype was designed to support language and was meant to be accompanied by verbal explanations (Burke 2009: 214; Neurath 2010: 105). Isotype's main rule was that larger quantities were depicted not through enlarging a symbol (e.g. a soldier icon), but through repeating the symbol at the same scale (e.g. in order to depict an army) thereby creating a 'kind of illustrated bar chart' (Burke 2009: 213) (Figure 8.3). Neurath believed Isotype was a 'neutral' communication system akin to cartography and that it would aid public debate by facilitating evidence-based arguments (Neurath 2010: 125).

Isotype has had a great influence on graphic design internationally, from the production of statistical charts, to the development of pictographic signage systems, to corporate identity programmes (Lupton 1986: 47). Its influence has been understood as both stylistic and ideological. Ellen Lupton has observed that the theory of communication exemplified by Isotype provides a visual rhetoric of scientific authority and empirical objectivity: it appears to be neutral, it is simplified, consistent and follows a strict set of rules. Using post-structuralist theory, Lupton counters this view of visual science by arguing that any attempt to fix a specific meaning to a visual icon, and to exclude interpretation, will fail because language (whether visual or verbal) is dependent on context and therefore is always in flux. Lupton argues that the continued influence of Isotype within graphic design disseminates a rhetoric of quasi-scientific objectivity and thus naturalizes the workings and positions of public institutions, governments and corporations (Lupton 1986: 55).

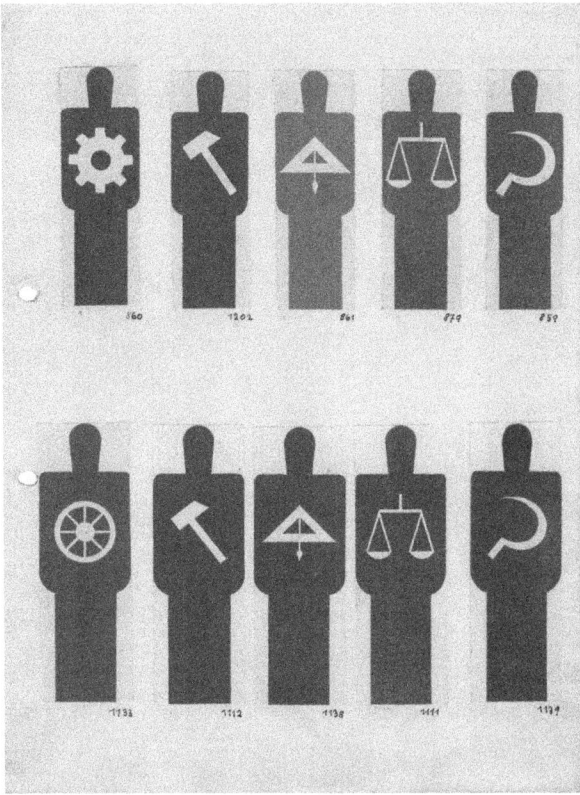

FIGURE 8.3 *Isotype 'Picture dictionary' leaf from binder, Gerd Arntz, 1929–33, 300 x 225 mm, permission Otto and Marie Neurath Isotype Collection, University of Reading.*

Infographics and journalism

Although information graphics can be found in journalism in the United States as early as 1920, for example in the *New York Times* (Bogost, Ferrari and Schweizer 2010: 38), its rise as a more rigorous activity in America has been identified with the late 1930s (Meyer 1997: 18). European émigré designers, including Ladislav Sutnar and Herbert Bayer, brought with them to the United States modernist graphic techniques emphasizing simplicity and functionalism (Meggs and Purvis 2006: 350–52). In the United Kingdom there was very little innovation in newspaper infographics prior to the 1960s. The reasons for this may include a professional newsroom culture that constrained innovative journalistic forms (Dick 2015: 2).

In the United States in the post-war years publishers with financial resources, such as that of *Fortune* magazine, were able to invest in information graphics (Bogost, Ferrari and Schweizer 2010: 39). During the 1950s and 1960s an emphasis on minimalism gave way to more expressive graphics, typified by the New York School 'chartoon' style. This approach saw designers apply illustrative detail and often cartoonish imagery to graphic displays of information in order to appeal to busy readers. Associated with the prolific British designer Nigel Holmes in the 1960s and 1970s (Bogost, Ferrari and Schweizer 2010: 39), 'explanation graphics' became a mainstay of

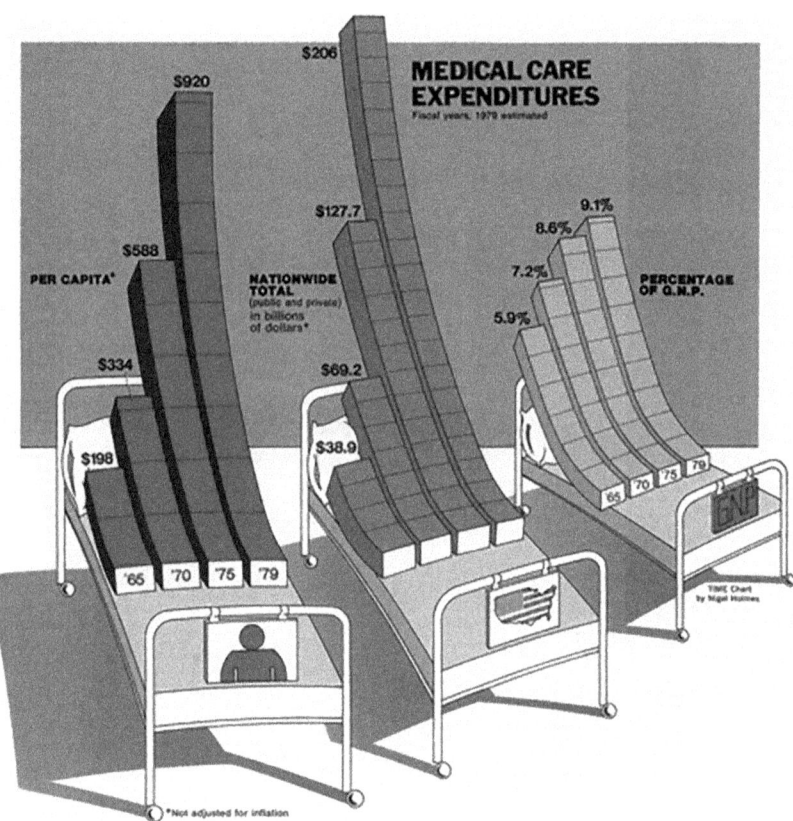

FIGURE 8.4 *'Medical Care Expenditures', explanation graphics for* Time *magazine, 1979. Design and permission Nigel Holmes.*

the influential USA Today and at popular news magazines such as Newsweek and Time, where Holmes was an art director from 1980 to 1994 (Holmes n.d.) (Figure 8.4).

USA Today

Since its launch in 1982 USA Today has been recognized as 'a catalyst of near revolution in the newspaper business'. Numerous major newspapers adopted its use of colour, illustrations, graphics, and its short form, 'digest-style' writing (Logan 1986: 74; Gladney 1993: 17). USA Today instigated an industry-wide adoption of 'factoids', a contemporary newspaper industry term for information graphics (Logan 1986: 76). Despite its self-proclaimed origin in the aesthetics of television, the style of USA Today's information graphics was, in fact, borrowed from Time and Newsweek. The information graphics used in these publications were, however, seen as 'unimaginative, [and] crude in execution'. Holmes' instigation of 'pop data graphics' for Time beginning in 1978 became a significant influence on USA Today's design language. In the 1980s and early 1990s US newspapers that invested in infographics saw increases in their circulation figures (Schoenbach 2004: 224).

The development of infographics was not confined to the print news media. It was also witnessed in other noteworthy publishing ventures, including Richard Saul Wurman's Access Press (founded in 1981), which focused on books on medicine, travel and sports. At the other extreme were the parodic and excessive charts of *Spy* magazine, launched in 1986. The journalistic emphasis on telling stories through infographics was also apparent in *USA Today*'s other predecessors, which included newspapers across the United States, such as the Chicago *Tribune*, Miami *Herald* and even the *New York Times*. The latter represented a significant precursor of the paradigmatic shift towards visual infotainment in American print media, under art director and assistant managing editor Louis Silverstein from 1976 (Miller in Lupton and Miller 1996: 145).

However, the fact that America's first national, mass circulation newspaper was driven by market and entertainment values resulted in a flood of criticism. Infographics and digest-style journalism at *USA Today* were seen as partners in an attack on in-depth, analytical reporting (Gladney 1993: 18). According to some critics (Postman 1985; Remnick 1987), information graphics do not allow readers to nurture the skills of comprehension required for more complex texts. Instead they encourage readers to passively 'watch' a newspaper like they would watch TV. Furthermore, it was thought that *USA Today*'s emphasis on graphics crowded out important news and opinion. Supporting these criticisms were the views of media professionals who had observed a turn away from complex, analytical and investigative reporting to infotainment (Gladney 1993: 33).

Some reporters and editors feared that designers were trivializing 'serious journalistic efforts with pretty pictures and fancy design' (Gladney 1993: 19). Aware of such criticisms of his own practice, Holmes wrote that designers should be 'prepared with arguments and reasons' for fusing information and illustrations. Warning that 'he or she will not have an easy ride' (Holmes 1984: 10), Holmes argued that infographics not only created more space for words, but that the journalist should 'be pleased that the attractiveness of the illustration will lead the viewer into reading' (Holmes 1984: 10).

At *USA Today, Time* and *Newsweek* Edward Tufte's preference of low ink to high data ratio in order to achieve visual clarity and avoid supposedly unnecessary decoration seemed never to have been considered (Miller in Lupton and Miller 1996: 148). Tufte criticized *Time* specifically for employing distorting and distracting 'chartjunk' (decorative devices, including cross hatching, moiré patterns, 3-D perspective and other forms of supposed decoration). In 1982 Tufte dismissively wrote that the purpose of chartjunk was 'to enliven the display' (Tufte 2001: 108). Holmes, whose work seemed to typify this expressive approach, presented his charts as sharing the lineage of Tufte's exemplar William Playfair and the functionalist Otto Neurath, whom he praised in his book (Holmes 1984: 12–21). It was precisely this attempt to engage viewers that was at the heart of Holmes' practice. As if countering Tufte, Nigel Holmes wrote in 1984 that a 'simple chart is no more than a set of statistics made visible … . It can engage the viewer by capturing his imagination' (Holmes 1984: 9). Aware of Tufte's minimalist method and his groundbreaking book of 1982, Holmes criticized pared-down functionalism for its inability to communicate data themes. 'To simply parade the numbers as a set of bars or a rising and falling line does only half the job. It gives no clue as to the subject being dealt with. [Thus] losing the interest of the consumer' (Holmes 1984: 9).

What Holmes asserted in 1984 was later proven correct: that people prefer (Inbar Tractinsky and Meyer 2007) and more easily interpret and remember (Bateman et al. 2010) chartjunk infographics (Dick 2015: 4). Research which reconsidered Tufte's rule of maximizing the data:ink ratio has concluded that other characteristics beyond clarity and efficiency, but especially aesthetic qualities, were needed to create 'impact' in data graphics. As one academic put it, 'I shudder to consider it, perhaps there is something to be learned from the success enjoyed by the multi-colored, three-dimensional pie charts that clutter the pages of *USA Today, Time*, and *Newsweek*. I sure hope not much' (Wainer 1990: 341).

By 1986 the industry-wide concerns regarding the dumbing down of news through *USA Today*-style reporting seemed to have diminished (Logan 1986: 76). Studies have shown that that *USA Today*-type design innovations, including the extensive use of information graphics 'do not clash with professional values' (Gladney 1993: 30; also Logan 1986). However, the more illustrative approach, for example where ethnic or gender stereotypes might be employed in an illustrated data chart, could strongly influence the meaning of a supposedly neutral information graphic (Lupton and Miller 1996:152). In fact, research has shown that biased illustrated infographics were extensively used for Conservative Party propaganda in the United Kingdom beginning in the mid-fifties at the well-financed *Daily Express* to promote the political interests of its proprietor Lord Beaverbrook (Dick 2015: 1).

Information visualization

As more sophisticated technology has allowed for access to, and manipulation of, larger data samples, traditional information graphics have given way to more complex information visualization. Information visualization or 'infovis' uses computers both for processing large bodies of data and for visualizing that data. The rendering of these large data sets – sometimes in the millions – helps to reveal underlying patterns (or networks), which may have escaped observation without being visually ordered (Bogost, Ferrari and Schweizer 2010: 44). Arguably, the recent interest in visualizing quantitative data and the representation of networks is a result of a need for clarity in a world of information overload. But, just how much information overload is there? How do we measure it? One way is to examine the environments in which we encounter information, whether visual or text-based. Consider the exponential rise of the World Wide Web. In 1990, Tim Berners-Lee and Robert Cailliau developed the concept of the World Wide Web, in which web nodes and hypertext pages were visualized by browsers within a network. Launched in December of that year, it grew to 130 websites in 1993. In June of 1998 it had increased to 2,410,067 sites and five years later to 40,936,076 indexed websites. By 2011 there were more than two hundred million (Lima 2011: 56). As of September 2014, this had more than doubled to 470 million (worldwidewebsize.com 2014).

Arguably, the production of data has increased so quickly that it has outrun our ability to control it. Some believe that we now suffer from a 'total dependency on instruments and data representations' (Bermúdez 2004: 357). Such enormous sums of information can lead to perceptual blindness in humans, it is argued, thus requiring further dependence on the interpretive capabilities of machines. However, this problem could be overcome through the aesthetic and communicative intervention of artists and designers. In a world of machine-produced 'unclear...sensorial output' artists and designers should become the 'prime cognitive faculty in making sense out of information' thus 'restoring society's perceptual ability to process data' (Bermúdez 2004: 357). While such a call to arms pits machines against humans and mechanical logic against human creativity, another way of critiquing this problem is via the underlying structures of networks, which are often used to visualize information.

Visual complexity

Lev Manovich has observed that information visualization and networks science are 'two key techno-cultural phenomena of our time' (Lima 2011: 11). Research ranging from online social connections and neural patterns, to airline routes and protein chains, suggests that 'the network is a ubiquitous structure present in most natural and artificial systems ... from power grids to proteins, the internet, and the brain' (Lima 2011: 15). Usually these are represented as network diagrams composed of nodes (from a person to a protein) and connecting lines that depict relationships between the nodes (from friendship to chemical exchange) (Lima 2011: 15). Used for millennia to represent everything from knowledge to biological structures, the tree may be one of the earliest and most long-standing visual metaphor and representation of a network (Lima 2014). Despite its pervasiveness, critics of root and branch analogies, Gilles Deleuze and Félix Guattari, have associated the symbol with despotism, authoritarianism and centralized power.

> We're tired of trees. We should stop believing in trees, roots, and radicles. They've made us suffer too much. All of arborescent [sic] culture is founded on them, from biology to linguistics. Nothing is beautiful or loving or political aside from underground stems and aerial root, adventitious growths and rhizomes. (Deleuze and Guattari 1987: 15)

Deleuze and Guattari instead offer the rhizome as a more decentralized, non-hierarchical and multiplicitous metaphor for political organization. As they describe it, the 'rhizome pertains to a map that must be produced, constructed, a map that is always detachable, connectable, reversible, modifiable, and has multiple entryways and exits and its own lines of flight' (Deleuze and Guattari 1987: 23).

The concept of the rhizome has had a profound effect on postmodern thinking, influencing everything from communication theory to hypermedia, and it has been especially influential on the way we imagine hypertext and the interconnectivity and growth of the world wide web. Beginning in the second half of the twentieth-century 'problems of organized complexity', ranging from stabilization of currencies and war planning to price fluctuation and social behaviour, and extending from the political and economic sciences to the study of medicine and psychology, became more extensive and have increasingly required design intervention as an interpretive solution. The tree metaphor cannot adequately visualize these recent complex, and often urgent, connected problems. So, information designers have turned to the rhizome, which allows for a more holistic, systems approach, including the properties of 'decentralization, emergence, mutability, nonlinearity, and ultimately, diversity' (Lima 2011: 44–45) (Figure 8.5). The rhizomic structure became the dominant form of the internet as pioneered by Paul Baran while working for the RAND Corporation. Baran's new interconnected communication system would resist attack because of its form; its many nodes avoided the vulnerabilities of a centralized or decentralized structure (Lima 2011: 54).

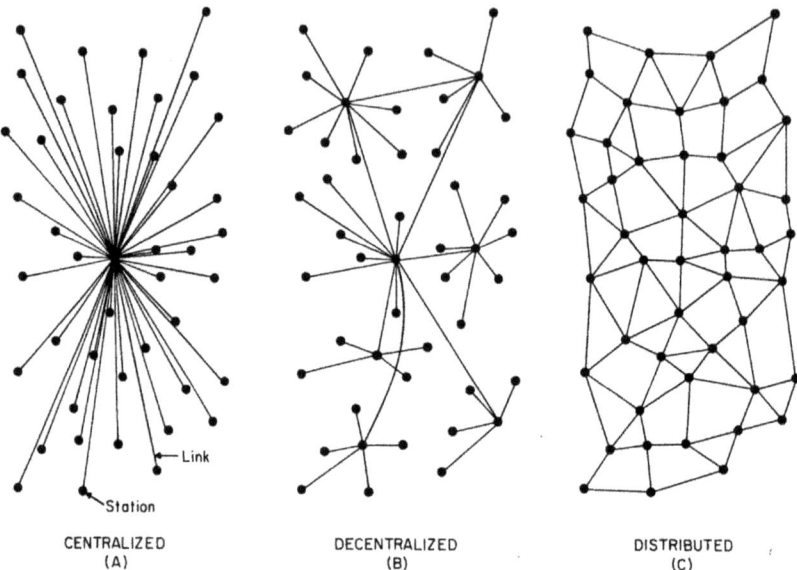

FIGURE 8.5 *Network Models. Three proposed models of the internet: centralized, decentralized and distributed, designed by Paul Baran, 1964. Permission from the RAND Corporation.*

The quantified self movement

The interconnected, rhizomic structure of the internet also allowed for sharing of personal data. Although data visualization is often understood as abstract and impersonal and dealing with distant subjects, a number of practitioners have used newer technologies, such as mobile phones, to record their own geo-spatial autobiographies. Recording GPS points over a period of several years can show a person's whereabouts and even reveal their emotional state at certain times and places. For his project 'Atlas of the Habitual' artist Tim Clark recorded his location and thoughts around Bennington, Vermont over a 200-day period between 2010 and 2011 (Figure 8.6). His atlas had clickable categories and time periods that created an interactive personal journal. The impact of this piece resides in its ability to shift from the prosaic and everyday, for example 'Running errands', to the highly personal and emotional, for example 'Reliving the breakup' with a long-term girlfriend (Yau 2013: 8).

The contrast between impersonal aesthetics and personal information is also found in the annual reports of Nicholas Felton, perhaps one of the better-known practitioners of the quantified self movement, particularly in the graphic design community (Figure 8.7). Felton designed his first report in 2005 and has continued to do so each year. In contrast to the corporate annual report and the family Christmas newsletter, his reports record the minutiae of his life, from his location to movies he has watched and books he has read. After his father died, he designed an annual report based solely on his dad's life, complete with data on his book collection and TV-watching habits, thus adding emotion to raw data, at least according to statistician and visualization expert, David Yau (2013: 11). On the other hand, perhaps the use of statistics and a seemingly neutral design aesthetic was a way of evading emotion while literally facing the facts of a difficult life event – the death of a parent.

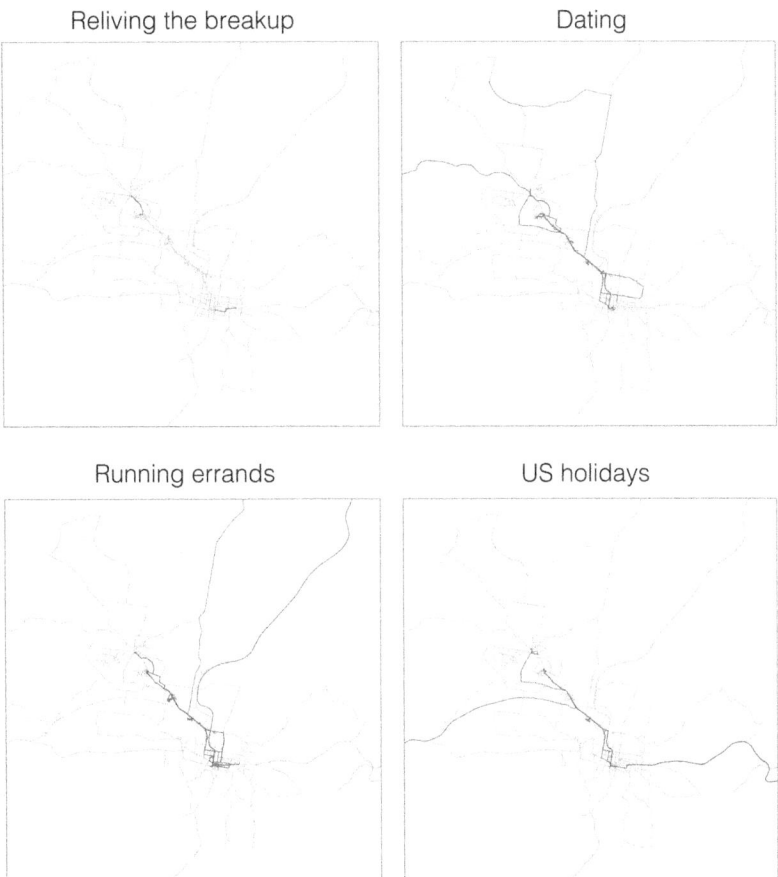

FIGURE 8.6 *Selection from an atlas of 64 maps, 'Atlas of the Habitual', 2010–2011, atlasofthehabitual.tlclark.com, design and permission Tim Clark.*

Conclusion

Information, whether personal data or bureaucratic statistics, has proliferated with the development of industrialized societies and multiplied with the more recent advent and accessibility of digital technology, from mobile devices that allow the documentation of one's life to the rise of vast data storage systems. This chapter surveyed some of the history of the graphical depiction of such information while challenging its supposed neutrality. Charles Joseph Minard's flow map (1861) of Napoleon's catastrophic 1812 march on Russia was analysed as an important example of the visualization of time, space and human life, but it was also recognized for its dark symbolism depicting the devastation of war. Charles Booth's pioneering maps of London poverty (1889–1902) visually communicated the scope and depth of economic deprivation. Apparently unbiased, the maps' use of neighbourhood colour coding (equating light with wealth and dark with poverty) reinforced existing cultural biases based on the oppositions of the bright middle classes and the grimy poor. The chapter considered the problematic modernism of Otto Neurath's Isotype

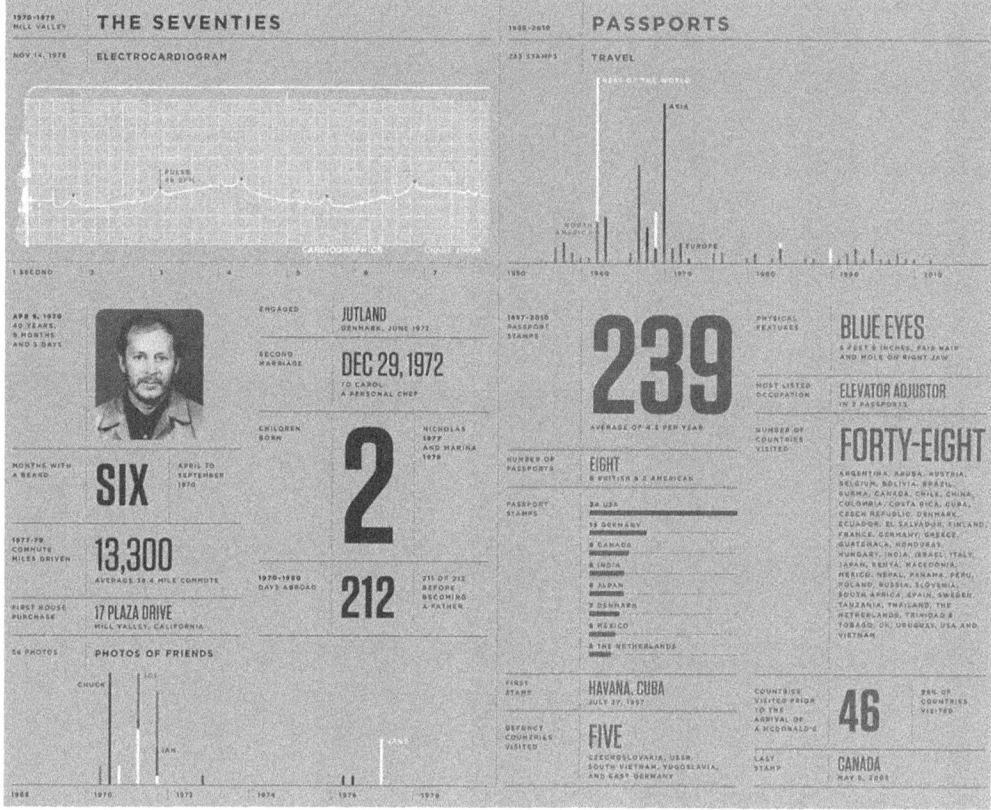

FIGURE 8.7 *Selected pages from 2010* Annual Report, *http://feltron.com. Design and permission Nicholas Felton.*

system: despite their idealism, Neurath and his collaborators sought to achieve neutral, universal communication through the depiction of data in consistent simplified form. Its minimalist language of figurative and object-based icons has influenced graphic designers stylistically, while also providing them with a visual rhetoric of apparent scientific authority, thus naturalizing the graphic communication of public and private institutions. Neurath's functionalism contrasts with the more expressive, illustrative 'explanation graphics' of Nigel Holmes of the 1960s and 1970s, an approach dismissed by the outspoken information graphics theorist, Tufte. While Tufte encouraged the removal of decorative 'chartjunk', Holmes used illustration to engage viewers' imaginations in order to make information more memorable, the efficacy of which was later proven by scientific research. This chapter discussed the political implications of network designs – whether branching (associated with centralized, authoritarian, top-down systems) or rhizomic (associated with decentralization and diversity). It ended with an investigation of the quantified self movement exemplified by Nicholas Felton's autobiographical annual reports with their personal and individual focus and quasi-scientific graphic aesthetic. Felton's emotive data expressed through corporate aesthetics inverted modernism's aim of universality and objectivity. The examples of the visual depiction of information outlined above illustrate the graphic designer's challenge to balance emotional engagement with neutrality, complexity and clarity.

References

Barton, Ben F., and Marthalee S. Barton. 1993. 'Ideology and the Map: Toward a Postmodern Visual Design Practice'. In Nancy Roundy Blyler and Charlotte Thralls (eds.), *Professional Communication: The Social Perspective*, 49–78. Newbury Park, CA: Sage.

Bateman, Scott, Regan L. Mandryk, Carl Gutwin, Aaron Genest, David McDine, and Christopher Brooks. 2010. 'Useful Junk? The Effects of Visual Embellishment on Comprehension and Memorability of Charts'. *Conference Proceedings of the 28th International Conference on Human Factors in Computing Systems*, CHI 2010, Atlanta, GA, 10–15 April, 2010.

Bumiller, Elisabeth. 2010. 'We Have Met the Enemy and He Is PowerPoint'. *New York Times*. 26 April: 1.

Bermúdez, Julio. 2004. 'Art and Design Cures for Society's Growing Data Perceptual Blindness?' *Leonardo* 37 (5): 357.

Bogost, Ian, Simon Ferrari, and Bobby Schweizer. 2010. *News Games: Journalism at Play*. Cambridge, MA: The MIT Press.

Bonsiepe, Gui. 1965. 'Visual/Verbal Rhetoric'. *Ulm*. 14/15/16 December: 30.

Burke, Christopher. 2009. 'Isotype: Representing Social Facts Pictorially'. *Information Design Journal* 17 (3): 211–23.

Deleuze, Gilles, and Félix Guattari. 1987. *A Thousand Plateaus*. Translated by Brian Massumi. Minneapolis: University of Minnesota Press.

Dragga, Sam, and Dan Voss. 2003. 'Hiding Humanity: Verbal and Visual Ethics in Accident Reports'. *Technical Communication* 50 (2003): 61–82.

Dick, Murray. 2015. 'Just Fancy That: An Analysis of Infographic Propaganda in *The Daily Express*, 1956-1959'. *Journalism Studies* 16 (2): 152–74.

Galloway, Alexander. 2011. 'Are Some Things Unrepresentable?' *Theory Culture Society* 28 (7–8): 85–102.

Gladney, George Albert. 1993. 'Imitators, and Its Critics: Do Newsroom Staffs Face an Ethical Dilemma?' *Journal of Mass Media Ethics* 8 (1): 17–36.

Holmes, Nigel. n.d. 'Explanation Graphics'. http://nigelholmes.com. Accessed 2 December 2015.

Holmes, Nigel. 1984. *Designer's Guide to Creating Charts and Diagrams*. New York: Watson Guptill.

Inbar, Ohad, Noam Tractinsky, and Joachim Meyer. 2007. 'Minimalism in Information Visualization-Attitudes Towards Maximizing the Data-Ink Ratio'. *Proceedings of ECCE (European Conference on Cognitive Ergonomics)*, 28–31 August, 185–8. London: ACM Press.

Kimball, Miles A. 2006. 'London through Rose-Colored Graphics: Visual Rhetoric and Information Graphic Design in Charles Booth's Maps of London Poverty'. *Journal of Technical Writing and Communication* 36 (4): 353–81.

Kinross, Robin. 1985. 'The Rhetoric of Neutrality'. *Design Issues* 2 (2): 18–30.

Lima, Manuel. 2011. *Visual Complexity: Mapping Patterns of Information*. New York: Princeton Architectural Press.

Lima, Manuel. 2014. *The Book of Trees: Visualizing Branches of Knowledge*. New York: Princeton Architectural Press.

Logan, Robert A. 1986. 'USA Today's Innovation and Their Impact on Journalism Ethics'. *Journal of Mass Media Ethics* 1 (2): 74–87.

Lupton, Ellen. 1986. 'Reading Isotype'. *Design Issues* 3 (2): 47–58.

Lupton, Ellen, and J. Abbott Miller. 1996. 'McPaper: USA Today and the Journalism of Hope'. *Design Writing Research: Writing on Graphic Design*, 143–56. New York: Princeton Architectural Press.

Meggs, Philip B, and Alston W. Purvis. 2006. *Megg's History of Graphic Design*. Fourth edition. Hoboken, NJ: John Wiley and Sons, Inc.

Meyer, Eric K. 1997. *Designing Infographics*. Indianapolis: Hayden Books.

Neurath, Otto, Matthew Eve, and Christopher Burke (eds.) 2010. *From Hieroglyphics to Isotype: A Visual Autobiography*. London: Hyphen Press.

Neurath, Marie, and Robin Kinross. 2009. *The Transformer: Principles of Making Isotype Charts*. London: Hyphen Press.

Postman, Neil. 1985. *Amusing Ourselves to Death: Public Discourse in the Age of Show Business*. New York: Viking Penguin.

Remnick, David. 1987. 'Good New Is No News.' *Esquire*. October: 156–65.

Schoenbach, Klaus. 2004. 'A Balance Between Imitation and Contrast: What Makes Newspapers Successful? A Summary of Internationally Comparative Research'. *Journal of Media Economics* 17 (3): 219–27.

Tufte, Edward R. 2001 (1983). *The Visual Display of Quantitative Information*. Cheshire, CT: Graphics Press.

Wainer, Howard. 1990. 'Graphical Visions from William Playfair to John Tukey'. *Statistical Science* 5 (3): 340–46.

Wildbur, Peter. 1989. *Information Graphics: A Survey of Typographic, Diagrammatic and Cartographic Communication*. London: Trefoil Publications.

worldwidewebsize.com. 2014. 'The Size of the World Wide Web (The Internet)'. Accessed 2 December 2015.

Yau, Nathan. 2013. *Data Points: Visualization That Means Something*. Indianapolis, IN: John Wiley & Sons.

PART THREE

On paper and on screen

9

How to? Visual techniques of persuasion in guidebooks and manuals

Grace Lees-Maffei

This chapter examines the ways in which words and images work together, using the example of how visual techniques operate within the largely textual format of advice books. Like advertisements, advice books are persuasive and informative texts, but advice books go further in enabling people to learn a variety of skills, from etiquette and home decoration, to business and cooking. An image is said to be worth a thousand words, and in the advice genre images are crucial in providing information about desired results (whether dishes of food or decorative schemes for rooms) to which readers may aspire. However, words and images do not always work in tandem to reinforce one another in these texts. In this chapter, I introduce a variety of visual techniques through representative examples organized into a concise typology.

Introduction: Words and graphic design

Images and words are distinct modes of communication: we might say that one shows and the other tells. Put another way, we can turn to semiotics to understand the difference between iconic signs which resemble the thing communicated, and indexical signs which require a learnt connection between the sign and the referent or thing referred to (see Chapter 1). Not all images function as iconic signs, of course. A depiction of a fire shows danger, and draws upon the viewers' experience of fire, and of fire signs, but a depiction of smoke necessarily relies on a learnt connection between smoke and fire. All textual communications rely on a learnt connection. We learn languages, whether our mother tongue or further acquired languages, by emulating and remembering, practising and developing.

Commentators have shared a variety of views about the primacy of words or images, with some people arguing that Western society and culture in the modern period has privileged words, whether written or spoken, and others remarking on the visual turn in our image-obsessed culture (Crow 2006). These polarized positions can obscure the fact that words and images are often used together in bi-modal communication.

Text sometimes appears entirely without visual imagery, as in the case of a novel without illustrations and with a plain or wholly text-based cover. And, an image can convey narrative without text, or at least a narrative can be communicated in only a small number of images. This is the basic function of stained glass windows, to communicate bible stories to an illiterate population in a series of images not unlike a cartoon strip. However, unlike the majority of stained glass windows, cartoons strips and comics also use words to explain and develop the narrative. In fact, images seldom appear without some words, and these words can take many forms, from brand names to captions, comments and descriptions.

The range of formats which rely on successful bi-modal communication using words and images is enormous. From the film with spoken dialogue or subtitles to the painting with a caption; from the reportage photograph in the columns of a newspaper to a print or TV advertisement featuring a brand name, logotype and strapline; and from an illustrated or graphic novel, to a food package featuring text which is both enticing and informative, word and image go hand in hand throughout our culture. And graphic designers play a central role in the management of word and image, and their relation, to communicate.

As this book shows, graphic design takes many forms, from page layouts and billboard posters, to logo design. As I have noted previously we often encounter design through words:

> From students attending lectures and seminars and researching and writing essays, to designers keeping up with current practice in professional magazines and on the websites and blogs of other design professionals, to shoppers browsing product specifications online, in catalogues and magazines, and in retail environments, to museum and gallery visitors reading labels. (Lees-Maffei 2012: 2)

Words and images combine in design and representations of design. Words are, therefore, crucial in both learning about design past, present and future, and in communicating what we know.

Graphic designers are expert in combining text and images to create effective communications. In fact, it would be wrong to regard graphic design as a wholly visual practice and to underestimate the extent to which graphic designers work with text: they set text into page layouts; sometimes they copyedit by searching out and removing textual errors; they deliver the text- and image-based information that makes the world function properly. Typographers shape the letters and words that we use to communicate textually. The design in graphic design is as much textual as it is visual, and indeed the borders between textuality and visuality are not clear cut in graphic design practice. As designer Michael Rock put it 'the ways a designer can be an author are complex and confused' (Rock 1996).

And, of course, graphic designers write. Design historian Gabriele Oropallo points out that 'practice and verbalization in design are intimately connected. Designers write to present and pitch their work, quote their influences, describe their methods and formulate their views on design history and theory' (Oropallo 2012: 205). Ellen Lupton and J. Abbott Miller have demonstrated the importance of writing through their studio Design/Writing/Research and their book of the same name (Lupton and Miller 1999). Their work entails relatively extensive textual ekphrasis or explanation, and reflection; for example, their 1999 (1996) book includes a timeline accompanied by a reference to Miller's reflective essay about timelines as ways of representing history (Miller 1988; on timelines see also Rosenberg and Grafton 2012). Teal Triggs is also exemplary of the designer-writer. A signatory of the 'First Things First 2000' manifesto (First Things First 1999), she has written consistently throughout her career, including books on fanzines (2010), type design (2003) and visual communication (1995).

Polly Cantlon and Alice Lo and have probed this relationship between words and graphic design in their study of the extent to which celebrated classic graphic design books are designed to match, or exemplify, the ideas about design that are communicated through the text. They make a close analysis of four books published between 1923 and 1960, the high period of modernism. They argue that scrutinizing the design of classic books on graphic design 'can reveal much about design practice, as well as indicate disjunctions between ideals and practice' (Cantlon and Lo 2012: 135). They state: 'The book was, crucially, the main channel through which modernism was theorized and debated; it functioned moreover as a vehicle for the embodiment as well as the communication of modernist ideals' (Cantlon and Lo 2012: 136). They conclude that while three of the four books they examined display a suitable relationship between form – book design – and content, the fourth book, Reyner Banham's *Theory and Design in the First Machine Age* (1960) relays in its book design 'the very opposite significant to its text: a message of unsophisticated and unquestioning use of convention of form and an apparent disregard of imaginative, visual or communicative values' (Cantlon and Lo 2012: 145).

This chapter examines advice books as examples of information and persuasion. These functions – information and persuasion – are key to the graphic designer's role. Much of what we read can be placed into a small number of core functions, or categories of discourse. The things we read usually aim to either inform, entertain or persuade us. In some cases, such as an infomercial, they aim to do all three of these. Rhetoric refers to the practice and study of persuasive speaking or writing – graphic designers use rhetorical strategies within visual layouts or other contexts, as we shall see.

The advice genre: Information, education, entertainment and persuasion

In this chapter, we will explore the persuasive function of word and image through the case study of advice books. Advice is offered via a wide variety of forms, from the conversations we have with friends, family, teachers, colleagues, mentors and others, to advertising and marketing, and from the films we watch at home, at the cinema and online, to the magazines, books and websites we read. There is a vast amount of advice published online and in mainstream media each year. Advice is given, and published, on every aspect of life. From childbirth, parenting, dating, weddings, business, travel, divorce and funerals, few parts of our lives are not addressed in published advice, and advice discourses extend across the life course from birth to death, from potty-training to dinner parties. This advice quickly dates, as social ideals and norms shift, so a continual stream of new advice books is produced in a range of formats, including both new advice titles and new editions of existing titles. When read retrospectively and against the grain, these books offer insights into the ideals people upheld, and shared, about the possibilities of domesticity, rather than evidence of actual practice.

This chapter focuses on advice which concerns the home in a variety of ways. Domestic advice books are one of several channels through which we receive guidance about what we do in our homes, along with magazines, advertising, marketing and instructional and edutainment broadcasting. Homemaking books tell us how to run our homes, and etiquette books tell us how to behave whether at home or beyond. These books have been produced in various forms for as long as the book market has existed, and in greater numbers from the eighteenth century to the present. Examining old advice books is very instructive: they may not tell us how to behave today, but they do shed light on shared *ideals* of domesticity that we promoted in the past. Today we have celebrity TV tie-ins such as those by UK crafter and erstwhile homefinder Kirsty Allsop and, in the United States, the apparently multitalented Martha Stewart. Outside of mainstream media, the maker movement has provided a focus for new ways of talking about domestic practices from hacking to upcycling.

Although these books are principally textual, they typically contain a valuable visual dimension as a resource for contemporary readers and retrospective readers alike. Various visual strategies are employed by domestic advice writers and graphic designers working together after the Second World War, to inform, entertain and persuade readers to adopt up-to-date and 'modern' homemaking practices and these form the focus of this chapter.

Designing domesticity: Visual techniques of persuasion

Showing more, telling more

One very straightforward way in which visual material contributes to advice books is through the provision of more information than is given in the text. This can take many forms, but to choose just one example, consider the following. Hosting domestic dinner parties without the assistance of staff is a major topic of twentieth-century domestic advice. Mary Wright and her husband, Russel Wright, a leading designer of casual mid-century modern ceramics, published their *Guide to Easier Living* in 1950, with a second edition in 1954 (Wright and Wright 1954 [1950]). In the book, the authors proclaim the social benefits of buffet suppers, as opposed to sit-down meals around a dinner table. They go further in recommending that hosts ask their guests to clear up after the meal. The textual advice is accompanied by illustrator James Kingsland's drawing of how the tradition-busting buffet supper works for home entertaining (Figure 9.1). The drawing is captioned 'The Kitchen Buffet is really cafeteria procedure. A stack of trays and tableware is laid out on the counter, and food is taken directly from the stove by the guests.' This paired-back textual description points only to the practical arrangements, but Kingsland's drawing shows guests interacting with one another as well as with the buffet meal, so that readers are *shown* the social benefits of the buffet arrangement as well as being *told* about them. This is reinforcing and more powerful than text alone.

FIGURE 9.1 *'The Kitchen Buffet'*, illustration by James Kingsland. Mary and Russel Wright, Guide to Easier Living, *New York: Simon and Schuster, 1954 (1950). Permission Russel Wright Studios CC-BY.*

Representing readers

One of the ways in which advisors and graphic designers have worked effectively to persuade their readers is by appearing to target them directly. If readers feel that they, personally, are being addressed, it is easier for them to also conclude that the advice being offered is relevant to them, and is something they should follow. This direct appeal is achieved in a number of ways, visual and textual, in advice books.

On the back cover of Sarah Maclean's *Pan Book of Etiquette and Good Manners* (1962), a photograph of a pensive woman is accompanied by a text box headed 'How often do you stop to wonder' followed by a number of questions. The juxtaposition of text and image here implies that the questions are those preying on the mind of the woman shown. The use of the word 'you' connects the woman's plight to that of the reader. In this example, then, the image becomes a representation of the reader with the effect that the questions posed are more direct and vivid. Although this is a depiction of anxiety in text and image, the questions the woman apparently asks are answered in the book, this cover implies. In this example word and image combine in an appeal to potential readers and purchasers of the book.

Book design and imagery can also function to connect with readers through the visual expression of inclusivity without text. The Good Housekeeping Institute's *Book of Good Housekeeping* of 1946 (also 1944 and 1945) makes an inclusive appeal to its readers in the endpapers used for the book by representing readers' homes. From a curvilinear modern house with horizontal fenestration and a suburban detached house to a thatched farmhouse and an Arts and Crafts style manor house, the endpapers for this advice book provide a synchronic representation of architectural heterogeneity, illustrating the variety of what home could be in 1946, and implying, therefore, that the book addresses a broad and varied readership. The endpapers are supported by the book's plates and line drawings. Readers would see in the endpapers either the house they lived in, or something like it, and/or something like the house in which they wished to live, if different from their current home. They might recognize similar homes from their neighbourhoods and from the magazines and other mediating channels they were consuming at the time of publication. Through this process of recognition, occurring at the first opening of the book with its endpapers, readers are already primed to accept the advice offered in this book before they have even read any text.

Comparisons: Good and bad, before and after

However, not all advice strategies are as inclusive as the attempts to represent and connect with the reader discussed so far. A strong theme of distinguishing between good and bad runs through the advice genre. Advisors aim to communicate taste, judgement, discernment and sensibility to

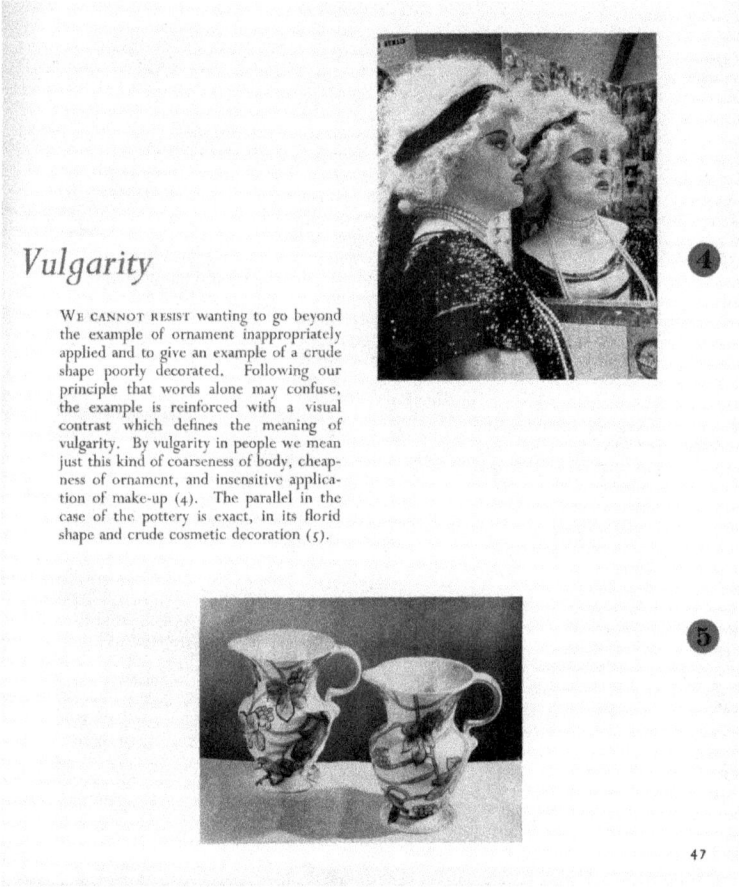

FIGURE 9.2 *'Vulgarity', portrait by John Deakin, jugs photographed by Elsie Collins, in Alan Jarvis*, The Things We See No. 1 Indoors and Out, *West Drayton, Middlesex: Penguin, 1946, 47. Permission Design Council / University of Brighton Design Archives. CC-BY.*

their readers. We see this in the government-sponsored advice of the Council of Industrial Design, later the Design Council, which aimed to educate consumers as well as designers into adopting ideals of good taste informed by the modern movement. In his book *The Things We See No. 1 Indoors and Out*, Alan Jarvis (Jarvis 1946) shows, under the heading 'Vulgarity', a portrait of a heavily made-up woman photographed by John Deakin with some jugs by Elsie Collins (Figure 9.2). Jarvis wrote 'by vulgarity we mean just this kind of coarseness of body, cheapness of ornament, and insensitive application of make-up. The parallel in the case of pottery is exact, in its florid shape and crude cosmetic decoration' (Jarvis 1946: 47). Jarvis demonstrates how visual rhetoric can communicate class and gender norms. And, he contributes to a tradition of teaching consumers to distinguish between good and bad, which extends back to nineteenth-century design reform. In *True Principles* (1841), Augustus Welby Pugin presents pointed or Gothic architecture positively as a truly indigenous English architectural style, whereas neoclassicism is critiqued as an imported Italian introduction. Jarvis, like Pugin, promotes a particular taste in design as a tool for making distinctions between people, so aesthetics are translated into class markers.

Good and bad comparisons are similar in strategy to before and after examples which also rely on visual comparison for their effectiveness. One example of this visual strategy is 'Chimneybreast before and after conversion' in Joyce Lowrie's *Practical Homemaking* (Lowrie 1965: 89). Lowrie's chimneybreast conversion removes the fireplace to create storage space, fitting for a period in which more homes adopted central heating in place of coal fires and no longer used fireplaces. This strategy was also attractive because post-war homes accommodated an unprecedented accumulation of domestic goods. Lowrie's book forms part of a wider effort to modernize Britain's Victorian housing stock after the Second World War. The appeal of this drawing is found in the viewer's satisfaction, not only at the process of modernization but also at the efficient, space-saving storage solution.

Modes of authority

The techniques domestic advisors used to persuade and inform readers can be understood with reference to founding sociologist Max Weber's identification of traditional, rational and charismatic modes of legitimation (Weber 1968: 212–45). In order to give advice, and especially published advice, an advisor needs to possess some sort of expertise – this might be a formal qualification, or it might be a body of experience on which the advisor bases her or his guidance. The basis upon which an advisor purports to offer advice is described in terms of authority. In order to be convincing, authority should be legitimated rather than simply asserted. Weber's tripartite model is usefully applied to text and image in advice discourses (Lees-Maffei 2014b: 15–31).

Traditional legitimacy

Traditional authority may be seen at work in the recycling and adaptation of images, as well as reiterated points of advice. Publisher Odhams Press used the same visual identity across genres and decades when it repurposed cover designs by illustrator Ésme (Florence Olive Ésme Eve) from *The Woman Week-End Book* numbers 1 (Woman 1950 [1949]) and 2 (Woman 1949) for the

FIGURE 9.3 *Cover, illustration by Ésme,* The Creda Housecraft Manual, *Stoke-on-Trent: Simplex Electric Co. and London: Odhams, 1958. Permission IPC Media, a Time Inc. Company. CC-BY-NC-ND. Copyright TI Media Ltd.*

FIGURE 9.4 *Cover, illustration by Ésme,* Woman Week-End Book, *London: Odhams Press, [1949] 1950. Permission IPC Media, a Time Inc. Company. CC-BY-NC-ND. Copyright TI Media Ltd.*

FIGURE 9.5 *Cover, illustration by Ésme,* Woman Week-End Book Number Two, *London: Odhams Press, 1949. Permission IPC Media, a Time Inc. Company. CC-BY-NC-ND. Copyright TI Media Ltd.*

Creda Housecraft Manual (Creda 1958) (Figures 9.3; 9.4; 9.5). While the Woman *Week-End Book*s are entertaining selections of short stories, and tips on beauty, housewifery, personal problems, cookery, knitting, and 'useful things to make', the *Creda Housecraft Manual* promotes a household appliance brand, forming an example therefore of the advertising cookbooks genre. Although the recycling of imagery may have been an expedient solution for the publisher, it also represents an instance of traditional legitimation because the 1958 book harks back to the two 1949 titles, using a visual style already associated with the advice genre.

Charismatic legitimation

Charismatic authority underpins direct personal appeals, such as advice presented in the form of a signed letter. Possessing no other qualification than being a celebrity, popular British film actress Anna Neagle (1904–86) helped to glamorize the act of baking on behalf of the Spiller's flour brand. The foreword to Spiller's advertising cookbook *How to be a Good Hostess* (Spillers 1950) engages charismatic legitimation powerfully personalized in the form of a letter, beginning 'How lovely to see you' and ending with an autograph 'Yours sincerely, Anna Neagle'. It bears comparison, therefore, with the graphic and textual techniques of the numerous film magazines of the era in its glamorous representation of a well-known actress.

While Neagle was a well-known personality, charismatic legitimacy does not rely on the personality being a real person in order to function. Published advice is sometimes given by invented authors, such as Betty Crocker. The cover for *Betty Crocker's Guide to Easy Entertaining: How to Have Guests - And Enjoy Them* (Crocker 1959) resembles needlepoint, a home craft, and the cover emphasizes traditional home comforts. A red-roofed home set in landscaped garden with a white picket fence is framed with a cartouche showing a teapot, roast turkey, leg of ham, pink iced celebration cake, and a pineapple, which is a symbol of hospitality. The cover features Crocker's 'signature', and the book has a possessive title, both further exemplifying charismatic legitimation, as well as some traditional legitimation.

Rational legitimation

Rational authority underpins the paired images of before and after comparisons, discussed above, as well as diagrammatic depictions of the organized and efficient home informed by Scientific Management in the Home, or Rational Housekeeping. In her discussion of 'Today's Kitchen', leading US etiquette writer Emily Post was influenced by Christine Frederick's application of Scientific Management to homemaking, and an emphasis on designing domestic spaces with a view to 'saving steps'. Her book *The Personality of a House* (1948 [1930]) shows a diagram by Stephen J. Voorhies of 'An Ideal Kitchen Arrangement'. Diagrams have a rational authority not found in more impressionistic illustrations because they are empirically grounded. Diagrams therefore have a special place in time-and-motion studies of the workplace and the home alike. See, for example 'Efficient grouping of kitchen equipment' (Frederick 1920: 22).

FIGURE 9.6 *Teen decorator, image 'Courtesy Dow Chemical Company', in* Teen Guide to Homemaking, *edited by Barclay, Marion Stearns and Frances Champion, New York and London: McGraw-Hill Book Company Inc., 1961, p. 205. Courtesy Dow CC-BY-NC.*

The professionalization of activities which take place within the home has extended across a range of fields from home economics to interior design (Lees-Maffei 2008). This process of professionalization is associated with rational legitimation too. The 1961 edition of the *Teen Guide to Homemaking* (Barclay and Champion 1961) shows girls designing rooms using swatches, models, paints, and so on. (Figure 9.6). They demonstrate creativity, competence and thrift by fitting a new slipcover to an old chair, and decorating a mirror frame (thereby beautifying their spaces and themselves). This book makes extensive use of formatting and layout to combine word and image in the form of text boxes, and side bars. The effect is one of ample information, communicated in clear and digestible chunks for efficient learning and revision.

From rational to fanciful: Text and subtext

As we have noted, part of the graphic designers' skillset is in bringing words and images together to form a coherent whole. This is complicated, though, not only because these two modes require wrangling into bi-modal communication through graphic design layout but also because one mode of communication may contradict the other, whether purposely, by accident or as a result of unsuccessful design.

In the main, the images in advice books reinforce the messages communicated in the texts. Illustrations are sometimes regarded as subordinate to the text which they illustrate. However, occasionally twentieth-century domestic advice features images which subvert the messages in the text, in various ways.

Romantic fantasy

One group of subversive images replaces rationality with fantasy is found in Pam Lyons' book *Today's Etiquette*. It contains a dry passage about dressing for the countryside: 'Clothes that co-ordinate to carry you through both smart and casual occasions are the order of the day' (Lyons 1967: 135). This is accompanied by Belinda Lyon's illustration of a man on horseback waving to a woman with flowing hair, holding some flowers. The line drawings do not offer enough detail to tell us much about the clothes being worn, but the woman shown in the image is not wearing smart casual garments and her setting outdoors, and the encounter with a man on horseback – a knight in shining armour – speak the language of romantic fantasy rather than work-to-evening sartorial solutions. This is not a failing of the illustrator but is rather a strategy more likely to capture the imagination and sympathy of a different reader than the conservative text would. Lyon's fashionable, informal illustrations engage readers on the younger side of the 1960s generation gap.

Futuristic fantasy

Two years later a 1969 book about *Tableware*, produced by the Design Council's Design Centre (Good 1969) shifts the emphasis from romantic fantasy to futuristic fantasy, if not science fiction. Ilana Henderson's ingenious revolving kitchen is presented as a window on a future in which householders require less storage capacity in their kitchens due to convenience foods, microwave cooking and disposable tableware. It follows Joe Columbo's Mini-kitchen for Boffi (1963) in replacing the kitchen with an object for use in any room. Henderson won a Bird's Eye/ Council of Industrial Design Award for this kitchen post. Sometimes the practical solutions for everyday life found in domestic advice books are punctuated by a fantastic or futuristic ideal.

Bad behaviour

But the ways in which images can subvert advice texts are not always fantastic. Sometimes they are all too real, more so than the ideals represented in advice books. I referred above to the worried woman depicted on the cover of Sarah Maclean's *Pan Book of Etiquette and Good Manners* (Maclean 1962) as a representative of the reader asking questions that are answered in the text, but the representation of her anxiety makes the image fairly unusual. Solutions are more usually depicted in the idealistic advice genre. An even more usual strategy, however, is the depiction of bad behaviour, not alongside good behaviour in an instance of the comparisons we looked at above, but on its own as the only visual depiction to accompany advice. This happens in Betty Allen and Mitchell Pirie Briggs' book *If You Please: A Book of Manners for Young Moderns* (1950 [1942]). Allen and Briggs' books show in the illustrations what is censured by the text. Scenes of teenagers having fun – listening to loud music, socializing without permission – carry disapproving captions. However, as with Belinda Lyon's illustrations for Pam Lyons' *Today's Etiquette* (1967) just mentioned, images of censured activity might provide the best scenarios of identification for young people, the things that they do in their social lives and want to do. These depictions of bad behaviour might function, whether purposely or unwittingly, as a subtext to gain the trust of an oppositional readership such as teenagers. Or, they might function as comic relief for more compliant readers who would benefit from the release of anxiety or embarrassment offered in this way.

Conclusion

This chapter has examined the interplay of text and image in persuasive discourses through the case study of post-war domestic advice books. Although principally textual, these advice books employ a significant range of visual techniques of persuasion. This chapter provides a brief typology of techniques to aid understanding.

At the most basic level, images are used in domestic advice books simply to provide more information than the text allows. More persuasively, authors and publishers have used text and images, and images alone, to represent the reader, whether as an individual or as a varied group. These depictions strengthen the connection between the reader and the guidance offered in advice books. At the next level, images are used comparatively to show two versions of the world, whether good and bad, or before and after. These juxtapositions enable readers to evaluate what they see and be persuaded by the evidence on the page.

The typology this chapter introduced incorporates Max Weber's tripartite model of traditional, charismatic and rational modes of authority, or legitimation. Traditional legitimation is exemplified here with the example of three books which strongly resemble one another, so that a visual language is recycled or repurposed and the newer book carries the associations of the older title. We saw two examples of charismatic legitimation, one in the form of a signed letter from a famous actress and the other in the form of an invented character who embodies a brand. Rational legitimation is discussed here through the examples of diagrams informed by the methods of scientific management and rational housekeeping, and education resources which present a professionalized image of interior design consumption.

The typology ends with instances in which images undercut, or subvert, the text that they purportedly illustrate. We considered a romantic fantasy as having very little to do with the practical advice it accompanied, and a futuristic fantasy as dispensing with the home as we know it in a radical vision that only the most fashion-forward early adopters would seriously have considered buying. Finally, we looked at an example in which the images depict bad behaviours. Although these are ostensibly cautionary depictions of what not to do, they have the potential to be viewed against the grain as a sub-textual and contradictory series of recommended behaviours, and thereby to engage an audience that would be alienated by the dominant discourse of the textual guidance, and/or to provide a friendlier form of advice with comic relief.

Persuasive discourse can take many forms. Graphic designers work with authors, illustrators and publishers to produce persuasive, informative and entertaining printed materials based on the combination of word and image. This chapter, about visual techniques of persuasion in post–Second World War domestic advice books, provides an instructive case study and the categories supplied in the brief typology can be seen at work across the print culture.

References

Allen, Betty, and Mitchell Pirie Briggs. [1942] 1950. *If You Please: A Book of Manners for Young Moderns*. Revised edition. Chicago: J. B. Lippincott Company.

Barclay, Marion Stearns, and Frances Champion (eds.) 1961. *Teen Guide to Homemaking*. New York and London: McGraw-Hill Book Company Inc.

Cantlon, Polly, and Alice Lo. 2012. 'Judging a Book by Its Cover: Or, Does Modernist Form Follow Function?' In Grace Lees-Maffei (ed.), *Writing Design: Words and Objects*, 135–47. London: Berg.

Creda. 1958. The Creda *Housecraft Manual*. Stoke-on-Trent: Simplex Electric Co. and London: Odhams.

Crocker, Betty. 1959. *Betty Crocker's Guide to Easy Entertaining: How to Have Guests - And Enjoy Them*. New York: Golden Press.

Crow, David. 2006. *Left to Right: The Cultural Shift from Words to Pictures*. Lausanne: AVA.

First Things First Manifesto 2000. 1999. *Eye* 33 (9). Available online http://www.eyemagazine.com/feature/article/first-things-first-manifesto-2000. Accessed 20 December 2017.

Frederick, Christine. 1920. *Scientific Management in the Home*. London: G. Routledge & Sons.

Good Housekeeping Institute. 1946 (1944, 1945). *Book of Good Housekeeping*. London and Chesham: Gramol Publications Ltd.

Good, Elizabeth. 1969. *Tableware: A Design Centre Publication*. London: Macdonald & Co. in association with the Council of Industrial Design.

Jarvis, Alan. 1946. *The Things We See No. 1 Indoors and Out*. West Drayton, Middlesex: Penguin.

Lees-Maffei, Grace. 2008. 'Introduction: Professionalization as a Focus in Interior Design History.' In *Professionalizing Interior Design, 1870-1970*, special issue, edited by Grace Lees-Maffei and Anne Wealleans. *Journal of Design History* 21 (1): 1–18.

Lees-Maffei, Grace. 2012. 'Introduction: Writing Design'. In Grace Lees-Maffei (ed.), *Writing Design: Words and Objects*, 1–16. London: Berg.

Lees-Maffei, Grace. 2014a. 'Designing Domesticity'. Online Image Gallery. Arts and Humanities Research Council. September. Available online at http://www.ahrc.ac.uk/research/readwatchlisten/imagegallery/2014galleries/designingdomesticity/. Accessed 8 January 2018.

Lees-Maffei, Grace. 2014b. *Design at Home: Domestic Advice Books in Britain and the USA since 1945*. Abingdon: Routledge.

Lowrie, Joyce. 1965. *Practical Homemaking*. London: Oldbourne.

Lupton, Ellen, and J. Abbott Miller. 1999. *Design Writing Research*. London: Phaidon.

Lyons, Pam. 1967. *Today's Etiquette*. London: Bancroft and Co. Ltd.

Maclean, Sarah. 1962. *Pan Book of Etiquette and Good Manners*. London: Pan.

Miller, J. Abbott. 1988. 'Tracking the Elusive Timeline'. *AIGA Journal of Graphic Design* 6 (2): 7.

Oropallo, Gabriele. 2012. 'Design as a Language without Words: A G Fronzoni'. In Grace Lees-Maffei (ed.), *Writing Design: Words and Objects*, 205–17. London: Berg.

Rock, Michael. 1996. 'The Designer as Author'. *Eye* 5 (20): 44–53. Available online at http://www.eyemagazine.com/feature/article/the-designer-as-author. Accessed 9 January 2018.

Rosenberg, Daniel, and Anthony Grafton. 2012. *Cartographies of Time: A History of the Timeline*. New York: Princeton Architectural Press.

Spillers. 1950. *How to be a Good Hostess*. London: Spillers Flour Limited.

Triggs, Teal (ed.) 1995. *Essays in Visual Communication*. London: B.T. Batsford.

Triggs, Teal. 2003. *Type Design: Radical Innovations and Experimentation*. London: Harper Design.

Triggs, Teal. 2010. *Fanzines*. London: Thames and Hudson.

Weber, Max. 1968. *Economy and Society: An Outline of Interpretative Sociology*. Edited by Guenther Roth and Claus Wittich, trans. Ephraim Fischoff et al. New York: Bedminster Press.

Woman. 1950 [1949]. Woman *Week-End Book*. London: Odhams Press.

Woman. 1949. Woman *Week-End Book Number Two*. London: Odhams Press.

Wright, Mary, and Russel Wright. 1954 [1950]. *Guide to Easier Living*. New York: Simon and Schuster.

10

Driving sales: Print and TV advertising of cars to women drivers

Grace Lees-Maffei

Graphic designers work as part of teams. They work closely with clients from manufacturers to marketing and advertising agencies, including creatives and account executives. Graphic designers need to understand how products are positioned in relation to potential markets, and how goods are presented as desirable to certain groups of consumers. This chapter looks at one example: how advertisers have tried to sell cars to women. It examines the ways in which advertisers have both represented and addressed women in the visual culture which surrounds automotive design, production, marketing or mediation and consumption or use, known as car culture. Women's influence on car purchase has long been recognized, but women have less often been recognized as drivers. Because no visual language existed through which to represent women drivers, car advertisements aimed at women have borrowed the language and imagery of fragrance and accessories advertising (Lees-Maffei 2002).

Sex sells, gender buys

In 1995, the Earls' Court Motor Show in London was promoted under the tagline 'See 500 sexy models reveal all.' Although the 'sexy models' referred to here could be of any gender, the fact that female models have traditionally been hired to host visitors to car shows means that readers of this slogan would have assumed the models were female. This slogan thereby provides a graphic reminder of the traditional role of women in car culture – as adjuncts rather than drivers. The fact that news outlets reported the retirement of so-called 'grid girls' from Formula 1 motor racing in 2018 suggests change, albeit slow change (Benson 2018). Examples abound: Stephen Bayley's 1986 essay *Sex, Drink and Fast Cars* typifies 'man's relationship' with his car as being all about power, as articulated by designers, stylists, advertising creatives and marketing professionals. For Bayley, a woman in a powerful car is 'at once titillating and de-masculating' and represents 'an overt sexual statement' (Bayley 1986: 32–3). The feeling is mutual, it seems, as shown by the female journalist who admitted: 'Men who are ambivalent about driving are not attractive to me. And it's not just me' (Cross 2000). Car culture has dramatized a polarized and stereotypical gender dynamic. And it continues. Even in 2017, Mark Walton, a contributing editor for *Car* magazine, bemoaned a 'motor show time-warp' in which car shows still feature women draped over new cars. This tactic works, but it does so by appealing to visitors' base instincts, Walton complained. For him, and not only him, this strategy is simply 'wrong in 2017' (Walton 2017). Readers' comments were supportive of Walton's position. Yet, the masculine dominance of car culture is sustained even though an increasing number of women drive and work as car journalists.

Where women have not been equated with cars as eroticized objects of desire, they have been cast by the producers of car culture as figures of influence on purchases by men. The 1920s US car producer Ned Jordan was acutely aware of the influence of women on car purchase, and the necessity of comfort, beauty and style in car design. However, Jordan also stands out as being thoroughly seduced by the ideal of an independent woman driver, as most famously exemplified in his 1920s fantasy 'Somewhere West of Laramie' (Figure 10.1). In the period between the two world wars (1919–1939), women's influence on car purchase was associated with an increasing

FIGURE 10.1 *'Somewhere West of Laramie'. Advertisement for Jordan Motor Car Company, Cleveland, Ohio. Original artwork by Fred Smith Cole, founder of the Jordan Motor Car Company. 23 June 1923. 11.5 × 8.5 inches. With permission from the Collections of The Henry Ford.*

emphasis on comfort and aesthetics. During the late 1920s and early 1930s, Harley Earl's Art and Color department at General Motors was viewed as excelling at feminized features such as style, colour and comfort. This was the case even though Earl himself was concerned to recruit only male employees in case 'any hint of femininity would handicap his struggle in the rough-and-tumble, masculine world of the automobile industry' (Gartman 1994: 87).

Concern about the corrupting influence of women consumers on the design of cars grew. Manufacturers excused model changes through reference to the influence of women upon the market. However, regular model changes were also consistent with the strategy of planned obsolescence (Packard 1960). This strategy sees manufacturers introducing subtle model changes or updates each year in order to foster a sense of distinction from one years' model to the next. This in turn breeds dissatisfaction among consumers and stimulates the market to increased purchases. Planned obsolescence thereby encourages buyers, who might otherwise have remained satisfied with their cars for a longer period of time, to make a new purchase.

In fact, the association of women with an aesthetic focus in car purchase, and as influencers in car purchase is not borne out by more recent research into women's primary concerns in purchasing cars. Qualitative consumer research has established that 'better fuel economy' is paramount for women, along with 'reliability and lower running costs'. The global recession of 2008 has been a factor in women's car purchase in the past decade, as has the 'rise in fuel prices to an all-time high in April 2010' (Mintel 2010).

Women driving

What is the reality of the role of women in car culture? Women have been driving in large numbers from the inception of widespread car use, as exemplified by the setting up of the Ladies Automobile Club of Great Britain in 1903. Women's driving in the First World War helped to dismantle stereotypical barriers (Scharff 1992). In 1933 women held 12 per cent of driving licences. In 1964, 13 per cent of all women held driving licences, compared with 56 per cent of all men. By the late 1970s, 30 per cent of all women and 68 per cent of all men were licensed to drive (O'Connell 1998: 43–8). By 1993, nearly half of driving licences were held by women, more than fourteen million in total, and more than a third of women drivers bought their own cars (Jackson 1993: vii). In the United Kingdom, the proportion of men passing their driving tests was higher for males each year from 1988 to 1998. However, the number of women passing their tests was higher each year in this period also. Therefore, and significantly, many more driving tests were taken by women than men in the decade from 1988 to 1998 and the number of licensed women drivers increased more quickly than the figure for men in the final decade of the twentieth century (Department of Environment, Transport and the Regions 1999: 'Private Motoring: Driving Tests, 1988-1998', Table 3.16). In 2015/16 women achieved a 44 per cent pass rate in their driving tests while men passed 51 per cent of their tests (Department for Transport 2016: 26), a comparable figure.

In the early phase of private car use, it was assumed in cases of joint ownership of one family car, that the male partner usually had the primary claim on the car. However, since then the number of cars owned by households has increased. In 1951, 13 per cent of households owned one car, and 1 per cent of households owned two. By 1986, 17 per cent of households owned two cars, whereas by 1996 this figure had increased to 23 per cent. Households with three or more cars increased from 3 per cent in 1986 to 5 per cent in 1996 (Department of Environment, Transport and the Regions 1999: 'Households with regular use of car(s): 1951–1998', Table 9.2; 'Private Motoring: households with regular use of cars', Table 3.14). By 1999/2000 42 per cent of cars were bought by women, and 80 per cent of car purchases involved a woman's input (Mintel 2000; Hacker and Cutler 2000; Coward 1999). In 2015, statistics for men and women's car use were largely similar. Men of all ages drove an average of 409 trips, while for women the figure was 353, although women made more trips as car passengers than men, and men drove longer distances (Table TSGB1113 (NTS0601), 'Average number of trips (trip rates) by age, gender and main mode, England: 2015' Department for Transport 2016: 315). In 2015, 80 per cent of men held driving licences (17.1 million men) and 68 per cent of women (15.1 million women) (Table TSGB0915 (NTS0201), 'Full car driving licence holders by age and gender, England: 1975/76 to 2015' Department for Transport 2016: 282).

Car advertisers have assumed that while men used their cars for work activities, women drive for leisure. However, once again there was a fault line between representation and reality at the turn of the millennium. For the period 1996–8, British men made more journeys for the purposes of commuting, business, education and leisure than women, who made more school runs and shopping journeys than men. However, at that time, approximately 20 per cent of school runs were followed by a journey to work (Number of Journeys by purpose and sex, 1996/98' Table 1.7, Dickson 2000: 47). So-called 'escort education' journeys increased from 3.2 per cent of all journeys in 1985/86 to 4.8 per cent in 1996/98, accounting for 3 per cent of journeys made by men, and 7 per cent of those made by women. Clearly, women have driven cars to help them combine work and childcare (Moorhead 1999). Therefore, the assumption that cars are leisure objects for women is erroneous, and trivializes the empowerment women have found, both personally and professionally, behind the wheel.

The facts about the influence women have on car-purchasing decisions, their own car purchases and the extent of their driving, seem not to have been fully recognized by the automotive industry. In 2010, market researchers Mintel reported on the basis of qualitative consumer research that:

> one of the most significant changes in UK society since the 1950s has been the growing independence of women and their diminishing reliance upon men for their economic welfare. … As a result, car usage among women rose as they sought independent transport of their own. Although more men than women are currently responsible for looking after a car, the proportion of women who are responsible for looking after a car has risen.

Indeed, 'over the period 2004–09, ownership of one car grew faster among women than among men'. It began rising in 2006 with a dip in 2008 for the recession and has continued since then. Yet, the report goes on, 'the automotive industry and its retail trade is still male-oriented, with insufficient consideration given to the different needs of a female car buyer and car user compared to her male counterpart' (Mintel 2010).

Representations of women drivers

So, women are not only influential on car purchases made by men. They (we) have been driving in increasing numbers, relying on cars to perform our various work and family roles, and buying more cars to the extent that we represent nearly half of all car purchasers. Little of this has altered the representation of women in car culture. Sean O'Connell points out that 'despite growing evidence of female competence at the wheel, the myth of greater masculine ability was not allowed to die' (O'Connell 1998: 59). In May 1987, *Your Car*'s regular day-in-the life column featured a driving instructor whose tutees are exclusively women described as lacking in confidence and competence ('An L of a Living' 1987: 66–7). These isolated examples are not drawn from a rich variety of representations of women in *Your Car*: women are absent from this publication to an astonishing extent. Two years later, *Your Car* offered a 'Reader's Lives' account of a mother's mismanagement of her car illustrated with a cartoon captioned 'Honest Mum – I was laughing with you, not at you' ('Reader's Lives' 1989: 11). The popularity of this strain of humour led Roy Bolitho, for example, to write *Woman at the Wheel*, a compendium of jokes about women's driving incompetence (Bolitho 1985).

The 1999 Road Survey Monitor for Northern Ireland provides interesting evidence of the mythical nature of man's greater driving competence. It reported that of the 75 per cent of men and 55 per cent of women who drove, 53 per cent of men and 37 per cent of women described themselves as 'well above' or 'above' average in their driving skills (Department of the Environment Central Statistics and Research Branch 1999). However, the greater confidence of male drivers in Northern Ireland, for example, is not explained by their success in driving tests. Sixty-one per cent of men passed their driving tests in the fourth quarter of 1996, as compared with 52 per cent of women. However, in the same period, 72 per cent of women passed the driving theory tests as opposed to 63 per cent of men (Department of the Environment (NI) Northern Ireland Information Service 1997).

A debate continues nevertheless about whether women or men are better drivers. The Transport Research Institute, the Automobile Association (AA) and the Royal Automobile Club (RAC) have publicized reports confirming that women drivers are 'safer and more skilful than their male counterparts'. Such statistics are countered by critics who claim that men do more driving, and are therefore more likely to become involved in an accident (Spinney 2000). Elsewhere biological explanations have been offered to 'prove' women's lesser competence, such as the fact that the part of the brain used for visualizing objects in three dimensions, estimating time and judging speed is smaller in women than in men (Hawkes 1999). Women's lack of confidence as drivers is exemplified by road-users' support projects such as the one set up by Devon County Council, which was attended almost entirely by women (Dodd 2000). Such a lack of confidence is unfounded, however, so much so that insurance companies routinely offered advantageous deals for women up to 2012, when the European Court of Justice (ECJ) ruled that insurers must not offer different prices for male and female drivers. Yet, recently the Automobile Association has noted that while 'male and female drivers can expect the same premium if all other elements of the quote are identical (car, mileage, occupation, address, driving record)', men are given higher insurance quotations than women 'due to other factors. Thus, according to the Index, men aged 17–22 can expect to pay £280 more than women in the same age group' (AA 2017: 4).

An extension of the support groups mentioned above, guidebooks published to support and advise car owners address the experience of women in a variety of ways. The first example, Dorothy Levitt's *The Woman and the* Car of 1909, advises on suitable dress and the need to carry a gun (indicative of the book's North American provenance). In 1915, etiquette writer Emily Post took a chauffeur-driven road trip from New York to California, and wrote about it for *Collier's Magazine* and as a book (Post 2004 (1916)). The articles and book were explicitly advisory in content. Later in the century, Longman's *Cars: A Consumer's Guide* of 1987 is trenchantly gender-neutral. It replicates the male-oriented nature of much car culture in that of nine case studies of car purchase and repair problems, only one mentions a woman, in a discussion of the legal intricacies of joint ownership. Among the aspects of car ownership and maintenance examined in this book are the experiences of those readers who feel marginal to car culture: 'Many people "switch off" when technical terminology is used – especially if they are unable to visualise "big ends" or "crankshafts" and understand their functions' (King 1987: 1). Although feeling out of depth technically is an issue common to the genders, women seeking car maintenance services have been regarded as technically incompetent and have been overcharged by mechanics in 80 per cent of cases (Agace 1995: 51–2).

By 1993 Judith Jackson's *Every Woman's Guide to the Car*, published by the pioneering feminist UK imprint Virago, discussed car retailing as an issue for woman drivers: 'Although the market recognises the rapidly growing numbers of female buyers, sadly, there are still dealers who regard solo woman customers as insignificant' (Jackson 1993: 9). By 2000, the situation was only marginally improved. Only 30 per cent of car sales staff were female and 80 per cent of women took a male companion with them when buying a car for a confidence boost, even though women bought almost half of cars at that time (Hacker and Cutler 2000). One solution suggested is the online sale of cars (Freeman 2000). However, although car buyers are increasingly happy to do their research online, as late as 2010 they remained largely unwilling to purchase cars online (Mintel 2010). By 2014, the newest trend in car retailing was a move from out-of-town dealerships to shopping centre showrooms, for Hyundai, Tesla and Seat for example (Sharman 2014) and towards a greater emphasis on retail experience in the existing dealerships. It is not easy to predict the impact this will have on female purchasers specifically.

Car design

One possible explanation for the lack of confidence felt by women in the driving seat might have to do with the sort of seat it is. Both men and women may experience discomfort from car design that is geared towards the 'international standards' of body shape and size formed by the Society of Automotive Engineers (Birch 2000a). Seat design has traditionally been aesthetically rather than ergonomically oriented, compounded by the fact that more than one-third of men drive with their legs extended and almost one-third of women sit too close to their steering wheels (Birch 2000b). But women experience additional, specific problems with car design. A 2000 article on women's seatbelt discomfort noted that while women buy around half of cars sold, their needs remain neglected in automotive design as shown by a seatbelt manufacturer's admission that the company's research and development has never entailed asking women about their experiences of car design (Langley 2000).

Part of the problem might be seen to be the lack of women involved in automotive design and engineering. Journalist Lesley Hazleton described Detroit designers working with 'paper clips taped to their fingers so that they'd know how it feels to open a car door when you have long nails' Hazleton 1999). In 1999, of the 8,500 members of Retail Motor Industry Training (ReMIT) only 5 per cent were women, and this was an improvement on previous years ('Have you the Drive to be an Engineer?' 1999). Ford set up a 'women's marketing panel' comprising female employees who suggested larger and simpler dashboard controls and tailgate handles. Japanese manufacturers have been quicker than US or UK car manufacturers to provide the compact cars women desired. Cars marketed at women drivers have included the Honda Logo, Nissan's Micra, the Seat Leon, the Twingo, Ford's Ka, the Yaris, the Matiz and the VW Lupo (Hacker 2000; Sawyer 2000; Wark 1999). Ford has sought to recruit more women into its design and engineering departments (Coward 1999). This activity is a necessary corrective to the association of men with technological know-how (Oldenziel 1999). Since the period of analysis in this chapter, though, women have become more prominent in the car industry. In 2009, BMW launched its Z4 model, designed by Juliane Blasi and Nadya Armaout. Mary Barra is the first woman to work as CEO of a global car manufacturer; she has been chairman and CEO of General Motors since 2014. It seems plausible to suggest that women will continue to make inroads into the car industry and that car culture may, eventually, become less masculine.

Gender bending/genre bending: Advertising cars to women

It is not only design that needs to take on board the issues particular to women if manufacturers are to fully realize that sector of the market: marketing, too, needs to address women purchasers. The advertising of cars has been as important to the continuation of the industry as stylistic and technical innovations. Cars are durable and purchasing a car is therefore something that can be postponed, for as long as one's current car remains roadworthy, as noted above in relation to planned obsolescence (Jones and Prais 1978 in Tomlinson 1999: 24). By the early 1970s the world market for cars had reached saturation point (Flink 1975: 211). Car advertisers have employed a range of co-existent approaches in order to stimulate the market. In the early twentieth century, car advertising was dominated by technical information, but in the 1920s a shift towards 'evocations of consumer desires for modernity, status, and autonomy' was recognized (Gartman 1994: 23, 42). Subsequently, the history of car advertising has ranged 'from plutocratic to sexual display, through environmental concern to latter-day technophilia' (Bayley 1986: 101).

The amount of money spent on car advertising is relatively enormous. In 1995, '46 car manufacturers spent pounds 500 million on 487 campaigns. They parked their advertisements on 15,830 press pages and motor-mouthed their way through about 3,000 radio ads. Their use of TV accelerated to the extent that, on average, people in the UK watched 702 car commercials last year – almost two a day' (Dwek 1996). Ford Fiesta alone was advertised more extensively than Kellog's Cornflakes and Guinness. In the same year, 'the average car manufacturer spent pounds 425 on advertising for every car it sold. The biggest spender, Alfa Romeo, splashed out pounds 1,600 per car' (Dwek 1996). Ten years later, in the United States, in 2005 car manufacturers spent an average of $630 on advertising per car, while luxury brand Aston Martin spent $3,698 for each car (Lutz and Lutz-Fernandez 2010).

But, does all this spending create an excellent product? Motoring journalist Penny Wark did not think so. Wark noted at the turn of the millennium:

> It is true that there are now several cars on the market that are designed specifically and accurately for women. But many men in the industry have yet to work out how to pitch them without resorting to "nippy runaround" and "women's car" cliches, which they whisper but never include in brochures or press releases because they are terrified of being politically incorrect. (Wark 1999)

Since the last decade of the twentieth century, advertisements aimed at women drivers have featured aspirational figures such as powerful career women, efficient mothers, women with desirable lovers and so on which simultaneously appeal to men and to women. One such example is provided by Renault's 'Nicole-Papa' campaign, which boosted sales to women to the extent that the Renault Clio was bought by men and women in equal numbers (Agace 1995: 51) (Figure 10.2). In a series of narrative television advertisements, a young woman expresses increasing independence from her father. Father and daughter engage in playful deceptions which communicate a British notion of French sophistication. This trope of French car, British designers and British market was again overlaid onto a relationship between a man and a woman in the 2005 'Twice the Va Va

FIGURE 10.2 *Renault 'Nicole-Papa' campaign for the Clio car ran for seven years from 1991. Image Courtesy of the Advertising Archive.*

Voom' campaign which followed the Va Va Voom campaign starring French footballer Thierry Henri, famous in the United Kingdom as a player for Arsenal football team (Jobling 2011). These narrative advertisements have the capacity to point obliquely both to technical advancements in Renault's car design, and to differences of national identity, within the context of a saga about the battle of the sexes that has as much in common with the soap opera genre as it does with the automotive industry's performance specifications.

Cars advertised as accessories

One significant recent trend in car advertising has been the promotion of them as fashionable accessories. Such an association is not exclusive to cars, however. Other technological products have been presented as fashion accessories, such as the Canon Ixus camera, which was advertised as jewellery (Figure 10.3). This approach may be seen as an attempt to make technology

FIGURE 10.3 *Advertisement for Canon Ixus, Permission from Canon, UK.*

accessible and appealing through recourse to familiar forms (for more on the market introduction of new technologies see, for example Forty 1986). In addition, such a technique implies the extent to which one's technological choices enhance personal identity and become, in a necessary corruption of McLuhan's dictum, an 'extension of woman' (McLuhan 1994). This approach is not new. In 1961 Volkswagen used miniaturization to advertise the Beetle. An image of a woman holding a toy model of a car has the strapline 'Your Car Madam' and the same copy accompanies a contemporaneous ad showing a VW seen through a foreground handbag handle and a gloved hand (Young 1993: 44, 32). Scale here is manipulated to connect the car with the woman's glove and handbag, thereby presenting the car as another of her personal accessories (Figure 10.4).

In 1993, Volkswagen ran a print advertisement with the strapline 'Discover the fragrance of Umwelt. By Volkswagen' (Figure 10.5). The closing line of text 'For man. For woman' recalls, however, the unisex fragrance CK One by Calvin Klein which offered a minimalist aesthetic at odds with the rococo extravagance depicted in this image of a man and woman in evening dress kissing on the bonnet of the car against a night cityscape. So while the text connects the ad to a particular

FIGURE 10.4 *'Your Car Madam'. Advertisement for Volkswagen Beetle. 1961. Permission from adam&eveDBD.*

FIGURE 10.5 *'Discover the fragrance of Umwelt by Volkswagen'. Appeared in* The Tatler *magazine, April 1993. Photography and permission Chris Simpson.*

fragrance campaign, the image and text combine to refer in general to the genre of fragrance advertising. The extended metaphor of this ad is continued in the provision of a piece of folded paper with the instruction 'open fold to experience umwelt' which recalls the samples of perfume offered in women's magazines. This ad appeared in magazines alongside genuine examples of the perfume advertisements it imitates. The intention here is that there is no scent to be discerned because, as the copy informs us, the Umwelt features a 'turbo charger for less smoke' and a 'catalytic converter for less toxic gases' to create 'a fragrance so subtle you'd wonder if it was there at all.' So while this ad aims to communicate technical information, it does so through the language and imagery of fragrance advertising, an essentially feminized sphere of visual culture. The fact that no fragrance is available here presents a humorous critique of the hype of fragrance advertising, on one level. More insidiously, though, it seeks to dissociate cars from pollution. When viewed in retrospect, following the VW emissions test scandal (Vizard 2016), the strategy adopted in this ad is cynical rather than romantic.

Peugeot has exploited the association of sex and cars more recently in a bid to meet and enhance the already buoyant female market for their cars. By 1995, women bought 60 per cent of Peugeot's new cars (Agace 1995: 51). Euro RSCG Wnek Gosper's television campaign for the Peugeot 106 featured a pastiche of the final scene from Ridley Scott's 1991 road movie, *Thelma and Louise*, itself a corruption of cinematic conventions of gender and genre (Hall 1997). The 1997 print campaign for the 106 Independence also worked with gender subversion to achieve its aim. A Peugeot 106 advertisement shows a car transfer tattooed onto a woman's hip under the words

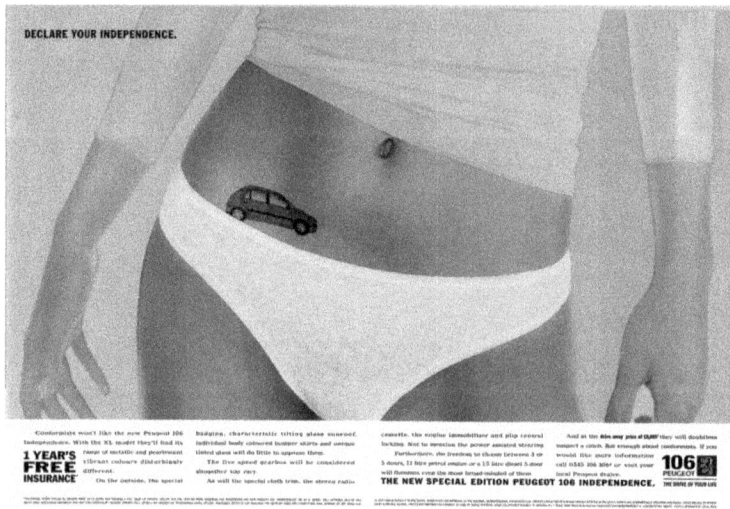

FIGURE 10.6 *'Tattoo' Peugeot 106 Independence advertisement, published as a centrefold in* The Observer, *June 1997. Part of a campaign for the 106, 206 and 306 initiated in 1993 to target women. Photo Peugeot / Euro RSCG Wnek Gosper. Photography and permission by Nadav Kander.*

'Declare your independence' (Figure 10.6). The imperative language is a call to arms that recalls discussions of the importance of cars for a sense of personal freedom, for both men and women. Judy Wajcman asserts that women's relation to cars depends on the practical issues of safety, mobility and independence (Wajcman 1991: 135). Penny Sparke is just one design historian to have noted the 'desire, narcissism, envy and a quest for self-identification' mobilized by cars for both men and women (Coward 1999). In 1999, Bayley rephrased his understanding of the meaning of cars echoing Wajcman's feminist analysis: 'The real emotional pull of the car is not sex, or social status, or all those things that we associate with car lovers – it is that the motor car gives you the sense that you are a free person' ('A classic of modern design' 1999).

The woman in the Peugeot tattoo ad is depicted without legs, in the manner of classical voyeuristic imagery from the history of art and – particularly as the image is spread across two pages in close-up – pornography. The woman is stripped down to her underwear, and displays to the viewer a personal physical feature suggestive of sexual proffering and intimacy. She remains anonymous in that we cannot see her face. Her mobility comes, it is implied, from the car she drives, but she has no car, only the image of one in the form of bodily ornament. She declares her independence by wearing a tattoo. While tattoos are intricately bound up with the expression of personal identity, historically of a tribal or sub-cultural nature, they are increasingly employed in the West as just another bodily adornment. Furthermore, the Peugeot woman is decorated not with jewellery or (as far as we can see) with make-up, but rather with a tattoo which would imply a permanent commitment to the car, if it were not a printed transfer. James Flink points out that the cosmetics and car industries are united by the fact that both insist on achieving unusually high profits (Flink 1975: 201). The conservatism of the ad is reflected in the text which, although beginning with 'Conformists won't like the new Peugeot 106 Independence', continues in a manner conforming to gender stereotypes by referring to the 'range of metallic and pearlescent colours', 'special badging', 'body coloured bumper skirts' and 'cloth trim'. Technical aspects mentioned include a 'racy' gearbox, stereo radio, central locking and power-assisted steering. This image, then, while superficially offering something of a challenge to the traditionally masculine emphasis of car culture, is found on closer inspection to echo the imagery and assumptions of traditional male-stream car culture.

Another attempt to communicate female power in a car advertisement is found in a Peugeot image of the 106 logotype shaved into a woman's hair (Figure 10.7). Like the tattoo ad, this example straddles both stereotypical and subversive approaches to the business of advertising cars to women. It carries identical copy to the tattoo image. Again, the shaved motif functions as a decorative expression of the woman's identity through the act of label-display and its associations of brand allegiance, like branded sportswear. However, for a woman to shave her head remains an act of visible rejection of the normative ideal of femininity. Both the haircut and the motif shaved into it associate the product with the masculine imagery of sub-cultural street style, behind which lie a raft of subtler contradictory references with pop cultural, racist, homoerotic and military nuances. All of these associations garner masculine power for the woman who presents herself in this manner.

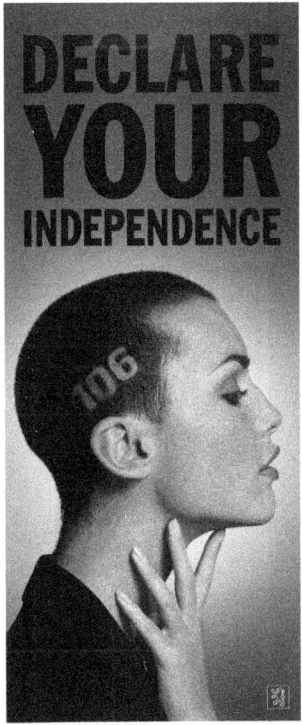

FIGURE 10.7 *'Shaved' Peugeot 106 Independence advertisement poster. This also appeared in a two-page format in magazines and newspapers including* The Guardian, *July 1997. Photo Peugeot / Euro RSCG Wnek Gosper. Photography and permission by Nadav Kandar.*

The two Peugeot 106 advertisements are interesting for the way in which they negotiate feminine stereotypes. On the one hand, these advertisements offer a new visual language, which places women in a position of power, as exemplified by the name '106 Independence'. On the other hand, the name belies the timeworn association of women with an ideal of femininity reminiscent of the sexualized women of extant car culture who function to titillate male viewers. These advertisements exemplify the traditional association of women with fashionability, vanity and a concern for aesthetics and in this case the emphasis on automotive aesthetics subsumes a concern for technical specification.

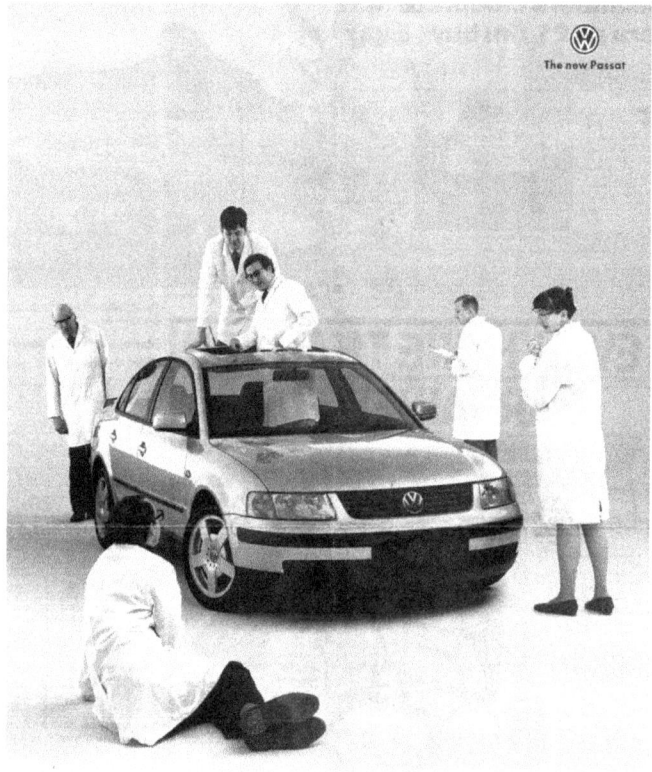

FIGURE 10.8 *'Obsession from Laboratoires Volkswagen'. Advertisement for The New Passat, Volkswagen. Printed in* The Guardian, *April 1997. This image mixes references to fragrance (Calvin Klein's Obsession) with shampoo (from Laboratoires Garnier) with stereotypes of German technical excellence. Photography and permission by Chris Simpson.*

In 1997, Volkswagen advertised its new Passat with the line 'Obsession from Laboratoires Volkswagen' (Figure 10.8). The text continues, 'The look of it. The feel of it. The fully galvanised body of it'. The word 'obsession', the typeface and washed-out, monochromatic image specifically recall advertisements for Calvin Klein fragrances. But another reference is made this time to Laboratoires Garnier. Obsession, unlike the unisex CK One, is sold separately for men and for women. This advertisement features five men and one woman in white coats attending to the car, suggesting that the advertisement intends to target a mixed audience, an assumption supported by the appearance of the ad in a national daily newspaper rather than a women's magazine. The mixed audience is consistent with Klein's unisex fragrances, including CK One. This advertisement reveals the narcissistic relation some consumers have with their cars, and the borrowed imagery, recalling a leading fashion company, suggests an emphasis upon the design values of the Volkswagen. This text references two distinctly recognizable beauty products, but the image, by featuring mainly males, appeals to a mixed audience.

Conclusion

This chapter has examined some advertising strategies adopted by car producers at the end of the twentieth century and the beginning of the twenty-first century to attract women purchasers. The advertisements discussed here represent a concerted effort on the part of car producers, via advertising and marketing professionals, to address the female sector of the car market. This is achieved through recourse to the language and imagery of fashion and beauty, realms associated with women. These advertisements subvert conventions of both gender and genre, thereby appealing to a knowing awareness in the target audience. However, such advertisements are only partly progressive. It appears that a transitional stage in the advertising of cars to women was occupied at this time, reflective of an ambiguous relation to stereotypes. References in car advertisements to unrelated women-centred areas of consumption such as fashion, fragrance and cosmetics are specific to a stage in which the traditional, sexualized, car culture had not yet thoroughly incorporated female consumers and necessarily referred instead to another feminized market sector. However, while advertisements are key tools for the enforcement of stereotype, they can also help to dismantle them.

References

'A Classic of Modern Design'. 1999. *The Guardian*. 17 July.
AA. 2017. *AA British Insurance Premium Index – 2017 quarter 2*. 24 July.
Agace, Melanie. 1995. 'Not Just a Pretty Bonnet'. *Vogue* (UK). November: 51–2.
'An L of a Living'. 1987. *Your Car*. May: 66–7.
Bayley, Stephen. 1986. *Sex, Drink and Fast Cars: The Creation and Consumption of Images*. London: Faber.
Benson, Andrew. 2018. Formula 1: 'Grid Girls' Will Not Be Used at Races This Season'. *BBC Sport*. 31 January. Online at http://www.bbc.co.uk/sport/formula1/42890261. Accessed 29 March 2018.
Birch, Stuart. 2000a. 'Are You the Wrong Shape for Your Car?'. *The Times*. 12 February.

Birch, S. 2000b. 'Why Car Seats Can Be Such a Pain in the Back'. *The Times*. 6 May.
Bolitho, Roy. 1985. *Women at the Wheel: A National Menace?* London: Futura Publications.
Coward, Ros. 1999. 'Into the Driving Seat'. *The Guardian*. 16 November: n.p.
Cross, Lucy. 2000. 'Driving Miss Crazy'. *The Guardian*. 28 February: n.p.
Department for Transport. 2016. *Transport Statistics Great Britain 2016*. December. London: Crown Copyright.
Department of the Environment Central Statistics and Research Branch. 1999. *Northern Ireland Road Safety Monitor*.
Department of the Environment (NI) Northern Ireland Information Service. 1997. 'Women Drivers are Better than Men – In Theory'. *Road Transport Statistics Bulletin*. 10 April.
Department of Environment, Transport and the Regions. 1999. *Transport Statistics Great Britain: 1999 Edition*. London: HMSO.
Dickson, M. 2000. 'Characteristics of the Escort Education Journey'. *Transport Trends 2000*. London: Department for Transport National Statistics.
Dodd, Celia. 2000. 'Wheel Thing: New Research Reveals Why Some Women Become Wimps in the Driving Seat – and Men Are to Blame'. *The Guardian*. 25 May.
Dwek, Robert. 1996. Are Car Advertisers Wasting Money? *Campaign*. 10 May. http://www.campaignlive.co.uk/article/car-advertisers-wasting-money/21528. Accessed 19 September 2017.
Flink, James. 1975. *The Car Culture*. Cambridge, MA: MIT Press.
Forty, Adrian. 1986. *Objects of Desire: Design and Society since 1750*. London: Thames and Hudson.
Freeman, Vaughan. 2000. 'Buy a New Car with your Baked Beans and Bleach'. *The Times*. 2 September.
Gartman, David. 1994. *Auto Opium: A Social History of American Automobile Design*. London: Routledge.
Hacker, Simon. 2000. 'Road Test Honda Logo and HR-V'. *The Guardian*. 1 May.
Hacker, Simon, and Sarah Cutler. 2000. 'The Price for You Madam'. *The Guardian*. 3 April: n.p.
Hall, Emma. 1997. 'Peugeot Unveils Latest 106 Execution'. *Campaign*. 30 May. http://www.campaignlive.co.uk/article/peugeot-unveils-latest-106-execution/30003. Accessed 19 September 2017.
'Have You the Drive To Be an Engineer?'. 1999. *The Guardian*. 16 October.
Hawkes, Nigel. 1999. 'Size Matters with Males Brain Lobe'. *The Times*. 11 December.
Hazleton, Lesley. 1999. 'Sex Drive'. *The Guardian*. 20 September.
Jackson, Judith. 1993. *Every Woman's Guide to the Car*. London: Virago.
Jobling, Paul. 2011. '"Twice the va va voom?": Transitivity, Stereotyping and Differentiation in British Advertising for Renault Clio III'. *Visual Studies* 26 (3): 244–59.
Jones, D., and S. Prais. 1978. 'Plant Size and Productivity in the Motor Industry: Some International Comparisons'. *Oxford Bulletin of Economics and Statistics* 40: 131–52.
King, Judith. 1987. *Cars: A Consumer's Guide*. Harlow: Longman.
Langley, Sophie. 2000. 'Designers Don't Care That Seatbelts Can Be a Sore Point for Women'. *The Times*. 12 February.
Lees-Maffei, G. 2002. 'Men, Motors, Markets and Women'. In Peter Wollen and Joe Kerr (eds.), *Autopia: Cars and Culture*, 363–70. London: Reaktion.
Lutz, Catherine, and Anne Lutz Fernandez. 2010. *Carjacked: The Culture of the Automobile and Its Effect on Our Lives*. London: Palgrave Macmillan.
McLuhan, Marshall. 1994. *Understanding Media: The Extensions of Man*. Cambridge, MA and London: MIT Press.
Mintel. 2000. 'Car Retailing'. March.
Mintel. 2010. 'Female Motorist (The)'. UK. May.
Moorhead, Joanna. 1999. 'Take a Walk on the Wild Side'. *The Guardian*. 30 June.
O'Connell, Sean. 1998. *The Car in British Society: Class, Gender and Motoring, 1896–1939*. Manchester: Manchester University Press.

Oldenziel, Ruth. 1999. *Making Technology Masculine: Men, Women and Modern Machines in America 1870–1945*. Amsterdam: Amsterdam University Press.

Packard, Vance. 1960. *The Waste Makers*. New York: David McKay Company, Inc.

Post, Emily. 2004 (1916). *By Motor to the Golden Gate*. Jefferson, NC: McFarland & Company.

'Reader's Lives'. 1989. *Your Car*. September: 11.

Sawyer, Miranda. 2000. 'Spanish Flyer'. *The Observer*. 11 June.

Scharff, Virginia. 1992. *Taking the Wheel: Women and the Coming of the Motor Age*. Albuquerque: University of New Mexico Press.

Sharman, Andy. 2014. 'Carmakers Chase Consumers into Shops and Online in Sales Drive' *Financial Times*. 26 October. https://www.ft.com/content/21b9c420-5b6d-11e4-b68a-00144feab7de. Accessed 15 September 2017.

Spinney, Laura. 2000. 'Once a Boy Racer…'. *The Guardian*. 14 February.

Tomlinson, Jim. 1999. 'The Government and the Car Industry 1945–1970'. *The Journal of Transport History* 20 (1): 17–29.

Vizard, Sara. 2016. 'Volkswagen Brand on Road to Recovery as it Launches First Campaign Since Emissions Scandal'. *Marketing Week*. 5 February. https://www.marketingweek.com/2016/02/05/volkswagen-brand-on-road-to-recovery-as-it-launches-first-campaign-since-emissions-scandal/. Accessed 19 September 2017.

Wajcman, Judy. 1991. *Feminism Confronts Technology*. Cambridge: Polity Press.

Walton, Mark. 2017. 'Motor Show Time-warp: Why Draping Women over New Cars Is Wrong in 2017'. www.carmagazine.co.uk. 6 June. http://www.carmagazine.co.uk/features/opinion/mark-walton/women-on-cars-at-motor-shows/. Accessed 13 September 2017.

Wark, Penny. 1999. 'Why Women Want Something Different'. *The Times*. 22 October.

Young, Daniel. 1993. *Advertising the Beetle 1953–1978*. London: Yesteryear Books.

11

Picturing music: The rise and fall of music packaging

Nicolas P. Maffei

The album cover has been almost entirely neglected as an area of academic study, and has been relegated to a profusion of uncritical coffee table books. In addition to its aesthetic appeal the album cover serves functional, economic, psychological and social roles: it protects the disc, advertises the recording, accompanies the music and finally, as a designed commodity, it is bought, collected and displayed (Inglis 2001: 84), thus aiding the development and expression of consumer identity. Despite being an aural medium, music is marketed through its visual and physical appeal. When Johnny Rotten of the Sex Pistols proclaimed, 'if people bought the records for the music, this thing would have died a death long ago' (Dean and Howells 1982: 23), he may have been referring to the album cover as a prop for identity formation and communication, shaping individuals internally and externally, psychologically and socially. On the one hand, 12-inch record sleeves provided canvasses for designers through which they primed listeners with messages about the music. On the other hand, their display, whether in bedrooms or front rooms, in crates or on shelves, communicated individual identity and group belonging.

This chapter concentrates on the 12-inch, long playing (LP) record, and it considers the development of smaller sized formats, including cassettes and compact disc (CDs) and the place of music packaging in the digital era (with the introduction of iTunes) where music packaging has been reduced to thumb nail icons on computer screens and mobile devices. Has music packaging today been transformed from physical engagement with record covers, sleeves and inserts to a series of screen taps and swipes: an ergonomic experience with minimal visual reference to the artists? What is gained and lost in this shift, both specifically in design terms and more broadly in terms of identity formation and social communication?

Focusing in particular on the relationship between the cover image and music this chapter first considers the fundamental qualities of the album cover. What makes it unique as an object? It then explores the evolution of music packaging beginning with its earliest history. The chapter provides a series of methodological approaches – from gender analysis to art historical visual interpretation. A range of issues, including the manufacture or national identity (the English Folk

Revival 1960s/70s) and representation of women (female singers of the 1970s) are reviewed. A historic overview of one group's album covers (the Beatles) observes their transformation from stereotype to innovative individuality. The physical collecting of albums is explored as a profound psychological and social activity, while an investigation of the digital music commodity – the MP3 file, the iTunes single, and so on – questions its ability to meet the needs of identity development and individual expression.

The essence of music packaging: Reuniting sound with image and object

The historian Kevin Edge has observed how prosaic music packaging turns immaterial and temporary sound into a concrete and symbolic consumer good. Album covers mark the physical presence of recorded sound with ink and paper and communicate the character of performers and the content of performances. Through this transformation the ephemeral becomes concrete and music is transformed into a saleable commodity (Edge 1991: 3). Arguably, the fusion of time-based, recorded music and static image makes the album cover a unique form of packaging, a point developed in *Coverscaping,* an academic study of album aesthetics edited by Øvind Vågnes and Asbjorn Gronstad (2008). They warn that studying the album cover as an independent art form may be impossible as music packaging is always inseparable from the music it contains (10). Thus, the album cover must be considered a kind of paratext, a term coined by the literary theorist Gérard Genette (1997), which in the context of a book can include everything that supports the main text: illustrations, the preface and even the author's name. Therefore, a text, whether a novel or a piece of music cannot be fully understood without considering these accompanying elements including cover art, inner sleeves, inserts, and so on.

The tension between sound and materiality at the heart of the album cover is explored by Corbett, a theoretically inclined music scholar who argues that throughout its history the music industry has been focused on 'over-coming the all-sonic recorded music object'. Corbett notes that as a result the 'graphic accompaniment' to recorded music commodities has become increasingly 'sophisticated' and the album cover has taken on a pivotal role in 'binding' 'aural/visual disarticulation' (Corbett 1990: 86), a disconnected relationship between sound and image at the heart of the album cover. The various visual and material strategies – whether colourful design or artist portraits, gatefolds or inner sleeves – have become an essential aspect of the music commodity. The centrality of design in music packaging can be interpreted as an attempt not merely to illustrate sound but, more fundamentally, to reinvest the aural with the visual and material. The picture disc where 'the visual is inscribed directly upon the surface of that which produces its absence' perhaps most explicitly represents the attempt to literally reunite the visual, aural (Corbett 1990: 86) and the material.

Combining Marxist and psychoanalytic theory, Corbett argues that desire is generated by the 'audio/visual tension' of the album cover, the purchase of which typifies the mechanics of capitalism. To illustrate his point Corbett cites W. F. Haug, the Marxist philosopher of commodification, who describes the process of purchasing the sexually provocative *Sticky Fingers* album designed by

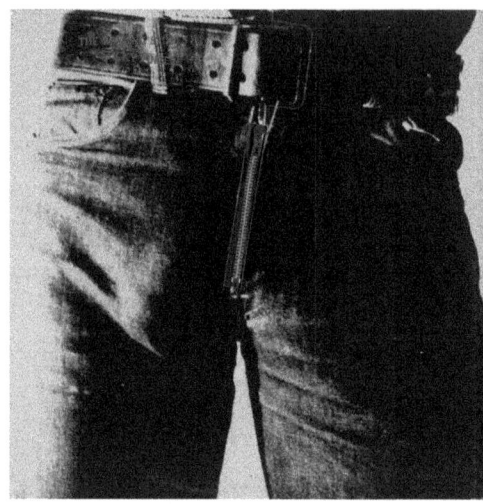

FIGURE 11.1 *Andy Warhol, Billy Name, Craig Braun, John Pasche, Rolling Stones Records, Album cover for The Rolling Stones* Sticky Fingers, *1971. New York, Museum of Modern Art. Lithograph with metal zipper, 12 x 12" (30.5 x 30.5 cm). Committee on Architecture and Design Funds. Inv. n.: 847.2014.© 2017. Digital image, The Museum of Modern Art, New York/Scala, Florence.*

Andy Warhol for the Rolling Stones (1971), the cover of which includes a photograph of a man's crotch and a working three-dimensional zipper (Figure 11.1):

> Whoever buys the record, purchases with it a copy of a young man's fly, the package identified by the graphic trick which stresses the penis and highly stylizes the promised content. The buyer acquires the possibility of opening the package, and the zip and finds … nothing. It is a reversal of the tale of the Emperor's new clothes: the tale of the buyers' new bodies. They buy only packages which seem to be more than they are. (Haug 1986: 86–7)

As a microcosm of commodification, Haug's example illustrates one theory of capitalism: desire is stimulated, purchase entails, followed by a lack of consumer satisfaction which generates more desire and more consumption. Corbett suggests that the separation of image from music plays a key role in this process. But, at what point did music and image become separated and what role did commodification (whether of LPs or digital files) play in this process?

From sound to image: Before the 12-inch LP

In the last quarter of the nineteenth century innovations in audio technology in America and Europe led to the development of musical box cylinders and 'nickel-odeon' metal discs which when played produced mechanical music rather than facsimile recordings. Beneath the lids of these unassuming music boxes could be found often colourful ornamental and idyllic imagery. Nickelodeon discs packaged in large paper and card albums prefigured the multi-paged record albums of the 1930s (Edge 1991: 91). Wax cylinders were available for home use in the 1890s. These were delicately cradled within lambs-wool lined boxes. Wrapped around the boxes was a variety of lithographic paper promoting the record company, its machinery, and its inventor Thomas Alva Edison (1847–1931), thus personalizing mass-produced goods (Figure 11.2). At this time, promotional imagery of recording artists had not appeared on the printed material (Steffen 2005: 159; Edge 1991: 92).

The ten-inch disc of 1901 signalled the demise of the wax cylinder. These early records did not provide imagery of the artists, but attracted consumers primarily through their improved ability to mimic music. Early shellac records were sold in plain paper or card 'bags' with cut-out circles to reveal the centre label. Often colourful, these labels were dominated by the music company's logotype or emblem (Steffen 2005: 160; Edge 1991: 92). Perhaps the most famous of these was HMV's (His Master's Voice) emblem, which included the dog (Nipper) fascinated by the gramophone player, apparently convinced by its life-like mimicry.

From the late 1920s record bags were produced in a wide range of coloured or plain card and paper. Big companies produced generic 'house' bags which displayed their logotypes and, continuing to develop the theme established by Nipper's obsession with mechanical verisimilitude, included written accounts promoting the technical achievements of their players and radios (Steffen 2005: 160; Edge 1991: 93). In the late 1940s the microgroove long playing album and single became widely available and its packaging offered high quality colour portraits of star performers, liner notes and biographies (Edge 1991: 92).

Because of their delicate surface, microgroove records required a new form of protection: a smooth paper bag as an inner lining and a strong card sleeve as outer packaging. Where once the centred, circular cut-out acted as a window for the record company, now the exterior card sleeve provided a stage for promotional imagery and text related to the performer. Information was usually

FIGURE 11.2 *Thomas Edison portrait on wax cylinder case, ca. 1902-1912, Victoria and Albert Museum, National Art Library, London.*

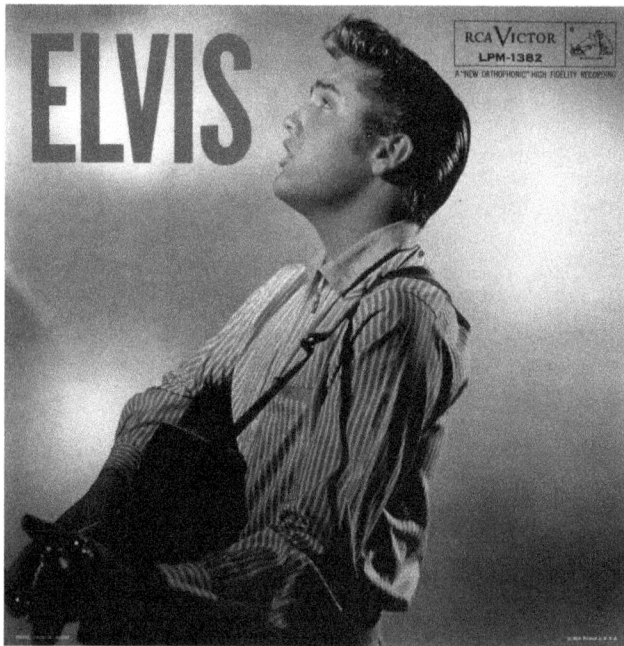

FIGURE 11.3 *Elvis Presley album cover for* ELVIS, *released 1956 by RCA. Photograph and permission from Michael Ochs Archive/Getty Images.*

in letterpress and printed in offset lithography. Appealing to a developing teenage market, sleeves began to display conventional portraits of Frank Sinatra and Elvis Presley (Figure 11.3) and other music stars (Edge 1991: 93). From the 1950s, sleeves were no longer interchangeable, functional, protective bags, but more thoughtfully considered, designed objects, which could promote and define the image of the performer and through ownership, identification and display communicate and develop consumer identity. In the 1960s the form of the record sleeve was further developed and began to include gatefolds, fold-out sleeves, and lyric sheets transforming what was once a functional bag into a 'fetishized commodity' (Edge 1991: 94). Examples of sleeve design discussed below illustrate the extent to which performers, designers and marketers developed the album cover as a form of graphic communication.

Approaches to album cover analysis: Gender, national identity and art history

The following section provides a series of analytical perspectives from which to investigate album covers. The first case study is of a series of Beatles album covers and presents a diachronic analysis, correlating the changes in cover design to changes in the band's music and members. The second example investigates the English Folk Revival movement of the 1960s and 70s and explores how national identity was communicated through album cover art. The third section provides a feminist investigation using quantitative analysis of the album covers of female singers (1973–1981). The section concludes with an art historical interpretation of a 1981 Bow Wow Wow album cover based on Édouard Manet's *Le Déjeuner sur l'herbe* (1862-63).

The Beatles' album covers, particularly *Sgt Pepper's Lonely Hearts Club Band*, illustrate the evolution and innovations in music packaging during the 1960s and have been lauded for their contribution to visual culture. According to popular music scholar Ian Inglis, their record covers were 'groundbreaking': their 'innovative' and 'imaginative' sleeves provided 'an early impetus for the expansion of the graphic design industry into the imagery of popular music' and were responsible for explicitly connecting art and pop (Inglis 2001: 83). In his article Inglis analyses the development of the Beatles' image through their album cover output over the course of their career. While the visual language of the early albums was largely conventional, consolidating and communicating the recognizable image of the Fab Four, Merseyside's moptops, the graphic design of the later LPs reveals a more independent, personally distant and visually innovative approach to their representation. For example, on *Rubber Soul* (1965) the four Beatles make an appearance, but three of them are looking away. Their faces are not smiling as in typical pop music promotion, but stretched and distorted, pointing perhaps to their increased use of drugs, but also to changes in their lives, as their wealth increased, their privacy diminished, and they encountered a more diverse range of people and ideas (Inglis 2001: 86). *Revolver* (1966) diverged even further from existing promotional practice, displaying a montage of small photographs of the band peering through Klaus Voorman's larger line drawings of the four musicians, looking in four different directions. Here the diversity in scale, medium and gaze evidences the band's rejection of the traditional visual language of popular music marketing. Thus, the experimental imagery of the album's exterior prepared the listener for the innovative music within.

Such design innovation was not restricted to the Beatles. Observers of album cover art pinpoint a significant shift in the visual language of sleeve design in the late 1960s and 1970s. In particular, progressive rock bands veered from the traditional portrait album cover to more expressive but identifiable album designs associated with the performer's style of music, including the psychedelic imagery produced by Martin Sharp for Cream's *Disraeli Gears*, Roger Dean's otherworldly illustrations for *Yes* and Barney Bubbles' geometric designs for *Hawkwind* and others, thereby achieving a kind of rock equivalent of Richard Wagner's *Gesamtkunstwerk*, where each element of a work of art, from the music to the imagery, expressed the same coherent aesthetic (Paytress 2008: 28), an approach established in album art by the Beatles' *Sgt Pepper* (1967).

Sgt Pepper arguably represents the culmination of the Beatles' increasingly innovative and independent approach to sleeve design (Figure 11.4). It has been hugely influential and inspired numerous parodies and homages (Twemlow 2014: 87). Evidencing the group's greater investment in aesthetics, the sleeve art cost $2,868, a large amount at the time (Twemlow 2014: 87). The increased financial commitment to design resulted in a pioneering album sleeve. It was the first album to have lyrics printed on the reverse of the cover and the first to include additional cardboard cut-out ephemera. The collage-like cover design of *Sgt Pepper* was as eclectic, complex and theatrical as its music, which combined brass band, music hall and psychedelia. The visually rich front sleeve, designed by Peter Blake and Jann Haworth and photographed by Michael Cooper, portrayed the band's alter ego, Sergeant Pepper's Lonely Hearts Club Band (the Beatles in colourful military band uniform), surrounded by contemporary and historical figures. These ranged from the Rolling Stones to Shirley Temple, along with marijuana plants, a television and an Indian

FIGURE 11.4 *The Beatles*, Sgt. Pepper's Lonely Hearts Club Band, *album cover, design by Peter Blake and Jann Haworth, 1967, Parlophone, UK. Courtesy Getty Images.*

goddess. This mixture suggested not only the rejection of the conventional pop star imagery, but also the diverse nature of the band's musical, intellectual and spiritual exploration. A year later the group's next album provided a stark contrast to *Sgt Pepper*: a completely white double album, simply embossed with the title '*The Beatles*'. This concept was developed by one of the earliest proponents of Pop Art, Richard Hamilton, who saw the cover not as an artistic statement but as a commercial strategy. The album would stand out from the crowd of lavishly decorated albums that had appeared in the wake of *Sgt Pepper* (Inglis 2001: 89). With its references to Dylan, Hollywood and Indian spirituality, *Sgt Pepper* looked outside of England to more global influences. However, it also played with the national stereotypes of England – the military brass band and the sounds of the music hall – seeming to simultaneously mock and celebrate Englishness while placing it in a wider context.

Around the time of *Sgt Pepper*'s appearance, English folk-rock groups, including Jethro Tull, Steeleye Span and Fairport Convention, appropriated the historical imagery of traditional working-class rural English life. The appropriation and representation of folk signifiers, whether May poles, Morris dancers, or bucolic village scenes, drew upon ideas of authenticity grounded in the artists, marketers and graphic designers' perceptions of history, thus re-presenting the English past as 'invented tradition', a term developed by historians Eric Hobsbawn and Terence Ranger in their discussion of relatively recent inventions of seemingly ancient traditions (Hobsbawn and Ranger 1983). Using the past to conjure nostalgia in the present, English folk-rock album design followed a practice established by Peter Blake's cover for The Beatles' *Sgt Pepper*, with its 'depictions of military pageantry from an imagined pre-World War I era, in which existed notional innocence and a sense of empire in the aftermath of a lost age of Merrie England' (Burns 2010: 107). In the late 1960s and early 1970s when American folk music was increasing in popularity, the employment of historic English vernacular imagery by British folk-rock performers was a way of reaffirming English identity in the face of American competition from artists ranging from the Beach Boys to Bob Dylan to the Eagles (Burns 2010: 108). Many of the artists under consideration above typify the male-dominated culture of rock. However, at the same time many female performers were challenging gender stereotypes found more widely in competing media.

Can album cover design offer a positive alternative to gender stereotypes found for example in advertising, television and film? An American study of album covers of women singers (1973–1981) observed that popular culture imagery of the period stereotyped women as 'housewifely, passive,' wholesome … blandly pleasing … intellectually inferior, hapless dependent, butt of humour … [and] childlike', citing scholars of gender representation including Erving Goffman (1979) Butler and Paisley (1980) Ferguson (1978) and Weibel (1977).

Looking at LP sleeve art of the same period and focusing on the female singers' album cover photographs the study analysed a set of imagery that challenged mass media stereotypes. The images most strongly communicated by the album covers were those of independence, confidence, strong will, control, competence and daring. In an effort to counter dominant sexist stereotypes, feminists of the period had long demanded such traits be included in the female characters of children's books, television shows, feature films and cartoons. At a time when 'images of women conveyed in … popular culture … [we]re sexist and shallow … limited and highly stereotyped' their positive depiction persisted on LP covers (Thaxton and Jaret 1985: 259). In the 1980s, concern regarding the depiction of women persisted as evidenced by the reaction to punk impresario Malcolm McLaren's provocative album cover concepts for Bow Wow Wow.

Ian Chapman's essay 'Luncheon on the Grass with Manet and Bow Wow Wow: Still Disturbing After All These Years' (2010) mixes art historical analysis with popular culture studies and focuses on a single album cover, British pop band Bow Wow Wow's *See Jungle! See Jungle! Go Join Your Gang Yeah! City All Over, Go Ape Crazy* (RCA 1981). (Figure 11.5). Chapman presents Malcolm McLaren as an auteur who used his art historical knowledge to shape the image of his artists and garner media attention while communicating ambiguity, female confidence and forbidden sexuality. Chapman compares Édouard Manet's, *Le Déjeuner surl'herbe* (1862-63) with Bow Wow Wow's album cover photographic re-enactment of Manet's painting, looking for 'associations and allusions' by interrogating the parody. In the Bow Wow Wow sleeve image the underage singer Annabella Lwin poses nude with two men in a wooded landscape. Chapman explores the paratexts of the album (lyrics, publicity shots, album cover (including the American alternative) and audio) as well as Malcolm McLaren's unrealized projects (a pornography magazine featuring children entitled *Chicken*) to interrogate the pop Svengali's use of adolescent sexuality as a promotional tool. Critics considered Bow Wow Wow's album exploitative, in particular because of its depiction of the under age, unclothed singer.

In the second half of the nineteenth century Manet's critics lambasted his painting as vulgar and obscene for its depiction of a nude woman in the woods with two men. More recently,

FIGURE 11.5 *Bow Wow Wow,* See Jungle! See Jungle! Go Join Your Gang, Yeah! City All Over! Go Ape Crazy, *album cover, 1981, RCA. Photography and permission by Andy Earl.*

commentators have praised the painting for its confrontational feminism: the unembarrassed stare of the nude woman towards the viewer was audacious at the time because it challenged dominant pictorial conventions and conventions of femininity. In addition, the image may have been considered disturbing because it lacked an obvious narrative: is it sexual or not? What has happened? What is about to happen? Thus, it broke the rules of allegorical painting and challenged dominant fine art traditions at the time. Chapman argues that McLaren's knowledge of art history meant he was aware of the ambiguity and rebellious potential of Manet's composition and used them strategically to promote his new band (Chapman 2010: 100).

The 12-inch sleeve has provided a substantial canvas for the representation of changing attitudes: of a single band (the Beatles) over time, of the communication of national identity through a musical genre and movement (English Folk Revival), of positive images of women performers in the 1970s and 1980s. However, with the advent of new media which limited the scope for graphic design – the cassette, CD 'jewel box', the digital music file and its accompanying thumbnail image – the opportunities for such representation became increasingly challenged.

The cassette threat and the rise of the CD

In the United States, the dominance of the 12-inch record was first threatened not by CDs but by the cassette. Cassettes and 8-track cartridges began to outsell vinyl records in the 1970s due to the introduction of cassette players in cars (Jones 1992: 37). Although the technology for the CD had been developed in the early 1970s it was not initially considered commercially viable and its launch was delayed until 1982 (1983 in the United States). By 1988 the sales of CDs had surpassed those of vinyl in the United States and by 1992 they outsold pre-recorded music cassettes (Straw 2009: 82–3).

The industry switch from vinyl records to CDs has been called 'probably the most significant change in the recorded music market in the second half of the 20th century' (Giles, Pietrzykowski and Clark 2007: 430). By 2002, twenty years after the CD format was launched, global sales of albums on CD surpassed 2.25 billion while vinyl albums sold only 8.5 million. The iPod and iTunes software were introduced in 2001 further altering the landscape of the music market (Giles, Pietrzykowski and Clark 2007: 430) and substantially challenging established traditions of music packaging, whether the 12-inch canvas of the vinyl album cover or the 6-inch CD square. By the end of 2005 iPod sales globally had reached 42 million units (Ogden, Ogden and Long 2011: 124). The billionth worldwide legal music download occurred in February of 2006 (Beer 2008: 71). Revenue from physical sales were roughly equal to those of 'digital channels' – including music downloads, ad-supported streaming services such as YouTube, and music subscription services like Spotify, and so on. They reached $6.85 billion in the United States in 2014 according to a 2016 report by the International Federation of the Phonographic Industry (2016).

Based on the cassette case developed in the 1960s, the first CDs were sold in 1983 in hinged plastic containers known as 'jewel boxes'. This square format was soon superseded by the 12-inch x 6-inch cardboard 'longbox' which was developed to increase visibility in the store, reduce theft and create more display space for word and images on the package itself. This shape was designed to fit into existing 12-inch LP bins and thus eased the CD into the retail environment, but it became a target of the environmentalist 'Ban the Box' movement in 1990, so by 1993, major record companies sought alternatives to the longbox (Straw 2009: 85–6).

The initial design of CD packaging was based on assumptions regarding consumer engagement with the 12-inch LP including relaxed contemplative listening and the reading of lyrics and liner notes. It was thought that listening would take place in an ideal environment of quiet and comfort, requiring spaces for display of jewel boxes. In such spaces listeners would physically interact with the images and text of CD packaging while absorbing carefully designed and informative booklets (Straw 2009: 86). However, with the advent of new audio technology, CDs could be played almost anywhere: on portable Sony Discmans, laptop computers, DVD players and with CD-compatible car stereos. These technologies encouraged CD owners to disaggregate the unadorned disc from its design packaging elements: the materiality, photography, illustrations, typography and colour of its packaging. Increasingly, the jewel box was left on the shelf at home. As part of its increased mobility the CD found homes in new forms of packaging from car visor holders to fanny packs, thus weakening the original packaging's paratextual usefulness. The introduction of recordable CDs (CD-Rs) allowed digital music to be recorded from computers onto blank discs which further challenged the place of design in music packaging (Straw 2009: 87). It dissolved the unity of image and music that has been recognized as the essence of the album cover, finally cutting the tenuous link between immaterial, time-based sound and its static, material representation.

With the technological transformation outlined above, 'any sense of the CD as a complex package, fully meaningful only through the interaction of music and its annotative accompaniments, withered'. Digital music had become 'migratory, detached from the surfaces and visual-textual adornments that might stabilize it in material and cultural terms' (Straw 2009: 87). The home-recorded generic CD-R with its lack of visual cues about the music it contained can be seen as a transitional object between the materially and visually rich LP sleeve and the invisible digital music file. Extending Straw's discussion, the MP3 file (and other similar formats) ushered in the ultimate separation of the album cover from the music. The digital music file denied the tripartite unity of physical, visual and aural, packaging design, graphic design and music, that had made the LP unique. Arguably the shift in format from 12-inch LP, which offered a vast canvas for display, to the thumbnail of the digital music file substantially impacted the way in which individuals communicated their identities through musical allegiance with particular recording artists.

Shaping identity: Collecting sleeves

Whether it involves virtual 'folders' of digital iTunes singles or physical shelves of 12-inch vinyl, collecting is a vital aspect of music consumption. The writer Evan Eisenberg has observed that collecting satisfies a number of human needs: 'To make beauty and pleasure permanent'; 'to comprehend beauty'; 'to distinguish oneself as a consumer'; 'to belong'; and the 'need to impress others, or oneself' (Eisenberg 1987 (2005):14–16). This section investigates the extent to which these needs can be met by physical and digital music commodities.

Collecting of records has other functions beyond aural enjoyment. Some scholars (Appadurai 1986; Douglas and Isherwood 1978) have observed that material possessions are bound up with the display of personal meaning and used as communicators of individual identity. Likewise, Russel Belk writes that in many societies 'possessions are regarded not only as a part of the self, but also as instrumental to the development of the self' (1988: 141). Thus the display of music packaging in one's home or elsewhere transfers symbolic meaning from the packaged product to the owner: 'the prominent display of a personal music collection on a living room bookshelf acts as a powerful statement of its owner's identity for the benefit of visitors' (Giles, Pietrzykowski and Clark 2007: 431) (Figure 11.6).

Collections contribute to the development of identity through their ability to express both the individuality and conformity of the collector (Csikzentmihalyi and Rochberg-Halton 1981). It is unlikely that any two record collections are the same. Yet, the act of record collecting is a widely shared social practice (Giles, Pietrzykowski and Clark 2007: 341). The physical record collection can perhaps be distinguished from the digital one in that the former provides a material cultural biography where specific albums are associated with life experiences (Lunt and Livingstone 1992). Whereas, with digital formats 'it is unlikely that such sentimental value would be accorded to individual music files, which can be easily deleted at the click of a mouse' (Giles, Pietrzykowski and Clark 2007: 431).

Giles et al observe a number psychological and social needs of vinyl album collectors, including 'records as sacred objects' where, like a well-known religious painting or holy relic, when on display in one's home makes an explicit visual statement about the taste of the owner while providing a link between the owner and the musical artist (Giles, Pietrzykowski and Clark 2007: 435). While such display is an outward and externalized form of communication, vinyl albums also offer opportunities for their owners to produce internal and private meanings, such as embarrassment about purchasing

FIGURE 11.6 *Teenager's bedroom with LPs on the wall, Norwich, photograph and permission by Martin Devenney, 2016.*

a particular LP (e.g. the 1992 UK novelty hit *Mr. Blobby*) which might be hidden in the back of a collection yet may still have some sentimental value (Giles, Pietrzykowski and Clark 2007: 437) or identification with the values of the recording artist be they social protest or patriotism.

Record collecting is a subcultural and oppositional practice where collectors of used vinyl records identify as a coherent outsider group countering the commercial imperative of the music industry (Crawford 2013: 13). Many LP collectors, with their aesthetic interest in packaging and music, perceive themselves as preservationists of a significant form of popular art acting in opposition to the music industry which views music as a disposable commodity (Shuker 2004; Hayes 2006). Album collectors often value their records as objects of posterity to be handed down to their family members thus continuing to influence their loved ones while transmitting cultural values to the next generation. Record collecting thereby acts generatively (McAdams and De St. Aubin 1998).

The experience of digital music played on a device such as an MP3 player or phone is arguably more focused on the aural experience – on the sensual and functional aspect of listening to music than the more explicit opportunities for identity formation provided by physical formats. The consumption of digitized music on a mobile device is often a private experience. The visual components (record album cover, sleeve notes, inserts, etc.) are reduced to a thumbnail image – a much more diminished expression of identity than a 12-inch album cover displayed on a living room wall or shelf. Paradoxically, though, digital music has enhanced social potential due to the ease with which music files can be shared.

The 'death' of the physical album, whether vinyl or CD, may be a long way off due perhaps to the psychological benefits they provide, including the expression of identity and the potential for generativity – the transfer of cultural values, personal taste and memories, down the generational line. This is supported by data showing that sales of vinyl have increased in the face of competing music-listening technologies, including digital files and CDs. In 2012 3.2 million vinyl record albums were sold in the United States (Resnikoff 2012) and sales continued to rise to 12 million in 2015 (Nielsen 2016: 5). This may come as a surprise to those in the music industry who embraced CDs as *the* music format in the early 1990s. While the CD's small size, portability and durability may have provided commercial advantages, many collectors saw its development as evidence of an interest in profits over aesthetics, as well as the rejection of other supposedly human qualities inherent in LPs and their use, including defects, fragility and physical interaction (Plasketes 1992). Applying Walter Benjamin's theory of aura (1978), where the unique is considered more authentic than mass-produced object, vinyl LPs can be considered more real than digital music files, which can be reproduced with ease, have no physical presence, do not seem to contribute to communicating one's identity through personal display, and appear to have a negligible role in social rituals.

Conclusion

Throughout its history, the packages for music, whether wax cylinder boxes, 12-inch record sleeves or digital thumb nails, have provided a significant canvas for the visual communication of technological innovation, a performer's brand image and graphic experimentation, whether through type, image or materials. In the process, the rise and fall of the record sleeve – its persistence as a significant cultural artefact despite its decline in sales – has provided an opportunity for discussion of a range of issues, from gender representation to consumer identity. The broadcasting of one's own musical preferences whether through the domestic display of 12-inch LPs or wearing band T-shirts (see Chapter 4) now runs in parallel to the use of social media to share one's musical taste in real time. The innumerable 'likes' broadcast via Twitter, Myspace and Facebook are perhaps a more important commodity than the digital file or the 12-inch record sleeve. Following the communications theorist Dallas Smythe's notion of the 'audience commodity', in the digital sphere it is the audience which is the main product. Smythe theorized that 'readers and audience members of advertising-supported mass media are a commodity produced and sold to advertisers *because they perform a valuable service for the advertisers*' (Smythe 1981: 8; Coté and Pybus 2007: 97). Smythe's contribution to our discussion – the audience as product – aids our understanding of the wider context of music packaging. While some music-consuming audiences – vinyl collectors for example – can be seen as subcultures who resist the commercial aims of the record companies in their attempt to preserve an authentic past, other audiences – online communities who share musical preferences – can be seen as a more ephemeral version of the LP-loving connoisseur. This perspective reveals the common ground between digital and physical music packaging: whether cardboard sleeves or virtual images, both products are commodities which in turn sustain audience communities.

References

Appadurai, Arjun. 1986. 'Introduction: Commodities and the Politics of Value.' In Arjun Appadurai (ed.), *The Social Life of Things: Commodities in Cultural Perspective*, 3–63. Cambridge: Cambridge University Press.

Beer, David. 2008. 'The Icon Interface and the Veneer of Simplicity: MP3 Players and the Reconfiguration of Music Collecting and Reproduction Practices in the Digital Age'. *Information, Communication & Society* 11 (1): 71–88.

Belk, Russell W. 1988. 'Possessions and the Extended Self.' *The Journal of Consumer Research* 15 (2): 139–68.

Benjamin, Walter. 1978. 'The Work of Art in the Age of Mechanical Reproduction'. In Hannah Arendt (ed.), *Illuminations*, 217–52. New York: Schocken Books.

Burns, Robert G. H. 2010. 'Depicting the "Merrie": Historical Imagery in English Folk-Rock'. *Music in Art* 35 (1/2): 105–17.

Butler, Matilda, and William Paisley. 1980. *Women and the Mass Media: Sourcebook for Research and Action*. New York: Human Sciences Press.

Chapman, Ian. 2010. 'Luncheon on the Grass with Manet and Bow Wow Wow: Still Disturbing After All These Years'. *Music in Art* 35 (1/2) (Spring–Fall): 95–104.

Corbett, John. 1990. 'Free, Single and Disengaged: Listening Pleasure and the Popular Music Object'. *October* 54 (Autumn): 79–101.

Coté, Mark, and Jennifer Pybus. 2007. 'Learning to Immaterial Labour 2.0: Myspace and Social Networks'. *Ephemera* 7 (1): 88–106.

Crawford, Casey. 2013. *Vinyl Junkies: An Investigation involving Record Collecting in the 21st Century*. MA Thesis, Omaha, NE: University of Nebraska.

Csikzentmihalyi, Mihaly, and Eugene Rochberg-Halton. 1981. *The Meaning of Things: Domestic Symbols and the Self*. Cambridge: Cambridge University Press.

Dean, Roger, and David Howells. 1982. *Album Cover Album: The Second Volume*. New York: A & W Publishers.

Douglas, Mary, and Baron Isherwood. 1978. *The World of Goods: Towards an Anthropology of Consumption*. Harmondsworth: Penguin.

Edge, Kevin. 1991. *The Art of Selling Songs: Graphics for the Music Business 1690-1990*. London: Futures Publications.

Eisenberg, E. 1987 [2005]. *The Recording Angel: Music, Records and Culture from Aristotle to Zappa*. Second edition. New Haven, London: Yale University Press.

Ferguson, Marjorie. 1978. 'Imagery and Ideology: The Cover Photographs of Traditional Women's Magazines'. In Gaye Tuchman, Arlene Kaplan Daniels, James Walker Benét. (eds.), *Hearth and Home: Images of Women in the Mass Media*, 97–115. New York: Oxford University Press.

Genette, Gérard. 1997. *Paratexts: Thresholds of Interpretation*. Translated by Jane E. Lewin. Cambridge: Cambridge University Press.

Giles, David C., Stephen Pietrzykowski, and Kathryn E. Clark. 2007. 'The Psychological Meaning of Personal Record Collections and the Impact of Changing Technological Forms'. *Journal of Economic Psychology* 28 (4): 429–43.

Goffman, Erving. 1979. *Gender Advertisements*. Cambridge, MA: Harvard University Press.

Haug, Wolfgang Fritz. 1986. *Critique of Commodity Aesthetics: Appearance, Sexuality and Advertising in Capitalist Society*. Translated by Robert Bock. Minneapolis: University of Minnesota.

Hayes, David. 2006. '"Take Those Old Records off the Shelf": Youth and Music Consumption in the Postmodern Age'. *Popular Music and Society* 29 (1): 51–68.

Hobsbawm, Eric, and Terence Ranger (eds.) 1983. *The Invention of Tradition*. Cambridge: Cambridge University Press.

Inglis, Ian. 2001. '"Nothing You Can See That Isn't Shown": The Album Covers of the Beatles'. *Popular Music* 20 (1): 83–97.

The International Federation of the Phonographic Industry. 2016. 'Digital Music in Figures'. http://www.ifpi.org/facts-and-stats.php. Accessed 9 June 2016.

Jones, Steve. 1992. *Rock Formation: Music, Technology, and Mass Communication*. Newbury Park, CA: SAGE Publications Inc.

Lunt, Peter K., and Sonia M. Livingstone. 1992. *Mass Consumption and Personal Identity: Everyday Economic Experience*. Buckingham: Open University Press.

McAdams, Dan P., and De St. Aubin (eds.) 1998. *Generativity and Adult Development: How and Why We Care for the Next Generation*. Washington, DC: American Psychological Association.

The Nielsen Company. 2016. '2015 Nielsen U.S Music Report'. http://www.nielsen.com/us/en/insights/reports/2016/2015-music-us-year-end-report.html. Accessed 30 March 2018.

Ogden, James. R., Denise T. Ogden, and Karl Long. 2011. 'Music Marketing: A History and Landscape'. *Journal of Retailing and Consumer Services* 18: 120–5.

Paytress, Mark. 2008. 'Art of Noise', *M: The MCPS/PRS Members Music Magazine*: vol. 30, p. 28.

Plasketes, George. 1992. 'Romancing the Record: The Vinyl De-evolution and Subcultural Evolution'. *Journal of Popular Culture* 26 (1): 109–22.

Resnikoff, Paul. 2012. 'Still Gaining: Vinyl Sales up 16.3 Percent in 2012'. *Digital Music News*. http://www.digitalmusicnews.com/permalink/2012/121004vinyl. Accessed 9 June 2016.

Shuker, Roy. 2004. 'Beyond the "High Fidelity" Stereotype: Defining the (Contemporary) Record Collector'. *Popular Music* 23 (3): 311–30.

Smythe, Dallas W. 1981. *Communications, Capitalism, Consciousness, and Canada*. Norwood, NJ: Ablex Publishing Corporation.

Steffen, David. 2005. *From Edison to Marconi: The First Thirty Years of Recorded Music*. Jefferson, NC: McFarland and Company.

Straw, Will. 2009. 'In Memoriam: The Music CD and Its Ends.' *Design and Culture* 1 (1): 79–92.

Thaxton, Lyn, and Charles Jaret. 1985. 'Singers and Stereotypes: The Image of Female Recording Artists'. *Sociological Inquiry* 55 (3): 239–63.

Twemlow, Alice. 2014. 'Sgt. Pepper's Lonely Hearts Club Band Cover'. In Grace Lees-Maffei (ed.), *Iconic Design: 50 Stories about 50 Things*, 84–7. London: Bloomsbury.

Vägnes, Øvind, and Gronstad, Asbjorn (eds.) 2008. *Image-Music-Text: Discovering Album Aesthetics*. Copenhagen: Museum Tuscalanum Press.

Weibel, Kathryn. 1977. *Mirror Mirror: Images of Women Reflected in Popular Culture*. Garden City, NY: Anchor Press.

12

E-Book, iBook, weBook, youBook: Declensions of digital design

Nicolas P. Maffei

Like the last chapter, this one considers the extent to which the introduction of new media has changed the landscape of established forms of communication. We will explore how the meaning and function of traditional media – the printed book in particular – has been challenged as a result of technological innovations centred upon a shift to digital delivery. The writer on new media, David Jay Bolter, has called this period 'the late age of print', a period of 'transformation of our social and cultural attitudes toward, and uses of, this familiar technology' (Bolter 2001: 3). Many commentators have predicted the death of the book during this period, especially with the advent of computer technology. Yet, even in the age of the e-reader the physical book continues to thrive. Books have often been regarded primarily as information carriers, responding to the human need for knowledge. Yet, information does not solely meet functional requirements: especially when delivered as a material and spatial experience it can also satisfy social, psychological and even sensual needs.

This chapter reviews the key debates – from the post-war period to the present – regarding the future of the book, ranging from the prescient predictions of media theorist Marshall McLuhan to the bold claims of Amazon CEO, Jeff Bezos, regarding the impact of the Kindle reader (Figure 12.1). The chapter explores publishers' and designers' responses to the advent of the electronic word: the possibilities and the perils, reviewing design outcomes that extend and challenge the form of the book, while examining experimentation in print and innovations in digital texts. While some publishing projects invite readers to collaborate with authors, others seek to challenge traditional modes of production and distribution. The former is exemplified by 'I Read Where I Am' (2011), an online book that makes every reader an editor. The latter is illustrated by the Espresso Book Machine, which prints a glued, trimmed and perfectly bound book in minutes, eradicating the need for warehousing and shipping. In this rapidly evolving landscape print publishers are innovating, exemplified by London-based Visual Editions and their radical remaking of both the traditional paperback and the notion of authorship. These developments are not only examined in light of new technology, including hypertext and app design, but in the context of literary theory, including postmodern notions of deconstruction and the death of the author.

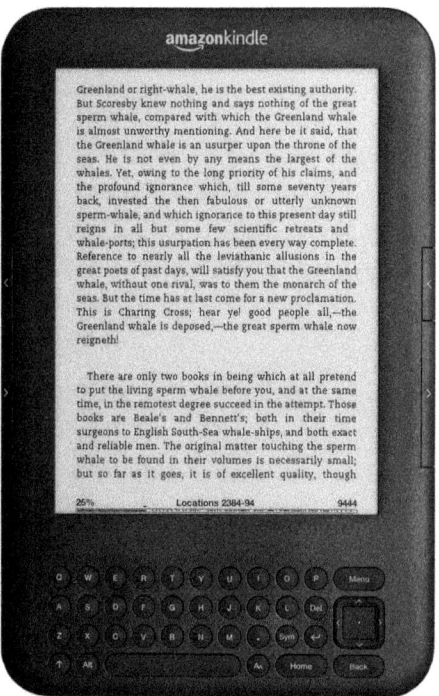

FIGURE 12.1 *Third-generation Amazon Kindle e-reader showing text from the novel* Moby Dick, *2010. Photograph by NotFromUtrecht - Own work, CC BY-SA 3.0, https://commons.wikimedia.org/w/index.php?curid=11658040.*

The death of the analog book?

A discussion of the future of the book must include the views of Marshall McLuhan, the pioneering and effusive theorist of new media. In 1965 McLuhan declared the book 'obsolescent', an odd, but precise word choice. Neither obsolete nor technologically advanced 'it is like the dinosaur just before he disappeared' (Ray 1966: 783). Such apparent doom-saying contributed to McLuhan's reputation as an enemy of books. However, McLuhan recognized the book as a societal necessity and sought to save print culture by learning how it communicates and works with other media: for example, viewing book reading as a sensory balance to the consumption of electronic media such as television (Neill 1971: 311–12).

Recent research confirms McLuhan's observations. In a study of contemporary reading practices in Europe, scholars of reading, Nossek, Adoni and Nimrod (2015) observed that many of their respondents divided their reading almost equally between print media (books, newspapers and magazines) and their digital counterparts (digital books, online newspapers and other digital information sites): 'The consequent functional interpretation is that different media fulfill different psychosocial needs. Thus, instead of displacement, we are witnessing the evolution of a new functional division of labor among print media and their digital equivalents' (Nossek, Adoni and Nimrod 2015: 381). Far from rendering the book obsolete, new technologies are simply complementing the functions already provided by printed texts.

At the launch of the Kindle in November 2007, Amazon CEO Jeff Bezos presented the physical book as an obsolete technology. But unlike McLuhan, obsolescence for Bezos really did suggest extinction, declaring 'books are the last bastion of analog'. Bezos emphasized the e-book's functionality and made three bold claims: the Kindle e-reader was akin to a book, surpassed the book, and made the book disappear. Bezos announced, 'If you're going to do something like this, you have to be as good as the book in a lot of respects.' Reassuring his audience by referring to the familiar print medium, he explained that the Kindle was designed to 'project an aura of bookishness'. The Kindle was more than a book: 'This isn't a device, it's a service,' one that allows change of font size, text searching, data storage, internet access and the purchase of goods. He described a Kindle reading experience where readers would lose themselves in the text, resulting in a book that 'disappears' (Levy 2007). With the Kindle, the physicality of the book – the constant turning of pages, the necessity of always finding your place – would vanish, allowing readers to purely enjoy the text. As book scholar Alessandro Ludovico explained, the Kindle 'achieves a transcendence of the physical medium' (2013: 87) The launch of the Kindle seemed to herald the end of our physical interaction with a technology with roots which extended to the invention of paper in China in 105 AD (Cope and Phillips 2006: ix).

Defenders of the physical book, likewise, argue its superiority from a utilitarian perspective, celebrating the fact that it is 'instant-on', needs no batteries, 'is a more reliable storage device than a hard disk drive, and it sports a killer user interface' (Levy 2007). This emphasis on functionality, rather than human satisfaction, has coloured comparisons of the two media. However, an emphasis on use often ignores the emotive and psychological aspects of human engagement with objects. It neglects the psychological and emotional benefits offered by interaction with materials. A book's texture, weight, size, smell, its relation to space and to one's body provides an experiential dimension, a physical pleasure in reading and handling.

Throughout these often-passionate debates many authors have displayed their love for tangible books, in some cases, presenting arguments that are more emotive than logical. Essayist Sven Birkerts, in his tellingly titled *Gutenberg Elegies: The Fate of Reading in an Electronic Age* (1994) provides an early and impassioned critique of the digital text, finding inhumanity in its immateriality and celebrating the traces of ink on paper:

> Nearly weightless though it is, the word printed on a page is a thing. The configuration of impulses on a screen is not – it is a manifestation, an indeterminate entity both particle and wave, an ectoplasmic arrival and departure. The former occupies a position in space – on a page, in a book, and is verifiably there. The latter, once dematerialized, digitized back into storage, into memory, cannot be said to exist in quite the same way. It has potential, not actual, locus. … The same word, when it appears on the screen, must be received with a sense of its weightlessness – the weightlessness of its presentation. The same sign, but not the same. (Birkerts 1994: 188)

It is precisely the 'weightlessness', the dematerialization of the book, that Bezos promoted as a tangible benefit, and Birkerts finds so problematic. Echoing Barthes' notion of the death of the author (see Chapter 1) Birkerts goes on to argue that the dematerialization of the word 'results in the toppling of a whole tradition of textual authority'. Birkerts' technological determinism perpetuates a traditional model of textual authority and belongs to a tradition of critique which locates authenticity and humanity in the technologies of the past (Striphas 2009: 24–5).

This technologically deterministic view has coloured much of book forecasting. In many discussions, it is assumed that new technology inevitably usurps traditional technology. It is true that some communication technologies are superseded. Yet, when faced with a seemingly superior competitor others continue to thrive in altered roles. The candle, for example, was not made obsolete by electric lighting. Once a primary source of illumination for reading, needlework, and so on in developed regions it now serves a mostly atmospheric effect, adding a sense of intimacy and romance. With the advent of television, the demise of radio was assumed. However, the two technologies developed in parallel serving different needs. Despite the dominance of the digital music format, vinyl records have maintained a thriving niche, due in part to meeting the social and psychological needs of their users (see Chapter 11). The publisher and writer Gerald Lange has observed, 'As electronic information transfer increasingly relieves the book of its informational responsibilities, perhaps the book is likewise freed from its utilitarian obligations' (Lange 2007: 383). As the book's role as primary information vessel is increasingly usurped, what role will it play in our lives and in our culture?

Concerns regarding the future of the book may seem largely confined to the last twenty years with the onset of the digital revolution. However, following advances in computer technology in the post-war period similar worries were raised. Once it was clear that digital technology posed a threat to the traditional book its ardent defenders began to sound dire warnings. Gordon N. Ray's 'The Future of the Book', the opening address of the American Library Association's 1966 conference, pleaded for books to be saved in the face of 'electronic devices' (e.g. radio and TV). Ray argued that books allowed for review, comparison, immediate reference and prolonged attention and thus informed argument and aided study, outweighing the advantages of electronic devices (Gilroy 1966: 24). Ray's worries presage those of the author Nicholas Carr, who in 2008 associated deep reading with deep thinking and asked if the internet was making us stupid.

While Ray was alarmist, an earlier forecaster was more open-minded. In 1955 the *Library Quarterly* published a contribution to this anxious discourse, Lester Asheim's 'Introduction: New Problems in Plotting the Future of the Book'. Asheim worried that his librarian colleagues were blinded by a nostalgic attachment to the book and were not ready to accept that 'the book of the future may well depart from its traditional form, content or usage' (Asheim 1955: 282). He believed that a lack of imagination regarding the printed book was more likely to hasten its death. His concern was for those who adamantly insisted on retaining, for twentieth-century purposes, the nineteenth-century form of the book and encouraged its re-examination to overcome its inadequacies (Asheim 1955: 282–3). This chapter investigates the outputs of book designers who, perhaps unknowingly, have embraced Asheim's perspective: innovators who have re-examined the book, its form, content and usage.

Hypertext and the end of books?

Reading on the internet in the twenty-first century can be a distracting experience: scanning a short passage here, watching a brief video clip there, perhaps a television show or Facebook feed streaming in the background. Internet reading is often branching (or rhizomic, see Chapter 8) rather than linear, superficial rather than deep. According to some this is not necessarily a bad thing. In 1992 the fiction author Robert Coover penned a provocatively titled text, 'The End of Books', responding to a concern that hypertext would kill paper text, while reflecting on its potential as a creative medium:

> unlike print, hypertext provides multiple paths between text segments ... [with] its network of alternate routes (as opposed to print's unidirectional page-turning) hypertext presents a radically divergent technology, interactive, polyvocal, favouring a plurality of discourses over definitive utterance and freeing the reader from domination by the author. Hypertext reader and writer are said to become co-learners or co-writers, as it were, fellow-travellers in the mapping and remapping of textual (and visual, kinetic and aural) components, not all of which are provided by what used to be called the author. (Coover 1992: np)

Coover is describing a scene not unlike the one we find ourselves in today where every internet user is potentially a 'co-writer', via comments, reviews, critiques and hacks. With the advent of hypertext the literary theories which predicted the death of the author seemed to have come to fruition, resulting in the wider appearance and acceptance of a narrative logic exemplified by 'fluidity, contingency, indeterminacy, plurality, [and] discontinuity' (Coover 1992: np) (Figure 12.2).

Some publishers, as we will see in the work of Visual Editions, seem to have responded to Coover's apparent enthusiasm for co-authorship and the reformulation of the text. Coover's perspective suggests optimism, seeming to herald the democratization of publishing through online authorship and reader involvement. But to what extent has this transformation of the reader–author relationship transformed the book? In the following sections, a few recent graphic

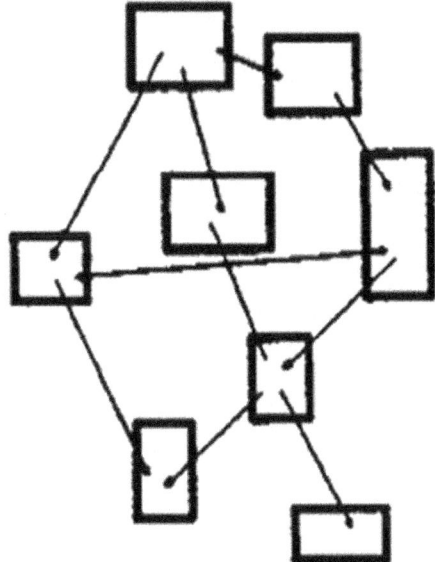

FIGURE 12.2 *Discrete (Chunk Style) hypertext from Ted Nelson's* Computer Lib/ Dream Machines, *1974 (faxed copy from Ted Nelson Studios 10.28.1998). Permission Ted Nelson.*

design examples illustrate in both print and electronic publishing how the traditional text has been reconsidered.

The sensual book: Challenging the form

The book has long been considered primarily 'a vehicle of information recording and delivery' (Jury 2007: 13). However, in the age of Kindle e-readers and Wikipedia, the online encyclopaedia, is this still the case? It is precisely the rise of the electronic book that has reminded readers and publishers of its many innate, unique qualities beyond the transfer of information. Because it is comprised of ink, binding, cloth, paper and glue, providing weight, texture, sound and scent, it offers a heightened sensorial experience in contrast to the electronic book. As discussed in Chapter 11, the book also includes paratextual elements such as the barcode, publisher's mark, the 'blurb' and much more. All of these physical elements are understood through the senses and communicate the character of the book whether precious or prosaic. As a result, they significantly impact reader interaction, perhaps suggesting reverence or disposability and thus influencing attitude, posture, touch and more (Feltham 2014: 9).

Focusing on the bodily experience of touch, weight, space, and so on graphic designer Esther Feltham's 'The Sensual Book' (2014) considered independent British publishers in the context of the digital publishing landscape. What she found was not the death of the book, but a renewed emphasis on tactility and physicality (Feltham 2014: 7). Feltham applied the theories of phenomenology, in particular those of philosopher Martin Heidegger, to understand how readers' physical subjective experiences, touch in particular, guided by social and cultural upbringing, acted as reference points in understanding the physical book (Feltham 2014: 7, 14; Heidegger 1996).

With their emphasis on the materiality of books, London-based Visual Editions, founded in 2010 by Anna Gerber and Britt Iverson, aimed to fill a gap between lavishly produced coffee table books and inexpensive paperbacks. Gerber has explained that one of their goals was to create affordable, culturally desirable paperbacks – treasured objects – in response to the widespread disposal of paperbacks as consumers increasingly took up e-readers. This effort to valorize the printed text within the ecology of new media is consistent with Marshall McLuhan's belief that print provides a needed antidote to electronic media. According to McLuhan, since the time of Gutenberg society has been biased psychologically and culturally to the visual experience (Figure 12.3). But with the advent of radio and television the bias towards the auditory and tactile has increased. In this new milieu, he understood print and reading as rebalancing this perceptual disparity (Neil 1971: 317).

According to Gerber one of Visual Editions goals was to produce materially engaging paperbacks that are cherished for aesthetic and emotional reasons, 'we want our books to be read, worn and loved' (Feltham 2014: 11). This emphasis on the audience and the object underlines the importance of the content and readability of the Visual Editions book, as well as its appeal as a physical artefact. Gerber's quote points to a key difference between digital and print publications: materiality allows for increased tactile engagement and thus encourages increased personal attachment.

The centrality of the senses in consumer engagement, whether in product appeal or retail environments, has been established in numerous studies (Rahman 2012; Schifferstein and Cleiren

FIGURE 12.3 *Gutenberg Bible, Johann Gutenberg, ca. 1455. Lenox Copy, New York Public Library, Rare Books Division, photo by NYC Wanderer (Kevin Eng). CC BY-SA 2.0.*

2005). Touch has been strongly linked with emotional attachment (Hertenstein et al. 2009). Furthermore, the role of tactile materials has a significant impact on whether an individual likes a particular object (Armel and Ramachandran 2003; Atakan 2014; Shu and Peck 2011). However, Visual Editions is not only interested in book materials. They have been keen to challenge form as well: by deconstructing and rearranging a book's generic elements (paper, glue, ink and board), they have confronted the long-held traditions of authorship and storytelling.

In September 2010, Visual Editions published its first book, a redesign of Laurence Stern's *The Life and Opinions of Tristram Shandy, Gentleman*. By choosing what is considered the earliest novel where image was as important as text, Visual Editions established their literary heritage while demonstrating their dedication to visual writing. Their second publication, Jonathan Safran Foer's *Tree of Codes*, was published in November 2010, and was considered revolutionary for its use of die-cutting, where passages were punched from the pages of the original novel, *The Street of Crocodiles* by Bruno Schulz, to reveal a new narrative (Figure 12.4).

The book seemed to ask, 'Who is the author, Foer or Schulz?', while it engaged in a radical transformation of its story and pages. Visual Editions' third book, *Composition No. 1* of August 2011, was produced as both a physical artefact and an app, illustrating the publisher's embrace of digital technology (Figure 12.5). The print version of *Composition No. 1* was an unbound, series of loose leaf pages within a hinged box. The lack of binding allowed readers to order their own experience and seemed to evidence a logical progression from the company's previous and more recognizably bookish projects.

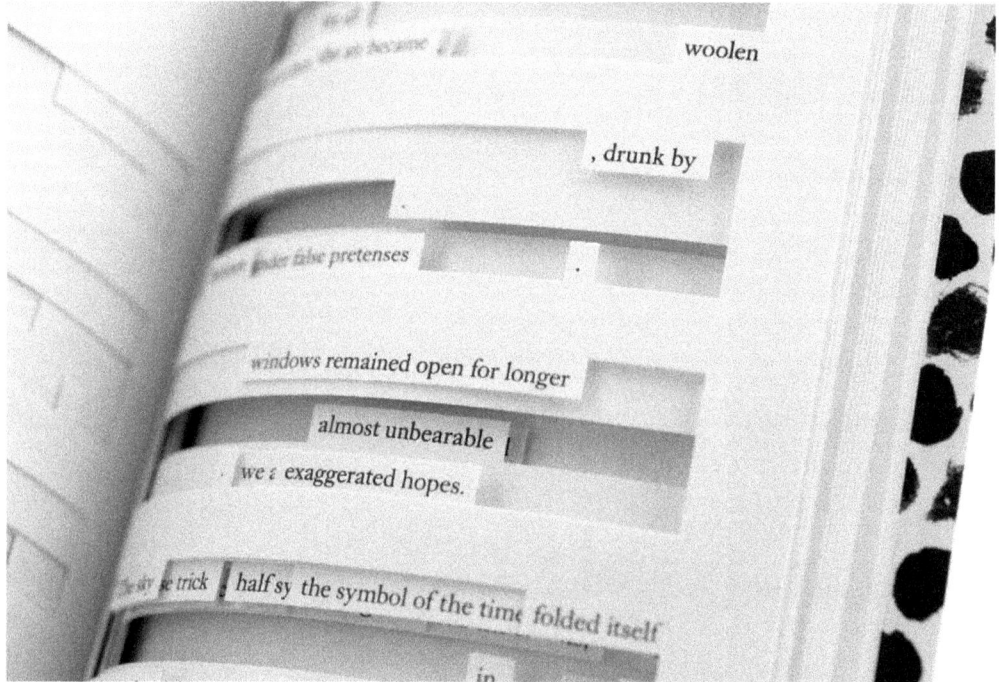

FIGURE 12.4 Tree of Codes, *by Jonathan Safran Foer, London, 2010. Permission Visual Editions.*

FIGURE 12.5 Composition No. 1, *by Mark Saporta, London, 2010. Permission Visual Editions.*

While the physical version allowed the readers to shuffle the pages in any order, the app rearranged them automatically (visual-editions.com). *Composition No. 1* provides an illuminating instance where the print and digital version of a publication, while originating from the same design concept of the unbound book, resulted in significantly different outcomes. Arguably, much of Visual Editions' success is based on its ability to push the form of the book to its limits. In this sense, it can be associated with the practices of the twentieth-century avant-garde, which was preoccupied to a large extent with formal experimentation.

Because of their literary pedigree and their relation to the formalist tradition of the avant-garde, Visual Editions' publications have the potential to impart social status to their owners through acquisition of cultural capital (Bourdieu 1984). As scholars of book consumption, Nossek et al have noted:

> From a sociological point of view, it is well documented (Bourdieu 1984; Escarpit 1971) that books as objects serve as signifiers of high social status. ... Moreover, many people like to read the 'right' print books and magazines in public, thereby asserting their social status and aspirations. (Nossek, Adoni and Nimrod 2015: 380)

Can an e-book impart the same cultural capital as a printed one? The following section continues to explore the role of the book as a social object focusing on the way in which recent technology has allowed readers to share and comment, thus creating online communities and indicating one's taste, education and identity.

Are books social media?

Assumptions that the book is merely a vessel of information and consumed by individuals in isolation discounts its many other attributes. The book can be shared via a range of media, whether this takes the form of emailing passages to friends via reading apps, discussing novels in book clubs, or disseminating a powerful idea on a global stage. In 2009, Bob Stein, director of the Institute for the Future of the Book, argued that the book has become a social space where readers can control its form, sequence and pacing. Stein offered a new definition of the book: 'A user-driven media where readers and sometimes authors congregate'. Stein's redefinition of the book in the digital age is consistent with other fields of design practice, including branding (see Chapter 2). In both instances the designed artefact, whether it be a publication or a logo, is not fixed but fluid: it is open to the influences typical of social media (comments, feedback, review etc.), as well as active interventions (hacks, online protests, crowdsourcing, etc.), or in the case of the book, rewriting and re-versioning.

In his book *Print is Dead: Books in Our Digital Age* (2008) Jeff Gomez explores the book as a social object. At the time of Gomez's writing there were a handful of social networking sites devoted to sharing book reading, including Library Thing (est. 2005), Shelfari (est. 2006) and Goodreads (est. 2006) (Gomez 2008: 157). On these sites users create profiles and 'virtual bookshelves' to inform others what they are reading (2008: 158). Such sites allow users to produce lists, collections, tags, recommendations, comments and reviews. This information sharing is intended to generate mutual social and intellectual connections and results in further like-minded recommendations, thus helping individuals to refine their reading (2008: 159).

Gomez's description suggests a pluralistic, polyvocal community of many independent sites critiquing and sharing the love of books. Amazon purchased Shelfari in 2008 and Goodreads in 2013 and merged them in 2016 (Wikipedia.org, https://en.wikipedia.org/wiki/Shelfari). This consolidation and commercialization of social reading online has coincided with the removal of some reader comments on sites such as Goodreads, potentially threatening the diversity of opinion and openness of online social reading (goodreads.com).

E-readers are implicated too. The Kindle website proclaims that its readers can share passages and notes not just with other Kindle users, but with 'authors, thought leaders', and 'professors' (Kindle 2016). Yet, such sharing may not be without consequences. The online traces of one's reading habits are recorded by the likes of Google and Amazon and may be shared not just with reader communities but with governments, commercial interests or hackers, thus raising concerns about the lack of protection of readers' data (Glanville 2012).

Despite the opportunities brought about by digital technologies to redefine the role of the book, as well as the author and the reader, for the most part big publishers still consider the book in old fashioned terms: a single-authored, completed text. However, these long-held traditions are increasingly challenged. Some of those involved in online publishing projects, such as Todd Sattersten of *Every Book is a Startup* (launched in July 2011), see text and authorship as fluid and open to change, whether through rewriting of the published work by the author, or through audiences continuously adding to the text in an act of co-creation. Observing a lack of innovation among the big book producers, Sattersten has been critical of the publishing industry, observing its conservative attitude and its unease with the possibilities of the electronic medium:

> What I never expected was how strongly the qualities of a book would be brought forward from the physical to the digital. Digital books have been designed to carry forward the same atomic quality of immutability of physical books. As I reached out to my colleagues working in the world of ebooks, the consensus was that no one had considered a reality where an author, given the ability to distribute directly and virtually cost free, would consider updating their work and the consequences that might have. Bits and atoms don't behave the same way, but we have built the next step forward in publishing as though they do. (Sattersten 2011)

One such project that counters established publishing practices, attempting in its design to bring bits and atoms together, is *I Read Where I Am: Exploring New Information Cultures*, published by Valiz in 2011. Edited by Mieke Gerritzen, Geert Lovink and Minke Kampman, designed by LUST, a multidisciplinary design studio based in The Hague, the book was developed in association with the Graphic Design Museum (now the Museum of the Image), Breda, The Institute of Network Cultures at the School of Interactive Media at the Hogeschool van Amsterdam. It is concerned with the future of reading. Consistent with this forward-looking emphasis, the print version of the book uses the visual language of hypertext while its online counterpart is editable by the public.

The now defunct online book allowed for editorial involvement from its internet audiences, such as poetic interjections, nonsensical screeds and counter arguments inserted in the middle of the prose of established authors, ranging from the technologist James Bridle to the curator Andrew Blauvelt. It illustrated both the democratic potential of shared authorship on the internet, and reflected the cacophony of the online echo chamber. With constant additions from users creating multiple hypertext links from clickable words in the text, the online version of the book became increasingly 'buggy', requiring constant technical updating with a decreased budget and was eventually abandoned (Léna 2016).

The print version of 'I Read Where I Am' sought to produce a new way of reading a physical book that was consistent with online engagement and extended LUST's design concept established in *Margeting: Inventing a Different Marketing Language* (2003) which, in a rejection of hierarchy, indexed every word in the book. *I Read Where I Am* replaced the traditional index and table of contents with an algorithmically derived 'Index of Word Frequency' where each word was printed in a range of grey to black according to how many times it appeared. The result was a text that looked more like a series of hyperlinks than a traditional collection of essays. Following the logic of a Twitter tweet the book also included an 'Index on First 140 Characters of Essay', providing a brief taster of each contributor's submission. With its attempt to apply lessons from online reading to the context of the printed book, *I Read Where I Am* reverses a tendency in online publishing in which, as Sattersten has noted, the traditions of the physical book predominate. The convergence of print and digital technologies is explored in the following sections as something that challenges not authorship but rather the traditions of production and distribution within the publishing industry.

The printing evolution: Marrying print and digital

In the late 1960s, Marshall McLuhan had predicted that the photocopier (Xerox machine) when wed with printing technology would increase the book's usefulness and dissemination resulting in a mass book production technology as an 'information service' (Anon, 1967: 1703). The Espresso Book Machine, a self-contained print-on-demand technology that has been called 'an ATM for books', seems to correspond to McLuhan's forecast (Figure 12.6). Developed by On Demand Books, it prints, binds and trims a 'bookstore quality', perfect-bound paperback in any language. The first beta version was installed in 2006 at the World Bank InfoShop in Washington D.C. and produced thousands of World Bank publications. As of June 2016, sixty-seven EBM machines have found homes in libraries, printing schools, and chain, university and independent book stores ranging from France, United States, South Africa, Dominican Republic, Egypt, The Netherlands, Japan and the United Arab Emirates. Because it has removed the traditional supply chain of the publishing industry, the EBM provides a decentralized, direct-to-consumer, production and distribution system (On Demand Books 2015).

The EBD can print from a digital network of more than 7 million titles, ranging from self-published, in-copyright and public domain. Authors can also design, edit and upload their books for the EBM to reprint. The advantages of the EBM include avoiding overstock and out-of-stock titles, creating a self-publishing community hub for retailers, as well as benefitting the environment through eliminating shipping and the pulping of returned books due to overstock of unsold books, a common occurrence in the publishing industry (On Demand Books 2015). While the EBM leverages the benefits of the physical and digital media, providing readers with the pleasure of ink on pages and offering a vast range of titles and instantaneous delivery, the machine is not yet able to achieve the attention to materials and nuance of design provided by innovative book publishers.

FIGURE 12.6 *Espresso Book Machine, permission On Demand Books.*

Conclusion

For several hundred years, printed books were humanity's primary information source. With many people, such as Amazon's Jeff Bezos, assuming that this central role has been usurped by digital media, designers and publishers are exploring the book's other quintessential qualities, innovating its form and enhancing its materials. This is exemplified by independent publishers such as Visual Editions, with book designs that surprise and engage readers as much as they question traditions of narrative linearity and challenge notions of authorship. Likewise, LUST's *I Read Where I Am* confronts the practices of digital publishing, which has largely followed the precedent of printed books, employing a similar information architecture (e.g. table of contents, index, chapter headings, page numbers, etc.). These projects and others provide useful models for designers. But technological developments such as the Espresso Book Machine challenge the very foundation of the publishing industry supply chain with its need for warehouses, vehicles and retail spaces.

Confirming McLuhan's view that different media meet different human needs, some scholars of reading have recently argued that the cultural practice of reading printed books meets personal and social requirements better than any other medium and therefore its continued survival is likely in the present media environment (Nossek, Adoni and Nimrod 2015: 367). Aware of the fundamental benefits of human engagement with books, whether print or digital, designers are developing publications which appeal to readers' sensual, social, psychological and informational needs. This chapter has largely focused on perhaps the main advantage of print over digital books: the sensual engagement of the reader. However, with the advent of the internet of things, books have the opportunity to become embedded with technology as sensing, communicating, networked devices: the book of the future may read us while we read it. Such a development would allow books to become sensitive, responsive and adaptive objects, potentially reversing the relationship humans have had with bound text since its inception.

References

Anonymous. 1967. 'A McLuhan Montage.' *Library Journal*. 15 April: 1701–3.
Armel, K. Carrie, and Vilayanur Subramanian Ramachandran. 2003. *Projecting Sensations to External Objects: Evidence from Skin Conductance Response*. http://web.stanford.edu/~kcarmel/papers/HandIllusion.pdf. Accessed 27 September 2015.
Asheim, Lester. 1955. 'Introduction: New Problems in Plotting the Future of the Book'. *The Library Quarterly* 25 (4): 281–92.
Atakan, Sukriye Sinem. 2014. 'Consumer Response to Product Construction: The Role of Haptic Stimulation'. *International Journal of Consumer Studies* 38 (6): 586–92.
Birkerts, Sven. 1994. *Gutenberg Elegies: The Fate of Reading in an Electronic Age*. New York: Fawcett Columbine.
Bolter, David Jay. 2001. *Writing Spaces: Computers, Hypertext, and the Remediation of Print*. New York and London: Routledge.
Bourdieu, Pierre. 1984. *Distinction: A Social Critique of the Judgment of Taste*. Cambridge, MA: Harvard University Press.
Carr, Nicholas. 2008. 'Is Google Making Us Stupid? What the Internet Is Doing to Our Brains'. *The Atlantic*. http://www.theatlantic.com/magazine/archive/2008/07/is-google-making-us-stupid/306868/. Accessed 15 June 2016.
Coover, Robert. 1992. 'The End of Books'. *The New York Times*. 21 June. Available online at http://www.nytimes.com/books/98/09/27/specials/coover-end.html. Accessed 16 June 2016.
Cope, Bill, and Angus Phillips (eds.) 2006. *The Future of the Book in the Digital Age*. Oxford: Chandos Publishing.
Escarpit, Robert. 1971. *Sociology of Literature*. London: Frank Cass.
Feltham, Esther. 2014. *The Sensual Book: An Exploration into How British Publishers Are Regenerating the Book as a Sensorial-led Object*. Unpublished MA Thesis, University of Brighton.
Gerritzen, Mieke, Geert Lovink, and Minke Kampman. 2011. *I Read Where I Am: Exploring New Information Cultures*. Amsterdam, Netherlands: Valiz Book and Cultural Projects.
Gilroy, Harry. 1966. 'Librarians Urged to Save the Book: Gordon Ray Tells Meeting of Electronic Limitations'. *New York Times*. 11 July: 24.
Glanvill, Jo. 31 August 2012. 'Readers' Privacy Is Under Threat in the Digital Age'. *Guardian*. Online https://www.theguardian.com/books/2012/aug/31/readers-privacy-under-threat. Accessed 5 July 2016.
Gomez, Jeff. 2008. *Print is Dead: Books in Our Digital Age*. London: Macmillan.
Goodreads.com. 2016. 'Goodreads Feedback Discussion: Announcements > Important Note Regarding Reviews'. http://www.goodreads.com/topic/show/1499741-important-note-regarding-reviews?page=1. Accessed 30 June 2016.
Heidegger, Martin. 1996. *Being and Time*. Translated by Joan Stambaugh. Albany: State University of New York Press.
Hertenstein, Matthew J., Rachel Holmes, Margaret McCullough, and Dacher Keltner. 2009. 'The Communication of Emotion via Touch'. *Emotion* 9 (4): 566–73.
Jury, David, ed. 2007. *Book, Art, Object*. Berkeley: Codex Foundation.
Kindle. 2016. 'Frequently Asked Questions: What Are Public Notes'. https://kindle.amazon.com/faq#PublicNotes0. Accessed 6 July 2016.
Lange, Gerald. 2007. 'The Key to the Survival of the Book.' In David Jury (ed.), *Book, Art, Object*. Berkeley: Codex Foundation.
Léna. 2016. 'I Read Where I Am: A Discussion with Thomas Castro from LUST'. Institute of Network Cultures. 20 April. http://networkcultures.org/outofink/2016/04/20/i-read-where-i-am-a-discussion-with-thomas-castro-from-lust/. Accessed 25 June 2016.
Levy, Steven. 2007. 'Amazon Reinventing the Book: Amazon's Jeff Bezos Already Built a Better Bookstore. Now He Believes He Can Improve upon One of Humankind's Most Divine Creations:

The Book Itself.' 17 November. http://europe.newsweek.com/amazon-reinventing-book-96909?rm=eu. Accessed 15 September 2016.

Ludovico, Alessandro. 2013. *Post-Digital Print: The Mutation of Publishing since 1894*. Eindhoven, Netherlands: Onomatopee.

Neill, Sam. 1971. 'Books and Marshall McLuhan'. *The Library Quarterly* 41 (4): 311–19.

Nelson, Ted. 1974 (1987). *Computer Lib/Dream Machines*. Self-published. (Second edition, Redmond, WA: Tempus Books/Microsoft Press).

Nossek, Hillel, Hanna Adoni, and Galit Nimrod. 2015. 'Is Print Really Dying? The State of Print Media Use in Europe'. *International Journal of Communication* 9: 365–85.

On Demand Books. 2015. 'Espresso Book Machine'. http://ondemandbooks.com. Accessed 22 April 2015.

Rahman, Osmud. 2012. 'The Influence of Visual and Tactile Inputs on Denim Jeans Evaluation'. *International Journal of Design* 6 (1): 11–25.

Ray, Gordon N. 1966. 'The Future of the Book'. *ALA Bulletin* 60 (8): 783–93.

Sattersten, Todd. 2011. 'The Paperless Book'. *TOC: Tools of Change for Publishing*. November 30. Online at http://toc.oreilly.com/2011/11/the-paperless-book.html. Accessed 30 March 2018.

Schifferstein, Hendrik N. J., and Marc P. H. D. Cleiren. 2005. 'Capturing Product Experiences: A Split-modality Approach'. *Acta Psychologica* 118 (3): 293–318.

Shu, Suzanne B., and Joann Peck. 2011. 'Psychological Ownership and Affective Reaction: Emotional Attachment Process Variables and the Endowment Effect'. *Journal of Consumer Psychology* 21 (4): 439–52.

Striphas, Ted. 2009. *The Late Age of Print: Everyday Book Culture from Consumerism to Control*. New York: Columbia University Press.

Visual-editions.com 2016. 'Our Books'. http://visual-editions.com/our-books. Accessed 6 July 2016.

Wikipedia.org 2016. 'Goodreads'. https://en.wikipedia.org/wiki/Goodreads. Accessed 30 June 2016.

Wikipedia.org 2016. 'Shelfari'. https://en.wikipedia.org/wiki/Shelfari. Accessed 30 June 2016.

Index

Note: Page numbers in **bold** denote a reference to an image on that page.

A&F Pears   126
Abercrombie & Fitch   74
Access Press   151
Adbusters   41, 45
Adoni, Hanna   208–9, 215
advertising   183–9. *See also* outdoor advertising
   advertising cookbooks   169
   cars   181–3
   citizen advertisers   68
   sex and gender   61–2, 175–7, 181–3
advice books   161–73
   as genre   163–4
AEG   37, 38–40, 126
   trademark   38
Afghanistan Powerpoint slide   144
Africa, apparel industry   77
Aicher, Otl   23–4
album covers   94–6, 192–204
   The Beatles   197–8, **198**
   a brief history   193–4
   CDs   200–2
   collecting   202–4
   English folk rock   198–9
   women singers   199–200
Alessi   125–41
   catalogue cover   **136**
   corporate identity case study   127–9
   factory employees   **128**
   Family Follows Fiction   132–3
   family portrait   **131**, 133, 139
   Italian crafts   134–5
   mediating design   129–30, 135–8
   mysqueeze and Juicy Salif   138–40
   from steel to plastic   130–31
Alessi, Carlo, 'Bombe' tea service   128, **129**
Alessi, Michele   **131**, 133, 135
Alessi, Stefano   133
Alessi Anghini, Alberto   128, **131**, 133, 135, 137, 138, 139

Alessi Anghini, Giovanni   128, **131**, 135
Alfa Romeo   181
Allen, Betty   172
Allsop, Kirsty   164
Amazon   216
   Kindle   **208**, 209, 212, 216
American Apparel   26, 68, 78
American Civic Association   55
American Institute of Architects   58
American Institute of Graphic Arts (AIGA)   2, 98
American Park and Outdoor Art Association (APOAA)   55
annual reports   127
anti-branding movement   41, 47
   billboard reformers   54–5
Apple Macintosh computers   2, 98
Armaout, Nadya   181
Arntz, Gerd   148, **149**
Arts and Crafts Movement   84
Asheim, Lester   210
Aston Martin   182
Attwood, Feona   73
authority, modes of   167–71, 172
Automobile Association   179
Aynsley, Jeremy   100

Bailey, David   110
Bangladesh, garment industry   77, 78
Banham, Reyner   163
Baran, Paul   153, **154**
Barnum, Phineas Taylor   52
Barra, Mary   181
barrio art   72–3
Barthes, Roland   1, 17–26, 28–9, 92
   continuing relevance of   25
   death of the author   21–2, 50, 91, 209–10
   fashion   76, 111
   replicated by Houze   6
   soap powders   1, 28
Baudelaire, Charles   84

Baudrillard, Jean   41, 94, 137
Bauhaus   84, 85, 88, 135
	cover of Alessi catalogue **136**
Bauman, Zygmunt   42
Bayer, Herbert   85, 149
	Universal typeface **86**
Bayley, Stephen   175, 186
Beard, Timothy, Bibliothèque   46
Beatles, the   197–9, **198**
Beaverbrook, Lord   152
Behrens, Peter   38–9, 126
Belair cigarettes   27
	advertisement **28**
Belk, Russel   202
Bellati, Nally   137
Benjamin, Walter   91, 204
Berger, Arthur Asa   25
Berger, John   107
Berners-Lee, Tim   152
Betty Crocker   170
Bezos, Jeff   209
Bhabha, Homi K.   107
Bibliothèque   46
	Ollo logo **47**
Bick, Paul   42
Bill, Max   23, 88
billboards. *See* posters and billboards; T-shirts
bi-modal communication (words and graphic design)   161–3
	authority 167–71
	contradictions 171–2
	persuasive function in advice books 163–4
	visual techniques of persuasion 164–7
binary oppositions   20, 28, 29, 31, 33, 92, 107, 148
Birkerts, Sven   209
Black Power   107
Blake, Peter   197
Blasi, Juliane   181
Blauvelt, Andrew   5, 216
'Blue Pencil' blog   6
BMW   181
Bolitho, Roy   179
Bolter, David Jay   207
'Bombe' tea and coffee set   **129**
Bonsiepe, Gui   24, 145
books
	death of 208–10
	definition 215
	Visual Editions 212–15
Booth, Charles   146–8
bottled water   27

Bow Wow Wow   199–200
	album cover **200**
BP logo   31
branding   25–8, 36–50. *See also* logos
	brand identity 25, 46–7, 125–9
	rejection of 23
Brandt, Marianne   135, 137
Brazilian Association of Advertisers   62–3
Breuer, Marcel   135
bricolage   42, 92, 98
Bridle, James   216
Briggs, Mitchell Pirie   172
Brighten the Corners   127
Brody, Neville   93–5, 97, 100
	The Face **93**
Brown, James, 'Cool Khaki'   **118**
Bubbles, Barney   197
Bürdek, Bernhard E.   24
button blankets   76

Cabaret Voltaire   94
Cailliau, Robert   152
Calvin Klein   184, 189, **189**
Campbell, Laura   119
Canon Ixus   183, **183**
Cantlon, Polly   163
Carr, Nicholas   210
cars
	advertised as accessories 183–9
	money spent on advertising 181–2
	women drivers 175–83
Carson, David   98–100
	'ra6belaisian without a clue' **99**
Casa da Musica   46
Cassina   135, 138
CBS Outdoor   63
CDs   200–2
Chaddha, Anmol   71–2
Chapman, Ian   199
Chatelain, Alex   110–11
	Vogue **112**
Cheang, Sarah   114, 120
Chermayeff and Geismar   37, 126
Chicago, billboards   54
Chicano culture   72–3
children and babies, T-shirts   69–70, 74
China, reorientalism   120
chinoiserie   104–8, 109–13
'Chinoiserie by Beaton'   109–10, **111**
Chiper, Sorina   42
citizen advertisers   68
City Beautiful Movement   55

Clark, Kathryn E. 202
Clark, Tim 154
    'Atlas of the Habitual' **155**
Clear Channel Communications 63
Clulow, Melanie 115
Coca-Cola 25, 30
co-creation, concept of 45
Cole, Shaun 7
collectors 202–4
    teenager's bedroom **203**
College Art Association (US) 3–4
Collins, Elsie 167
    photograph **166**
Collins, Michael 137
colonialism 106–7
Comme des Garçons 111, 116
Condé Nast 108. See also Vogue
Conran, Terence 139–40
Conservative Party propaganda 152
consumer society 41, 105, 117
Coomber, Lee 30
    Unilever logo **30**
Cooper, Michael 197
Cooper Union logo 46
Coover, Robert 211
Corbett, John 193
corporate identity 125–7. See also identity design
    Alessi SpA case study 127–9
Council of the Preservation of Rural England (CPRE) 59
counterculture 70. See also DIY; punk
Countryside and Footpaths Preservation Conference 59
Cox, Patrick 116
Craig, Robert L. 108
Creda Housecraft Manual 168–9, **168**
Crystal Goblet 85–6
CuteCircuit 78–9

Danish design 104
Davidson, Carolyn 37
Deakin, John 167
    'Vulgarity' **166**
Dean, James 69, **70**
Dean, Roger 197
death of the author 207, 211
    Barthes 21–3, 50, 92, 209–10
Deleuze, Giles 92, 153
de Marco, Tony 62
    photograph **62**
design
    design history 3–9

and national identity 103–5
Design and Industries Association (DIA) 59
Design Council 126, 167, 171
Designers and Art Directors Association 2
Design/Writing/Research 162–3
desire 108–9
De Stijl 88
Dewey, Thomas 70
Dilnot, Clive 4
Dingbats 100
Dior 113
Di Palma Associati 129
DIY 71
domesticity 164–7
Dosa 113
Doyle and Partners 46
Dresser, Christopher, design reinterpreted by Alessi **132**, 136–7
Dwiggins, William Addison 2

Earl, Harley 177
East India Company 105
Easton Pearson 112
Edge, Kevin 193
Edison, Thomas Alva 195
    portrait **195**
Eisenberg, Evan 202
English folk-rock groups 198
E-readers (Kindle) **208**, 209, 212, 216
Eskilson, Stephen J. 5, 23
Ésme (Florence Olive Ésme Eve) 167–8
    illustrations **168**, **169**
Espresso Book Machine 217–18, **218**
ethical consumption 77–8
etiquette books 161, 171, 172. See also advice books
Euro RSCG 185
Experimental Jetset 47

Facebook, 'like' button 45, 204
Factory, The (poster) **95**
Factory Records 95, 100
Fallan, Kjetil 84, 90
Family Follows Fiction 131–3, **132**, 136, 137
Farrelly, Liz 98
Featherstone, Mike 135
Feltham, Esther 212
Felton, Nicholas 127, 154
    Annual Report **156**
feminism
    nudity 98
    Wonderbra billboard campaign 61

Feng Shui   116, 119
Firat, Fuat   41–2
First World War, women drivers   177
Flagg, James Montgomery   57
    'Wake up, America!'   **56**
Flink, James   186
Foer, Jonathan Safran   213
    Tree of Codes   **214**
folk-rock   198–9
Ford   181
form follows function   1, 84, 85, 100, 137
Fornari, Franco   137
Fortune   149
Foucault, Michel   18, 22, 92
Frampton, Jez   44
Frankfurt School   41
Fratelli, Enzo   135
Frederick, Christine   170

Galliano, John   113
Gap gaffe   43–9
    logo generator   **44**
Gardner, Helen   5
Garrett, Malcolm   6, 94, 97
Geczy, Adam   107–8
gender
    advertising cars to women   181–3
    album covers of women singers   199
    feminism   61–2, 98
    male gaze   107
    modernism   90
    sex sells, gender buys   175–7
    stereotypes   104
    T-shirts   73–5
General Motors   177, 181
Genette, Gérard   193
Gerber, Anna   212
Gerritzen, Mieke   216
Gerstner, Karl   88
Gesamtkunstwerk   8, 84, 197
Gibb, Bill   110
Giles, David C.   202
Gill, Rosalind   73
Giorgio Armani   116
Giovannoni, Stefano   138
Glass, Aaron   75–6
globalization   103, 104, 119, 121
Goldman, Robert   43
Gombrich, E. H.   5
Gomez, Jeff   215
González, Laura   139
Good Housekeeping Institute   165–6
Goodreads   215, 216

Google   216
Google AdWords   64
Gorman, Carma   4, 8, 127
Gosper, Wnek   185
    Peugeot ads   **186**, **187**
graffiti   26
Granny Axu   76
graphic design. *See also* bi-modal communication
    in an expanded field   8–9
    as a professional field   1–3
    semiotics and structuralism   22–5, 33
    text and words   161–3
Graphic Design Museum, Breda   216
Graves, Michael   130, 133
    'Kettle with a Whistling Bird'   **131**
Greenwell, Mary   118
greetings cards   9, 10, 18
Greiman, April   97–8
    self-portrait   **96**
Gropius, Walter   39, 85
Gruendler, Shelley   86
Guattari, Félix   92, 153
Guevara, Che   **71**, 71–2
guidebooks. *See* advice books
Gutenberg Bible   **213**

Habermas, Jürgen   41
Haiti, refashioned logos   42–3
Hall, Sean   24
Hamilton, Richard   198
Hamnett, Katharine   68, **69**
Hansen, Marka   44
Hassan, Ihab   90, 92
Haug, W. F.   193
Hauschild, Frank   45
Haworth, Jann   197
Hazleton, Lesley   181
Heath, Stephen   20, 23
Hebdige, Dick   42
Heidegger, Martin   212
Heller, Steven   108
Helvetica   6, 26, 88
    film poster   **89**
Helvin, Marie   110
Hempel, Anouska   113
Henderson, Ilana   171–2
Henrion, F. H. K.   36–7, 50, 126
Henri, Thierry   182–3
Herzigová, Eva   **61**, 62
Higgins, Hannah   6
Highway Beautification Act (US)   60
Hine, Thomas   90
HMV (His Master's Voice)   195

Hoberman, Brent   139
Hobsbawn, Eric   198
Hochschule für Gestaltung (HfG)   23, 24, 88
Hoffmann, Eduard   88
Holmes, Nigel   149, 150, 151
Hoppen, Kelly   113
Houze, Rebecca   6
Huli tribesmen   120
Hunt, Corrine Hunt, T-shirt design   **75**
Huppatz, D. J.   4–5, 23
Hurricane Katrina   74–5
hybridity   92, 107–8, 121
hypertext   210, 211, 216
    discrete (Chunk Style)   **211**

IBM   38–40, 126
    logo   **40**
identity design
    MIT Media Lab   46, **46**
    national identity   103–4
    Olins   126, 127
    terminology   8, 127
    Whitney Museum   47, **48**
Impey, Oliver   105–6
'Index of Word Frequency'   217
'Index on First 140 Characters of Essay'   217
India, T-shirt manufacture   77
infographics   144–56
    Isotype pictograms   148, **149**
    journalism   149–52
    London poverty map as historical precedent   145–8, **147**
    quantified self movement   154–5
    rhetoric   145
    visualizing complex networks   152–4
Inglis, Ian   197
Institute for the Future of the Book   215
Interbrand   44
International Design Alliance   2
iPods   201
I Read Where I am   216, 217
isms   90
Isotype   148–9, **149**
Italian crafts   **134**, 134–5
italianità   132, 134
    'Made in Italy' myth   104
Iverson, Britt   212
Izenour, Steven   91

Jackson, Judith   180
Jacobson, Dawn   105, 106, 119
Jacques, Alison   74
Jameson, Frederic   91, 100, 118

Japan, globalization and tradition   120
japonisme   104–8, 109–13
Jarvis, Alan   167
    'Vulgarity'   **166**
JCDecaux   63
Johnson, Philip, AT&T building   96
Jones, Anthony Armstrong (Lord Snowdon), photograph   109, **110**
Jones, Carla   119, 119
Jordan, Ned   176
'Juicy Salif'   130, 139
    in Alessi family photo   **131**, 133
Julier, Guy   139

Kamekura, Yusaku   37
Kampman, Minke   216
Kang
    MIT Media Lab identity design   **46**
Kang, E. Roon   46
Kapoor, Anish   127
Kassab, Gilberto   62–3
Kawakubo, Rei   111, 116
Kegel, Denis   85
Kegler, Richard   85
Kemp, Martin   31
Kenzo Takada   109
Kettemann, Bernhard   27
'Kettle with a Whistling Bird'   **131**
Kim, Christina   113
Kimball, Miles A.   145
Kindle   **208**, 209, 212, 216
Kingsland, James   164
    'The Kitchen Buffet'   164
Kinross, Robin   25, 145
Kircherer, Sibylle   133, 135
Klein, Naomi   41
Knight, Nick   113
Knott, Kim   118
Kraidy, Marwan   107
Kreiter, Roland   139–40, **140**
Kress, Gunther   25
Kwakwaka'wakw   75–6

Laakkonen, Tiina   113
Laboratoires Garnier   189
Lacan, Jacques   23
Lacroix, Christian   118
Ladies Automobile Club   177
Laird and Partners   44
Landor Associates   126
Lange, Gerald   210
Lasn, Kalle   41
Las Vegas, Pepsi advertisement   **26**

Le Corbusier   90, 135
legitimation (Weber)   167, 169, 170, 171, 172, 173
Leshkowich, Ann Marie   119
Lever Brothers   29, 126
Levi-Strauss, Claude   20, 42
Levitt, Dorothy   180
Liberty Bond posters   56–7
Life and Opinions of Tristram Shandy, Gentleman, The   213
'likes'   45, 204
Lissitzky, El   88
Lo, Alice   163
Lodge, David   18
logos
    AEG trademark   **38**
    IBM   **40**
    MIT Media Lab   **46**
    Ollo   **47**
    responsive   43–9
    static   36–8
    Tate   **48**
Lohse, Richard Paul   88
London
    Chinatown   **115**
    poverty maps   146–8, **147**
Love, Courtney   73
Lovink, Geert   216
Lowrie, Joyce   167
LPs. *See* album covers
Ludovico, Alessandro   209
Lupton, Ellen   24, 148, 162–3
LUST   216
Lutz, Tina   110
    'Chinoiserie by Beaton'   **111**
Lwin, Annabella   199
Lynchburgh Bill Posting Co.   **54**
Lyon, Belinda   171
Lyons, Pam   171

McChrystal, General   144
McCracken, Grant   108–9
Macintosh computers   2, 98
MacKenzie, John M.   107
Mackintosh, Rennie   135
McLaren, Malcolm   199–200
Maclean, Sarah   165, 172
McLuhan, Marshall   184, 208, 212, 217, 218
McNeil, Peter   112, 120
McQueen, Alexander   113
'Madam Butterfly'   109, 118
Madonna   73
magazines   108–9. *See also Vogue*
infographics and journalism   149–52
maker movement   164
Maldonado, Tomás   23
Male, Alan   23
Manchester United   76
Manet, Édouard   199
Manovich, Lev   153
manuals. *See* advice books
Margeting: Inventing a Different Marketing Language   217
Margolin, Victor   3, 7
Marshall, Esmé   110, **112**
Marx   27
Masami Suga   120
Matsumoto, Hiroko   109, **110**
Maugham, Syrie   90
mediation   7, 23
    Alessi SpA   129–30, 135–8
Meggs, Philip   5
Mendini, Alessandro   130, 138
Miedinger, Max   88
Miller, Abbott   24, 162–3
Minard, Charles Joseph   145–6
    map   **146**
Mintel   178
MIT Media Lab   46
    identity design   **46**
Miyake, Issey   111, 116
modernism   4, 83–101. *See also* postmodernism
    Bauhaus   85
    Isotype   148
    moderne   90
    modernisms   83–5, 89–90
    typography   85–8
Moholy-Nagy, László   85, 88
Mollerup, Per   27
Monster.com   46
Moor, Liz   37, 126–7
Mori, Hanae   109
    Vogue image   **110**
Morris, William   84, 119
Moss, Kate   113
Mostyn, Melissa   113
MP3 player   203
Mr. Blobby   203
Müller-Brockmann, Josef   88
Mulvey, Laura   107
Murray, Jeff   41
museums
    Alessi   135
    Tate   47

Whitney   47
music packaging. *See* album covers
mydeco.com   139–40
mysqueeze   138–40, **140**
Mythologies   6, 22, 25, 28

Napoleon's army, infographic   145–6, **146**
National Committee for Restriction of Outdoor Advertising (NCROA)   58
national identity   103–4, 105
Nazi Germany   85, 88
NBC peacock   37
Neagle, Anna   169
Nelson, Ted, hypertext   **211**
Neurath, Marie   148
Neurath, Otto   148, 151
Newell and Sorrell   31
   Pharmacia and Upjohn logo   **32**
Newlyn, Miles   30
   Unilever logo   **30**
New Order   95
Newsweek   150, 151
New York
   billboards   **53**
   subway   6
   Times Square   **64**
New York Times   144
   infographics   149
Niagara Falls, billboards   54
Nickelodeon discs   194–5
'Nicole-Papa'   **182**, 182–3
Nike   77, 78
   swoosh   37, 42–3, **43**
Nimrod, Galit   208, 215
Northern Ireland, driver competence   179
Nossek, Hillel   208, 215
Noyes, Eliot F.   39

Occupy movement   127
O'Connell, Sean   179
Odhams Press   167
O'Donnell, Kate   113
Ogilvy & Mather   29
Olins, Wally   29, 30, 45, 104, 126–7
   Wolff Olins   29, 30, 45, 47
Olivetti   135
Ollo   46–7
   logo   **47**
Omo   28, 29
On Demand Books   217
onomatopoeia   19–20
orientalism   103–21

design theory   104–8
   typology of signifiers   114
Oropallo, Gabriele   162
Ortiz, Fernando   107
'other' ('otherness')   106, 113
outdoor advertising   52–65
   a brief history   52–4
   digital signage and electronic billboards   63–5
   First World War   56–7
   highways   57–8
   lorry bills   59–60
   regulation   53, 54–5, 57, 58, 60, 62–3, 65
Outdoor Advertising Association of America   60
overswooshification   43
Ozanne, Julie   41

Panzani foods advertisement   **21**
Papson, Stephen   43
paratext   193, 199, 201, 212
Parkin, Alan   37, 50, 126
pastiche   103, 115, 118
Peirce, Charles Sanders   18–20, 27
Penguin Books   88
Penney, Joel   69
Pentagram   97, 126
Perriand, Charlotte   135
persuasion. *See* advice books
Peugeot   185–8
   advertisement   **186**, **187**
Pevsner, Nikolaus   1, 4, 6
Pharmacia and Upjohn   31
Phelan, Kate   118
   'Cool Khaki'   **118**
pictograms   148
Pieroni, Lucia   119
   'Cool Khaki'   **118**
Pietrzykowski, Stephen   202
Pilditch, James   126
plastic   130–2, 136–8
Playfair, William   145, 151
Poiret, Paul   107
Polinoro, Laura   130
postcolonialism   103
Post, Emily   170, 180
posters and billboards   56–7
   empty billboard   **62**
   examples   **56**, **57**, **59**, **61**
postmodernism   83–101
   after postmodernism   100–1
   postmodern pastiche   118
   what is   90–2

Poynor, Rick   6, 94
Presley, Elvis   **196**, 196
'Printing Should be Invisible'   85–6
privacy concerns   65
propaganda, infographics   152
Pugin, Augustus Welby Northmore   119, 167
punk   2, 42, 94, 96, 199

quantified self movement   154, **155**

Race, Kane   27
Ramamurthy, Anandi   108
Rand, Paul   23–4, 38–40, 126
RAND Corporation   **154**
    network models   **154**
Ranger, Terence   198
'ra6belaisian without a clue'   **99**
Ray, Gordon N.   210
Ray Gun   99–100
Renault   182
Rhizome logo   45
rhizomes   92, 153
Rietveld, Gerrit   135
Riot Grrrl   73–4
Robertson, Frances   6
Rock, Michael   162
Romania, logo refashioning   42
Roth, Ed   70
Rotten, Johnny   192
Ruskin, John   119

Sadre-Orafai, Stephanie Neda   115
Sagmeister and Walsh   46
Said, Edward   108, 109, 117, 119
    binary oppositions   92
São Paulo   62–3
    empty billboard   **62**
Saporta, Mark, *Composition No. 1*   **214**
Sattersten, Todd   216, 217
Saussure, Ferdinand de   17–20, 24–7, 33, 92
Saville, Peter   6, 94, 95, 96, 97, 98, 100
Scarzella, Patrizia   129
Scenic America   63
Scheffler, Karl   38
Schlemmer, Oskar   84
Schmid, Lothar   116
Scholl, Inge   23
Schulz, Bruno   213
Schweimer, Daniel   72
Scott Brown, Denise   91

Selle, Gert   138
semiotics   17–33, 92, 161
sensuality   212–15
Sex Pistols   192
Sharp, Martin   197
Shaw, Paul   6
Shell   59, 60
    'See Britain' poster   **59**
Siegel+Gale   46
silk   116
Silvano, Dalton   62
Silverstein, Louis   151
Simons, Raf   98
Skov, Lise   111
Sloboda, Stacey   106, 120
slogans. *See* T-shirts
Smythe, Dallas   204
Snowdon. *See* Jones, Anthony Armstrong
social media   44–5, 204
    books as   215–17
Society for Checking the Abuses of Public Advertising (SCAPA)   54, 59
'Somewhere West of Laramie'   **176**, 176–7
Sottsass, Ettore   138
space-time-story graphics   145, **146**
Sparke, Penny   186
Spencer, Herbert   4–6, 94
Spice Girls   74
Spiller's flour   169
Spy   151
stained glass windows   162
Starck, Philippe   130, 133, 139, 140, **140**
statistics. *See also* infographics
    billboards   54, 63
    car advertising   181–2
    vinyl sales   203–4
    women driving   177–8, 179
Stein, Bob   215
Stein, Jesse Adams   6–7
Sterne, Laurence   91
Stewart, Martha   164
Sticky Fingers   193–4
    album cover   **194**
Straw, Will   201–2
Street of Crocodiles, The   213
structuralism   17, 20–2
    and graphic design   22–5
Sullivan, Louis. *See* form follows function
Sunlight soap   29, 126
Surface.de   45
surfing community   99

Suterwalla, Shenaz   120
Sutnar, Ladislav   149
Swiss School typography   87–9
   rejection of   92

Tableware   171–2
tape cassettes   200, 201
Tate museums   47
tattoo ad   **186**, 186–7
Tea and Coffee Piazza   130, 140
Teen Guide to Homemaking   **170**, 171
Teller, Juergen   113
Thatcher, Margaret   68, **69**
TheGreenEyl   46
   MIT Media Lab identity design   **46**
Thelma and Louise   185
theory-in-action approach   25
This Is a Printing Office   **87**
Thomson, Ellen Mazur   2
Threadless   78
Thun, Matteo   138
Time   **150**, 151
trademarks   26, 27, 37
   AEG   **38**
   IBM   39–40, **40**
Tree of Codes   213, **214**
transculturation   92, 107–8
trees   153
Tresidder, Richard   24
Triggs, Edward   24
Triggs, Teal   163
Troy, Nancy   107
Tschichold, Jan   88, 94
   influence of   96
T-shirts   68–79
   barrio art   72–3
   a brief history   68–71
   Che Guevara   **71**, 71–2
   gender   73–5
   group belonging   75–6
   Hunt Memorial Potlatch T-shirt   **75**
   Thatcher and Hamnett   68, **69**
Tufte, Edward R.   145–6, 151–2
Twemlow, Alice   98
Twitter   217
typefaces
   Dingbats   100
   Neville Brody's   94
   Universal   **86**
Typographische Mitteilungen   88

typography   85–6. *See also* Helvetica; Swiss School typography; typefaces

Unilever   28–33
   logo   **30**, 31
Universal typeface   85, **86**
USA Today   150–2
US military   68–9, 144

Vågnes and Gronstad   193
van Leeuwen, Theo   24
Va Va Voom   182–3
Venkatesh, Alladi   41–2
Venturi, Robert   91
Venturini, Guido   138
vinyl records   201–4, 210. *See also* album covers
Virago   180
Visual Editions   211, 212–15
visual identity. *See* identity design
Vogue   108–20
   Bayer in Berlin   85
   'Cool Khaki'   **118**
   Hiroko Matsumoto   **110**
   typology of orientalism   113–17
   'Vogue in China'   **112**
   Yves Saint Laurent   **117**
Volkswagen   184–5, 189
   advertisements   **184**, **185**, **188**
Voorhies, Stephen J.   170
Voorman, Klaus   197
Vreeland, Diana   114

Wagner, Karin   31, 32
Wajcman, Judy   186
Walker, Tim   120
Walton, Mark   176
Wannamaker, John   53
Ward, Gemma   120
Warde, Beatrice   85–6, 87
   This Is a Printing Office   **87**
Warhol, Andy   194
   album cover   **194**
Wark, Penny   182
Watson, Thomas J. Jr.   39
wax cylinders   195, **195**
Weber, Max   167, 172
Wedgwood, Josiah   125
Weil, Daniel   137
Weisbeck, Marcus   45
Whitehouse, Denise   4
Whitney Museum   47
   'Responsive W'   47, **48**

Wikipedia   212
Wildbur, Peter   145
Willer, Marina   47
Williams, Zoe   119
Williamson, Judith   27
Winnicott, Donald   137
Wizard of Oz, The   69
Wolff, Michael   29. *See also* Wolff Olins
Wolff Olins   29, 30, 36, 45, 47
Wollen, Peter   107
Woman *Week-End Book*   **168**
Wonderbra billboard campaign   **61**, 61–2
Woodham, Jonathan   2
World Bank publications   217
World Privacy Forum   65

World Wide Web   152–3
Wray, Adam   98
Wright, Mary and Russel   164
   'The Kitchen Buffet'   **165**
Wurman, Richard Saul   151

Yamamoto, Yohji   97, 111
Yau, David   154
Your Car   179
Yu, James, logo generator   **44**
Yves Saint Laurent   116
   Rive Gauche   **117**

Zen Buddhism   112, 116, 119
Zumtrobel   127